Film Review 1986-7

Film Review 1986-7

INCLUDING VIDEO RELEASES

F. Maurice Speed

COLUMBUS BOOKS
LONDON

First published in Great Britain in 1986 by
COLUMBUS BOOKS LTD
19-23 Ludgate Hill, London, EC4M 7PD

Designed by Fred Price

British Library Cataloguing in Publication Data
Film review: including video releases. —
1986-7
1. Moving-pictures — Periodicals
791.43'05 PN1993

ISBN 0–86287–299–5
ISBN 0–86287–300–2 Pbk

Phototypeset by Falcon Graphic Art Ltd
Wallington, Surrey
Printed and bound by R. J. Acford,
Chichester, Sussex

Contents

Introduction

F. MAURICE SPEED

If, as I somewhat understandably hope, you are a regular reader of this annual, you may recall that last year I commenced this introductory review feature with some quotations which, I felt, contained some important statements on the film business. Among these was a statement made by Professor Basinger which was something of a warning to all moviemakers: 'When we go out to a movie it's not simply to spend time. We're only getting our money's worth if we are being entertained. They [the moviemakers] ought to think about it: a film should be good, not long.'

These words are, I think, well worth repeating for they are as relevant to this (or next) year's crop of movies as they were to last year's. And I'd like to see them writ in letters of fire over the entrance of every film studio in the world.

This year I want to preface my own comments with another quotation, this time from an article by Will Tusher published in a January (1986) issue of *Variety*. During the whole twelve months I have read nothing, anywhere, to compare in salutary straightforwardness and sheer commonsense with Mr Tusher's words. The article contained so much that was so good in these terms that I wish I could reprint the (pretty lengthy) feature in full – had I the space and, of course, the author's blessing! But as it is, I shall have to be content with taking from this gold-mine of celluloid home-truths just a few of the writer's shinier nuggets.

Mr Tusher, writing about the many changes in management and ownership that have occurred in Hollywood recently, starts off by saying: 'Will it really matter whether Ted Turner runs MGM instead of Kirk Kerkorian, whether Rupert Murdoch* instead of Marvin Davis calls the shots at Fox, whether Coca-Cola performs a bottling-industry marketing transplant at Columbia Pictures . . . or whether erstwhile Paramount *wunderkind* Michael Eisner instead of Ron Miller and Richard Berger attends Disney's master planning board?

'In a nutshell – to a town occupationally petitioning for miracles – not very likely. Happy endings are more easily contrived on-screen than off-screen. In the real Hollywood the only sure thing remains uncertainty. In the real Hollywood, failure inexorably exceeds success. In the real Hollywood, genius – corporate or creative – is a pretentious word carelessly turned loose to impute intention to dumb luck. It has ever been thus and ever will remain thus.

'The more conglomerates take over, the more likely Hollywood will rely increasingly on audience and market research, less on instinct or taste . . . If by the use of such yardsticks the new film tycoons are convinced that the public is thirsting for trash, the thing to do . . . is to slake that thirst with premeditated trash. Yes, even when it means making a bad movie on purpose. Hollywood remains what it is destined forever to be – the Las Vegas of the world of entertainment, where every picture is a roll of the dice . . . The motion picture industry is perhaps unique in that disasters are no deterrent to those on the outside wanting in. No matter the industry slumps, no matter how unstable the pattern of ownership, there always is someone – or some conglomerate – bursting out of the wings, confident that the odds can be beaten.'

There's a whole lot more in similar vein, to be read, digested and – inevitably – ignored by the men who control this most wickedly glamorous of industries. They will recognize it as the truth, but for diverse unreasonable reasons will be unable to accept it.

Certainly we have had our fair share of celluloid rubbish over this past twelve months, movies which one can only watch with astonished disbelief, wondering what utter insanity impelled their makers to take them from what must have been a poor script on to the studio floor?

But such movies appear to be endemic to the trade; they have always played a part in the year's production schedules, unfortunately, and presumably they always will. Possibly it is just a trick of fading memory that makes one think there were fewer celluloid turkeys in the past than appear on the modern menu. To compensate, to some degree, there has always been, are now, and will be, please God, the occasional artistic and/or commercial movie that is beautifully crafted and intelligently made; imaginative and entertaining masterworks which make the whole business of movie-going worth while. After a half-dozen horrors one such movie always seems to pop up to restore one's faith in the art, and in the artists working in the motion-picture medium.

Looking back through yellowed cuttings and forgotten comments and reviews, one realizes that it is just a matter of history once more repeating itself, and that I was saying all this, in so many words, five, ten and twenty years ago.

*Late in 1985 press baron Murdoch became the new and sole private owner of 20th Century-Fox Films for a purchase price of $487 million after having owned a half-share of the company for some time.

Opposite, Producer Steven Spielberg and director Joe Dante on the set of *Gremlins*, the science-fiction film about a Christmas present which turns sour, *very* sour; released over the Christmas period of 1984-5. In the spring of 1986, at their annual awards ceremony, Spielberg was presented with the highest honour that the British Film Academy of Film and Television Arts can offer, their Fellowship award.

Fred Schepisi, who has been responsible for the success of some outstanding Australian films in the immediate past, but is now working in Hollywood, directing Meryl Streep and Tracey Ullman (centre) in the RKO Radio–Thorn EMI production *Plenty*.

Then, as now, a few, just a few celluloid classics seemed to come along every year.

This year having seen the completion of the British Film Year, it is now possible to draw up some sort of advance balance sheet. Yes, it *has* been a success, quite how great a success will only be known later. Though official attendance figures for British cinemas are unfortunately no longer issued by the Department of Trade, the cinemas themselves and the Cinema Advertising Association reckon that following a dramatic fall in the sale of cinema tickets during the previous twelve months, UK cinema attendances in British Film Year showed a recovery by as much as 40 per cent. Now it is up to both the moviemakers and the movieshowers to see that the trend continues and the recaptured patrons become regulars by maintaining a flow of entertaining films showing in clean, comfortable and technically first-class cinemas.

It is time to forget all about those misbegotten so-called 'youth-aimed' movies which have formed such a large part of recent output. They have not, in any case, proved the financial success which their creators hoped they would, in either America or Britain. Instead, moviemakers should try making more 'family' films, movies which contain less foul language, less mindless violence and less vulgarity than have played too large a part in too many recent movies – even if the general standard for 1985–6 has been higher than it was for the period immediately preceding it.

The claim that British attendance figures rose dramatically during British Film Year was certainly supported by the end-of-year Rank Organization balance sheet, which recorded a profit for 1985 from the Group's cinema, distribution and studio (Pinewood) interests of some £11 million, £4 million above the previous year's figure. It appears that attendance at the Group's cinemas rose during the period by a remarkable 44 per cent.

It is ironic, by the way, that the bad British summer, which it was generally agreed had encouraged cinema-going, was followed by an even worse winter, which must have had a correspondingly adverse effect on movie-going.

But the generally cheerful and optimistic mood engendered by the success of British Film Year was soured somewhat when the news broke about the financial crisis at Goldcrest Films, the company generally accepted as the flagship of Britain's moviemaking industry after the international, artistic and commercial success world-wide of such productions as *Chariots of Fire* and *Gandhi*. Partly the crisis was caused by the company's rushing into production – after a year's lay-off – with several big-budget movies scheduled to cost £42½ million in total, and the over-running of the budgets of some of them. For instance, the unfortunate *Revolution* ran £3 million over a budget of £19 million. It appears now that the future of the company rests considerably on the success or failure of two of its 1986 releases: the

Though thoroughly castigated by the American critics (didn't they like an Englishman directing the film of their famous stage musical?) *A Chorus Line* met a far better reception from the British critics and general applause from the public on both sides of the Atlantic. Considerable credit must go to Richard Attenborough, who took over the direction when others had walked away from what was always accepted to be a difficult – and dangerous – job, and made the film at least entertaining. With Attenborough, his stars: Michael Douglas and Alyson Reed.

original and lively musical *Absolute Beginners* – which cost about £8 million – and *The Mission* (about £17 million).

Brought back to sort things out, former Goldcrest boss Jake Eberts reckoned he could weather the storm and continue to make movies. Let's hope he is right, because the failure of Goldcrest would have a considerable effect on all British moviemaking, and would make it all the harder in future to raise production money.

In the spring of 1986 Goldcrest defiantly announced a plan to make or buy-in some ten films a year from 1987; it hopes to raise the cash to finance this programme largely from American sources. Promises of financial backing are indeed said to have materialized, but another blow to the increasingly optimistic company fell in July, when it was announced that Goldcrest's most successful producer, David Puttnam (*The Killing Fields, Chariots of Fire, Local Hero* and *The Mission*, which was a major prize-winner at the 1986 Cannes Film Festival) has accepted an offer from the Coca-Cola-owned Hollywood giant Columbia Pictures to take over as its production chief. His contract calls for him to make about a dozen major movies over a period of 3½ years at a cost of about $200 million, for a personal reward of about $2 million a year. Long pondered by Puttnam, his decision to go was obviously encouraged by his resentment of the encroachments into the British film industry (production and exhibition) by the Cannon Group.

Another unsettling event during British Film Year was the decision of the giant Thorn EMI Group to sell off its Entertainment Division (its cinema, film production and distribution, and video interests). Both Rank and Cannon showed interest but in many quarters there was a sigh of relief when a deal was struck between the company and the management by which the latter bought out the division for £110 million, broken down, apparently, into £35 million for the 105-cinema circuit (295 screens), £6 million for Elstree Studios and the balance for the company's film library and video assets.

Having taken over the Entertainment Group from Thorn EMI, the company formed by the old management – Screen Entertainment Ltd – went to the Australian Bond Corporation for finance to complete the deal. However, owing to circumstances not at this point clear (to me), Bond (which, it seems, had envisaged itself as a comparatively minor shareholder in the new company) suddenly found itself funding and owning the whole set-up – something which did not appeal. Its ownership was to last just one week. At the end of that period, Cannon's top two, Menahem Golan and Yoram Globus, on their way to the Cannes Film Festival, dropped off in London and, within a few hectic hours, had their £175 million offer for the company accepted. (Remember that Cannon's original, rejected bid had been for £110 million.) What *is* clear is that, with this purchase, the Cannon Group has suddenly become the most powerful force in the British film industry: quite apart from its studio and video interests, it now owns 485 screens in Britain, or 39 per cent of the total (against Rank's 216 screens). This seemingly unstoppable takeover is certain to cause further controversy.

After it had seen the conclusion of the Thorn EMI deal, the Rank Group, apparently in acquisitive mood, made a bid to take over the Granada Leisure Group, with its small cinema circuit, chains of bingo halls and retail shops, TV interests and service stations. Latest news is that this deal seems to have fallen through.

In terms of film production the British graph seems to have remained pretty steady. Although for several worrying months at the beginning of 1985 Pinewood had only four of its 13 stages in operation, a later burst of activity made up for the lull and brought the end-of-year figure very close to that of 1984. The horrific rise in production costs meant there could be no real rise in production levels. *Variety*, which keeps a careful finger on the celluloid pulse, reckoned that the average cost of a British film in 1986 would emerge as some 47 per cent higher than the 1985 figure, with the budget rising from £2¼ to £3½ million. However, three unusually lavish British productions helped to throw the figures out of balance, and what must be taken into consideration is that some 11 productions were actually brought in under the £1 million mark. But despite their low budgets, few of these are likely to make a profit owing to the difficulty of obtaining a decent release outside the British Isles; even a low-budget film needs a reasonable showing in America and elsewhere if it is ever to go into the black. But according to Joy Pereths, vice president and sales acquisitions manager for the International Film Exchange in New York, there is a growing demand from specialist cinemas in both New York and Los Angeles for the good British so-called 'art film'. Ms Pereths reckons that such demand could soon guarantee about half the budget (say $1 million) of a modest British 'quality' production, with that income about equally divided between cinema showings and videocassette sales. This forecast figure is more than double the revenue such films are currently earning in the US.

Incidentally, some of the more successful lower-budget movies that *have* had an American release include *Giro City, Laughterhouse, She'll Be Wearing Pink Pyjamas, Wetherby* and *My Beautiful Laundrette*. The number of small releasing companies dealing with specialist films is growing rapidly in America, as it is in Britain, and Ms Pereths reckons she can now count on getting several competing offers for the release of a quality British movie.

On the subject of British production, once more, something which damped down the British studios' optimistic calculations for the future was the increasing use by cost-conscious producers of non-specialized buildings (low-rent disused factories, in the main) for film production at the expense of established studios such as Pinewood and Elstree. For instance, Stanley Kubrick hired a former gasworks in which to shoot some of the sequences in his new production; nearby, concurrently, Virgin was making a film in another old building.

However, this has not stopped the British studios from investing in their future. The Lee Brothers, for example, were rumoured to be spending some £15 million on improving their recently acquired Shepperton Studios and 1985 saw the completion of rebuilding of the famous 007 stage at Pinewood after its total destruction by fire the previous year.

Not entirely unconnected with the success of British Film Year and the recovery in the attendance figures was the news of a number of new British cinema projects in this country. After opening its 10-screen complex in Milton Keynes, ABC started work on an 8-screen complex in Manchester, while CIC announced plans to erect a multiple-screen cinema in High Wycombe, Bucks. Other companies announcing similar projects include American Multi-Cinemas and the Rank Group, which is on record as saying that if it could find suitable sites it would embark on the erection of similar cinema complexes. Meanwhile in the spring (of 1986) Capital Leisure announced it was considering two possible

The moviemakers: the team which brought lots of laughter to the British screens with *Clockwise*, director Christopher Morahan, writer Michael Frayn, producer Michael Codron and star John Cleese, who was back in top *Fawlty Towers* style in the movie.

sites for the first British drive-in cinema (never before tried in the UK) with additional ozoners, as they are sometimes called, in Manchester, the Midlands and – bravest throw of the dice – in Scotland.*

Cannon, too, will almost certainly remain in an acquisitive mood for some time to come. The international growth of this remarkable set-up is a great success story. Menahem Golan and Yoram Globus, that extraordinary Israeli duo, having taken over the Classic Group in 1982 and spent a fortune on refurbishing and updating those cinemas (incidentally turning something like a £2 million loss into a £1½ million profit by the end of 1985 and achieving a rise of a million in audience figures), acquired the Star circuit in 1985. This made Cannon the second-largest cinema exhibition group in Britain, with some 216 screens in 95 cinemas. At this point came their acquisition of the ABC chain of cinemas, as previously mentioned.

In addition to its world-wide film distribution interests, the Cannon Group is one of the most prolific of international moviemaking companies, with plans for four major productions in Britain in 1986. During 1985 Cannon put no less than 22 films into production (with the indefatigable Mr Golan personally directing one of the most important, *Delta Force*, and lining up more personal production chores for the months ahead).

Cannon has in the more immediate past been accused of making a succession of sensational celluloid pot-boilers, and it would be difficult to argue against that. But now it looks as if these accusations may have been taken to heart and at least a part of the group's future product will be going up-market. For instance, it has engaged Bill (*Gregory's Girl*) Forsyth to direct Oscar-winning star Diane Keaton in a film called *Housekeeping*, and there are other similarly ambitious plans in the production folder including four major features for Warner release (including two Sylvester Stallone starrers) and the fourth *Superman* movie. No wonder the year's activities included a move into impressive new headquarters in Los Angeles.

Although the major Hollywood film companies made fewer films in 1985 – at 105, down by 25 from 1984 – the grand total of American films went up from 318 to 330, thanks to the activities of independent moviemakers.† In fact more films were started in 1985 than has been the case for some 12 years.

A possible brake on future major productions will be the news that during 1985 only 40 per cent of films were anything like financial successes, as against about 50 per cent for several years previously (these figures apply only to American cinema release, of course: later income from non-American showings and release on video-cassette often turns a potential loser into a winner). One pleasant sidelight on all this is that of the 'foreign' films shown in the US it is the British imports that seem to have done the best business.

*If you think that open-air cinemas in the UK are impractical, the response from the open-airers is that they run some very successful drive-ins in Nova Scotia!

†According to a mid-term report, feature-film production by the major Hollywood production companies shot up for the first three months of 1986 to more than 50 per cent over the same period in 1985; figures from the independents were also up, by almost 10 per cent. During the period the Hollywood 'majors' had started 29 films, in comparison with last year's 19. The same review indicated that both the British and the Australian studios were less busy during the period; an overall drop of 21 per cent.

The moviemakers: Richard Zanuck (son of famous father Darryl), Lili Fini Zanuck and David Brown, the partners of the Zanuck-Brown production company whose films include two of the most successful ever made: *Jaws* and *The Sting*. This photo of the trio in fact comes from the set of their most recent winner, *Cocoon*.

One good piece of American production news was that (in contrast to Britain) the cost of making a movie during 1985–6 was no longer rising at the horrific rate of the previous few years. According to *Variety* (that marvellous source of all world-wide showbiz information – what *should* we do without it?) the average budget for the 138 films made by the Hollywood 'majors' during 1985 worked out at $10,700,000, with the projected costs for 1986 productions rising by only 5 per cent above that.

An interesting item, 1986 American production news was Dino de Laurentiis's purchase of Embassy Pictures from the Coca-Cola conglomerate (which, as you might recall, now owns Columbia Pictures) with the idea of transforming the company into a major one; not only making a continuous flow of movies but also distributing other producers' films. At the time of writing it seems that Dino has hopes of releasing eight Embassy banner productions before the end of 1986.

A 1986 production news item of major nostalgia value concerned an announcement that RKO Radio were back in business (many great films were made under the RKO banner in the past), with co-production interests in half a dozen Australian films and a similar number of New Zealand productions.

In contrast to the rising attendance figures in Britain for 1985–6, the year ending in December 1985 was a tale of doom and gloom for American managements, with an estimated 11 per cent drop in the admission figures for the period, though one mustn't forget that even the lower figure still topped the billion mark!

The drop caused dismay and anger in the ranks of the cinema-owners. A lot of that ire was directed at that old enemy the video-cassette, with a vociferous demand that there should be a statutory six-month gap between the cinema showing of a film and its release on home video. It was pointed out that in France the minimum period, by law, is one year.

The clouds had cleared somewhat by the spring of 1986, when it was revealed that US cinema admissions were running at a steady 3 per cent over the same period last year. Announcing these cheerier statistics, *Variety* commented: 'Too many junk films caused last year's recession, and the recent crop of hits (*Out of Africa, Delta Force, Pretty in Pink, Down and Out in Beverly Hills* and *The Color Purple* among them) has turned the business around. Nothing more, nothing less.'

In terms of movie-goers' behaviour it seems our American cousins show up pretty badly compared with their British counterparts. According to a *Wall Street Journal* report in March (1986), on an average night American movie-goers toss enough rubbish on to the floor to fill 10 large plastic sacks. And one, more serious, movie-goer complained that he had to change seats twice during the screening of a feature because of the – largely youthful – audience's general rowdiness and the 'lecherous shouts' of teenage girls!

It seems, according to the managements, that in Britain the type of film being shown has a direct influence on the amount of litter dropped and bad behaviour exhibited. One manager went on record as saying that when he showed a 'class' film audiences were pretty decent and took their rubbish home with them. But when they showed a film such as *Rambo* the rubbish problem becomes a major one. Another manager was quoted as saying that with films like *Nightmare on Elm Street* he had to employ seven or eight security guards to help out his regular staff.

A sad event for London's more serious movie-goers was the closure in April 1986, after some 50 years, of the Academy Cinemas in Oxford Street. Opening as The Picture House in 1913, changing its name and policy in 1928, the Academy since 1944 had been run by George Hoellering (who died in 1980) and his stepson Ivo Jarosy, who premièred many outstanding films (they introduced Bergman to British movie-goers) which otherwise would never have had a showing in Britain. Another sad departure from London's specialist-cinema scene (though in this case the cinema itself remained open under new management) was that of David and Barbara Stone, who once ran four cinemas but in 1985 decided to sell the last of these – The Gate at Notting Hill – and go into the restaurant business. But these specialist cinemas *can* still be successful, as witness the statement by Romaine Hart of Mainline Films that while it had anticipated that 180,000 seats would be occupied in their Screen-on-the-Green cinema during 1985, in fact it ended the year with a figure in excess of 240,000.

Now let's turn to a number of diverse matters, some serious, some amusing, all relevant, I think, and all contributing to an overall picture of the cinematic year.

By 1986 Britain had the third-largest number of video recorders in the world, with a total in excess of 8½ million sets. The same survey suggested that 42 per cent of all British homes now have a second TV set (and 25 per cent, incidentally, now own a micro-computer). On the other hand, a survey suggested that one in every dozen purchasers of a video recorder discards it within the first year and that the total of such sets now gathering dust amounts to almost 1¼ million.

Cable TV has certainly not yet taken off in Britain. *Variety*'s survey of the situation suggested that while 1986 has seen an extension of the territory covered, there has actually been a fall in the number of subscribers.

Technically the year has seen nothing of great importance, although there have been a few stories worth recording. For instance, in his film *Power*, Sidney Lumet tried out a new computerized editing process that allows the editor to arrange, re-arrange and view film almost immediately, thus eliminating the comparatively slow and laborious process of cutting and splicing. Already in use in TV and video, the new process proved so successful in *Power* that it seems likely to eventually be adopted by most film producers of the future.

Another interesting technical advance has been an electronic subtitling system which, the technicians claim, will in due course take over from the old methods of superimposing dialogue. In the new system lines appear in red letters *outside* the picture area, either just below or just above the image on a computer-controlled display screen. The display can accommodate two lines of dialogue at the same time.

Subtitling certainly needs improving. Too often now the captions appear so fleetingly that there is no time to read them before they have vanished, and they demand so much concentration that you are apt to miss the visual images.

Unless I am mistaken things were better in the past, when one had a chance both to see the film and to read the caption. Maybe they try to squeeze in more of the dialogue now than they used to in the past. Do readers think my complaint is justified?

A further technical innovation unveiled in London in the summer of 1985 was a new high-speed 16mm colour negative film designed for shooting night scenes and dim interiors. It was claimed to make such sequences sharper and provide an improved image.

Although it was primarily for television presentation, MGM spent some £12 million with a firm called Colour Systems Technology to convert 100 films in its black-and-white movie library into full colour, starting with *Yankee Doodle Dandy* (suddenly topical again after the death of its star, James Cagney, in the spring). Disney at about the same time contracted the same firm to convert 16 of its Shirley Temple films in the same way, and it is not difficult to imagine that sooner or later we shall be seeing at least some of these in the cinema – although it is a moot point whether discerning audiences will hail the colouring up of classic movies conceived in black-and-white as an improvement.

Having lost its Eady Fund contributions of about £½ million the British Film Institute's production wing found itself in considerably straitened circumstances, reckoning that its reduced income would mean it could only make one small-budget film a year, as against the four or more it would otherwise have produced. The average BFI budget stands at about the £½ million mark, *Distant Voices* having been brought in for less than that and *Caravaggio* more (both were released during 1986). It looks as if the BFI will have increasingly to depend on Channel 4 for its funding, and in fact Channel 4 has become the major and sometimes only source of hope for many independent producers.

In 1985 a total of some 60 million Hungarians went to the cinema, the money-making local production being *Colonel Redl*. The several other Hungarian films which reached us were invariably gloomy, often shot in black-and-white.

In Italy, too, there was plenty of gloom in 1985. Italian studios produced only 90 films – the first time in a long, long while that the figure has dropped below the three-figure mark. And the attendance figures for the twelve months from the summer of 1984 to summer 1985 showed a considerable slackening-off.

In Germany, both East and West, figures suggested that movie-going was on the decline. In East Germany the total of 70 million showed a drop of some 3½ million, and in the West attendance slipped to the lowest figure recorded since the war.

In France, too, after several years of rising totals the cinema-going figure showed a reduction of some 8 per cent. Incidentally, production figures for French films were no more optimistic, with 10 fewer features made during 1985 than were made in 1984 (151 against 161), and this unhappy trend continued well into 1986. But one item from France was interesting in more than one way: the announcement of the first Indian-European co-production (France-Belgium-Switzerland-India), to be directed in India by Mrinal Sen.

In Spain, where about 48½ million people went to the cinemas during 1985, local productions appeared to hold little attraction (with one or two exceptions); of the 15 top box-office moneytakers only one was homemade, and the government's efforts to get the industry blossoming – to the extent of contributing a subsidy of up to 50 per cent of production costs – seemed to be having little impact.

In Egypt – the so-called 'Hollywood of the Middle East' – things are not well. The total of cinemas operating in the country has dropped over the years from 350 to less than 200 (Cairo, with its population of 10 million has only ten cinemas now) and many of these are apparently in a pretty poor state of repair. Production has slacked off, too, to about 50 films a year, many of which are pretty mediocre.

From Turkey, too, the story is a sad one: falling attendance figures and fewer productions. A local critic there is on record as saying that only 60,000 went to the cinemas in Istanbul in the last quarter of 1984, as compared with 160,000 during the same period the previous year. In 1970 the national attendance figure was 250 million movie-goers going to 2,400 cinemas, but by the end of the 'seventies those totals were down by two-thirds and half respectively. And whereas in the not-too-distant past Turkey was turning out some 200 movies a year, that figure has sunk to below 80.

One has to turn to India for some of the year's cheeriest statistics. There within the past twelve months box-office takings have made a 12 per cent jump and the numbers of operating cinemas has risen by 164 to a grand total of 12,448.

The USSR, too, has been the source of some optimistic stories recently. It seems that a new air of relaxation has spread to the moviemakers there. Without any observable frowns from above, the Soviet producers are aiming to make

The Taviani brothers, Paolo and Vittorio, one of the rare examples of successful shared direction, on the set of their film *The Night of San Lorenzo – La Notte di San Lorenzo*, one of many classic Italian films they have produced since their *Padre Padrone* (1977) became the first film ever to win both the Golden Palm Grand Prix and the International Critics' prizes at the Cannes Film Festival.

An interesting point about recent releases has been the number of silent – and sound – screen classics which, generally refurbished with clear, bright new prints and specially created musical scores have met with success, although in some cases they have also been shown on television. They have included Douglas Fairbanks' *The Black Pirate*, *High Noon* (both illustrated), *Black Narcissus*, *Alice in Wonderland*, *Citizen Kane*, *Pandora and the Flying Dutchman*, *The Life and Death of Colonel Blimp*, *M* (the 1951 film), *The Wages of Fear* and *Les Diaboliques*.

films of wider national and international appeal; indeed, they claim that already the new-style Soviet movies have created such a wide interest abroad that there are not enough to satisfy the demands of the various film festivals. The USSR is also taking ever more non-Soviet films, including American ones, and is in turn making a big effort to export its own movies – to the USA, amongst other countries. Additionally, it is showing a much greater interest than heretofore in the possibility of international co-productions.

The fashion (started by Kevin Brownlow with his reconstruction of Abel Gance's silent epic *Napoleon*) for new presentations of silent classics continues at an ever-increasing pace. Carl Dreyer's *Joan of Arc* has recently undergone reconstruction, too, and was premiered at an Amsterdam cathedral, while Paris saw a rejuvenated *Intolerance* (D.W. Griffith). Early 1986 saw Alexander Volkoff's *Casanova* getting the treatment – and a starry premiere in Paris (made in 1927, the film now has a specially composed musical score by Georges Delerue).

Meanwhile Brownlow and David Gill were doing that same kind of restoration work on Erich von Stroheim's gargantuan 1924 film *Greed* and the 1925 *Ben-Hur*, though in these cases it appears likely that the films will be seen on television before they are shown in the cinemas.

As an interesting footnote to this subject, at the last Barcelona Film Festival *The Wind* (1928), starring Lillian Gish, was voted the most popular film of the festival.

After the success of the series of special film-star stamps put on sale by the Post Office to coincide with British Film Year (see illustration) the USA announced that it would be releasing a special Laurel and Hardy issue in 1987 to commemorate the anniversary of the initial teaming of the pair.

Having had a flop with the initial launch of his 'straight' 1940s period detection piece *It's Called Murder Baby*, director Anthony Spinelli and producer Billy Thornberg hauled it back into the cutting room, added an explicit sex sequence and re-issued it with the title *Dixie Ray, Hollywood Star*, with which label the film walked away with the 'Best Direction', 'Best Picture', 'Best Screenplay', 'Best Editing', 'Best Photography' and 'Best Art Direction' Awards at the 9th annual prizegiving of the Adult Film Association of America!

The ever-spreading panic caused by Rock Hudson's highly publicized death from AIDS resulted in the Screen Actors' Guild of America demanding that in future producers must notify actors and actresses in advance if their roles call for any 'open-mouth' kissing, so that players may opt out if they are nervous of catching the disease. The worried producers did their best to allay such fears but nobody was prepared actually to *guarantee* that infection was impossible. SAG is therefore continuing to press for a ruling in its favour.

The most financially successful half-dozen movies to be shown in the USA and Canada during 1985, in cash order, were: *Back to the Future, Rambo, Rocky IV, Beverly Hills Cop, Cocoon* and *The Goonies*, while *Silverado* came 22nd, *The Killing Fields* 25th and *A Passage to India* 27th. Incidentally, by the end of 1985 *Amadeus* had taken £50 million from box-offices around the world and the money was still pouring in during 1986.

You might watch out for a film called *Clue* if it hasn't already come your way. Four different endings were shot for it, to play simultaneously at four different cinemas, the producers hoping that the gimmick will mean cinema-goers seeing more than one version in order to find out what happened in the other last reel! Well, it's original, anyway.

Though unfamiliar in the UK – as far as I can recall only one of the several features has been shown in Britain – Asterix is a greatly beloved and popular comic strip cartoon in his native France and his fame has been spreading around the world. The books of his colourful adventures have sold more than 160 million in 33 different languages. Now Gaumont is making two more feature animation films about the little Gaul; the first of these, *Asterix v. Caesar*, was actually finished in time for a Christmas release and the second, *Asterix and the Britons*, is well into production, if not already completed. I hope we'll get a chance to see at least the latter, in view of that title . . .

Russ Meyer, a producer well known, though perhaps not internationally famous, for his porno features, has been spending all his spare time – and more than $1 million in cash – in making his Big Movie (about himself!) at present titled *The Breast of Russ Meyer*, which he reckons will run

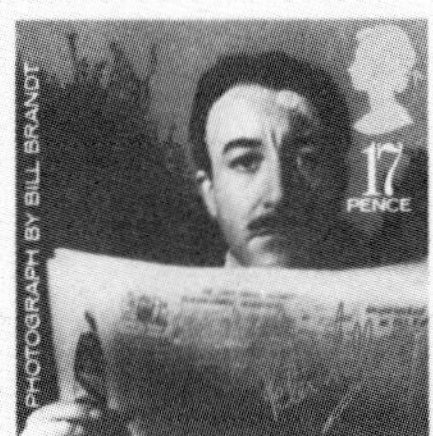

To join in the British Film Year celebrations, the Post Office produced a special issue of 'film star' stamps on 9 October 1985 and kept them on sale for some weeks. The set's values and stars were as follows: top left, 17p – Peter Sellers; top right, 22p – David Niven; centre, 29p Charles Chaplin; bottom left, 31p – Vivien Leigh; 34p – Alfred Hitchcock.

for more than twelve hours and will be the mamillary movie to end all mamillary movies! The film will be largely autobiographical, and Meyer says that although his epic will be a soft- rather than a hardcore sex movie, he was considering adding a hardcore sequence featuring himself 'and a lady friend'.

Germany, by the way, seems to have found its equivalent to France's always-controversial Jean-Luc Godard in Herbert Achternbusch, whose *Das Gespenst (The Ghost)* depicts Jesus coming to Earth and taking the job of a barman in a convent! Though it outraged many, it apparently did not enjoy much box-office success on its home ground.

Now a couple of end-pieces to add to any trivia items you may be collecting. Early in 1986 Ginger Rogers filed suit in the New York Federal Court in an effort to block distribution of the new Fellini film *Ginger and Fred*. Miss Rogers was asking for £2 million compensatory damages and a further £3¼ million in exemplary damages, claiming that the producers had not sought her consent to use her name. The infuriated Miss Rogers claimed the film showed her in a false light and suggested that she and Fred had been lovers!

During a big economy drive in the Disney studios *Variety* reported that 'in a minuscule but nevertheless symbolic action the Disney studio barber has been clipped'.

Happy movie-going.

TV Feature Films of the Year

In this section you will find all the made-for-television feature movies show on BBC1 and BBC2, ITV and Channel 4 during the period covered by the annual. The date given in brackets after each title is the year the feature was made. In the case of repeat broadcasts, the date of the previous broadcast is given along with a note of the *Film Review* in which they were first listed.

Accounts (1983). TV film of considerable status, which captures realism in its warm and moving story about the 'widder-woman' and her two lively teenage sons trying to make a go of their small farm in the Border country. One of the most completely acceptable TV films of 1986. Cast: Elspeth Charlton, Robert Smeaton, Michael McNally, etc. Dir: Michael Darlow. Screenplay: Michael Wilcox. Channel 4, 6 February 1986.

American Dream (1981). The problems of a Chicago family whose pecuniary state forces them to move down-market when the size of their family demands larger accommodation. And it works out far more interestingly than you might imagine, thanks to a good script and splendid performances. Featuring Steven Macht, Hans Conreid, John McIntire and Karen Carlson. Dir: Mel Damski. Screenplay: Ronald Cohen, Barbara Corday and Ken Hecht. Channel 4, 16 July 1985.

Anatomy of an Illness (1983). Heart-warming, real-life story of the power of mind over matter; telling how an American *Saturday Review* editor fought and cheerfully won his battle against a rare and crippling bone disease. A really rewarding two hours of TV. Featuring Eli Wallach, Edward Asner and Millie Perkins. Dir: Richard T. Heffron. Screenplay: Laurence Roman; based on the book by the editor Norman Cousins. Channel 4, 26 November 1985.

Another Time, Another Place (1982). This brilliant TV feature, which earned a cinema showing in the summer of 1983, depicts a tragic war-time love affair between a restless farmer's wife and one of the Italian POWs working on her husband's farm in bleakest north-east Scotland. A beautifully observed picture of the contrasting ways of life of the dour Scots and the warm, sensual Italians, with a marvellous performance by Phyllis Logan. See *Film Review 1984–5* for full details. Channel 4, 4 July 1985.

Any Second Now (1969). A former hero in British films, Stewart Granger, is a villain in this his first TV film feature, playing a photographer whose plan to murder his wealthy wife goes very, very sour . . . Also featuring: Lois Nettleton, Dana Wynter, Katy Jurado, etc. Dir and Screenplay: Gene Levitt. ITV, 8 March 1986.

Assignment Munich (1972). Baddies and goodies (US agents) after $5 million worth of gold, the location of which was only known by a dead man. All the weaving and dealing occurs in the German town of the title. Cast: Roy Scheider, Richard Basehart, Lesley Ann Warren, Keenan Wynn, etc. Dir: David Lowell Rich. Screenplay: Eric Bercovici and Jerry Ludwig. ITV, 28 June 1986.

Bad Blood (1981). Reconstruction of a sensational New Zealand murder hunt during World War II when a farmer in a remote community ran amok and shot seven people before being finally besieged by the police (four of whom die during the proceedings). Cast: Jack Thompson, Carol Burns, Dennis Lill, etc. Dir: Mike Newell. Screenplay: Andrew Brown; based on the book *Manhunt* by H. A. Willis. Channel 4, 20 February 1986.

Bad Hats (1982). The odyssey of two World War I soldiers, one French, the other British, both deserters from the Somme trenches, who meet, team up and sail to Ireland. Star Mick Ford helped with the screenplay. Also featuring Marcel Bozzuffi and Catherine Lachens. Dir: Pascal Ortega. Screenplay: Robert Hickson and Ford. Channel 4, 14 November 1985.

Bill (1981). An outstanding performance by Mickey Rooney as a mentally retarded character winning through (and winning viewers' hearts) in the harsh and unfriendly climate of New York. Memorable and well worthy of the Best Actor Emmy award that Mickey won for this. Dir: Anthony Page. No writing credit. Channel 4, 3 December 1985.

Billion-dollar Threat (1979). See *Film Review 1984–5*. ITV, 25 August 1986. Originally shown on same channel on 25 August 1983.

Blood Hunt (1985). Dour story of a man seeking revenge for the killing of his brother; and how the man with whom the accidental killer takes shelter tries to bring about some sort of reconciliation. It all takes place in the Scottish Highlands. Cast: Iain Glen, Michael Carter, Nigel Stock, etc. Dir: Peter Barber-Fleming. Screenplay: Neil Gunn; based on the book by Stewart Conn. BBC2, 16 March 1986.

Born Beautiful (1982). The problems facing models when they reach 30 and the jobs start to tail off. Luckily for her, our heroine is made of tough stuff and switches careers effectively. Featuring Erin Gray, Lori Singer, Polly Bergen and Joe Coffee. Dir: Harvey Hart. Screenplay: Rose Goldembeeg. Channel 4, 12 November 1985.

Boy of the Muddy Shore (1982). And now a TV feature from South Korea – a somewhat sentimental but occasionally touching tale about a small boy and his grandmother taking refuge in a small fishing village when they are driven away from their home by the war, c. 1953. Fascinating backgrounds. Cast: Kang Tae-Ho, Han Eun-Chin. Dir: Chang Hyong-il. Screenplay: Kim Ha-Rim; from a story by Han Nam-Choi. BBC2, 18 April 1986.

Broken Promise (1980). Seriously treated story of a quintet of kids who are left to fend for themselves in Kansas, and the efforts of the eldest (an extremely able performance by Melissa Michaelsen) to find a way through the red tape and keep the family together. Also featuring Chris Saradon, George Coe, McKee Anderson and David Haskell. Dir: Don Taylor. Screenplay: Stephen Kandel; based on the book by Alex Lazzarino and Kent Hayes. BBC2, 14 August 1985.

Bronk (1975). Another version of the familiar story about a dedicated cop, Bronkov (Jack Palance) who, although an innocent victim, is forced to resign from the police and then, with the mayor's blessing, sets out to uncover the drug-running crooks. Rest of cast: Tony King, Joseph Mascolo, etc. Dir: Richard Donner. Screenplay: Ed Waters, Al Martinez, Carroll O'Connor and Bruce Geller. ITV, 31 May 1986.

The Capture of Grizzly Adams (1981). ITV, 2 September 1985. Previously shown on same channel 25 December 1983. See *Film Review 1984–5*.

A Caribbean Mystery (1983). ITV, 22 May 1986. Originally shown on same channel on 23 March 1984. See *Film Review 1984–5*.

Champions – A Love Story (1979). While they're obviously no Torvill and Dean, Joy LeDuc and Paul Vincent McNichol appear to be able enough skaters in this story about a young couple with championship aspirations who come up against parental opposition to their love and their sporting ambitions. Also featuring Tony Le Bianco and Shirley Knight. Dir: John Alonzo. Screenplay: John Sacret Young. BBC1, 14 July 1985.

Chiller (1985). Rather unpleasant little horror piece about a young man, revived from a deep-freeze sleep after ten years, whose personality has been chilled to murderous intent in the interim . . . Cast: Michael Beck, Paul Sorvino, Beatrice Straight. Dir: John Hobbs. Screenplay: Richard Ommanney. BBC1, 12 May 1986.

The Christmas Coal Mine Miracle (1977). A real-life story about an American mine disaster which happened on Christmas Eve, 1951, and the aftermath of social unrest when workers and boss met head-on in a struggle about increased safety measures. Featuring Kurt Russell, Mitchell Ryan, John Carradine and Barbara Babcock. Dir: Jud Taylor. Screenplay: Dalene Young. ITV, 16 December 1985.

Christmas Present (1985). Seasonal tear-jerker about an unlikely bank director and his search for a deserving family in Camden Town, knowing that if he can't find them, there will be no job to go back to after the holiday! There are plenty of giggles among the tears. Featuring Bill Fraser, Peter Chelsom and Clive Parker. Dir and Screenplay: Tony Bicat. Channel 4, 19 December 1985.

City Killer (1984). Pretty Heather Locklear suffers from the very unwelcome attentions of a psycho who expresses his passion for her by blowing up a large office building – killing all inside – and then threatening to do more explosive mayhem unless . . . Lots of well-generated tension and some nice acting. Also featuring: Gerald McRaney, Terence Knox, Audrey Totter. Dir: Robert Lewis. Screenplay: William Wood. ITV, 5 January 1986.

Climb an Angry Mountain (1972). Remember Fess Parker as Daniel Boone in the TV series? Well, this feature hoped to re-launch him as a Northern Californian lawman, but didn't hit the nail on the head hard enough, so it was aborted. But it's still an interesting movie, showing him and his New York cop team-mate tracking an erring Indian and his hostage through the high snows. Also featuring: Barry Nelson, Stella Stevens, etc. BBC2, 16 May 1986.

The Concrete Cowboys (1979). Tom Selleck and Jerry Read as two hobo-ish cowboys who end up penniless in Nashville and, after accepting an offer to turn detective and trace the missing sister of a singer, straightaway jog into danger. Also featuring Morgan Fairchild and Lucille Benson. Dir: Burt Kennedy. Screenplay: Jimmy Sangster. ITV, 2 December 1985.

Counting Sheep (1982). TV movie from Czechoslovakia, and one for the kids, too. A marvellous performance by 11-year-old Zaneta Fuchsova as the happy little girl living in a clinic, whose eyes are opened about life outside her closed world by a new member of the staff. Dir: Karel Kachyna. Screenplay: Kachyna and J. Cabradek. BBC2, 5 April 1986.

The Cradle Will Fall (1983). About a lady assistant D.A. whose overnight stay in the local hospital after a car accident and her subsequent enquiry into an apparent suicide lead to her becoming the nasty's next target. Featuring Lauren Hutton, Ben Murphy and James Farentino. Dir: John Llewellyn Moxey. Screenplay: Jerome Coopersmith; based on the book by Mary Higgins Clark. BBC1, 19 October 1985.

Crowhaven Farm (1970). Neat little frightener about a woman who has scary dreams about a crowd of threatening Puritans; only later does she learn the dark secret of the New England farm which she and her husband have bought. Featuring Hope Lange, Paul Burke, John Carradine and Lloyd Bochner. Dir: Walter Grauman. Screenplay: John McGreevey. ITV, 7 November 1985.

A Cry for Love (1980). Another truth-based TV movie, but this one is a sorry, sordid tale about overdoing drugs and drink and the knock-on effect this produces in friends and family. Not one pleasant character nor one lighter moment relieve the sordid gloom. Ugh! Featuring Susan Blakely, Powers Boothe, Gene Barry and Edie Adams. Dir: Paul Wendkos. No screenplay credit listed. Channel 4, 5 November 1985.

Cry Panic (1974). Why do the small-town cops refuse to believe that John

Forsythe has knocked down and killed a pedestrian? What are they, and the local population, trying to cover up? Well-made thriller. Also featuring: Anne Francis, Earl Holliman, etc. Dir: James Goldstone. Screenplay: Jack B. Sowards. ITV, 13 May 1986.

Dangerous Company (1982). A serious movie based on the question as to whether imprisonment is the only answer for all criminals. Loosely modelled on a true story, it tells of a long-time lawbreaker who after 27 years in jails became socially conscious and found a new life helping other criminals on to the straight and narrow. Featuring Beau Bridges, Carlos Brown, Karen Carlson and Jan Sterling. Dir: Lamont Johnson. Screenplay: Christopher Keane; based on Ray Johnson's story of his life. BBC2, 21 August 1985.

Deadly Messages (1985). Splendid, stylish thriller, with everything to make the watcher sit on the edge of his seat as it tells a story about a girl pursued with evil intent by a maniacal killer who appears already to have done away with her friend . . . Featuring Kathleen Beller, Michael Brandon and Dennis Franz. Dir: Jack Bender. Screenplay: Bill Bleich. ITV, 15 September 1985.

Death at Love House (1976). When screen-writers Robert Wagner and Kate Jackson start to research for a film about silent star Lorna Love (Mariana Hill), they find more than enough material – to their peril! And how marvellous to see veterans Sylvia Sidney, (the late) Joan Blondell, Dorothy Lamour and John Carradine in the cast. Dir: E. W. Swackhamer. Screenplay: Jim Barnett. ITV, 19 June 1986.

Death Cruise (1974). Sea-going whodunit with the passengers getting the chop one by one, like Agatha Christie's 'Ten Little Indians', from a mysterious killer, on board their luxury liner. It's the ship's doctor turned 'tec who, a few bodies later, finds the solution. Killing fun. Cast: Michael Constantine, Polly Bergen, Celeste Holm, Edward Albert, Richard Long, etc. Dir: Ralph Senesky. Screenplay: Jack B. Sowards. ITV, 3 June 1986.

Death Penalty (1980). Based firmly, though perhaps not quite fairly, on the subject of American killers lined up along Death Row awaiting their turn for the chop, this story is about the fight to save a young Puerto Rican murderer from joining the queue. Featuring Dana Elcar, Colleen Dewhurst and Frank Robles. Dir: Waris Hussein. Screenplay: Edward Adler. ITV, 9 November 1985.

Death Squad (1973). Remember that tough cop 'Dirty Harry', played by Clint Eastwood? Well, this is the TV version of his *Magnum Force* feature. Rest of cast: Melvyn Douglas, Robert Forster, Michelle Phillips, etc. Dir: Harry Falk. Screenplay: James David Buchanan and Ronald Austin. ITV, 26 June 1986.

Death Stalk (1975). Escaped jailbirds (played by Vic Morrow and Neville Brand) abduct the terrified wives of a couple of holidaymakers river-tripping on a raft, and hold them hostage. Featuring Vince Edwards, Anjanette Comer, Robert Webber and Carol Lynley. Dir: Robert Day. Screenplay: Steven Kandel and J. W. Bloch. ITV, 28 November 1985.

Deep Water (1983). German TV movie thriller based on one of Patricia Highsmith's books, a psychological murder tale about the turbulent undercurrents of a marriage which, on the surface, is all loving calm. Featuring Peter Bongartz and Constance Engelbrecht. Dir: Franz Peter Wirth. Screenplay: Wirth and Leopold Ahlsen. BBC2, 27 December 1985.

The Defection of Simas Kudirka (1977). That fine actor Alan Arkin on top form in another TV movie based on a true story: it concerns a Russian sailor who decided when his ship docked in America (in 1970) that he would like to swop Eastern oppression for Western decadence. So he leapt on to the US Coastguard boat drawn up alongside, causing a considerable strain on international relations. Also featuring Richard Jordan, Donald Pleasence and Shirley Knight. Dir: David Lowell Rich. Screenplay: Bruce Feldman. BBC1, 8 November 1985.

Delta County, USA (1977). Things still seethe in America's Deep South, it appears, and there are lots of seethes here in this small and fading town, with jealousy, revenge, sex, drink and raw passion to keep it bubbling. Quite a familiar theme, but quite a well-handled re-tread. Featuring Doney Oatman, Jeff Conaway, Joanna Miles, Peter Donat and Lola Albright. Dir: Glenn Jordan. Screenplay: Thomas Rickman. BBC1, 6 September 1985.

The Disappearance of Azaria Chamberlain (1983). The documentary-style story of the bizarre Australian trial of the early '80s, when, although they protested that a dingo was responsible, the parents of baby Chamberlain were arraigned on a charge of killing their child. Cast: Elaine Hudson, John Hamblin, etc. Dir: Judy Rymer. Screenplay: Frank Moorehouse. ITV, 25 June 1986.

Don't Look Back (1981). Baseball films have generally been the kiss of death to the British cinema and it's doubtful whether they are any more popular on the small screen. This is the factually based story of a Negro 'pitcher' star who, in spite of prejudice, rose from reformatory to the game's big-time. Featuring Louis Gossett Jr, Cleavon Little, Ossie Davis and Donald Blakely. Dir: Richard Colla. Screenplay: Rob Rubin. BBC2, 20 November 1985.

Drying up the Streets (1978). The sad situation of an (ex-) professor hooked on heroin who finds his long-lost daughter is also on the stuff and has, moreover, if reluctantly, taken up the trade of hooker! Strong stuff from Canadian TV. With Don Franks, Len Cariou and Sarah Torgov. Dir: Robin Spry. Screenplay: B. A. Cameron. Channel 4, 19 July 1985.

Due to an Act of God – Im Zeichen des Kreuzes (1983). A scary and highly topical West German TV film, first released in British cinemas. (See *Film Review 1984–5* for details.) BBC2, 1 March 1986.

An Early Frost (1985). The first time on either large or small screen that the fatal disease AIDS has motivated a fictional film. And a pretty sober treatment it gets too. Cast: Gena Rowlands, Sylvia Sidney, Aidan Quinn, Ben Gazzara. Dir: John Erman. Screenplay: Ron Cowen and Daniel Lipman. ITV, 3 May 1986.

Enola Gay (American title: **Enola Gay: the Men, the Mission, the Atomic Bomb** (1980). Carefully constructed, straightforward relating of the dropping of the Bomb on Hiroshima. Cast includes Patrick Duffy, Billy Crystal, Kim Darby, James Shigeta, Henry Wilcoxon and Ed Nelson. Dir: David Lowell Rich. Screenplay: James Poe and Millard Kaufman; based on the book by Gordon Thomas and Max Morgan-Witts. Channel 4, 6 August 1985.

Every Move She Makes (1984). Highly competent thriller from Australia with the familiar screen story about an unfortunate young lady hounded by the psycho who becomes obsessed with her. Cast: Julie Nihill, Doug Bowles, James Laurie, etc. Dir and Screenplay: Catherine Millar. ITV, 21 April 1986.

Every Picture Tells a Story (1984). Nice little film made by James Scott as a tribute to his artist father. Though made for the small screen it was first shown on the large one, at the Minema in March 1985. See *Film Review 1985–6*, Releases of the Year. Channel 4, 27 October 1985.

The Eyes of Birds (1982). Grim French-made prison drama about life in a South American jail and the story of some of its unhappy inmates. Cast: Philippe Clevenot, Roland Amstutz, etc. Dir and Screenplay: Gabriel Auer. Channel 4, 13 March 1986.

Evil Roy Slade (1972). Another feature introduction to a series which – alas, in view of its comic quality – was stillborn. A welcome return to the western genre, with John Astin as the villain of the title who hears those romantic old bells when he kisses a schoolteacher (Pamela Austin), victim of his *banditismo*! Also featuring Mickey Rooney, Dick Shawn, Dom DeLuise, Milton Berle and Edie Adams. Dir: Jarry Paris. Screenplay: Garry Marshall and Jerry Belson. Channel 4, 30 July 1985.

Family Reunion (1981). With her retirement gift of a bus pass without limits, schoolmarm Bette Davis sets out to visit long-lost relatives, returning only to find she must deal with dirty politicians and crooked businessmen who plan to sell off part of her home town. As usual with Bette, she *is* the film. Also featuring Roy Dotrice and Peter Weller. Dir: Fielder Cook. Screenplay: Allan Sloane. In two parts: BBC1, 26 July and 2 August 1985.

Fatal Vision (1984). Many recent TV feature films have been based on true stories and this rather better-than-average small-screen movie is no exception: its basis is the stranger-than-fiction investigation of the murder of an army captain's entire family at Fort Bragg, Carolina in the winter of 1970. The problem facing the cops was whether the Captain was the victim or the killer. Featuring Karl Malden, Eva Marie Saint, Gary Cole, Andy Griffith and Barry Newman. Dir: David Greene. Screenplay: John Gay; based on the book by Joe McGinniss. In two parts: BBC1, 2 and 4 September 1985.

Fellow Travellers (1983). A thriller from Israel about a popstar from that country who becomes, because of his pro-Arab leanings, embroiled in a fight between an Arab terrorist and the Israeli anti-terrorist force. Cast: Gidi Gov, Yossi Pollak, etc. Dir: Yehuda Judd Neeman. Screenplay: Neeman and Amnon Lord. Channel 4, 17 April 1986.

Fifty Fifty (1984). The pilot feature which was successful enough to launch a new TV series about a couple of women – one a photographer and the other a musician – who inherit their husbands' private-eye business – a sort of privatized *Cagney and Lacey*. Cast: Linda Carter, Loni Anderson, Eileen Heckart. Dir: Harry Faulk. Screenplay: Leonard Stern and Jeffrey Lane. ITV, 24 March 1986.

Firehouse (1972). Racial tension in a big US city when arson is the suspected cause of a ghetto fire. It splits the fire-fighters into factions, too – young blacks *versus* white veterans (played, for example, by Richard Roundtree and Vince Edwards). Also featuring Andrew Duggan, Richard Jaeckel and Sheila Frazier. Dir: Alex March. Screenplay: Frank Cucci. ITV, 22 November 1985.

First Love – Sharma and Beyond (1984). Channel 4, 9 January 1986. Originally shown on same channel, 24 May 1984. See *Film Review 1984–5*.

Five Desperate Women (1971). Four in fact; the fifth of the quintet, who rub each other the wrong way on meeting again at their college reunion, is murdered. When they realize that they are similarly threatened, the remaining quartet come closer together. Cast: Stephanie Powers, Anjanette Comer, Joan Hackett, Juli Sommars, Robert Conrad. Dir: Ted Post. Screenplay: Norman and Walter Black. ITV, 28 April 1986.

Frankie and Johnnie (1985). Local reporter Hywel Bennett isn't happy at the suicide verdict when two teenagers are found dead in their car, so he follows the trail right back into TV's Holiest of Holies, BBC Television Centre in London – where he finds more than dirt under the carpet. Also featuring: Madoc Thriepland, Samuel West, etc. Dir: Martin Campbell. Screenplay: Paula Milne. BBC2, 2 February 1986.

Friendships, Secrets and Lies (1979). (They wouldn't get away with such a title in the cinema!) This is a whodunit with an all female cast and a high proportion of women on the other side of the cameras. The question: who killed the baby, found after a score of years in the rubble of a college? Cast includes Stella Stevens, Paula Prentiss, Tina Louise and Sondra Locke. Dir: Anna Zane Shanks and Marlene Laird. Screenplay: Joanna Jane; based on the novel by Babs H. Deal. ITV, 7 October 1985.

Fun and Games (1980). Aimed at all chauvinist pigs, like the anti-hero of this feminist film, whose efforts to get little Carol to sleep with him end up with a crusade on the woman's part, which rises from the factory floor to her union and the firm's head office, as she fights against male sexual attitudes. Cast: Valerie Harper, Cliff de Young, Jobeth Williams, etc. Dir: Alan Smithee. Screenplay: David Smilow and Elizabeth Wilson. BBC1, 17 February 1986.

Getting Married (1978). Light romantic comedy about a man who, finding his secret love is about to get married, decides to throw caution to the winds and carry out a top-speed wooing to make her change her mind – and choice of future husband. Featuring Bess Armstrong, Richard Thomas and Van Johnson. Dir: Stephen Stern. Screenplay: John Hudock. BBC2, 14 September 1985.

The Gift of Love (1978). BBC2, 16 November 1985. Previously shown on same channel 2 July 1983 See *Film Review 1984–5*.

Gnomes (1980). Channel 4, 21 December 1985. Previously shown on same channel 26 December 1984. See *Film Review 1985–6*.

The Golden Gate Murders (1979). Did he fall or was he pushed off 'Frisco's Golden Gate Bridge? A detective (David Janssen in one of his last roles) sets out to prove that a priest's death was murder and not suicide, as decreed by the initial verdict, with the unlikely assistance of a nun, played by Susannah York. Also featuring Lloyd Bochner, Kim Hunter and Tim O'Connor. Dir: Walter Grauman. Screenplay: David J. Kinghorn. ITV, 25 August 1985.

Good and Bad at Games (1983). Channel 4, 30 January 1986. Originally shown on same channel, 4 December 1983. See *Film Review 1984–5*.

Green Eyes (1976). BBC2, 31 July 1985. Previously shown on same channel, 3 October 1985. See *Film Review 1984–5*.

A Guide for the Married Woman (1978). Screenwriter Frank Tarloff's efforts to repeat the successful formula of his *A Guide for the Married Man* of ten years ago. Cybill Shepherd in her TV feature debut, stars as the bored housewife who finds dallying with men isn't always that exciting. With the comedy, some sharp shafts aimed at contemporary American life-styles. Also featuring: Charles Frank, Eve Arden. Dir: Hy Averback. Screenplay: Frank Tarloff. BBC1, 12 April 1986.

Hans Christian and the Geographic Society (1980). A lovely little comedy from Swedish TV featuring a butcher who becomes sick at the sight of blood, and many other oddball characters – a gallery of delightful eccentrics. Cast: Ernst-Hugo Jaregard, Per Oscarsson, etc. Dir: Lars-Lennart Forsberg. Screenplay: Goran Tunstrom; based on his novel. Channel 4, 8 May 1986.

Hear No Evil (1982). Made deaf in a baddie's attempt to blow him up in his car, 'Frisco cop Gil Gerard gallantly carries on his work of bringing to justice the motorcycle gang he suspects of being involved in drugs trafficking. Cast: Bernie Casey, Wings Hauser, etc. Dir: Harry Falk. Screenplay: Tom Lazarus. ITV, 20 January 1986.

Heatwave (1974). Made when 'disaster' movies were all the rage, this TV model is about a town threatened by abnormally hot weather. Luckily the place is full of good performers like Ben Murphy, Bonnie Bedelia, Lew Ayres and Lionel Johnson. Dir: Jerry Jameson. Screenplay: P. A. Fields and M. Weingart. ITV, 19 July 1985.

Her Life as a Man (1984). Predictable complications when a female aspirant who has been turned down for a sports reporting job disguises herself as a male applicant and gets the position. Cast: Robyn Douglass, Marc Singer, Joan Collins, Robert Culp, etc. Dir: Robert Ellis Miller. Screenplay: Diane English and Joanna Crawford; from 'My Life as a Man' feature in *The Village Voice* (New York City newspaper) by Carol Lyn Mithers. BBC1, 19 April 1986.

Hijack (1973). On the ground this time around: truckers David Janssen and Keenan Wynn find that the offer to renew their suspended licences if they'll take a secret cargo from Los Angeles to Houston in double-quick time has some hair-raisingly unexpected and murderous strings attached. Good, fast fun. Also featuring: Tom Tully, Lee Purcell, Jeanette Nolan. Dir: Leonard Horn. Screenplay: Michael Kelly. ITV, 4 June 1986.

Honest, Decent and True (1985). Another peep into the advertising world which is much more convincing and amusing when it stays in the office, far less so when it follows the people concerned to their homes. Cast: Derrick O'Connor, Yvonne French, Lyndsay Russell etc. Dir: Les Blair. Screenplay: presumably by the director. BBC2, 9 February 1986.

Hotel du Lac (1985). Beautifully acted British TV film adaptation of the prize-winning novel about a lady novelist, getting over an emotionally traumatic event, on an out-of-season holiday at a small Swiss lakeside hotel; after a period of calm, she has to face up to more emotional upsets. In the acting, the quality of the photography and general standards, it is way above the run-of-the-mill TV film. Cast: Anna Massey, Denholm Elliott, Googie Withers, Julia McKenzie, Patricia Hodge, Irene Handl, Barry Foster, Ann Firbank, etc. Dir: Giles Foster. Screenplay: Christopher Hampton; based on the novel by Anita Brookner. BBC2, 2 March 1986.

Hotline (1982). TV's Wonder Woman Lynda Carter plays as the victim of a self-confessed killer whose telephone calls eventually advise her that she is next on the list. Well made, routine stuff. Also featuring Steve Forrest, James Booth and Frank Stallone. BBC1, 16 November 1985.

The House on Greenapple Road (1970). BBC1, 8 March 1986. Originally shown on same channel 9 May 1983. See *Film Review 1983–4*.

A Husband for Caterina (1982). Utterly captivating Italian film about a father who 'buys' his spinster daughter (she's 30!) a husband but then finds he's purchased a lot of trouble along with the handsome rogue. It was good enough to merit a cinema release, at least in its country of origin. Cast: Stefano Madia, Anna Melato, Donato Petilla. Dir: Luigi Comencini. BBC2, 8 March 1986.

Ill Fares the Land (1983). Channel 4, 23 January 1986. Originally shown on same channel, 19 May 1983. See *Film Review 1983–4*.

In Like Flynn (1985). With plenty of big names to support her (such as TV 'tec William Conrad as well as Eddie Albert) in this feature pilot for a planned series, Jenny Seagrove plays a tough lady novelist turned snooper when she decides to investigate why the body of a long-missing Vietnam soldier has washed ashore in Jamaica. Well up to top TV drama standard. Dir: Richard Lang. Screenplay: Glen Larson. ITV, 4 January 1986.

Insurance Man (1985). Dramatist Alan Bennett brings his own quirky style of comedy-drama to a film about, or rather centred on, Franz Kafka, whom he presents not as the famous Czech author he was but as the accident insurance claims processor which was his normal job. This gives Bennett plenty of opportunities to comment upon bureaucratic indifference to the unfortunate individual. Idiosyncratic but, even though its flaws are increasingly evident as the film unfolds, still very fascinating. Featuring: Trevor Peacock, Alan MacNaughton, Robert Hines, etc. Dir: Richard Eyre. Screenplay: Alan Bennett. BBC2, 23 February 1986.

Ishi, the Last of his Tribe (1979). BBC2, 13 November 1985. Previously shown on same channel 19 September 1983. See *Film Review 1984–5*.

I Want to Keep My Baby (1976). Mariel Hemingway in her first TV feature as a 15-year-old going through difficult times as an unmarried mother. The script was apparently inspired by some actual case histories. Also featuring Susan Anspach, Jack Rader and Rhea Pearlman. Dir: Jerry Thorpe. Screenplay: Joanna Lee. BBC2, 7 August 1985.

The Jericho Mile (1979). TV feature released in Britain as a cinema movie on 2 December 1980 (see 'Releases in Detail' section of the 1980–81 *Film Review*). About a prison inmate who *unofficially* won the mile running gold medal in the Olympic Games! Featuring Peter Strauss and Brian Dennehy. BBC1, 9 December 1985.

Joe Dancer: The Big Black Pill (1981). One of a trio of TV films featuring private eye Joe Dancer (Robert Blake) who, in this episode, gets dangerously involved in political plots. Of a type, but watchable. Also featuring: Jobeth Williams, Wilford Brimley, Eileen Heckart, Carol Wayne. Dir: Reza Badiyi. Screenplay: Michael Butler. ITV, 18 November 1985.

Kentucky Woman (1983). Swallow this one if you can: glamorous Cheryl Ladd (late of *Charlie's Angels*) as the coal-miner's daughter who takes dad's place underground! What will they try to get away with next? Also featuring: Ned Beatty, Tess Harper, Brett Johnson. Dir and screenplay: Walter Doniger. Channel 4, 29 October 1985.

The Kid from Not-So-Big (1978). When the newspaper of the California town of Not-So-Big looks like folding with the death in a fire of its owner, brave 12-year-old granddaughter Jenny decides to carry on! Real homey stuff set in the pioneering 1870s. Cast: Jennifer McAllister, Robert Viharo, Veronica Cartwright. Dir: Bill Grain. Screenplay: Desmond Nakano. ITV, 5 May 1986.

Killer by Night (1972). ITV, 15 March 1986. Originally shown on BBC1, 7 August 1984. See *Film Review 1985–6*.

Killing at Hell's Gate (1981). Shades of (the cinema film) *Deliverance*! Here is the same plot about two men on a holiday trip down the rapids on a raft, who find something more dangerous than rough water when they go through the gorge of the title. Cast: Robert Urich, Lee Purcell, Deborah Raffin, etc. Dir: Jerry Jameson. Screenplay: Lee Hutson. BBC1, 17 May 1986.

The Killing of Randy Webster (1980). BBC1, 23 May 1986. Originally shown on same channel on 22 October 1984. See *Film Review 1985–6*.

A Killer in the Family (1984). Another TV feature based on a real incident: a brutal jailbreak from the Arizona State Prison, organized by the two sons of a convicted killer. Featuring Robert Mitchum, James Spader, Lance Kerwin and Eric Stoltz as the Tison family. Dir: R. T. Heffron. Screenplay: Robert Aller. ITV, 31 August 1985.

The King and Queen (1985). These TV features are getting more international by the week . . . This one is from Spain, is set in Madrid in 1936 and is about a lovely duchess hiding in her own republican-occupied stately home, and her mysterious Fascist-spy night visitor. Cast: Omero Antonutti, Nuria Espert, etc. Dir: José Antonio Paramo. Screenplay: Paramo and Luis Arino; based on a novel by Ramon José Sender. Channel 4, 27 March 1986.

Lady Doctor (1980). She's played by Susan Sullivan, who finds herself torn between love and duty, and there's lots of supporting drama/comedy from her various patients. Also featuring: Tony Bill, Paula Prentiss, Carol Lynley, Wayne Rogers. Dir: Richard Michaels. Screenplay: Elizabeth Clark. ITV, 3 February 1986.

Legs (1983). And lots of them, too; shapely, well-muscled and very mobile . . . and all belonging to the Rockettes, the famous New York Radio City Music Hall dance troupe. The film is about three pretty aspirants and what happened to them. Fiction with a fascinating factual background. Cast: Sheree North, Gwen Verdon, Maureen Teefy, John Heard. Dir and Screenplay: Jerrold Freedman. Channel 4, 27 August 1985.

Letter to an Unknown Lover (1985). From France with love, this complicated satiric story – set *c*. 1943 – about an escaped POW who finds he has exchanged one prison for another with the sisters who shelter him. Superior drama in all departments. Cast: Cherie Lunghi, Yves Beneyton, Ralph Bates, Andrea Ferreol, etc. Dir: Peter Duffell. Screenplay: Jan Narcejac; based on the novel *Les Louves* by Pierre Boileau. Channel 4, 5 June 1986.

Lieutenant Schuster's Wife (1972). Lee Grant as a New York cop's widow who can't believe her late husband was on the 'take' and sets out to prove that he wasn't. Also featuring: Jack Warden, Nehemiah Persoff, Eartha Kitt. Dir: David Lowell Rich. Screenplay: Steven Boscho and Bernie Kukoff. ITV, 12 July 1985.

Like Normal People (1979). Yet another based-on-fact/social-problem picture, this time about mentally retarded youngsters who fall in love but, when they want to marry, come up against the state law against such things. And it's a very professionally presented mix of tears and smiles. Cast: Shaun Cassidy, Linda Purl, Hope Lange, James Keach, etc. Dir: Harvey Hart. Screenplay: Joanna Lee. BBC2, 23 May 1986.

Little Gloria . . . Happy at Last (1982). Some outstanding performances in an outstanding TV feature film, shown in two parts, which relates the custody 'battle of the century', with the mother and the aunt of the 'richest 10-year-old in the world' – the Vanderbilt heiress – struggling to gain custody of her. Cast: Bette Davis, Angela Lansbury, Glynnis Johns, Christopher Plummer, Martin Balsam, Maureen Stapleton, etc. Dir: Waris Hussein. Screenplay: William Hanley; based on the book by Barbara Goldsmith. ITV, 23 and 24 June 1986.

The Loneliest Runner (1976). The miseries of boyhood incontinence, as told in this story of American athlete John Curtis, whose weakness led to isolation and concentration on running training – and his eventual triumph on the track. An unusual subject. Featuring: Lance Kerwin, Michael Landon, Brian Keith. Dir and Screenplay: Michael Landon. BBC2, 8 September 1985.

The Longest Hundred Miles (1967). Routine war drama set in the Philippines in 1945 with GI Doug McClure, priest Ricardo Montalban, pretty nurse Katharine Ross and sundry others (including children) fleeing in an ancient bus from the advancing Japanese, and learning a lot about each other during the hazardous 100 miles. Dir: Don Weis. Screenplay: Winston Miller. BBC2, 14 August 1985.

Longstreet (1971). Successful pilot feature that led to the TV series of the same title, with James Franciscus as the insurance company detective whose wife is killed and whose own sight is impaired by the crooks who want him off the case. First-rate. Also featuring: Martin Beswick, Bradford Dillman, John McIntire, Jeanette Nolan. Dir: Joseph Sargent. Screenplay: Stirling Silliphant. ITV, 20 December 1985.

The Mad Dog Gang (1983). A gang of kids find that a haunted castle contains more than spooks . . . Nice family fun. Featuring: Buddy Ruruku, Ian Templeton, Julie Wilson. Dir: Ross Jennings. Screenplay: Ian Mune. ITV, 3 January 1986.

The Making of a Male Model (1984). Routine story about a young man who is taken up and exploited as a body-beautiful model, and learns the hard way that it isn't all fun and games – even after making it to the bed of his mentor, played by Joan Collins. Also featuring: Jon-Erik Hexum, Kevin McCarthy, Arte Johnson. Dir: Tony Wharmby. No writing credit. ITV, 14 September 1985.

Man on the Outside (1975). A good enough pilot feature to convince the powers-that-be to go ahead with the *Griff* series. Here Lorne Greene is the retired cop who returns to action when his private-eye son is murdered for no obvious reason. Also featuring: Lorraine Gary, Jean Allison, James Olson. Dir: Boris Sagall. Screenplay: Larry Cohen. ITV, 25 May 1986.

Marilyn (1980). TV movie that was released in British cinemas in November 1981 with the somewhat misleading title *Marilyn: The Untold Story*. 'Pretty superficial' was the comment in the 'Releases of the Year' section of *Film Review 1982–3*. Featuring Catherine Hicks. ITV, 18 December 1985.

Meantime (1983). Channel 4, 28 November 1985. Previously shown on same channel, 1 December 1983. See *Film Review 1984–5*.

The Million-dollar Face (1979). Get this: beautiful Sylvia (*Emmanuelle*) Kristel as an archaeologist's daughter chosen as 'The Face to Launch a million lipsticks'. A slice of scented soap . . . opera! Also featuring: Tony Curtis, David Hoffman, Gayle Hunnicutt, Lee Grant, Roddy McDowall, Murray Matheson, Polly Bergen. Dir: Michael O'Herlihy. Screenplay: Jud Kinberg and Robert Hamner. ITV, 11 November 1985.

Missing Pieces (1983). Investigator Elizabeth Montgomery sorts out the pieces which, when in place, will solve the mystery of who murdered her husband. Also featuring: John Reilly, Louanne, David Haskell. Dir and Screenplay: Mike Hodges. BBC1, 14 December 1985.

Mistress of Paradise (1981). Channel 4, 25 September 1985. Previously shown on ITV, 31 July 1984. See *Film Review 1985–6*.

The Monkey Mission (1981). Robert Blake as the tough (but soft-hearted) Los Angeles private eye employed to steal back a stolen work of art from a gallery with a daunting array of safety gadgets. With the aid of a monkey and a one-armed electronics wizard, he decides to have a go . . . Routine caper movie, but very watchable. Also featuring: Keenan Wynn, Michele Ryan, Sondra Blake . . . not forgetting Willy (the monkey). Dir: Burt Brinkerhoff. Screenplay: Robert Crais. ITV, 21 October 1985.

Murder at the Mardi Gras (1978). BBC2, 16 October 1985. Previously shown on same channel, 21 September 1983. See *Film Review 1984–5*.

Murder Is Easy (1981). BBC1, 25 May 1986. Agatha Christie whodunit originally shown on ITV on 24 December 1983. See *Film Review 1984–5*.

Murrow (1985). Excellent TV feature about famous American broadcaster Edward R. Murrow, who against all the odds spoke out strongly on his TV programme against Senator Joe McCarthy and his anti-Communist witchhunt – a programme that caused a stir which echoed from one coast of the United States to the other. Cast: Daniel J. Travanti as Murrow, Dabney Coleman, etc. Dir: Jack Gold. Screenplay: Ernest Kinoy. Channel 4, 3 April 1986.

Nadia (1984). Mainly for gymnastics fans: the story of Nadia Comaneci, the 14-year-old Romanian star of the 1976 Olympics who, for the first time in athletics history, won perfect marks. Cast: Joe Bennett, Jonathan Banks, Leslie Weiner, Johann Carlo, Carrie Snodgress, etc. Dir: Alan Cooke. Screenplay: J. R. McGinn. BBC1, 5 May 1986.

The Nativity (1978). Some nice performances, the occasional scenic splendour, and a welcome conventionality sum up this Hollywood rendition of the story of the birth of Christ, set against the social unrest in the Holy Land under the Romans. Featuring: Freddie Jones, John Rhys-Davies, Kate O'Mara, Jane Wyatt, Audrey Totter. Dir: Bernard Kowalski. Screenplay: Millard Kaufman and Mort Fine. BBC2, 21 December 1985.

Nelly's Version (1983). Yet another amnesia epic, about a woman who finds she has far too many banknotes in her travelling case and doesn't know how they got there, or even what her name is. All very enigmatic. Featuring: Eileen Atkins, Susannah York, Nicholas Ball. Dir and Screenplay: Maurice Hatton; based on the novel by Eva Figes. Channel 4, 21 November 1985.

Nightmare (1973). Echoes of Hitchcock's *Rear Window* are to be seen and heard in this thriller about a man who is sure he's seen a man shooting a gun from a nearby apartment window. When called, the cops can't find any sign of the act, but when they go, nasty things start to happen to the worried onlooker . . . Featuring: Richard Crenna, Patty Duke Astin, Vic Morrow. Dir: William Hale. Screenplay: David Wiltse. ITV, 5 December 1985.

No Man's Land (1984). Pilot feature for a hoped-for new western comedy series about a widow who, with her three daughters, takes on her late sheriff husband's job. With Stella Stevens as the most glamorous law-upholder in cinema history, the failure of the film to win support for a series is regrettable! Also featuring: Terri Garber, Melissa Michaelsen, Donna Dixon, Estelle

Getty, Sam Jones. Dir: Rod Holcomb. Screenplay: Juanita Bartlett. BBC1, 6 July 1985.

The Norliss Tapes (1973). It all starts with a young widow letting fly with a gun at her late husband when he walks back into her house . . . The action carries on in that vein in this able flesh-creeper. Featuring: Roy Thinnes, Angie Dickinson, Hurd Hatfield. Dir: Dan Curtis. Screenplay: William F. Nolan. ITV, 18 July 1985.

Northstar (1985). Science-fiction stuff about an astronaut, Greg Evigan, who after being caught outside a shuttle during a solar storm finds he has been given something very like magical powers – an IQ of 1000! Dir: Peter Levin. Screenplay: Howard Lakin. ITV, 27 December 1985.

One of My Wives Is Missing (1976). First-rate mystery thriller about a newly wedded man, whose wife has vanished, suddenly faced by a strange lady who claims to be his spouse. Nicely tailored twists, turns and puzzles. Cast: Jack Klugman, Elizabeth Ashley, James Franciscus, etc. Dir: Glenn Jordan. Screenplay: Pierre Marton. ITV, 1 March 1986.

One Shoe Makes It Murder (1982). BBC1, 26 October 1985. Previously shown on same channel, 30 October 1983. See *Film Review 1984–5*.

Only One Day Left Before Tomorrow or **How to Steal an Airplane** (1971). Take your pick – this TV feature has had both titles! It stars Pete Duel and Clinton Greyn as a couple of youngsters sent to Central America to repossess and bring back a stolen airplane, but finding it not that easy an assignment. Also featuring: Claudine Longet, Katherine Crawford, Sal Mineo. Dir: Alex Singer. Screenplay: Robert Foster and Philip Degeure Jr. BBC2, 24 July 1985.

Orphans of the Earth (1984). From Brazilian TV comes this award-winning atmospheric feature about the struggle of a mother to keep her four children fed in spite of catastrophic drought conditions. A fascinating window on another world and way of life. Cast: Tania Alves, Arnoud Rodrigues, etc. Dir: Paulo Alfonso Grisolli. Screenplay: Aguinaldo Silva. BBC2, 15 March 1986.

Our Family Business (1981). A TV film echo of the large screen's *Godfather*, with Sam Wanamaker as the 'Family' boss out to take revenge on the 'mouth' who sent him to jail for six years on a tax avoidance charge. Old hat, but slickly directed and played. Cast also includes: Ray Milland, Vera Miles, Ted Danson. Dir: Robert Collins. Screenplay: Lane Slate. ITV, 8 November 1985.

Out of the Darkness (1985). Yet another based-on-fact TV film, this time the story of the American cop whose enthusiasm for the job of tracking down the notorious 'Son of Sam' multi-murderer is a contrast with the tragedy of his own life. The actual cop advisers (and small-part players) help to stamp authenticity on the movie. Cast: Martin Sheen, Hector Elizando, Matt Clark, etc. Dir: Jud Taylor. Screenplay: Tom Cook. ITV, 22 February 1986.

A Perfect Match (1980). Yet another of the many TV features based on actual human problems: this time the search for a bone marrow donor and the discovery that the only suitable one is the since-adopted illegitimate child of the heroine. A lot of heartache for those involved if not for the viewer. Featuring: Linda Kelsey, Michael Brandon, Charles Durning, Hildy Brooks. Dir: Mel Damski. Screenplay: John Sayles; from a story by Demski and André Guttfreund. BBC2, 2 October 1985.

The Phantom of Hollywood (1974). About the mysterious killer who lives in old film sets at the MGM studios and strikes those who want to sell the place and do him out of his hide-out home . . . and it is all quite fun! Cast: Jack Cassidy, Broderick Crawford, John Ireland, Peter Lawford, Jackie Coogan, etc. Dir: Gene Levitt. Screenplay: Robert Thom and George Schenk. ITV, 12 March 1986.

Pleasure Palace (1980). Real-life card-playing expert Omar Sharif plays a famous gambler who comes to the aid of a Las Vegas lady in her attempt to defeat the nasties trying to take over her casino. Also featuring: Victoria Principal, Hope Lange, José Ferrer. Dir: Walter Grauman. Screenplay: Blanche Hanalis. BBC1, 27 July 1985.

Pray TV (1981). The way they 'do' religion in America. Ned Beatty as the very business-like television evangelist, selling God to the viewers in return for revenue of something like a $1 million a week! Quite an astonishing, revelatory TV film, with the 'gospelcasters' downgrading God. Lots of fuel for controversy here. Also featuring: John Ritter, Madolyn Smith. Dir: Robert Markowitz. Screenplay: Lane Slate. Channel 4, 19 November 1985.

Prime Suspect (1981). What happens when investigative journalism goes too far – in this case, a TV team trying to pin a murder on an innocent man, who isn't helped by the unsympathetic and suspicious cops. Featuring: Mike Farrell, Teri Garr, Lane Smith, Veronica Cartwright. Dir: Noel Black. Screenplay: Douglas Graham. BBC1, 23 November 1985.

Prisoner Without a Name, Cell Without a Number (1983). So many of the more recent TV movies are very serious indeed and based on true stories. This one concerns an Argentinian newspaper owner who lost his battle of words with the *junta* and suffered imprisonment, torture and humiliation. Strong stuff, with Roy Scheider, Liv Ullmann, Zach Galligan, Michael Pearlman and Sam Robards. Dir: Linda Yellen. Screenplay: Yellen, J. Platnick and Oliver P. Drexell Jr. BBC2, 9 October 1985.

Prototype (1983). An update of the old Frankenstein story, with Christopher Plummer as the inventive scientist whose robot-like creation is 'borrowed' by the Pentagon for (Plummer suspects) the worst possible reasons. So he steals back his 'Michael' and flees, with the annoyed authorities hard on his heels . . . A pretty good thriller, hailed as one of the best TV features of its year. Also featuring: David ('Michael') Morse, Frances Sternhagen. Dir: David Greene. Screenplay: Richard Levinson and William Link. BBC1, 14 July 1985.

The Questor Tapes (1974). Science fiction on a par with most cinema movies: about an android computer ('robot' to those who are simple-minded like me!) which tries to find out what has happened to its mysteriously missing creator. Good fantasy fun it is, too. Cast: Robert Foxworth, Mike Farrell, Lew Ayres, Dana Wynter, James Shigeta, etc. Dir: Richard Colla. Screenplay: Gene Roddenberry. ITV, 17 May 1986.

Rainbow (1978). Judy Garland biopic with 14-year-old stage star Andrea McArdle playing Judy (up to her adolescence). Though it's all routine stuff, Miss McA does know how to belt out a typical Judy number. Also featuring: Piper Laurie, Don Murray, Nicholas Pryor, Martin Balsam. Dir: Jackie Cooper. Screenplay: John McGreevey; based on the book by Christopher Finch. Channel 4, 9 July 1985.

Rearview Mirror (1984). Another psychopathic killer (Michael Beck) on the loose, and another unlucky lady (Lee Remick) as his hostage – and she has to use all her wits to stay alive on the long drive towards Florida. Also featuring: Tony Musante, Don Galloway, Ned Bridges. Dir: Lou Antonio. Screenplay: Lorenzo Semple Jr; based on a novel by Caroline Cooney. ITV, 26 October 1985.

A Reason to Live (1984). Remember little Ricky Schroder? He was the kid who did a lot of scene stealing in *The Champ* and now has his own American TV series. Here he is trying to persuade his depressed dad (lost job, lost wife) to stick it out. Also featuring: Peter Fonda, Deidre Hall, Carrie Snodgress. Dir: Peter Levin. Screenplay: Robert Lewin. ITV, 23 November 1985.

The Red Light Sting (1984). Yet another TV movie based on a true story: this time an utterly incredible, if amusing, one about American cops spending almost half a million dollars to buy a whorehouse as a lure and trap for a gangster they have not been able to bring to book. Neat performances by Farrah Fawcett and Beau Bridges. Dir: Rod Holcomb. Screenplay: Howard Berk. ITV, 2 November 1985.

Red Monarch (1982). The 'Monarch' of the title is Stalin, and this story of the Soviet premier and his unhappy times is treated with a mixture of black comedy and broad satire, with performances getting near, if never quite going over, the top. Cast: Colin Blakely, David Suchet, Carroll Baker, Brian Glover, etc. Dir and Screenplay: Charles Wood; from stories by Yuri Krotkov. Channel 4, 16 January 1986.

Rehearsal for Murder (1982). Robert Preston as the playwright who uses a reading of his new play by the cast to discover who killed his lady love, knowing that one of the thespians must be guilty. Some nice support from Lynn Redgrave and Patrick MacNee. Dir: David Greene. Screenplay: Richard Levinson and William Link. BBC1, 4 August 1985.

Remembrance of Love (1983). Kirk Douglas with his young son Eric Douglas in a TV movie that resembles his large-screen film *The Final Countdown*. In this one, Douglas plays a man suffering from periodic nightmares of the Holocaust as he searches for his long-lost love. Also featuring: Pam Dawber, Michael Goodwin, Robert Clary. Dir: Jack Smight. Screenplay: H. J. Bloom. Channel 4, 22 October 1985.

The Return of the Man from U.N.C.L.E. (1983). ITV, 7 October 1985. Previously shown on same channel, 21 April 1984. See *Film Review 1984–5* .

Reunion at Fairborough (1985). And the fourth teaming of Robert Mitchum and Deborah Kerr in this good, old – British – romantic tale about a disillusioned ex-pilot who returns to England for his old squadron's reunion and finds more than he bargained for. Also featuring: Red Buttons, Judi Trott, Barry Morse, etc. Dir: Herbert Wise. Screenplay: Albert Ruben. ITV, 23 March 1986.

The Revolt of Job (1983). Another TV film from Hungary; this one is about how a Jewish couple's joy when they adopt a small Christian boy is ruined by Nazi intervention. Cast: Hedi Temessy, Ferenc Zenthe, Gabor Feher, etc. Dir: Imre Gyongyossy and Barna Kabay. Screenplay: Katalin Petenyi, Gyongyossy and Kabay. Channel 4, 24 April 1986.

Right of Asylum (1978). A real hybrid – a Spanish TV feature based on a Cuban story – which shows a lovely Latin sense of ironic wit. A story about a young man who knows how to make himself indispensable. Cast: Xavier Elorriaga, Susana Mara, etc. Dir: Pascual Cervera. Screenplay: Solly Wolodarsky. BBC2, 4 April 1986.

Right of Way (1983). Beautiful performances by Bette Davis and James Stewart (the first time they have ever co-starred together) as two mellow old people who want to decide the time and way of their deaths, and run into opposition from family and authorities. Dir: George Schaefer. Screenplay: Richard Lees; based on his own stage play. BBC2, 24 July 1985.

Rodeo Girl (1980). Another very creditable directing job by ex-child star Jackie Cooper: semi-fictionalized, biographical film about American rodeo star Sue Pirtle (a very likeable performance from Katharine Ross). Also featuring: Bo Hopkins, Candy Clare. Dir: Jackie Cooper. Screenplay: Kathryn Powers. BBC2, 23 October 1985.

The Russian Soldier (1985). Down on the farm, lethal things begin to bubble out of the ground . . . and one misty morning, life starts to offer some nasty problems for farmer Warren Clarke. Also featuring: Patrick Malahide, Alan MacNaughton, etc. Dir: Gavin Millar. Screenplay: Brian Phelan. BBC1, 9 March 1986.

Saigon – Year of the Cat (1983). ITV, 20 November 1985. Previously shown on same channel, 29 November 1983. See *Film Review 1984–5* .

Sakharov (1984). Somewhat propagandist TV film about the famous Soviet dissident and his equally committed wife, now exiled to far-away Gorki after a long and persistent struggle against the Soviet authorities. With Jason Robards and Glenda Jackson as the couple; also Nicol Williamson, Frank Finlay, Michael Bryant. Dir: Jack Gold. Screenplay: David W. Rintels. BBC2, 28 August 1985.

The Savage Bees (1976). American TV film released in the UK on 23 April 1979 as a cinema feature. It concerns some South American killer bees on the loose in New Orleans. BBC1, 2 December 1985. See *Film Review 1978–9* 'Releases of the Year'.

Scorned and Swindled (1984). A pretty awful title for a pretty good TV movie about a lovely woman (played by Tuesday Weld) conned by crooked Peter Coyote, who goes off with her money. But the lady, with the help of another victim (Keith Carradine) sets off to bring him to justice. The pace and the passion hot up as they travel the long road. Also featuring: Sheree North, Fionnula Flanagan, etc. Dir: Paul Wendkos. Screenplay: Jerome Kass and Karol Ann Hoeffner. ITV, 27 January 1986.

Scott Joplin (1977). Biopic about the ragtime composer whose music helped to make *The Sting* such a memorable movie. This is not memorable stuff, though, even if the music is there in all its honkytonk glory. Featuring: Billy Dee Williams as unhappy Joplin; also Art Carney, Clifton Davis and Taj Mahal. Dir: Jeremy Paul Kagan. Screenplay: Christopher Knopf. BBC2, 30 March 1986.

The Screaming Woman (1972). Olivia de Havilland in *Hush, Hush, Sweet Charlotte* thriller country again – in this case, her own considerable estate, where weird things happen after her recovery from a mental breakdown. As usual, she makes the whole thing more than satisfactorily mysterious and exciting. Also featuring: Joseph Cotten, Walter Pidgeon, Ed Nelson, Laraine Stephens. Dir: Jack Smight. Screenplay: Merwin Gerard; based on a story by Ray Bradbury. ITV, 26 July 1985.

A Shining Season (1979). Good old-fashioned tear-jerker based on the true story of athlete John Baker – played by Timothy Bottoms – who suddenly learns that cancer gives him only a few months to live, and courageously devotes a lot of that golden time to training a girls' running team to victory on the track he loves so well. Also featuring: Allyn Ann McLerie, Rip Torn, Ed Begley Jr. Dir: Stuart Margolin. Screenplay: William Harrison; based on the book by William Buchanan. Channel 4, 3 September 1985.

Sister, Sister (1982). Family friction in the American Deep South when Rosalind Cash returns from Chicago to the house where her two sisters (Diahann Carroll and Irene Cara) have lived since childhood and begins to stir up memories and uncover old scars. Also featuring: Dick Anthony Williams, Paul Winfield and Christoff St John. Dir: John Berry. Screenplay: Maya Angelou. BBC1, 6 June 1986.

The Snowman (1982). Outstanding British half-hour cartoon feature about the Christmas Eve adventures of a little boy and the snowman he builds which comes to life. Oodles of charm, fun and beautiful draughtsmanship: quite outstanding. Dir: Diane Jackson. Animation by Hilary Audus, Joanne Fryer and others; from the book by Raymond Briggs. Channel 4, 24 December 1985.

Someone's Watching Me (1978). That expert spine-chiller of the large screen, John (*Halloween*) Carpenter, here brings his skill to TV with great success in this story about a lady in a lush Los Angeles apartment, whose life is turned into a nightmare when she becomes aware that someone is watching her every movement – with what evil intention? Grand scary stuff. Featuring: Lauren Hutton, David Birney, Adrienne Barbeau. Dir and Screenplay: John Carpenter. BBC1, 2 November 1985.

Song of Experience (1985). Atmosphere-dripping British TV film about three Yorkshire lads who set off one (1960s) day to do a bit of train spotting but end up spotting a great deal more than they bargained for. Cast: Trevor Moffatt, Alan Bell, Paul Darlow, etc. Dir: Stephen Frears. Screenplay: Martin Allen. BBC2, 16 February 1986.

Sparkling Cyanide (1983). ITV, 4 April 1986. Agatha Christie whodunit originally shown on same channel on 26 April 1984. See *Film Review 1984–5* .

Special Bulletin (1983). An American TV station is the unhappy intermediary between a group who threaten to explode an atom bomb if their demands are not met, and the US government. The tension is cleverly built up as the moment of truth comes ever closer and the sense of reality is reinforced by the video techniques usually only employed by TV news programmes. Featuring: Ed Flanders, Kathryn Walker, Roxanne Hart. Dir: Edward Zwick. Screenplay: Marshall Herskovitch. ITV, 4 December 1985.

Spring Symphony (1983). A West German TV movie previously shown in the cinema in Great Britain. See *Film Review 1985–6*, 'Releases of the Year'.

Starflight One (1982). Excitement and danger on board a new 4000 mph transport plane on its maiden flight, when it comes into the path of a satellite missile . . . Sharing the fun are Lee Majors, Ray Milland, Gail Strickland, Lauren Hutton and many more. Dir: Jerry Jameson. Screenplay: Robert Malcolm Young. ITV, 29 December 1985.

Strawberry Fields (1985). A rather minor effort from West Germany about youthful neo-Nazism, which never attempts to examine what is an important social problem, rather is content to present it as a basis for a quite ordinary melodrama. Cast: Beate Jensen, Rolf Zacher. Dir: Christian Kuhn. Screenplay: Stephen Poliakoff. Channel 4, 20 March 1986.

Success Is the Best Revenge (1984). It is unlikely that many British cinemagoers when they first saw this film in November 1984 (see *Film Review 1985–6*) realized it had, apparently, been made primarily for television. Channel 4, 26 June 1986.

Sybil (1976). BBC2, 15 and 16 April 1986. Although now presented as a made-for-TV feature (in two parts), this re-make of a 30-year-old film (*The Three Faces of Eve*) was released in Britain as a cinema film a few years back. See *Film Review 1980–81* 'Releases of the Year'.

Thirteen for Dinner (1985). And one of them is found dead on the morrow. Typical evergreen Agatha Christie whodunit re-made for TV, with lots of false leads and suspects until the usual 'surprise' revelatory ending. Hercule Poirot – alias Peter Ustinov – sorts it all out in spite of Faye Dunaway playing dual roles. Dir: Lou Antonio. Screenplay: Rod Browning; based on the novel by Agatha Christie. ITV, 8 June 1986.

Thou Shalt Not Kill (1979). Familiar story about an innocent man sent to jail for a crime he did not commit, who becomes the subject of prison brutality and a guard's deadly venom. Cast: Lee Grant, Robert Culp, Albert Salmi, etc. Dir: I. C. Rapoport. Screenplay: Lonne Elder III and Rapoport. BBC1, 19 April 1986.

A Touch of Scandal (1984). The murdered man on her doorstep does little to help Angie Dickinson win the position of State Attorney General for which she is campaigning. This is the other side of the Los Angeles coin, a shadowy, vice-flickering city far from the tinsel town more often seen. Also featuring: Tom Skerritt, Roger Loggia, Jason Miller. Dir: Ivan Nagy. Screenplay: Richard Guttman. ITV, 25 November 1985.

Trackdown: Finding the Goodbar Killer (1983). TV sequel of 1979-released cinema film, *Looking for Mr Goodbar*, in which Diane Keaton gave a fine performance as a Jekyll-and-Hyde woman who is children's teacher by day and sex-seeking bar haunter by night. In this, George Segal (his TV film debut) is effective as the detective assigned to solve the girl's brutal murder. It works out quite well, even if you do know whodunit before the cop does. Also featuring: Shelley Hack, Shannon Presby, Marek Johnson, Barton Heyman. Dir: Bill Persky. Screenplay: Albert Ruben. ITV, 29 September 1985.

Trapped (1973). With the title *Doberman Patrol,* this 'straightforward, generally convincing thriller' was cinema-released on 30 June 1976 (see *Film Review 1975–6*). ITV, 21 November 1985.

Travis Logan, DA. (1971). Another example of a feature which, it was (mistakenly as it happens) hoped, would launch a new series about a lawyer who turns to murder investigation as a sideline. Cast: Vic Morrow, Hal Holbrook, Brenda Vaccaro. Dir: Paul Wendkos. Screenplay: Andy Lewis. BBC2, 30 May 1986.

The Trial of Chaplain Jensen (1975). Stoutly anti-Womens' Lib, fact-based TV movie about a US Navy cleric who was court-martialled for having committed adultery with the wives of two of his men. With the female duo painted as something akin to harlots, the scriptwriter shows where his sympathies lie! Featuring: James Franciscus, Charles Durning, Joanna Miles, Lynda Day George. Dir: Robert Day. Screenplay: Lorinda Mandel; based on the book by Chaplain Andrew Jensen and Martin Abramson. Channel 4, 10 December 1985.

Trouble in the High Timber Country (1980). Reliable Eddie Albert as the little man against big business among the Idaho trees. This was a pilot film, made for a series that apparently ran for just a fortnight! Also featuring: Belinda Montgomery, James Sikking, Martin Kove. Dir: Vincent Sherman. Screenplay: Jeb Rosebrook. BBC2, 30 October 1985.

240-Robert (1979). This was the feature pilot which preceded an action-packed TV series of the same title, about the hectic adventures of San Francisco's Emergency Corps. Phew! Cast: John Bennett Perry, Mark Harmon, Joanna Cassidy, etc. Dir: Paul Krasny. Screenplay: John Furia (well named!). ITV, 1 June 1986.

Walter (1982). A repeat of the sensational film that opened Channel 4, with its marvellous performance by Ian McKellen as the mentally retarded man who finds life pretty scary and hard when his protective mother dies, and he has to fend for himself. Also featuring: Barbara Jefford, Arthur Whybrow, Tony Melody. Dir: Stephen Frears. Channel 4, 19 September 1985.

W.E.B. (1978). The pilot feature for a series about television which didn't run for long. Cast: Pamela Bellwood, Alex Cord, Richard Basehart. Dir: Harvey Hart. Screenplay: David Karp. BBC1, 18 April 1986.

A Whale for the Killing (1981). Forced by a storm to stay in a Newfoundland fishing village, Peter Strauss and his family become involved with the struggle to save a stranded whale. Also featuring: Richard Widmark, Dee Wallace, Kathryn Walker, Bruce McGill. Dir: R. T. Heffron. Screenplay: Lionel Chetwynd; based on the book by Farley Mowat. BBC1, 24 January 1986.

When We Are Old (1983). A Japanese TV feature which dealt sympathetically with family relationships and the crisis that occurs when Father is taken to hospital. Cast: Chishu Ryu, Aiko Nagayama, etc. Dir: Seikph Iyoda. Screenplay: Taichi Yamada. Channel 4, 27 March 1986.

Whodunit? Murder in Space (1985). The TV film novelty of the year (1985): it was up to viewers to solve this murder that takes place in space in the 21st century. In an international competition, a million pounds in prize money was scattered around the globe for the clever amateur sleuths who could pick out the killer (or killers). The correct answer to this murder puzzle was not divulged until September, when the film was repeated with a new, ten-minute dénouement added. Featuring: Wilford Brimley, Arthur Hill, Martin Balsam, Alan Jordan. Dir: Steven Hilliard Stern. Screenplay: Wesley Ferguson. ITV, 13 August 1985.

The Wicked Lady (1983). Apparently, and surprisingly, this re-make of the famous 1945 Gainsborough feature was made for TV, although it had a cinema release in Britain in 1984 (see *Film Review 1983–4* 'Releases of the Year'.) and only now gets a TV première. All very confusing! ITV, 19 April 1986.

Winter Kill (1974). Superior whodunit, set in a ski resort, about a series of cold-blooded murders in a cold climate, and the efforts of the local sheriff to catch the killer . . . or maybe killers? Excellently done in all departments, from script to acting. Cast: Andy Griffith, Sheree North, Nick Nolte. Dir: Jud Taylor. Screenplay: Joseph Michael Hayes. ITV, 22 March 1986.

With This Ring (1978). A none-too-serious story of the last-minute doubts and worries of three couples on the brink of matrimony. Featuring: Dick Van Patten, Diana Canova, Donny Most, Joyce DeWitt. Dir: James Sheldon. Screenplay: Terence Mulcahy. BBC2, 7 September 1985.

Witness for the Prosecution (1982). Another TV remake of a popular stage and screen success: an Agatha Christie whodunit. This time, for the small screen, it is packed with expensive stars such as Ralph Richardson, Deborah Kerr, Beau Bridges, Wendy Hiller, Donald Pleasence, Peter Sallis, Diana Rigg and others, making the court scenes fascinating. Dir: Alan Gibson. Screenplay: John Gay; based on the Agatha Christie play. BBC1, 26 August 1985.

Women of San Quentin (1983). The sometimes difficult, occasionally dangerous existence of the female guards in San Quentin, a male prison, is highlighted when one of them is held hostage by a crazy convict in a jail riot. Cast includes: Stella Stevens, Debbie Allen, Amy Steel, Yaphet Kotto, Rosana de Soto. Dir: W. A. Graham. Screenplay: Mark Rodgers. ITV, 7 September 1985.

Releases of the Year

In this section you will find details of films released in Great Britain from 1 July 1985 to the end of June 1986 – the period covered by all the reference features in the book. The precise dating of some of these releases is a little tricky in view of the current lack of any rigidity in the release pattern, but dates given refer to the general release and not pre-release.

In the case of films sent out on a 'floating' release I have added, wherever possible, the date of the film's first London showing because usually this is also the first British showing.

The normal abbreviations operate as follows: Dir – for Director; Pro – for Producer; Assoc Pro – for Associate Producer; Ex Pro – for Executive Producer; Pro Ex – for Production Executive; Pro Sup – for Production Supervisor; Pro Con – for Production Controller; Co-Pro – for Co-Producer; Pro Co-Ord – for Production Co-Ordinator; Ph – for Photographer; Ed – for Editor; Art – for Art Director; Pro Des – for Production Designer; M – for Music; and a few others which will be obvious.

Abbreviations for the name of film companies are also pretty obvious when used, such as Fox for 20th Century-Fox, Rank for Rank Film Distributors, UA for United Artists and UIP for Universal International Pictures. Where known, the actual production company is given first, the releasing company last.

When it comes to nationality of the film you will find that this is noted wherever possible – those films without any mention of country of origin can be taken as being American – but in these days of increasing international co-productions between two, three and even four countries it is sometimes a little difficult to sort out where the premier credit is due.

Finally, unless otherwise specified (i.e. in black-and-white), it can safely be taken that the film is made in Technicolor or some similar colour process.

Censorship certificates: the position now is that *U* represents films suitable for persons of any age; *PG* (Parental Guidance) represents films which some parents might consider unsuitable for their children; *15* means no persons under that age will be admitted and films certified with an *18* (approximately the old 'X' certificate) means that nobody under that age will be admitted to the cinema while that film is showing.

Note: 'No cert' means that no certificate had been issued by the initial showing of the film but this does not mean that one was not issued at a later date.

Absolute Beginners. An enormous amount of energy – as well as money – must have gone into the production of this novel British musical, which is based on the teenage revolution of the 'fifties. The climax is the Notting Hill race riots – presented as a ballet! The film produces a kaleidoscope of rainbow-hued action and sound. There is no story worth mentioning, but stretches of rather daft and superfluous commentary. Plenty of lively performances from such stars as David Bowie, James Fox, Lionel Blair, Anita Morris, Eddie O'Connell and others. Rest of cast: Patsy Kensit, Ray Davies, Eve Ferret, Steven Berkoff, Sade, Graham Fletcher Cook, Mandy Rice-Davies, Bruce Payne, Tenpole Tudor, Tony Hippolyte, Alan Freeman, Chris Pitt, Paul Rhys, Julian Firth, Joe McKenna,

Left, friendly neighbour Big Jill (Eve Ferret) is watched by Eddie O'Connell in the Palace/Virgin/Goldcrest fast-paced musical *Absolute Beginners*. Above, David Bowie as the villain.

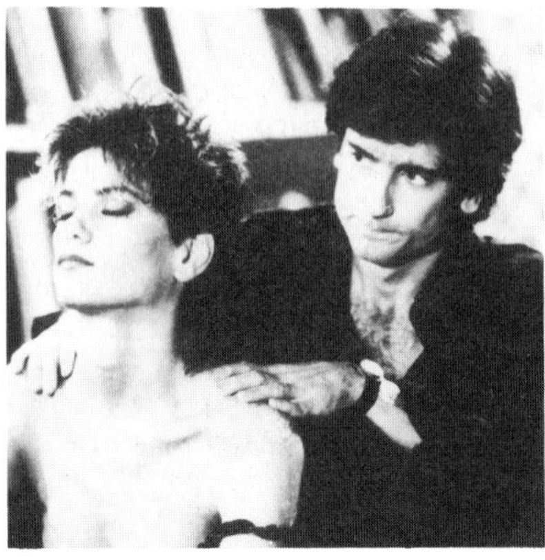

Going to SoHo – Manhattan – to meet Marcy (Rosanna Arquette), Paul (Griffin Dunne) soon finds himself meeting various other weird characters, including sculptress Kiki (Linda Fiorentino, right) in Warner's Scorsese comedy *After Hours*.

Ronald Fraser, Irene Handl, Sylvia Syms, Eric Sykes, Peter Hugo Daly, Johnny Shannon, Amanda Jane Powell, Robbie Coltrane, Gary Beadle, Jess Conrad, Slim Gaillard, Smiley Culture, Ekow Ebban, Robert Austin, Gerry Alexander, Jim Dunk, Johnny Edge, Carmen Ejogo, Paul Fairminer, Hugo First, Pat Hartley, Astley Harvey, Colin Jeavons, Alfred Maron, G. B. (Zoot) Money, Sandie Shaw, Bruno Tonioli, etc. Dir: Julien Temple. Pro: Stephen Woolley and Chris Brown. Ex Pro: Nik Powell, Al Clark and Robert Devereux. Assoc Pro: David Wimbury. Screenplay: Richard Burridge, Christopher Wicking and Don MacPherson; based on the novel by Colin MacInnes. Ph: Oliver Stapleton. Ed: Michael Bradsell, Gerry Hambling, Richard Bedford and Russell Lloyd. Pro Des: John Beard. Art: Stuart Rose and Ken Wheatley. M: David Bowie, Ray Davies, Gil Evans, Paul Weller, Patsy Kensit, Sade, Nick Lowe, Tenpole Tudor, Jerry Dammers, Ekow Ebban and Working Week. (Palace–Virgin/Goldcrest) Rel: 11 April 1986. 108 mins. Cert 15.

After Hours. Or, poor Paul's 'terrible, terrible' night in Manhattan's SoHo district where he goes to meet Marcy (Rosanna Arquette). He also encounters a collection of odd characters, but when he tries to return to the haven of his home, he finds that, if it was easy to get into SoHo, it is *very* difficult to get out of the district, thanks to some *very* queer adventures. Rightly described as 'a surreal comedy', this film by Martin Scorsese (which won him the 'Best Director' Award at the 1985 Cannes Film Festival) is based on an original script by a film school student. Cast: Griffin Dunne, Rosanna Arquette, Verna Bloom, Thomas Chong, Linda Fiorentino, Teri Garr, John Heard, Richard 'Cheech' Marin, Catherine O'Hara, Dick Miller, Will Patton, Robert Plunket, Bronson Pinchot, Rocco Sisto, Larry Block, Victor Argo, Murray Moston, John P. Codiglia, Clarke Evans, Victor Bumbalo, Bill Elverman, Joel Jason, Rand Carr, Clarence Felder, Henry Baker, Margo Winkler, Victor Magnotta, Robin Johnson, Stephen J. Lim, Frank Aquilino, Maree Catalao, Paula Raflo, Rockets Redglare. Dir: Martin Scorsese. Pro: Amy Robinson, Griffin Dunne and Robert F. Colesberry. Assoc Pro: Deborah Schindler. Screenplay: Joseph Minion. Ph: Michael Ballhaus. Ed: Elma Schoonmaker. Pro Des: Jeffrey Townsend. M: Howard Shore. (Double Play Pro/Geffen Co–Warner) Rel: floating; first shown London (Warner), 30 May 1986. 97 mins. Cert 15.

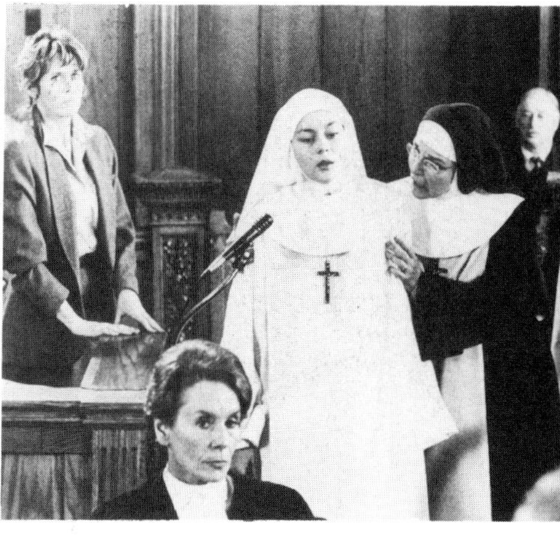

Left, Mother Superior Anne Bancroft and psychiatrist Jane Fonda share an off-duty joke in Columbia's *Agnes of God*. Above, both in far more serious mood in the courtroom scene where a young nun, Meg Tilly, stands accused of murdering her baby.

Agnes of God. John Pielmeier's adaptation of his own Tony Award-winning stage play which concerns religious faith and secular logic in opposition. A psychiatrist (Jane Fonda) is appointed by the court to assess whether a young nun (Meg Tilly), who has given birth and apparently murdered the babe, is fit to go on trial for her alleged crime; something that the sophisticated Mother Superior (Anne Bancroft), an ex-wife and mother, is determined shall not happen. The battle of wills between the two strong-minded women as the investigation continues, brings them to mutual respect and more, and also reveals their respective doubts as to what really happened: seduction of a simple-minded girl, something like a miracle, or strength of faith? Though the final practical problems are resolved and the court is satisfied, niggling doubts remain in the minds of the two women. Brilliant performances from stars and supporting cast, lovely photography, unusual locations (Quebec) and a perceptive, highly intelligent script add up to one of the year's superior movies. Rest of cast: Anne Pitoniak, Winston Rekert, Gratien Gelinas, Guy Hoffman, Gabriel Arcand, Françoise Faucher, Jacques Tourangeau, Janine Fluet, Deborah Grover, Michele George, Samantha Langevin, Jacqueline Blais, Françoise Berd, Mimi D'Estée, Rita Tuckett, Lillian Graham, Norma Dell'Agnese, Muguette Moreau, Janine Bryan, Agnes Middleton, France Arbour, Laurel Lyle, Victor Desy, Charlotte Laurier, Peter Langley, Nicole Marie Abbat, Matthew Armstrong, Chava Mandlsohn, Charles S. Pottie, Gerry Huckstep, Marc Denis, Herbert Luft, André Lacoste, Jennifer Jewison, Carole Chatel, Daniel Tremblay. Dir and (with Patrick Palmer) Pro: Norman Jewison. Assoc Pro: Charles Milhaupt and Bonnie Palef-Woolf. Screenplay: John Pielmeier; based on his stage play. Ph: Sven Nykvist. Ed: Antony Gibbs. Pro Des: Ken Adam. M: Georges Delerue. (Columbia Delphi IV–Columbia) Rel: 21 February 1986. 98 mins. Cert 15.

Agony – Agonia. Confused – and confusing – Russian film, made in 1974 but not even shown in Russia until its Moscow Film Festival première in 1981. Interspersed with chunks of newsreel footage, it purports to relate the tragic events of the last five years of the Russian monarchy (condensed so that they appear to occur within one year), a period which saw the evil influence of Rasputin. Though there are some memorable scenes, the concept of the film would seem to have been both grander and worthier than its realization, though the mystery of its years on the shelf may possibly partly explain this: some say it was savagely cut after completion, others that it was padded out. The mystery remains. Cast: Velta Linne, Alisa Freindlikh, Anatoly Romashin, Alexei Petrenko, A. Romantsov, S. Muchenikov, Y. Katin-Yartsev, B. Ivanov, A. Pavlov, L. Brontevoi, B. Omarov, P. Pankov, M. Danilov, V. Osenev, P. Arzhanov, A. Arkadev, V. Raikov, B. Romanov, A. Trishkin, A. Maikova, N. Pshennaya, M. Svestin, etc. Dir: Elem Klimov. Pro: S. Kutikov. Screenplay: Semyon Lunghin and Ilya Nusinov; from the story by A. Kalyagin. Ph: Leonid Kalashnikov. Ed: Valery Belovoi. Art: Y. Liublin. M: Alfred Schnitke. (Mosfilm – Thorn EMI Classics). Rel: floating; first shown London (Camden Plaza and Chelsea Cinema) 28 November 1985. 148 mins. Cert PG.

A.K. In some ways, this French documentary by Chris Marker is a mite superficial, as it never attempts to delve far into the personality of its subject,

Akira Kurosawa. But this record of the master shooting his magnificent film *Ran* on the slopes of Mount Fuji in the winter of 1984 brilliantly captures the spectacle of vast armies of extras being directed in the complex battle scenes which were such a magnificent part of this classic movie; and both technically and visually it is a fine piece of moviemaking. Dir, written and narrated (originally) by Chris Marker (though the English version was shown in Britain). Ph: Frans-Yves Maresco. M: Toru Takemitsu. (Virgin) Rel: floating; first shown London (ICA), 21 March 1986. 71 mins. No cert.

Alamo Bay. Louis Malle's film about friction between Texan fishermen and unwelcome new arrivals (and rivals) – the refugees from Vietnam – which results in armed sea battles and the introduction of the Klu Klux Klan as a scare element. An almost documentary start leading to a somewhat melodramatic finish. Not on par with Malle's best work but still very watchable, with Ed Harris as the roughneck bully leader of the anti-Vietnamese faction and Amy Madigan as his girl, the only one who can see both sides of the argument. Rest of cast: Ho Nguyen, Donald Moffat, Truyen V. Tran, Rudy Young, Cynthia Carle, Martino Lasalle, William Frankfather, Lucky Mosley, Bill Thurman, Michael Ballard, Gary Basaraba, Jerry Biggs, Mark Hanks, Khoa Van Le, Tony Frank, Caroline Williams, Max Evers, Buddy Killen, Doris Hargrave, Harvey Lewis, Ed Opstad, Christopher Blum, Xuan Thi Le, Lan Ti Do. Le Nguyen, Tuan Tran, Carolyn Farnsworth, Jeannette Hudson Gray, David Ivanowski, Mary Carroll Kinnett, Barbara Opstad, Norman Spells, Ken West, Ray Benson Seiffert, Johnny Gimble, Tony Anastasio, Richard Hormachea, Wally Murphy, Reese Wynans, Donna Callaway Nugent, Laura Casterline, Vic Magnotta, Konrad Sheehan, Reatheal Bean, Jay Patterson, Sally Sockwell, Jimmy Ray Weeks, Stan Wilson. Dir: Louis Malle. Pro: Louis and Vincent Malle. Ex Pro: Ross Milloy. Screenplay: Alice Arlen. Ph: Curtis Clark. Ed: James Bruce. Pro Des: Trevor Williams. M: Ry Cooder. Assoc Pro: Ken Golden. (Tri-Star) Rel: floating; first shown London (ICA), 31 January 1986. 98 mins. Cert 18.

Above, roughneck fisherman Ed Harris brings up the Klu Klux Klan as reinforcements to support his sea battle against the unwelcome Vietnamese refugee rivals in Louis Malle's *Alamo Bay*, released by Tri-star. Right, unhappy onlookers: Amy Madigan and Ho Nguyen.

Alice in Wonderland. Finally released for cinema showing, this combined puppet-and-live version of the Lewis Carroll classic fairyland tale was made, in Nice, as a British–American–French venture way back in 1951 – and was immediately put on the shelf. The Rank Group helped with the cash and with the then untried Ansco-Technicolor method of colour. At the time, Disney was making his *Alice*, and the American studio took Leo Bunin to court to try to stop him from releasing this film at the same time (the case failed but other factors did the job for Disney). The puppets were animated by stop motion and it shows; they also illustrate how much film puppetry has advanced in the 25-year interim. However, despite this, the film is a very interesting museum piece and it is amusing to compare it with the other 'Alice' released in 1986 (*Dreamchild*). Dir: Dallas Bower. Pro: Leo Bunin. Screenplay: Henry Myers, Albert E. Lewin and Edward Eliscu; based on Lewis Carroll's novel. Ph: Gerald Gibbs (live action), Claude Renoir and Erwin Broner. Animators: William King, Ben Radin and Oscar Fessler. Sup Ed: Inman Hunter. Pro Des (puppets): Bernice Polifka. Art: Irving Block. M: Sol Kaplan. Choreography: Roland Petit. Human cast: Carol Marsh, Stephen Murray, Pamela Brown, Felix Aylmer, Ernest Milton, David Read, Raymond Bussières, Elizabeth Henson, Joan Dale; puppet voices by the above with: Joyce Grenfell, Jack Train and Ivan Staff. (Bunin, USA/Union Générale Cinématographie, Paris/J. Arthur Rank, GB–Electric Pictures) Rel: floating; first shown London (Everyman), 27 December 1985. 75 mins. Cert U.

American Warrior (**American Ninja** in USA). Fourth in the Cannon martial-arts movies series, with Michael Dudikoff as the chip-on-shoulder GI Joe who seems to upset everyone but his C.O.'s lovely daughter, whose life he saves when some real nasties working for a crooked arms-dealer set their sights on her. With three successful 'Ninja' movies already released, this one, though a slight notch down, will probably also satisfy the more easily pleased action-liking movie-goer. Rest of cast: Steve James, Judie Aronson, Guich Koock, John Fujioka, Don Stewart, John LaMotta, Tadashi Yamashita, Phil Brock, Tony Carreon, Roi Vinzov, Manolet Escudero, Greg Rocero, Berto Spoor, Michael Hackbart, Jerry Bailey, Rohy Barliwala, James Gaines, Steve Cook, Brian Robilliard, Zenon Gill, Willie Williams, Christopher Hoss, Joey Galvez, Nick Nicholson, Eric Hahn, Jacon Mendoza, Avi Charupe, Esther Zewko. Dir: Sam Firstenberg. Pro: Menahem Golan and Yoram Globus. Assoc Pro: Avi Kleinberger, Gideon Amir and Ken Metcalfe. Ph: Hanania Baer. Screenplay: Paul de Mielche; from a story by Kleinberger and Amir. Sup Ed: Michael J. Duthie. Pro Des: Adrian Gorton. M: Michael Linn. (Golan/Globus–Cannon Films) Rel: floating; first shown London (Cinecenta), 11 October 1985. 95 mins. Cert 18.

The Angelic Conversation. A series of images by director-photographer Derek Jarman, largely of the male body and largely erotic to some degree, accompany a reading by Judi Dench of some dozen Shakespeare sonnets. An idiosyncratic little British movie of somewhat limited appeal. Pro: James Mackay, who also shared the Ph with Jarman. Ed: Cerith Wyn-Evans and Peter Cartwright. M: Coil. Also sharing the reading credits: Paul Reynolds and Phillip Willamson. (BFI in assoc with Channel 4) Rel: floating; first shown London (Everyman) 18 October 1985. 81 mins. Cert PG.

Anne Devlin. With this very serious, thoughtful – and initially very slow – movie about the farmer's daughter who aided Robert Emmet in his – eventually unsuccessful – uprising against the Brits in Dublin at the beginning of the 19th century (and who, as a consequence, spent several years in jail), writer–director–producer Pat Murphy draws attention to the plight of women who have been neglected by history. The Irish government financed this 1984, made-in-Ireland movie; and it is noteworthy that the film was released in Britain by 'The Cinema of Women'. Cast: Brid Brennan, Bosco Hogan, Des McAleer, Gillian Hackett, David Kelly, Ian McElhinny, Chris O'Neill, Pat Leavy, Marie Conmee, John Cowley, Bernie Downes, Niall O'Brien, Eamonn Hunt, Martin Dempsey, Noel

Collector's piece: Carol Marsh as Alice in the 1951 British-French puppet and live-action *Alice in Wonderland*, which, never released in British cinemas, was taken off the shelf by Electric Pictures for a Christmas 1985 season.

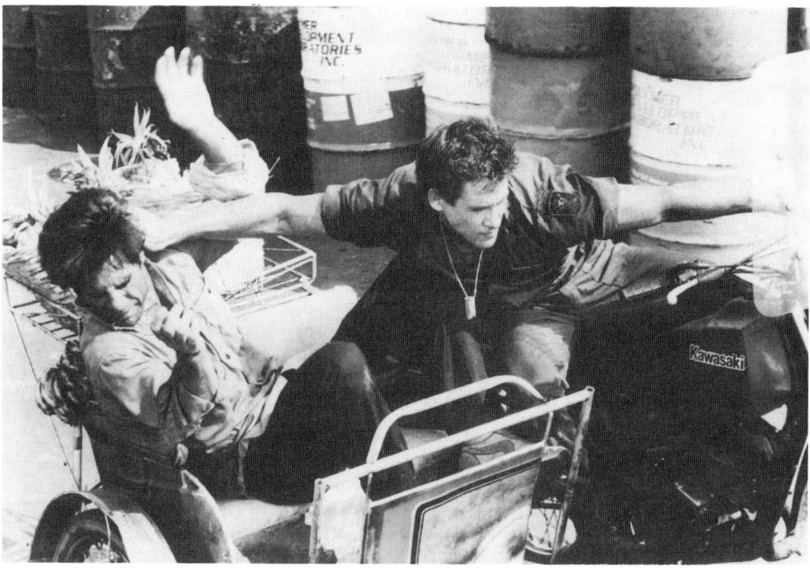

Michael Dudikoff shows how to ride a motorcycle and at the same time fight off an ill-wisher in Cannon's all-action *American Warrior*.

O'Donovan, Vinnie Murphy, etc. Dir, Screenplay and Pro: Pat Murphy. Ex Pro: Tom Hayes. Ph: Thaddeus O'Sullivan. Ed: Arthur Keating. Pro Des: John Lucas. M: Robert Boyle. (Aeom Films/Bord Scannan na hEireann/Irish Film Board/Arts Council in assoc with RTE–Cinema of Women) Rel: floating; first shown London (Everyman), 14 March 1986. 120 mins. Cert PG.

Antonio Gaudi. A feature documentary about Spain's premier architect made by Japan's Hiroshi Teshigahara in both English and Japanese versions. (ICA and Arts Council) Rel: floating; first shown London (ICA) 30 November 1985. 72 mins. Cert U.

Argie. This one-man-band British-made movie from Argentinian writer-director-producer-editor-star actor Jorge Blanco is described as 'an amalgamation of black comedy and political home movie'. Its oblique object is to show what it was like to be a loyal Argentinian in Britain during the Falklands War. Made on a shoestring – as is always obvious – it is the story of 'Pablo's' one-man war against his hosts, the British, and as a movie it works out as a mixture of the good, the bad and the indifferent. Rest of cast: Christine Plisson, Christine von Schreitter, Ella Blanco, David Janes, Philip Hartley, Bill Evans, Leon Redler, Rike Schwall, Orlando Diaz, Juan Carlos Ghirimoldi, Roberto Massey. Dir, Pro, Ed and (with Sylvie Rousseau) Screenplay: Jorge Blanco. Ph: Michael Amathieu and Jeanne Lapoire. (GIE Plisson-ICA Projects) Rel: floating; first shown London (ICA) 6 November 1985. 85 mins. No cert.

Madhur Jaffrey and Deborah Kerr in the outstanding British film *The Assam Garden* (Contemporary Films).

The Assam Garden. Beautifully made and brilliantly acted British chamber-work, small and modest in intent but large and brilliant in achievement. It tells the story of a widow whose late husband, a retired tea-planter, created and cared for an exotic Indian garden on a Gloucestershire hillside – and died from the effort. The widow struggles to keep the place tended and tidy ready for the promised visit of the publisher of *Great British Gardens* in which she hopes it will be included, as her husband had so ardently wished and worked for. Also about her friendship with an Indian woman living on a nearby new estate. A film full of subtlety, tenderness and moving insight and with a quiet, delicious sense of humour. Outstanding performances from Deborah Kerr and Madhur Jaffrey. Rest of cast: Alec McCowen, Zia Mohyeddin, Anton Lesser, Ian Cuthbertson. Tara Shaw, Dev Sagoo, Paul Bown, Simon Hedger, Maiser Aschar, Paula Jacobs. Dir: Mary McMurray. Pro: Nigel Stafford-Clark. Screenplay: Elisabeth Bond. Ph: Bryan Loftus. Ed: Rodney Holland. Art: Jane Martin. M: Richard Harvey. (Moving Picture Co–Contemporary Films) Rel: floating; first shown London (Academy), 5 July 1985. 92 mins. Cert U.

Back to the Future. Dubbed a 'Summertime Hit' by *Variety* (it was released in the United States in June 1985) this very jolly Steven Spielberg game with time makes pretty good Christmas fare too. After some 20 minutes in the here-and-now in a small American town, our young hero is whisked back some 30 years, courtesy of a nutty inventor and his DeLorean car Time Machine. That's when the film really settles down and begins to be fun. The changing setting (old movie house becoming a porno cinema, American car saleroom switching to Toyotas, small neighbourhood shops giving way to a supermarket, and so on) is as amusing as the main story about the hero and his scientist pal re-arranging time and events. Cast: Michael J. Fox, Christopher Lloyd, Crispin Glover, Lea Thompson, Claudia Wells, Thomas F. Wilson, James Tolkan, Marc McClure, Wendie Jo Sperber, George DiCenzo, Frances Lee McCain, Jeffrey Jay Cohen, Casey Siemaszko, Billy Zane, Harry Waters Jr, Donald Fullilove, Lisa Freeman, Cristen Kauffman, Elsa Raven, Will Hare, Ivy Bethune, Jason Marin, Katherine Britton, Jason Hervey, Maia Brewton, Courtney Gains, Richard L. Duran, Jeff O'Haco, Johnny Green, James Abbott, Sachi Parker, Robert Krantz, Gary Riley, Karen Petrasek, Tommy Thomas, Granville 'Danny' Young, David Harold Brown, Lloyd L. Tolbert, Paul Hanson, Lee Brownfield, Robert De Lapp. Dir: Robert Zemeckis. Pro: Bob Gale and Neil Canton. Ex Pro: Steven Spielberg, Frank Marshall and Kathleen Kennedy. Screenplay: Gale and Zemeckis. Ph: Dean Cundey. Ed: Arthur Schmidt and Harry Keramidas. Pro Des: Lawrence G. Paull. Art: Tod Hallowell. M: Alan Silvestri. (Amblin Entertainment–Universal–UIP) Rel: 20 December 1985. 116 mins. Cert PG.

Before Stonewall. American documentary, the sub-title of which tells all: 'The Making of a Gay and Lesbian Community'. About the rise from hidden underground to floodlit overground by these gay and lesbian communities and something of the fight that brought about the change. Dir: Greta Schiller. Pro: Schiller, Robert Rosenberg and John Scagliotti. Ph: Sandi Sissel, Jan Kraepelin and Cathy Zheutlin. Ed: Bill Daughton. M: Lori Seligman and Roy Ramsing. (Before Stonewall Inc. The Study for the Centre of Filmed History–The Other Cinema) Rel: floating; first shown London (Metro 1 and Everyman), 24 January 1986. 76 mins. Cert 15.

Best Defense. Comedians Dudley Moore and Eddie Murphy (teamed but never together in a single celluloid

Right, Steven Spielberg's *Back to the Future* (a Universal–UIP release) was first-rate film fun about an adventurous youngster (Michael J. Fox) who journeys into the past with the crazy inventor (Christopher Lloyd) in the latter's (DeLorean car!) Time Machine.

Below right, inventor Dudley Moore has no defence against boss Helen Shaver in Paramount–UIP's *Best Defense*, in which Eddie Murphy (below left) played co-star.

Left, daredevil WW1 ace pilot Biggles (Neil Dickson), and his support group (left to right, Bertie, James Saxon, Algy, Michael Silberry, and Ginger, Daniel Flynn) Above, with the young American (Alex Hyde-White) of 1968 who becomes mixed up in their heroics in the UIP release *Biggles*.

frame) showing how wholly unfunny both can be when appearing in this sort of wild and woolly comedy. Initially about a disastrous new tank guidance system, the film really defies reasonable description. Rest of cast: Kate Capshaw, George Dzundza, Helen Shaver, Mark Arnott, Peter Michael Goetz, Tom Noonan, David Rasche, Paul Comi, Darryl Henriques, Joel Polis, John A. Zee, Matthew Laurance, Christopher Mahar, Lorry Goldman, Stoney Richards, Tyler Tyhurst, Eduardo Ricard, William Marquez, Deborah Fallender, Raye Birk, Ellen Crawford, Gene Dynarski, John Hostetter, David Paymer, Dennis Redfield, Jerry Hyman, Hugo L. Stanger, Tracey Ross, Michael Scalera, Rob Winninger, Gary Bayer, Ronald Salley, Paul Eiding, Stephen Bradley, Sanford Jensen, Gerald Jann, Jennifer Wallace, Renny Temple, Ziporah Tzabari, Gabi Amrani, Rozsika Halmos, Diane Carter, Jake Dengel, Billy Ray Sharkey, Burton Collins, Bill Geisslinger, Itzhak Bbi Neeman, Jim Jansen, Javier Grajeda, Patricia Pivaar, Julie Ellis, Yulis Ruval, Pamela Stonebrook, Elizabeth Kubota, Rick Dees, 'Commander' Chuck Street. Dir: Willard Huyck. Pro: Gloria Katz. Screenplay: Katz and Huyck; based on the novel *Easy and Hard Ways Out* by Robert Grossbach. Ph: Don Peterman. Ed: Sydney Wolinsky and M. A. Stevenson. Pro Des: Peter Jamison. M: Patrick Williams. (Paramount–UIP) Rel: floating; first shown London (Plaza), 3 January 1986. 92 mins. Cert 15.

Beyond the Walls – Me Achovei Hasovagim. Grim, sordid and powerful Israeli prison drama which examines the situation of Jewish criminals and Arab terrorists confined in the same cell block and in so doing reflects the tensions, hostility and lack of understanding between the communities in the larger world outside. However, the film's message is that the two races *can* live together in – uneasy – peace, both in jail and therefore, surely, in the world outside. Winner of International Critics' Prize at 1984 Venice Film Festival and of six 1985 Israeli 'Oscars'. Cast: Arnon Zadok, Muhamad Bakri, Hilel Ne'eman, Assi Dayan, Boaz Sharaabi, Adib Jahashan, Roberto Polak, Naffi Salach, Loueteof Noussir, Edward Muallem. Youssuf Abed A'Nur, Jacon Ayali, Issa Mugrabi, Salach Houssain, Ali Al'Azaari, Haim Shinar, Ezra Rafael, Eliezer Albala, Ramzi Esmar, Shlomo Neer, Rami Livne, Shlomo Knafo, Iris Kanner, David Kedem, Micha Sharfstein, Motti Goldstein, Danny Bassan, Yehuda Cohen, Nachman Klilyan, Moshe Blieman, Avi Abuav, Jacob Naim, Yossef Fayumi, Dana Katz, Dina Ladani, Shura Greenhoise, Omri Marian, Dan Raviv, Muhamad Ali. Dir: Uri Barbash. Pro: Rudy Cohen. Assoc Pro: Katriel Schory. Screenplay: Uri and Benny Barbash and Eran Preis. Ph: Amnon Salomon. Ed: Tova Asher. Art: Eitan Levy. M: Ilan Virtzberg (song by Nurit Hirsh and Shimrit Or). (April Films – Cinegate) Rel: floating; first shown London (Gate, Notting Hill) 3 October 1985. 114 mins. Cert 18.

Biggles. A good tongue-in-cheek comedy based on a time-warp idea which somehow only fires on four of its possible six cylinders. It is the story of a young American executive in the 'sixties who is periodically pitchforked (latterly with his girl-friend) into heroic World War I adventures with daredevil British flying ace Biggles, and their efforts to stop the Germans bringing into deadly service a secret heat-ray weapon. Some nice performances, headed by Neil Dickson as the ace. Rest of cast: Alex Hyde-White, Fiona Hutchison, Peter Cushing, Marcus Gilbert, William Hootkins, Alan Polonsky, Francesca Gonshaw, Michael Siberry, James Saxon, Daniel Flynn, Roy Boyd, Terry Mountain, Fanny Carby, Alice Parsons, Patricia Ford, Pam St Clement, Christopher Robbie,

Jonathan Steward, Frank Singuinean. Dir: John Hough. Pro: Kent Walwin and Pam Oliver. Ex Pro: Adrian Scrope. Co-Ex Pro: Paul Barnes-Taylor. Assoc Pro: Peter James. Screenplay: John Grove and Kent Walwin; based on characters created by W. E. Johns. Ph: Ernest Vincze. Ed: Richard Trevor. Pro Des: Terry Pritchard. M: Stanislas. (Compact Yellow in assoc with Tambarle–UIP) Rel: floating, first shown London (Plaza) 22 May 1986. 92 mins. Cert PG.

Billy the Kid and the Green Baize Vampire. Described as a 'musical with a bite'(!), this uneven, stylish, promising little British film combines snooker (with a tense, 'sudden death' climax), crookery, comedy vampirey, music and much else in a novel, if not wholly successful way. But it's all mild fun – and games. Cast: Phil Daniels, Alun Armstrong, Bruce Payne, Louise Gold, Eve Ferret, Richard Ridings, Don Henderson, Neil McCaul, Zoot Money, David Foxe, Johnny Dennis, Trevor Laird, Daniel Webb, Ben Cole, Paul Cooke, Trevor Cooper, Chrissie Cotterill, Sarah Crowden, Ricky Diamond, Teresa Garraway, Peter Geeves, Glyn Grimstead, Tracie Hart, Sam Howard, Gareth Kirkland, Edwina Lawrie, Claire Lewis, Kevin Lloyd, Sarah London, Christina Matthews, Liz Morton, Paul Mulrennan, Clive Panto, Robert Pereno, Caroline Quentin, Nick Revell, George Rossi, Liza Sadova, Roger Tebb, Claire Tomlin, Tim Whitnall, Justin Case, Tony Chinn, Joe Fordham, Lisa Hart, Johnny Irving, Arnold Lee, Lindsay Neil, Joan Rhodes, Fiona Sloman, Gillian de Terville. Dir: Alan Clarke. Pro: Simon Mallin. Pro Sup: Bill Kirk. Screenplay: Trevor Preston. Ph: Clive Tickner. Ed: Stephen Singleton. Pro Des: Jamie Leonard. Art: Andy Harris. M: George Fenton (Zenith Pro in assoc with ITC–ITC) Rel: floating, first shown London (Cannon cinemas, Chelsea and Tottenham Court Road), 9 May 1986. 93 mins. Cert 15.

T.O. ('The One' – Bruce Payne) keeps a watchful eye on his snooker-player protégé Billy (Phil Daniels) in ITC's *Billy the Kid and the Green Baize Vampire* – the latter played by Alun Armstrong (right).

The Black Cauldron. Fantasy, fun, frolic and some fearsome characters in Disney's colourful, conventional, occasionally charming and technically silk-smooth cartoon fairy tale about a brave boy pig-keeper who braves the nasty behaviour of the devilish horned king to stop him getting his claws (literally) on the magic cauldron and raising an army of dead warriors with whose support he can rule the world. Luckily our young hero finds a magic sword and is assisted by a very pretty princess, an affectionate piglet with magical powers, a greedy little creature called Gugi and Fllewddur Fflam, an old minstrel with a mean harp. First-class family entertainment (though including frequently macabre and horrific visual images). But where oh where are the shameless sentiment, endearing charm and sheer moving magic of Disney's earlier cartoon features like *Dumbo* and *Bambi*? The voices: John Huston (introduction), Grant Bardsley (boy), Susan Sheridan (princess), John Hurt (king), Freddie Jones, Nigel Hawthorne, Arthur Malet, John Byner, Lindsay Rich, Brandon Call, Gregory Levinson, Eda Reis Maerin, Adele Malis-Morey, Billie Hayes, Phil Fondacaro, Peter Renaldy, James Almanzar, Wayne Allwin, Steve Hale, Phil Nibbellink, Jack Laing. Dir: Ted Berman and Richard Rich. Pro: Joe Hale. Ex Pro: Ron Miller. Ex in charge of Pro: Edward Hansen. Story by various writers based on the series of books by Lloyd Alexander, 'The Chronicles of Prydain'. Additional dialogue by Rosemary Anne Sisson and Roy Edward Disney. Ed: James Melton, Kim Koford and Armetta Jackson. M: Elmer Bernstein. (Walt Disney in assoc with Silver Screen Partners 11 – Walt Disney Pro – UK Film Distributors Ltd) Rel: 20 December 1985. 80 mins. Cert U.

Two scenes from one of Disney's better modern feature cartoons, *The Black Cauldron*, good family entertainment telling an old fairytale about a brave lad who defies and defeats the nasties and wins the pretty princess in the bargain.

Black Moon Rising. Complicated (and not very convincing) action melodrama about the revolutionary, 'space age' 350-mph car of the title – as well as an odd government agent on the run who hides his evidence in it, the lady-led gang who steal the car, and the inventors' and agent's efforts to recover car and evidence in a 'death defying climax'! Cast: Tommy Lee Jones, Linda Hamilton, Robert Vaughn, Richard Jaeckel, Lee Ving, Bubba Smith, Dan Shor, William Sanderson, Keenan Wynn, Nick Cassavetes, Don Opper, William Marquez, David Pressman, Stanley DeSantis, Richard Angarola, Edward Parone, Bill Moody, Al White, Lana Lancaster, Dalton Cathay, Townsend Coleman, Dave Adams, Rudy Daniels, E. J. Castillo, Peterson Banks, Frank Dent, Steve Fifield, Carl Ciarfalio, Don Pulford, Vincent Pandoliano, David Donham, Doug McHugh, Eric Trules, Lisa London. Dir: Harley Coklis. Pro: J. B. Michaels and Douglas Curtis. Screenplay: John Carpenter, Desmond Nakano and William Gray; based on Carpenter's story. Ph: Misha Suslov. Ed: Todd Ramsey. Pro Des: Bryan Ryman. M: Lalo Schifrin. (Thorn EMI Classics) Rel: floating; first shown London (ABC Edgware Road), 13 June 1986. 100 mins. Cert 18.

Blue Mountains – Golubye Gory Ely. Wittily directed Soviet – in fact, Georgian – comedy about a young author who finds everyone in the publisher's office friendly and co-operative, but without the faintest interest in their jobs or his story. A marvellous collection of shrewdly observed and gently satirized character studies – all ending when the ceiling falls in! Cast: Ramaz Giorgobiani, Vasili Kakhnishvili, Teimuraz Chirgadze, Ivan Sakvarelidze, Darejan Sumbatashvili. Dir: Eldar Shengelaya. Screenplay: Revaz Cheishvili. Ph: Leva Paatashvili. Art: Boris Tskhakaya. M: Ramaz Giorgobiani. (Gruziafilm–The Other Cinema) Rel: floating; first shown London (Metro), 20 April 1986. 97 mins. No cert.

Body Double. Brian de Palma's visually fascinating, carelessly unconvincing and sometimes very nasty (e.g. murder most foul by a giant power-drill) thriller, with hints of Hitchcock, tells of an unemployed Hollywood actor who drifts into the porno-movie business as he tries to solve a homicide mystery in which he becomes equivocally involved. The story, when there is one, is always loosely threaded. However, the almost magical silent sequences show de Palma at his considerable best, even if he has done it all before. Cast: Craig Wasson, Gregg Henry, Melanie Griffith, Deborah Shelton, Guy Boyd, Dennis Franz, David Haskell. Dir and Pro: Brian de Palma. Ex Pro: Howard Gottfried. Screenplay: R. J. Avrech and de Palma; from the latter's story. Ph: Stephen H. Burum. Ed: Jerry Greenberg and Bill Pankow. Pro Des: Ida Random. M: Pino Donaggio. (Columbia Delphi 11 – Columbia) Rel: 20 September 1985. 109 mins. Cert 18.

The Book of Mary – Le Livre de Marie. Pedestrian half-hour French-Swiss film about the break-up of a marriage as seen through the eyes, and ears, of the couple's 11-year-old daughter, who is torn between her parents. Cast: Rebecca Hampton (Mary), Bruno Cremer, Aurore Clément, Copi, Valentine Mercier, Clea Redalier. Dir, Screenplay and Ed: Anne-Marie Mieville. Ph: Jean-Bernard Menoud, Caroline Champetier, Jacques Firmann and Yvan Miclass. (The Other Cinema) Rel· floating; first shown London (Metro 1), 11 October 1985. 30 mins. No cert.

The Boys Next Door. After her 'youth' feature *Suburbia*, director Penelope Spheeris is again concerned with the young ones; this more ambitious effort relates an appalling story of an apparently inexplicable murder by an American college student whose excuse (sic) is the 'angry stuff that's inside him'. A hair-raising visit to the world of the psychopath. Cast: Maxwell Caulfield, Charlie Sheen, Patti d'Arbanville, Christopher McDonald, Hank Garrett, Paul C. Dancer, Richard Pachorek, Lesa Lee, Kenneth Cortland, Moon Zappa, Dawn Schneider, Kurt Christian, Don Draper, Blackie Dammett, Phil Rubenstein, James Carrington, Grant Heslov, Michael Lewis, L. O. Turner, Vance Colvig, Jeff Prettyman, Claudia Templeton, Ron Ross, Carlos Guitarist, Helen Brown, Hettie Lynne Hurtes, Sarah Lilly, Jimmy Ford, James Bershad, Joseph Michael Carla, Mary Tiffany, Marilou Conway, Mark Stanton, Kevi Kendall, Kenneth Gilman Sr, Carmen Filpi, Christina Beck, John Davey, Geof Brewer, Toby Iland, Richard Halpern, John Escobar, Ray Lykins, Jadie David, The Street Band. Dir: Penelope Spheeris. Pro: Keith Rubenstein and Sandy Howard. Ex. Pro: Mel Pearl and Don Levin. Screenplay: Glenn Morgan and James Wong. Ph: Arthur Albert. Ed: Andy Horvitch. Art: Jo-Ann Chorney. M: Great White. (New World Pictures–Cannon/Gala) Rel: floating; first shown London (Cannon Cinemas at Leicester Square and Oxford Street, after London Film Festival showing), 22 November 1985. 88 mins. Cert 18.

Brewster's Millions. According to *Variety* at least five films have previously been made of the 1906 stage play by this name, itself based on the novel by George Barr McCutcheon; the first film was made in 1914 and another (a British musical made in 1935) starred Jack Buchanan. It's pretty difficult to imagine, however, that any of the quintet (including the 1921 movie starring Roscoe Arbuckle and those starring Dennis O'Keefe in 1945 and Jack Watling in 1961) could have been less amusing than is Walter Hill's frantic-paced new version starring Richard Pryor as the surprised inheritor of a fabulous multimillion-pound legacy providing he can spend a somewhat smaller amount within a short stipulated period, at the end of which he must wind up penniless if he is not to forfeit the inheritance. A sadly misplaced and miscast Pryor is the big spender; he plays a

Maxwell Caulfield and Charlie Sheen, the highly unpleasant young neighbours in Cannon's *The Boys Next Door*, a story of mindless murder.

minor baseball team member of limited talent and outlook, making the character considerably less endearing than he should be. In fact, what performance credit there is must go to John Candy as Pryor's fat white fellow baseball-player pal. Rest of cast: Lonette McKee, Stephen Collins, Jerry Orbach, Pat Hingle, Tovar Feldshuh, Hume Cronyn, Joe Grifasi, Peter Jason, David White, Jerome Dempsey, David Wohl, Ji-Tu Cumbuka, Milt Kogan, Carmine Caridi, Yakov Smirnoff, Rick Moranis, Gloria Charles, Yana Nivana, Grand Bush, Conrad Janis, Rosetta Le Noire, Joseph Leon, Robert Ellenstein, Reni Santoni, Alan Autry, Joseph G. Medalis, Malachy McCourt, Roger Til, Allan Miller, Mike Hagerty, Kelly Yaegermann, Regina Hooks, Allan Graf, Archie Hahn, Jeff Mylett, Richard Hochberg, R.D. Call, Frank Slaten, Lin Shaye, Wesley Thompson, Strawn Bovee, Matt Landers, Kip Waldo, Shaka Cumbuka, Brad Sanders, Bill McConnell, Margot Rose, Joel Weiss, Candy Jennings, Bennie Dobbins, Gary Alexander, Joey Banks, Steven Benson, Mike Paciorek, Ken Medlock, Robbie T. Robinson, Ken Knighten, Hank Robinson, Art Reichle. Dir: Walter Hill. Pro: Lawrence Gordon and Joel Silver. Ex Pro: Gene Levy. Screenplay: Herschel Weingrod and Timothy Harris; based on the novel by George Barr McCutcheon. Ph: Ric Waite and Leroy Patton. Ed: Freeman Davies and Michael Ripps. Pro Des: John Vallone. M: Ry Cooder. Assoc Pro: Mae Woods. (Universal – UIP) Rel: 16 August 1985. 102 mins. Cert PG.

Richard Pryor as the black Brewster in yet another twist to the famous old stage play *Brewster's Millions* (Universal–UIP), with John Candy (right) as the faithful friend to the get-rich-quick character.

The Bride. Something of an elaborate and well produced mish-mash of the old Frankenstein, Pygmalion, and Beauty and the Beast legends in a story about the bad baron's storm-born creation of a suitable companion for his original patchwork male friend. This time he (Sting) creates such a beautiful – and strong-minded! – damsel (Jennifer Beals) that he falls in love with her. But, as in most previous Frankenstein epics, he is finally killed by his original male creation. The two best (scene- if not film-stealing) performances come from Clancy Brown as the Creature and David Rappaport as his dwarf mentor and friend. Rest of cast: Anthony Higgins, Geraldine Page, Alexei Sayle, Phil Daniels, Veruschka, Quentin Crisp, Cary Elwes, Tim Spall, Ken Campbell, Guy Rolfe, Andrew de la Tour, Tony Haygarth, Matthew Guinness, Tony Brutus, Gary Shall, Carl Chase, Bernard Padden, Janine Duvitski, John Sharp, Jack Birkett, Gerry Crampton, Fenella Fletcher, Robert Pereno, Joe Kay, Stromboli, Karen Furness, John Alexander, Jacqueline Russell, Tod Cody, Laurence Temple, Gerard Naprous, Vera de Vel, Sally Oultram, Joel Baland, Miss Irta, Annie Roddam, Dir: Franc Roddam. Pro: Victor Drai. Co-Pro: Chris Kenny. Ex Pro: Keith Addis. Screenplay and Assoc Pro: Lloyd Fonvielle. Ph: Stephen H. Burum. Ed: Michael Ellis. Art: John King and Damien Lanfranch. M: Maurice Jarre. (Columbia) Rel: 22 November 1985. 118 mins. Cert 15.

Partners in crookery Peter Bland and Phillip Gordon in the hilarious New Zealand comedy *Came a Hot Friday*. Right, Billy T. James as the scene-stealing Maori who thinks he's a Mexican bandit.

Bring on the Night. Feature documentary about the singer/songwriter Sting and the planning, formation, rehearsing and final public debut of his new musical combination, a rock/jazz mix. Well up to top standard for this kind of thing, with some humour, candid comments and even a close-up of the birth of Sting's baby. Dir: Michael Apted. Pro: David Manson. Ex Pro: Gil Friese and Andrew Meyer. Ph: R. D. Bode. Ed: Robert K. Lambert and Melvin Shapiro. M: Sting. Art: Ferdinando Scarfiotti. (Miracle) Rel: floating; first shown London (Prince Charles), 27 June 1986. 97 mins. Cert PG.

Sting as the bad Baron Frankenstein and Jennifer Beals as his lovely robot creation (with a mind of her own) in Columbia's thriller *The Bride*.

Came a Hot Friday. A brilliantly funny comedy from New Zealand, which is full of technical and dramatic talent, this is set in 1949 and concerns a couple of roving crooks whose target is normally the local bookies. The crooks' run of success stops short at Tainula Junction, where they become the unwilling keys to the unlocking of a Pandora's box of crime ranging from simple bootlegging to murder. Outstanding performances include those of Billy T. James as a sort of folklore character, Peter Bland, Philip Gordon and Erna Larsen. Rest of cast: Michael Lawrence, Marshall Napier, Marise Wipani, Phillip Holder, Don Selwyn, Patricia Phillips, Michael Morrissey, Marshall Napier, Erna Larsen, Bruce Allpress, Roy Billing, Hemi Ropata, Bridget Armstrong, Stephen Tozer, Sean Duffy, Ian Watkin, Norm Keesing, Derek Hardwick, Duncan Smith. Dir: Ian Mune. Pro: Larry Parr.

Screenplay: Mune and Dean Parker; based on the novel of the same title by Ronald Hugh Morrieson. Ph: Alun Bollinger. Ed: Ken Zemke. Pro Des: Ron Highfield. M: Stephen McCurdy. (Mirage – Miracle) Rel: floating; first shown London (Odeon, Kensington) 20 December 1985. 105 mins. Cert PG.

Camila – Camille. Superior, finely crafted, tear-jerking melodrama from Argentina based on an actual event of the mid-1800s: the passionate, ultimately tragic love affair between a headstrong young Buenos Aires socialite and a young Jesuit priest. Denounced by the authorities for sacrilege, the couple flee to the provinces where they open and run a school, but are eventually recognized by a priest who denounces them to the local military governor. He reluctantly obeys orders to have them shot, even though the girl is pregnant and may not lawfully be executed. This moving story conveys a strong political message reminding us that Argentina has often suffered in the past from brutal military dictatorships and that its Church has not dared to denounce openly the atrocities committed by such regimes. Beautifully acted, especially by Susu Pecoraro and Imanol Arias as the tragic couple; firmly directed and superbly photographed. Rest of cast: Hector Alterio, Elena Tasisto, Carlos Muñoz, Hector Pellegrini, Claudio Gallardou, Boris Rubaja, Mona Maris. Dir: Maria Luisa Bemberg. Pro: Angel Baldo, Hector Gallardo and Edecio Imbert. Ex Pro: Lita Stantic. Assoc Pro: Paco Molero. Screenplay: Bemberg, Beda Docampo Feijoo and Juan Bautista Stagnaro. Ph: Fernando Arribas. Ed: Luis Cesar D'Angiolillo. Art: Miguel Rodriguez. M: Luis Maria Serra. (GEA Cinematográfica, Argentina/Impala, Spanish Co-Production-Enterprise Pictures) Rel: floating; first shown London (Curzon, Mayfair) 27 September 1985. 107 mins. Cert 15.

Caravaggio. Another provocative, idiosyncratic film with strictly limited appeal from Derek (*Sebastiane*) Jarman; a partly factual, partly fictional biopic about the Italian Renaissance artist Michelangelo Merisi da Caravaggio. Effectively produced on a shoestring budget, with some beautifully posed scenes, the accent is on homosexual love and lots of – nearly – nude male bodies. Quirky humorous touches include 16th-century characters using typewriters, pocket calculators and even motorbikes; and it all becomes increasingly hard going as it progresses. Cast: Nigel Terry, Sean Bean, Garry Cooper, Dexter Fletcher, Spencer Leigh, Tilda Swinton, Nigel Davenport, Robbie Coltrane, Michael Gough, Noam Almaz, Dawn Archibald, Jack Birkett, Una Brandon-Jones, Imogen Claire, Sadie Corre, Lol Coxhill, Vernon Dobtcheff, Terry Downes, Jonathon Hyde, Emil Nicolaou, Gene October, Cindy Oswin, John Rogan, Zohra Segal, Lucien Taylor, Simon Turner. Dir and Screenplay: Derek Jarman; based on an original idea by Nicholas Ward-Jackson. Pro: Sarah Radclyffe. Ex Pro: Colin McCabe. Pro Ex: Jill Pack. Ph: Gabriel Beristain. Ed: George Akers. Pro Des: Christopher Hobbs. Art: Mike Buchanan. M: Simon Fisher Turner, assisted by Mary Phillips. (BFI in assoc with N. Ward-Jackson and Channel 4) Rel: floating; first shown London (Lumière), 24 April 1986. 93 mins. Cert 15.

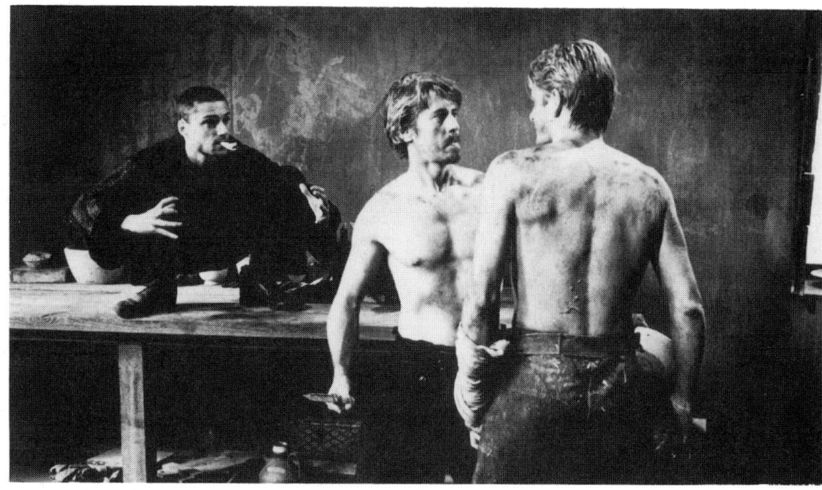

Confrontation between artist and model in BFI's Derek Jarman film *Caravaggio*, the artist being the Renaissance painter of the title, played by Nigel Terry (centre).

The Care Bears Movie. Animation feature about the very popular toys, aimed fairly and squarely, and very

Tenderheart Bear and his Care Bear Cousins (Bright Heart Racoon and Lotsa Heart Elephant) in the Samuel Goldwyn Company's children's feature cartoon *The Care Bears Movie* (Miracle Films).

Foster-parents Peter Whitford and Robyn Nevin with 6-year-old orphan PS (Nicholas Gladhill), subject of a bitter tug-of-love in *Careful He Might Hear You.*

successfully, at the kiddies. Certainly it drew them into the cinemas in droves during the school hols. Dir: Arna Selnick. Pro: Michael Hirsh, Patrick Loubert and Clive Smith. Ex Pro: Carole MacGillvray, Robert Unkel, Jack Chojnacli and Lou Gioia. Screenplay: Peter Sauder. Ph: David Altman, Jim Christianson and Barbara Sachs. Sup Ed: John Broughton and Rob Kirkpatrick. M: John Sebastian. Voices by Mickey Rooney, Georgia Engel, Harry Dean Stanton, Jackie Burroughs, Sunny Besen Thrasher, Eva Almos, etc. (American Greetings Corp/CPG Products-Nelvana Productions-Samuel Goldwyn Productions-Miracle Films) Rel: floating; first shown London (Classics) 26 July 1985 and subsequently widely released during August. 75 mins. Cert U.

Careful He Might Hear You. Another distinguished Australian film, based on a famous best-selling novel. This depicts the bitter, tug-of-war struggle between two sisters, one poor, plain and motherly (Wendy Hughes), the other rich and haughtily beautiful (Robyn Nevin), for the right to bring up their late sister's child. He, 6-year-old 'PS' (Nicholas Gledhill), has been deserted by his shiftless, basically unreliable, gold-seeking father. Thanks to the lovingly re-created 'thirties backgrounds, superb performances by the two women and others of the cast, plus a quite remarkable one by the lad (everyone concerned takes unusual care to see that their lines are clearly audible), the film is strongly emotional and often genuinely moving. Rest of cast: Peter Whitford, John Hargreaves, Isabelle Anderson, Geraldine Turner, Colleen Clifford, Julie Nihill, Beth Child, Pega Williams, Steve Fyfield, Jacqueline Kott, Kylie Burgess, Toby Blanchard, Virginia Portingale, Michael Long, Edward Howell, Len London, Colin Croft. Dir: Carl Schultz. Pro: Jill Robb. Screenplay: Michael Jenkins; based on the book by Sumner Locke Elliott. Ph: John Seale. Ed: Richard Francis-Bruce. Pro Des: John Stoddart. Art: John Carroll and John Wingrove. M: Ray Cook. (Syme International in assoc with N.S.W. Film Corp-Cannon/Gale), Rel: floating; first shown London (Berkely, Tottenham Court Road, and Arts, Chelsea) 12 July 1985. 113 mins. Cert PG.

Car Trouble. Though not the most refined and subtle of comedies, some may find this very broad British comedy-farce hilarious as it relates the plight of a couple enjoying illicit sex in the back of a car which runs away, resulting in a crash which prevents the lovers from physically separating! This leads them – still locked in embarrassing embrace – into a main road, causing a multiple pile-up. And while the fire brigade try to extricate them, the woman's infuriated husband watches it all on TV! Cast: Julie Walters, Ian Charleson, Vincenzo Ricotta, Stratford Johns, Hazel O'Connor, Dave Hill, Anthony O'Donnell, Vanessa Knox-Mayer, Roger Hume, Veronica Clifford, Laurence Harrington, John Blundell, Jeff Hall, Roy Barraclough, Sheila Bernette, Sally Hughes, Haydn Gwynne, Charles Cork, Kit Jackson, Roger Blake, Roy Heather, Michael Mears,

The End! Husband Ian Charleson 'at home' after watching his wife betraying him – caught in *vaginismus in extremis* by the TV cameras in Thorn EMI's very broad British farce *Car Trouble*.

Dave Arlen, Michael Melia, Winston Crooke, Betty Romaine, Dave Cooper, Simon Vyvyan, Justin Clark. Dir: David Green. Pro: Howard Malin and Greg Di Santis. Ex Pro: Howard Goldfarb and Laurence Myers. Co-Ex Pro: Max Meltzer. Assoc Pro: Redmond Morris. Pro Co-Ord: Sarah O'Brien. Screenplay: James Whaley and A. J. Tipping. Ph: Mike Garfath. Ed: Barry Reynolds. Pro Des: Hugo L. Wyhowski. Art: Celia Barnett. M: no credit listed. (Double-Helix Films–Thorn EMI) Rel: 28 February 1986. 93 mins. Cert 18.

Catholic Boys. Lively, often very funny and always entertaining re-working of the old story about a boy growing up and learning about life, this time against the background of a Brooklyn Catholic seminary where the pupils and Fathers are the normally mixed bunch, teachers varying from young, cigarette- and beer-liking to openly sadistic, boys from nice lad to sex-obsessed would-be bully. Along with the laughs come some sharply etched comments on the Holy Roman Catholic Church. Very well acted by all concerned. Cast: Donald Sutherland, John Heard, Andrew McCarthy, Mary Stuart Masterson, Kevin Dillon, Malcom Danare, Jennifer Dundas, Kate Reid, Wallace Shawn, Jay Patterson. Dir: Michael Dinner. Pro: Dan Wigutow and Mark Carliner. Assoc Pro: Kenneth Utt. Screenplay: Charles Purpura. Ph: Miroslav Ondricek. Ed: Stephen A. Rotter. Pro Des: Michael Molly. M: James Horner. (Silver Screen Partners-Thorn EMI) Rel: floating; first shown London (Cinecentre) 25 October 1985. 103 mins. Cert 15.

Below, the story of a lad growing up and finding out about adult life was treated with humour and understanding in Thorn EMI's *Catholic Boys*, about pupils and masters at a Brooklyn Catholic school, the headmaster of which is played by Donald Sutherland (right).

Cat's Eye. A three-story package of Stephen King's work first dreamt up on the set during the filming of the writer's *Firestarter*. An original screenplay is followed by two transcriptions of his thrillers: the first about a protective cat and a nasty troll hiding in the bedroom wall of a little girl played by Drew Barrymore (star of *Firestarter*); the second about a cat being used in a practical demonstration of the evils of

Drew Barrymore and the Cat which plays an important part in all three episodes that make up the Dino de Laurentiis thriller *Cat's Eye* (Thorn EMI).

smoking; the third concerning feline involvement in some marital cheating. All three pieces combine some slight humour with (not too shocking) thrills, and the acting in all three is of high quality. Rest of cast: James Woods, Alan King, Kenneth McMillan, Robert Hays, Candy Clarke, James Naughton, Tony Munafo, Mary D'Arcy, Court Miller, Russell Horton, Patricia Benson, James Rebhorn, Jack Dillon, Susan Hawes, Shelly Burch, Sal Richards, Jesse Doran, Patricia Kalember, Mike Starr, Charles Dutton. Dir: Lewis Teague. Pro: Martha J. Schumacher. Co-Pro: Milton Subotsky. 2nd Unit Dir: Glenn Randall Jr. Screenplay: Stephen King. Ph: Jack Cardiff. Ed: Scott Conrad. Pro Des: Giorgio Postiglione. 'Creatures' by Carlo Rambaldi. Art: Jeoffrey Ginn. M: Alan Silvestri. (Dino de Laurentiis–MGM/UA–Thorn EMI) Rel: 8 November 1985. 94 mins. Cert 15.

Cease Fire. Modest, very serious treatment of the familiar Vietnam vets problem with a nervous, irritable and nightmare-haunted hero brought up against reality when his similarly placed pal commits suicide. Cast: Don Johnson, Lisa Blount, Robert F. Lyons, Richard Chaves, Rick Richards, Chris Noel, Jorge Gil, John Archie, Christina Wilfong, Josh Segal, Darcy Shean, Richard Styles, Rooney Kerwin, Buddy Boylan, Lucy Pereda, Michele Dubou, Ed Fernandez, Christina Page, Dan Fitzgerald, Claudia Robinson, Bill Hindman, Eric Fredrickson, Father Morras, Julian Byrd, Jeff Muldovan, Carl Behm, Don Blakely, Charles Harris, Tim Hawkins, Gerry Stanley, Larry Ashlock. Dir: David Nutter. Pro: William Grefe. Ex Pro: George and Ed Fernandez. Screenplay: George Fernandez; based on his play *Vietnam Trilogy*. Ph: Henning Schellerup. Ed: Nutter, Julio Chaves and R. R. Clemente. Art: Alan Avchen. M: Gary Fry. (Double Helix Films–ELF Pro–Odyssey Video) Rel: floating; first shown London (Odeon, Kensington), 30 May 1986. 97 mins. Cert 18.

Chinese Boxes. Sharing the style, location (Berlin) and confusion of his *Flight to Berlin*, this over-plotted Christopher Petit piece (West German, English-speaking) depicts some unlawful and fairly unlikely events involving revenge, killings, drug trafficking and whatever against a would-be *Third Man* background. Cast: Will Patton, Gottfried John, Adelheid Arndt, Robbie Coltrane, Beate Jensen, Susanne Meierhofer, Jonathan Kinsler, L.M. Kit Carson, Chris Sievernich, Martin Muller, Jochen Von Vietinghoff, Ben de Jong, Michael Buttner, Michael Maichle, Edgar Hinz, Christopher Petit. Dir and (with L.M. Kit Carson) Screenplay: Christopher Petit. Pro: Chris Sievernich. Ex Pro: Stephen Woolley and Nik Powell. Pro Co-Ord: Ulla Swicker. Ph: Peter Harvey. Ed: Fred Srp. Art: Edgar Huinz and Klaus Beiser. M: Gunther Fischer. (Road Movies-Palace Pictures), Rel: floating; June/July 1985. 87 mins. Cert 15.

A Chorus Line. Richard Attenborough does his considerable best in bringing this big, essentially static musical show to the screen (apparently after a number of other hands had touched and, for various reasons, dropped it). The story of the selection of a chorus line for a new Broadway musical, it ventures into the private worlds of the finally chosen few who make the grade. It may not be (and probably never could have been) great stuff, but it is first-class entertainment, making the most of the material on hand. Cast: Michael Blevins, Yamil Borges, Jan Gan Boyd, Sharon Brown, Gregg Burge, Michael Douglas, Cameron English, Tony Fields, Nicole Fosse, Vicki Frederick, Michelle Johnston, Janet Jones, Pam Klinger, Audrey Landers, Terrence Mann, Charles McGowan, Alyson Reed, Justin Ross, Blane Savage, Matt West. Dir: Richard Attenborough. Pro: Cy Feuer and Ernest H. Martin. Ex Pro: Gordon Stulberg. Asso Pro: Joseph M. Caracciolo. Pro Sup: Michael S. Glick. Screenplay: Arnold Schulman; book of the play: James Kirkwood and Nicholas Dante. Ph: Ronnie Taylor. Ed: John Bloom. Pro Des: Patrizia von Brandenstein. Art: John Dapper. Choreography: Jeffrey Hornaday. M: (score) Marvin Hamlisch; (arr) Ralph Burns; (lyrics) Edward Kleban; based on the stage play conceived, choreographed and directed by Michael Bennett. (Embassy Films/Polygram Pictures–Rank Film Dist.) Rel: 28 February 1986. 118 mins. Cert PG.

The Clan of the Cave Bear. Prehistoric tale of a blonde orphan girl, reluctantly adopted by the hairy clan of the title, who has a rough time of it before she emerges as a sort of early Queen Boadicea, the first warrior woman and practising feminist. Beautifully photographed in wildest Canada. The other item on the credit side of a pretty dull balance sheet is Daryl Hannah's winning performance as the girl with prehistoric guts. Rest of cast: Pamela Reed, James Remar, Thomas G. Waites, John Doolittle, Curtis Armstrong, Martin Doyle, Adel C. Hammoud, Mike Muscat, John Wardlow, Keith Wardlow, Barbara Duncan, Gloria Lee, Janne Mortil, Lycia Naff, Linda Quibell, Bernadette Sabath,

Penny Smith, Joey Cramer, Rory L. Crowley, Nicole Eggert, Emma Floria, Pierre Lamielle, Paul Caravotes, Mary Reid, Samantha Ostry, Shane Punt, Christian Boyce, Catherine Flather, Guila Chiesa, Shauna Fanara, Amy Cyr, Colin Doyle, Natino Bellantoni, Rick Vanquette, Alan Waltman. Dir: Michael Chapman. Pro: G. I. Isenberg. Co-Pro: Stan Rogow. Ex Pro: Jon Peters, Peter Guber, Mark Damon and John Hyde. Co-Ex Pro: Sidney Kimmel. Screenplay: John Sayles; based on the novel by Jean M. Auel. Ph: Jan de Bont. Ed: Wendy Greene Bricmont. Pro Des: Kelly Kimball. M: Alan Silvestri. (Producers Sales Org. in assoc with Guber/Peters–Jozak/Decade Pro–Rank Film Dist.) Rel: 6 June 1986. 99 mins. Cert 15.

Audrey Landers shows off her talent – and shape – during rehearsals for a new Broadway musical, the Rank release *A Chorus Line*, during which producer Michael Douglas tries to dissuade ex-star Alyson Reed from joining the 'line' (right).

Clockwise. John Cleese returning to something like his famous *Fawlty Towers* character, and in funny form, in an essentially British farce about the headmaster of a comprehensive school, due to be honoured by his more illustrious Harrovian and Etonian peers, trying in spite of every possible accident and other nightmarish obstacles to get to the occasion on time. And it makes for good, and such pleasantly clean, fun.

Below, it's late, it's late . . . clock-conscious headmaster John Cleese makes his driver Penelope Wilton cry and his pupil Sharon Maiden sorry for her in Thorn EMI's *Clockwise*. Below left, with time pressing, all the phone boxes are either occupied or vandalized!

Rest of cast: Alison Steadman, Penelope Wilton, Stephen Moore, Joan Hickson, Sharon Maiden (a delightful performance), Chip Sweeney, Constance Chapman, Clint Jonathan Bowwater, Mark Burdis, Penny Leatherbarrow, Robert Wilkinson, Mark Bunting, John Bardon, Nadia Carina, Dickie Arnold, Angus Mackay, Peter Needham, Peter Lorenzelli, Ann Way, Ann-Marie Gwatkin, Mohammed Ashiq, Pat Keen, Geoffrey Hutchings, Geoffrey Greenhill, Richard Ridings, Geoffrey Davion, Charles Bartholomew, Sheila Keith, Christian Regan, Alan Parnaby, Tony Haygarth, Michael Aldridge, Ronald Sowton, Alan Granton, Susan Field, Leslie Scofield, Mike Glynn, Benjamin Whitrow, Geoffrey Palmer, Nicholas le Provost, Peter Cellier, David Conville, Patrick Godfrey, Rupert Massey, John Row, Philip Voss, Jeffrey Wickham, Nick Stringer, Graeme Green, Sidney Livingstone, Michael Percival, Peter Jonfield, Brian Portsmouth. Dir: Christopher Morahan. Pro: Michael Codron. Ex Pro: Verity Lambert and Nat Cohen. Assoc Pro: Gregory Dark. Screenplay: Michael Frayn. Ph: John Coquillon. Ed: Peter Boyle. Pro Des: Roger Murray-Leach. Art: Diana Charnley. M: George Fenton. (Thorn EMI) Rel: 27 March 1986. 97 mins. Cert PG.

Clue. Hilarious, campy, black-comedy send-up of the familiar whodunit, with every trick – and cliché – of the trade wittily played to the hilt in 90-odd minutes of fast-moving fun and thrills. The (largely unfamiliar) cast exploit their chances with gleeful expertise – especially Tim Curry, Lesley Ann Warren, Eileen Brennan, Martin Mull and Colleen Camp, And in the US, the film offered three different endings from which to choose! Rest of cast: Madeline Kahn, Christopher Lloyd, Michael McKean, Lee Ving, Bill Henderson, Jane Wiedlin, Jeffrey Kramer, Kellye Nakahara, Will Nye, Rick Goldman, Chere Bryson, John-Clay Scott, Don

Below, *another* body? Left to right, Lesley Ann Warren, Eileen Brennan and Madeline Kahn wonder whose will be next in Paramount's hilarious whodunit send-up *Clue*. Right, Tim Curry as the butler-cum-mastermind at the centre of the blackly comic goings-on.

Camp. Dir and Screenplay: Jonathan Lynn; from a story by Lynn and John Landis, based upon the Parker Bros board game 'Clue' ('Cluedo' in UK). Pro: Debra Hill. Ex Pro: Lynn, John Peters and Peter Guber. Assoc Pro: Jeffrey Chernov. Ph: Victor J. Kemper. Ed: David Bretherton, Richard Haines and Michael Kaplan. Pro Des: John Lloyd. M: John Morris. (Paramount in assoc with PolyGram Pictures and Debra Hill Pro–UIP) Rel: 9 May 1986. 96 mins. Cert PG.

Soft drink-manufacturing rivals Bill Kerr (left), the Australian independent, and Eric Roberts, the American Coca-Cola would-be take-over agent, in *The Coca-Cola Kid* (Palace Pictures).

The Coca-Cola Kid. From the idiosyncratic Yugoslav director of *WR: Mysteries of the Organism* and *The Telephone Operator* comes this equally idiosyncratic comedy about the mission of an American sales wizard sent to subdue and conquer the last independent soft-drinks stronghold in Australia (where the film was made). With plenty of chuckles on a basis of irony, the rambling format and crazy construction sink the film long before it becomes the satirical classic it might so easily have

Above, a large section of the cast including Wilford Brimley (left foreground) and Brian Dennehy (right ditto) and, background left to right, Tyrone Power Jr, Maureen Stapleton, Hume Cronyn, Steve Guttenberg, Mike Nomad, Tahnee Welch, Don Ameche, Jessica Tandy and Gwen Verdon in *Cocoon* (20th Century-Fox). Left, veterans Cronyn and (right) Verdon and Ameche.

been. But good, *very* individualistic fun nevertheless. Cast: Eric Roberts, Greta Scacchi, Bill Kerr, Max Gillies, Kris McQuade, Tony Barry, Chris Haywood, Tim Finn, Paul Chubb, David Slingsby, Colleen Clifford, Rebecca Smart, Esben Storm, Linda Nagle, Julie Nihill, Fiona Hallett, Angelo D'Angelo, Gia Carides, Steve Dodd, John Ewing, Annie Semmler, Jane Markey, Ian Gilmour, Ian Nimmo, David Bracks, David Argue, Peter Armstrong, Pola Negri., Dir: Dusan Makavejev. Pro: David Roe. Pro Sup: Susan Wild. Pro Co-Ord: Suzanne

Donnelly. Screenplay: Frank Moorhouse; based on his own short stories. Ph: Dean Semler. Ed: John Scott. Pro Des: Graham (Grace) Walker. M: William Motzing. (Songs, 'Coca-Cola Jingle' and 'Home from my Heart' by Tim Finn. (Cinema Enterprises Pty Ltd/ Smart Egg Pictures Ltd–Palace Pictures) Rel: 19 July 1985. 98 mins. Cert 15.

Cocoon. *E.T.* with heart – topped up by a layer of honest sentiment. A clever mixture of Outer Space fiction and very human comedy-drama, it shows how some extra-terrestrial beings arrive on Earth in human guise hoping to recover some of their cocooned friends, who lie waiting at the bottom of the sea. Their expedition is interfered with by a group of old people who find the waters of the swimming-pool, in which the recovered cocoons rest, have a marvellously rejuvenating effect. It is all done with commendable restraint and good taste. A wonderful cast headed by such great veterans as Don Ameche, Wilford Brimley, Hume Cronyn, Jessica Tandy, Brian Dennehy, Maureen Stapleton and Gwen Verdon, plus such promising newcomers as Tyrone Power Jr and Tahnee Welch. Rest of cast: Jack Gilford, Steve Guttenberg, Herta Ware, Barrett Oliver, Linda Harrison, Clint Howard, Charles Lampkin, Mike Nomad, Jorge Gil, Jim Ritz, Charles Rainsbury, Wendy Cooke, Pamela Prescott, Dinah Sue Rowley, Gabriella Sinclair, Cyndi Vicino, Russ Wheeler, Harold Bergman, Ivy Thayer, Fred Broderson, Mark Cheresnick, Bette Shoor, Mark Simpson, Robert Slacum Jr, Rance Howard, Jean Speegle, Charles Voelker, Irving Krone, Clarence Thomas, Ted Science. Dir: Ron Howard. Pro: Richard D. Zanuck, David Brown and Lili Fini Zanuck. Assoc Pro: Robert Doudell. Screenplay: Tom Benedek; from a story by David Saperstein. Ph: Don Peterman. Ed: Daniel Hanley and Michael J. Hill. Pro Des: Jack T. Collis. M: James Horner. (Zanuck/Brown Productions-Fox) Rel: 11 October 1985. 117 mins. Cert PG.

Code of Silence. This cops-and-robbers (in fact drug-dealing gangsters) thriller-fantasy has toughie Chuck Norris as a dedicated, incorruptible Chicago lawman who takes on and wipes out single-handedly (with a small, radio-controlled tank as his back-up) an entire gangster army and rescues the fair, if self-willed maiden in distress. Though totally incredible, the result is a well produced, smartly directed, rip-roaring action melodrama good enough to carry it high in the box-office popularity stakes. Rest of cast: Henry Silva, Bert Remsen, Mike Genovese, Nathan Davis, Ralph Foody, Allen Hamilton, Ron Henriquez, Joseph Guzaldo, Molly Hagan, Ron Dean, Wilbert Bradley, Dennis Farina, Gene Barge, Mario Nieves, Miquel Nino, Ronnie Barron, Joe Kosala, Lou Damiani, Nydia Rodriquez Terracina, André Marquis, John Mahoney, Dennis Cockrum, Zaid Farid, Howard Jackson, Alex Stevens, Don Pike, Les Podewell, Trish Schaefer, Martha Oton, Jack Kandel, James Fierro, Tom Letui, Jeff Hoke, Gary T. Pike, Catalina Caceres, Frank Strocchia, Shirley Kelly, Angela Zimm, Jack Decker, Sue Kelly, Michael E. Bradley, Sally Anne Waranch, Jerry Tullos. Dir: Andy Davis. Pro: Raymond Wagner. Screenplay: Michael Butler, Dennis Shryack and Mike Gray; from a story by Butler and Shryack. Ph: Frank Tidy. Ed: Peter Parasheles and Christopher Holmes. Pro Des: Maher Ahmed. M: David Frank. (Orion–Rank Film Dist.) Rel: 20 September 1985. 100 mins. Cert 18.

Tough Chicago cop Chuck Norris views the result of a gang argument in *Code of Silence* (Orion–Rank) and, right, faces up to an unfriendly gangster boss, played by Henry Silva.

Colonel Redl – Redl Ezredes. A handsome Hungarian historical film which, though based on fact, has a lot of fictional trimmings, changes and suppositions in its story of a poor young lad who through luck, a certain talent and an adoring loyalty to his Emperor becomes a member of the elite Military Academy and thereafter rises resolutely and ruthlessly to the position of Lieut-Col. Redl, Head of the Secret Police, during the period immediately preceding the outbreak of the 1914–18 war. But Redl's homosexuality and his unfortunate destruction of a plot set up by the Crown Prince lead to his arrest and eventually to a forced suicide. As no reliable account of these events exists, the film is also based to some extent on John Osborne's controversial play *A*

Duel to the death between one-man-army Arnold Schwarzenegger and erstwhile companion-in-arms Vernon Wells in Fox's *Commando*.

Patriot for Me. Overall it is a fine example of artistic collaboration, in this case between the writer, director and star, the trio who a few years ago made *Mephisto* such a critical and public success. Spectacular scenes, such as the gala ball with beautifully juxtaposed moments of intimacy, culminating in the disturbing suicide sequence. A Hungarian/West German/Austrian co-production, winner of the Jury Prize at Cannes, 'Best Actor' and 'Best Film' Awards at Budapest Festival, 'Best Actor' and 'Best Film' German Golden Band Awards. Cast: Klaus Maria Brandauer (Redl), Armin Muller-Stahl, Gudrun Landgrebe, Jan Miklas, Dorottya Udvaros, Athina Papadimitriu, Andras Balint, Karoly Eperjes, Laszlo Galffi, Laszlo Mensaros, Robert Rathonyi, Tamas Major, Gyorgy Banffy, Agnes T. Katona, Hans-Christian Blech, Gabor Svidrony, Eva Szabo, Maria Majlath, Gyorgy Racz, Dora Lendvai, etc. Dir: Istvan Szabo. Sup Pro: Manfred Durniok. Pro Sup: Judit Hugar. Screenplay: Szabo and Peter Dobai. Ph: Lajos Koltai. Ed: Zsuzsa Csakany. Art: Jozsef Romvari. M: Zdenko Tamassy. (Mafilm Studio Objectiv Mokep, Budapest, Manfred Durniok Pro for Film und Fernsehen, West Berlin/ZDF, Mainz/ORF (Vienna) – Cannon-Gala). Rel: floating; first shown London (Cannon Première and Minema), 22 November 1985. 149 mins. Cert 15.

Commando. Strongman Arnold Schwarzenegger out-Rambo-ing *Rambo* in a violent farce which can be seen as either riotous comic-strip comedy or repellently violent trash, according to one's outlook or mood. A.S. plays an invincible one-man army decimating legions of a king-crook's private martial forces, with only occasional help from larky and quite delightful Rae Dawn Chong. He ends up with just a scratch and she's quite intact as they clamber over a mountain of corpses to free his young kidnapped daughter. Rest of cast: Dan Hedaya, Vernon Wells, James Olson, David Patrick Kelly, Alyssa Milano, Bill Duke, Drew Snyder, Sharon Wyatt, Michael deLano, Bob Minor, Mike Adams, Carlos Cervantes, Lenny Juliano, Charles Meshack, Chelsea Field, Julie Hayer, Hank Calia. Dir: Mark L. Lester. Pro: Joel Silver.Assoc Pro: Joseph Loeb III and Matthew Weisman. Co-Assoc Pro: Stephanie Brodie and Robert Kosberg. Screenplay: Steve E. de Souza; from a story by Loeb, de Souza and Matthew Weisman. Ph: Matthew F. Leonetti. Ed: Mark Goldblatt, John F. Link and Glenn Farr. Pro Des: John Vallone. M: James Horner. (Fox) Rel: 21 February 1986. 90 mins. Cert 18.

Commando Leopard. Blood and thunder in a South American country where the son of a local landowner and a British milady set out to unseat the dastardly president and his evil military henchman. Cast includes: Lewis Collins, Klaus Kinsky, Hans Leutenegger, Manfred Lehmann, Christina Donadio, John Steiner, Franco Derosa, etc. Dir: Anthony M. Dawson. Pro: Erwin C. Dietrich. Screenplay: Roy Nelson. Ph: Peter Baumgartner. (Entertainment Film Dist.) Rel: 29 November 1985. 103 mins. Cert 15.

Compromising Positions. Minor, mixed-up whodunit about the murder of a wealthy, philandering, Long Island dentist and, alongside the official investigation, the amateur sleuthing by a housewife (a former reporter) to the increasing irritation of her husband. Cast: Susan Sarandon, Raul Julia, Edward Herrmann, Judith Ivey, Mary Beth Hurt, Joe Mantegna, Anne de Salvo, Josh Mostel, Deborah Rush, Joan Allen, Kaiulani Lee, Tanya Berezin, William Youmans, Amanda Lyons, Chris Cunningham, Jason Beghe, Timothy Jerome, Jack Gilpin, Bill Cobbs, Harris Laskawy, John Polito, Paul Butler, Pat Harper, Elkan Abramowitz. Dir and Pro: Frank Perry. Ex Pro: Sarah M. Hassanein. Screenplay: Susan Isaacs; based on her novel. Ph: Barry Sonnenfeld. Ed: Peter Frank. Pro Des: Peter Larkin. M: Brad Fiedel. (Paramount–UIP) Rel: 13 June 1986. 98 mins. Cert 15.

Le Cop – Les Ripoux. Delightful, amoral, witty and beautifully played (Philippe Noiret gives his best performance in years) French farce based on police corruption in the seedier parts of Paris. Having double-crossed his erstwhile team-mate and policeman pal, René (Noiret) sets out to make sure that the honesty of his new young partner doesn't survive for long! Decorated and promoted, René eventually oversteps the mark but, out of jail after two years, finds his partner waiting for him with the legal ownership of the pub René has always wanted. Crime, apparently, does pay and no wonder the film caused some comment in France when it was shown there . . . It won three of the much sought-after French César awards, including those for 'Best Direction' and 'Best Film of the Year'. Rest of cast: Thierry Lhermitte, Régine, Grace de Capitani, Claude Brosset, Albert Simono, Julien Guiomar, Henri Attal, Abou Baker, Pierre Baton, Bernard Bijaoui, Jean-Claude Bouillaud, Julien Bukouski, François Cadet, Jocelyn Canoen, Kamel Cherif, Jean Cherlian, Louise Chevalier, Salah Cheurfi, Jacques Ciron, Gérard Couderc, Madette Marion, Michel Cremardes, Alain David, Cheik Doukouré, Michel Ducjezeau, Richard Fiardo, James Fitzgerald, Pierre Frag, Jacques Frantz, Olivier Granier, Jacques Santi, Michel Hardy, Nicholas Hawtrey, Hélène Hily, Guy Kerner, Menzan Kouassi, Karine Lafabrie, Jean Lanier, Henry Laurent, Hector Melamaud, Pascal Martin-Granal, Simone Mickael, Georges Montillier, René Morard, Michael Morris, Pascal Pistacio, Francis Rousseff, Tiky, Régine Teyssot, Marius Yelolo, Abbas Zahmani. Dir and Screenplay: Claude Zidi; the latter based on an idea by Simon Mackael. Dialogue: Didier Kaminka. Pro Sup: Brigitte Faure. Ph: Jean-Jacques Tarbes. Ed: Nicole Saunier. Art: Françoise de Leu. M: Francis Lai. (Films 7/Editions 23–Cannon/Gala) Rel: floating; first shown London (Cannon cinemas at Leicester Square and Tottenham Court Road) 31 January 1986. 100 mins. Cert 18.

Cop au Vin – Poulet au Vinaigre – Chicken with Vinegar. A typical Chabrol whodunit, set against the background of a wickedly and wittily observed small French provincial town, with its factions, frictions and dark undercurrents of villainy. Wheelchair-bound Mme Cuno and her teenage son defy threats and refuse the financial carrots offered them by a trio of on-the-make locals (doctor, lawyer and butcher) who want the invalid's property for a development which will make them each a fortune. But after a mysterious death, the first of several, an out-of-town 'tec arrives to snoop, probe (sometimes roughly) and eventually to uncover the dirt that has been swept under the municipal carpet. A deft Chabrol mixture of sly perception, humour and thrills. Cast: Jean Poiret, Stéphane Audran, Michel Bouquet, Caroline Cellier, Lucas Belvaux, Jean Topart, Pauline Lafont, Andrée Tainsy, Jean-Claude Bouillaud, Josephine Chaplin, Jacques Frantz, Dominique Zardi, Albert Dray, Henri Attal, Marcel Guy, Jean-Marie Arnoux. Dir: Claude Chabrol. Pro: Marin Karmitz (of MK 2 Productions). Assoc Pro: Catherine Lapoujade. Screenplay: Chabrol and Dominique Roulet; based on the latter's book *Une Mort en trop*. Ph: Jean Rabier. Ed: Monique Fardoulis. Pro Des: Françoise Benoit-Fresco. M: Matthieu Chabrol. (MK2 Productions–Virgin Films) Rel: floating; first shown London (Screen-on-the-Hill), 11 October 1985. 110 mins. Cert 15.

Crazy Family – Gyakufunsha Kazoki. (The Japanese title means 'Reverse-Jet Family', referring to an airplane-landing hazard caused by a pilot's mental aberration.) The story of a Tokyo flatdweller and office worker whose problems begin when he achieves a longed-for house, and increase – due to his odd-ball father, his not over-bright son, his sex-obsessed daughter (who can't make up her mind between becoming a wrestler or a pop singer) and his unfaithful and immoral wife – to explosion point. A wry comedy with a social sting in the tail. Cast: Katsuya Kobayashi, Mitsuko Baisho, Yoshiki Arizono, Yuki Kudo, Hitoshi Ueki. Dir: Sogo Ishii. Pro: Kazuhiko Hasegawa, Yoyoji Yamane and Shiro Sasaki. Asso Pro: Sasumi Hiyakasa and Syosuke Taga. Screenplay: Ishii, Yoshinori Kobayashi and Fumio Konami; from a story by Ishii. Ph: Masaki Tamura. Ed: Junichi Kikuchi. Pro Des: Terumi Hosoichi. M: '1984'. (The Other Cinema) Rel: floating; first shown London (Metro One), 21 February 1986. 106 mins. Cert 18.

Creepers – Phenomena. Italian film made in (hilariously atrocious) English. It concerns a 14-year-old girl who is quite a character: she can communicate with insects, follow a trail of maggots to a psychotic monster killer and call up a cloud of flies to save her from awful death. And there's that nasty fellow who not only kills the girl's schoolmates but retains odd bits of their bodies as keepsakes! All this from Dario Argento, who has been called a 'master of modern Gothic horror movies' – and after this, aptly so. Cast: Jennifer Connelly, Daria Nicolodi, Dalila di Lazzaro, Patrick Bauchau, Donald Pleasence, Fiore Argento, Frederica Mastroianni, David Marotta, Fausta Avelli, Marta Biuso, Sophie Bourchier, Paola Gropper, Ninke Hielkema, Mitzy Orsini, Geraldine Thomas, Fiorenza Tessari, Mario Donatone, Francesca Ottaviani, Michele Soavi, Franco Trevisi. Dir, Pro and (with Franco Ferrini) Screenplay: Dario Argento. Pro Ex: Angelo Jacono. Ph: Romano Albani. Ed: Franco Fraticelli. (Dacfilm–Palace Pictures) Rel: floating; first shown London (Cannon, Panton Street), 18 April 1986. 83 mins. Cert 18.

Hardly a pleasant outlook for the glass breaker in the Palace Picture thriller *Creepers – Phenomena.*

Crimes of Passion. Overwrought, pretentious and all-but-pornographic sex film from Ken Russell about a girl (Kathleen Turner, who looks lovely with or without her wig) leading a double life: that of a successful and quite staid fashion designer by day and a voracious, no-holds-barred prostitute by night; in the latter role she meets a repressed young husband (John Laughlin) whose liberated sexual ardour brings a deeper response from the hooker. Lurking in the background, devoured by a twisted sexuality, is a priest (played with hysterical abandon by Anthony Perkins), with a deadly steel phallus in his ditty bag and an expert line in smutty talk, whose actions precipitate the climax of this ludicrous story. Rest of cast: Randall Brady, Norman Burton, James Crittenden, Bruce Davison, Peggy Feury, Dan Gerrity, Lisa Hayslip, Terry Hoyos, Gordon Hunt, Janice Kent, Christina Lange, Stephen Lee, Roxanne Mayweather, Yvonne McCord, Vince McKewin, Pat McNamara, Thomas Murphy, Deanna Oliver, Gerald S. O'Loughlin, Ian Petrella, Annie Potts, Janice Renney, John Rose, John D. Scanlon, Louis Sorel, Patricia Stevens, Seth Wagerman, Carol Ann Williams, John D. Scanlon, Joseph Chapman, Pamela Anderson, Jan Robson. Dir: Ken Russell. Pro: Barry Sandler and Donald P. Borchers. Ex Pro: Larry A. Thompson. Screenplay: Barry Sandler. Ph: Richard Bush. Ed: Brian Tagg. Pro Des: Richard MacDonald. Art: Steve

Marsh. M: Rick Wakeman. (New World Pictures–Orion–Rank Film Dis.) Rel: floating; first shown London (Odeon, Haymarket) 6 September 1985. 106 mins. Cert 18.

Crimewave. Apparently also shown in the United States with the alternative title of **Broken Hearts and Noses**. Black-tinged comedy-cum-comic-strip crime thriller, with the hero falsely condemned to death for a murder not committed, and only saved by the last-minute arrival of the heroine with her vital testimony. Cast: Louise Lasser, Paul L. Smith, Brion James, Sheree J. Wilson, Edward R. Pressman, Bruce Campbell, Reed Birney, Richard Bright, Antonio Fargas, Hamid Dana, John Hardy, Emil Sitka, Hal Youngblood, Sean Farley, Richard de Manicor, Carrie Hall-Schalter, Wiley Harker, Julius Harris, Ralph Drischell, Robert Symonds, Patrick Stack. Phillip A. Gillis, Bridget Hoffman, Anne M. Gillis, Frances McDormand, Carol Brinn, Matthew Taylor, Perry Mallette, Chuck Gaidica, Jimmie Launce, Joseph French, Ted Raimi, Dennis Chaitlin. Dir: Sam Raimi. Pro:Robert Tapert. Co-Pro: Bruce Campbell. Ex Pro: Edward R. Pressman and Irvin Shapiro. Assoc Pro: Cary Glieberman. Pro Co-Ord: Shalini Waran. Screenplay: Raimi, and Ethan and Joel Coen. Ph: Robert Primes. Ed: Kathie Weaver. Sup Ed: Michael Kelly. Art: Gary Papierski. M: Arlan Ober. (Pressman/Renaissance–Embassy Pictures–Rank Dist.) Rel: floating; first shown London (Cannon cinemas, Chelsea and Panton Street), 25 April 1986. 86 mins. Cert PG.

Nobody hears Sheree Wilson's screams as she is abducted by one of the villains (Brion James) in Embassy/Rank's *Crimewave*.

Kathleen Turner in her tart part (as opposed to her other life of serious business woman) in Ken Russell's *Crimes of Passion* (Orion–Rank), in which an all-stops-out Anthony Perkins plays the sex-crazed cleric.

Dangerous Moves – La Diagonale du Fou. This Swiss movie won the 1985 Oscar for 'Best Foreign Language Film', and it is indeed an excellent suspense drama about – of all things – world championship chess! Surely the first time that that leisurely game has been the theme for a motion picture? It's the struggle between the old master from Moscow and his wild young rival who, though also Russian, now lives in European exile. And the players themselves become pawns in a larger game played around them. Director Richard Dembo in his debut creates some fine suspense, while at the same time managing to make chess absorbing to watch

– quite a triumph. Cast: Michel Piccoli. Alexandre Arbatt, Leslie Caron, Liv Ullmann, Daniel Olbrychski, Michel Aumont, Serge Avedikian, Pierre Michael, Pierre Vial, Wojtek Pszoniak, Jean-Hugues Anglade, Hubert Saint-Macary, Bernhard Wicki, Benoit Regent, Jacques Boudet, Jean-Paul Eydoux, Albert Simono, Sylvia Granotier, Alain Rimoux, Willy Nicoidsky, Yaseen Khan, Marcel Tassimot, Matthiew Schiffman, Guy Braucourt, Piotr Kaminski, Olivier Beer, Constantin Melnik. Dir and Screenplay: Richard Dembo. Pro: Arthur Cohn. Ph: Raoul Coutard. Ed: Agnes Guillemot. Art: Ivan Maussion. M: Gabriel Yared; based on César Frank's Prelude Op.18. (Cohn–Enterprise) Rel: floating; first shown London (Academy), 6 February 1986. 95 mins. Cert PG.

D.A.R.Y.L. In spite of the fact that it is totally incredible, there's plenty of very pleasant entertainment in this story about a small test-tube-born boy with a computer where his brain should be, who becomes very human when exposed to family love and affection. A very exciting if never really explained start, and an equally fast-moving, completely unbelievable but warmly satisfying climax – and a very good performance by young Barret Oliver as **D**ata **A**nalyzing **R**obot **Y**outh **L**ifeform! Rest of cast: Mary Beth Hurt, Michael McKean, Kathryn Walker, Colleen Camp, Josef Sommer, Ron Frazier, Steve Ryan, David Wohl, Danny Corkill, Amy Linker, Ed L. Grady, Tucker McGuire, Richard Hammatt, Charlie Gudger, Stacy Woods, Pat Fuleihan, Noreen Lange, Joseph Reed, Jessica Johnson, Ginny Light, Danielle Le Moine, Patrick Branner, Susan West, Benjamin Peterson, Hardy Rawls, Dalton Poole, Wayne Shindoli, Sean Hower, Brian Stafford, James La Pointe, James H. Armfield, Ski Collins, Russ Wheeler, Nevil O'Neill, Paul Darby, Blain Fairman, Robert Arden, William Roberts, Christopher Muncke, Burtt Harris, Major Wiley, James Fitzpatrick, Mike Deluna, Matt Butler, John Moio, Suzanne Vaucher. Dir: Simon Wincer. Co-Pro: Burtt Harris and Gabrielle Kelly. Ex Pro: John Heyman. Pro Sup: Jennifer M. Ogden and Ted Morley. Screenplay: David Ambrose, Allen Scott and Jeffrey Ellis. Ph: Frank Watts, Ed: Adrian Carr. Pro Des: Alan Cassie. M: Marvin Hamlisch. (Columbia) Rel: 27 March 1986. 100 mins. Cert PG.

With a computer where his brain should be, young Daryl (Barret Oliver) is at home with the real thing in Columbia's warm and very human science-fiction feature *D.A.R.Y.L.*

Death in a French Garden – Péril en la Demeure. Stylish, imaginatively filmed and inventively directed (by Michel Deville) French movie which is consistently intriguing as it spins the ambiguously presented story of a somewhat naïve young music teacher (Christophe Malavoy), who quickly becomes erotically involved with the sexually open mother (Nicole Garcia) of his nubile young pupil (Anaïs Jeanneret). Add to this the girl's disturbingly dubious father (Michel Piccoli), a mysterious professional killer (Richard Bohringer) – whose motives for befriending the young man are questionable – and a young woman neighbour (Anemone) who, at their first meeting, talks about the fascination of women's sex and variations in pubic hair, and then sends the lovers video-cassettes of their lovemaking, and you have one of the most puzzling and altogether original movies from any country to be seen during 1986. Rest of cast: Jean-Claude Jay, Hélène Rousell, Elisabeth Vitali, Frank Lapersonne, Daniel Vérité. Dir and (with Rosalinde Damamme) Screenplay: Michel Deville; adapted from the novel *Sur la Terre au Ciel* by René Belletto. Pro: Emmanuel Schlumberger. Ex Pro: Damamme. Pro Co-Ord: Paul Gueu. Ph: Martial Thury. Ed: Raymonde Guyot. Art: Philippe Combastel. M: Brahms (Trio No. 1), Granados (Scherzo in B flat major) and Schubert (3rd Momente Musicale). (Gaumont/Elefilm–TFI Films–Artificial Eye) Rel: floating; first shown London (Chelsea Cinema), 23 January 1986. 100 mins. Cert 18.

Death Wish 3. Charles Bronson once more back on the job of removing thugs from the world the hard way, bringing his kind of rough justice to those nasties that the cops can't seem to touch. And along with the killings there's the occasional wry chuckle. Set in New York, but made largely in London. And so,

Back into lethal action action against the city's anti-social characters he has sworn to wipe out, one-man citizen army Charles Bronson forms an uneasy alliance with cop Ed Lauter in Cannon's *Death Wish 3*, a film in which the stuntmen (left) really had to earn their money.

on to . . . *Death Wish 4*? Rest of cast: Deborah Raffin, Ed Lauter, Martin Balsam, Gavan O'Herlihy, Kirk Taylor, Alex Winter, Tony Spiridakis, Ricco Ross, Tony Britts, Joseph Gonzalez, Francis Drake, Mirina Sirtis, David Crean, Nelson Fernandez, Alan Cooke, Bob Dysinger, Topo Grajeda, Barbie Wilde, Ron Hayes, Jerry Phillips, Leo Kharibian, Hana-Maria Pravda, John Gabriel, Mildred Shay, Kenny Marino, Birdie M. Hale, Hayward Morse, Ronald Fernee, Sandy Grizzle, Dinah May, Steffanie Pitt, Billy J. Mitchell, Lee Patterson, Olivia Ward, Manning Redwood, Joe Cirillo, Ralph Monaco, William Roberts, Mac McDonald, Sam Douglas, Ron Travis, Mark Stewart, Peter Banks, Tom Hunsinger, Nick D'Avirro. Dir and Co-Pro: Michael Winner. Pro: Menahem Golan and Yoram Globus. Assoc Pro: Michael Kagan. Pro Sup: Malcolm Christopher. Screenplay: Michael Edmonds. Ph: John Stainer. Ex Ed: Chris Barnes. Ed: Arnold Crust (Michael Winner). Pro Des: Peter Mullins. M: Jimmy Page (Golan–Globus Pro–Cannon) Rel: 17 January 1986. 90 mins. Cert 18.

Defence of the Realm. Quite a lot of political and moral ground is covered by this fast-paced British thriller about the near-crash on British soil of a atom-bomb-carrying US warplane, and the subsequent ruthless efforts of the government and MI5 to see that the public don't learn of the crisis. However, it is found out and investigated to the point of no return by a young reporter anxious to atone for his pillorying of an innocent-but-framed MP. Smartly directed, adequately acted. Cast: Gabriel Byrne, Denholm Elliott, Greta Scacchi, Ian Bannen, Fulton Mackay, Bill Patterson, David Calder, Frederick Treves, Robbie Coltrane, Annabel Leventon, Prentis Hancock, Michael Johnson, Mark Tandy, Daniel Webb, Lyndon Brook, William Job, Oliver

Top, enthusiastic young investigative reporter Gabriel Byrne and blasé old-timer Denholm Elliott share a drink and a secret in the Rank release *Defence of the Realm*. Above, Ian Bannen as the pilloried politician at the heart of the matter.

Ford Davies, Daniel Benzali, Graham Fletcher-Cook, Steven Woodcock, Beverley Anderson, Harriet Bagnall, John Challis. Dir: David Drury. Pro: Robin Douet and Lynda Myles. Ex Pro: David Puttnam. Screenplay: Martin Stellman. Ph: Robert Deakins. Ed: Michael Bradsall. Pro Des: Roger Murray-Leach. M: Richard Hartley. (In Britain, Enigma in assoc with National Film Finance Corp–Rank Film Dists.; in US, Warner) Rel: floating. 96 mins. Cert PG.

Delta Force. Fast-and-furious, all-action melodrama quite impressively helmed by the (in some British film circles) controversial Cannon co-magnate Menahem Golan, who has obtained the most from all the superficial possibilities of this exciting yarn and has jettisoned any significance that the theme obviously has. Starting off with a long introduction which echoes recent hijacking history (in Athens), the story switches to pure fiction as American heroes Chuck Norris and Lee Marvin, with incredible valour and equal amount of luck, take on and defeat the might of the Arab villains. For moviegoers who don't suffer from high brows, it's all great fun. Rest of cast: Martin Balsam, Joey Bishop, Robert Forster, Lainie Kazan, George Kennedy, Hanna Schygulla, Susan Strasberg, Bo Svenson, Robert Vaughn, Shelley Winters, William Wallace, Charles Floye, Steve James,

Chuck Norris with his James Bond-ish motorbike goes into battle against the Amal enemy in Cannon's all-action *Delta Force*.

Kim Delaney, Gerry Weinstock, Marvin Freedman, Bob Levit, Chelli Goldberg, Chris Ellia, Jerry Lazarus, Natalie Roth, Jerry Hyman, Gael Lehrer, Hank Leininger, Howard Jackson, Eric Norris, Zipora Peled, Aaron Kaplan, Caroline Langford, Yehudi Efroni, David Menahem, Shai K. Ophir, Avi Loziah, Uri Gavriel, Panos Nicolaou, Elki Jacobs, Menahem Eini, Assaf Dayan, Jack Cohen, Adin Gahshan, Hain Sirafi, Mosco Alkalai, Larry Price, Susan Ophir, Jack Messinger, Janet Harshman, Ezra Kafri, Danny Friedman, Richard Salano, Andy Shulman, Joe Sapel, Richard Peterson, Eugene Klein, Albert Amar, Ben Ami Shmueli, Moti Shirin, Itzik Aloni, Boaz Ofri, Albert Iluz, Osnat Vishinski, David Leshnik. Dir: Menahem Golan. Pro: Golan and Yoram Globus. Assoc Pro: Rony Yacov. Pro Sup: Itzhak Kol. 2nd Unit Dir: Carlo Gil. Screenplay: Golan and James Bruner. Ph: David Gurfinkel. Ed: Alain Jakubowicz. Pro Des: Lucisano Spadoni. M: Alan Silvestri. (Cannon) Rel: floating; first shown London (Warner), 31 May 1986. 128 mins. Cert 15.

Aidan Quinn and Rossanna Arquette, who give charming performances in the comedy *Desperately Seeking Susan* (Orion–Rank).

Desperately Seeking Susan. A likeable comedy which gets better and funnier as it goes along, spinning a somewhat complicated story about a bored young housewife (with an insufferable husband – there's a clearly observable feminine though not feminist slant to the movie) who follows up a personal-column advertisement placed by a young man seeking to contact his lost Susan. Thus she becomes involved (largely after a knock on the head) with murder, theft, nasty characters and other people's love affairs – leading to one of her own. It is all considerably helped along by a delightful performance from Rosanna Arquette, and introduces to the screen pop star Madonna, who often looks and sounds like a small young edition of Mae West. Rest of cast: Aidan Quinn, Mark Blum, Robert Joy, Laurie Metcalf, Anna Levine, Will Patton, Peter Maloney, Steven Wright, John Turturro, Anne Carlisle, José Santana, Giancarlo Esposito, Richard Hell, Rockets Red Glare, Steve Bosh, Daisy Bradford, Annie Golden, Richard Edson, Ann Magnuson, John Lurie, Mary Joy, Rosemary Hoschschild, Iris Chacon, Victor Argo, Shirley Stoler, J. B. Waters, Arto Lindsay, Henry Adler, Marty Gold, Alvey West, Michael R. Chin, John Patrick Hurley, Timothy Carhart, Curt Dempster, Shirley Kaplan, Lazaro Perez, John Hoyt, Gary Ray, Gary Binkow, Michael Bramon, Joyce Griffen, Paul Austin, Richard S. Lowy, Donna Ritchie, Kim Chan, Michael Badalucco, Elie J. Boubli, Harsh Nayyar, Keita Whitten, Adele Bertei, Peter Castellotti, Wende Dasteel, Steve Eidel, Michael Kaufman, Ilene Kristen, Carol Leifer, Richard Portnow, Isabel Garcia-Lorca, Timothy R. Wilson, Gilda Tortorello, Stanley Burns. Dir: Susan Seidelman. Pro: Sarah Pillsbury and Midge Sanford. Ex Pro: Michael Peyser. Screenplay: Leora Barish. Ph: Edward Lachman. Ed: Andrew Mondshein. Pro Des: Santo Loquasto. Art: Speed Hopkins. M: Thomas Newman. (Orion-Rank Film Dist.) Rel: 6 September 1985. 103 mins. Cert 15.

Detective. Another Godard movie, with the usual formlessness, confusing

and general do-it-yourself atmosphere, from which the talented performers – who struggle along gamely – along with the cameraman and music, emerge with considerable credit. But don't expect a synopsis of the story because it is virtually impossible to discover what it is. Cast: Nathalie Baye, Claude Brasseur, Johnny Hallyday, Stéphane Ferrara, Eugène Berthier, Emmanuelle Seigner, Cyril Autin, Julie Delpy, Laurent Terzieff, Jean-Pierre Léaud, Anne Gisèle Glass, Aurèle Doazan, Alain Cuny, Pierre Bertin, Alexandra Garijo, Xavier Saint Macary. Dir: Jean-Luc Godard. Pro: Alain Sarde. Pro Sup: Claude Bertonazzi and Louis Grau. Screenplay: Sarde and Philippe Setbon (Adaptation: Anne-Marie Mieville and Godard; Dialogue: Godard). Ph: Bruno Nuytten. Ed: Marilyne Dubreuil. Art: no credit. M: Wagner, Schubert, Honegger, etc. (Sara Films/JLG Films–Artificial Eye). Rel: floating; first shown London (Camden Plaza and Metro), 7 March 1986. 95 mins. Cert 15.

Diary for My Children – Napló Gyermekeimnek. Another sombre, political drama (with a surprisingly critical theme) from Hungary in black-and-white. It tells the story of a rebellious young girl who scorns the adoption plans for her made by a dedicated party member who becomes the female warden of the local jail. Overall the film paints a grim picture of slogan-spouting Stalinist commies and the suppression of anyone who dares to stray from the party line, no matter how intelligent, or how diligent a worker, they may be. Cast: Zsuzsa Czinkóczi, Anna Polony, Jan Nowicki, Tamás Tóth, Pál Zolnay, Mark Szemes. Dir & Screenplay: Márta Mészáros. Ph: Miklós Jancsó Jr. M: Zsolt Dome. Ed: Eva Karmento. Pro Des: Eva Martin. (Mafilm, Budapest-Artificial Eye). Rel: floating; first shown London (Camden Plaza), 18 July 1985. 106 mins. Cert PG.

Dim Sum – A Little Bit of Heart. The story of a Chinese expatriate family living in San Francisco and the relationship between the parents and the children. Leisurely, loving, optimistic and beautifully photographed; resulting in a warm glow and a conviction which makes this one of the most enjoyable American films of its year. Cast: Laureen Chew, Kim Chew, Victor Wong, Ida F. O. Chung, Cora Miao, John Nishio, Amy Hill, Keith Choy, Mary Chew, Nora Lee, Joan Chen, Rita Yee, George Wu, Elsa Cruz Pearson, Helen Chew, Jarrett Chew. Dir: Wayne Wang. Pro: Wang, Tom Sternberg, and Danny Yung. Assoc Pro: Emily Leung. Screenplay: Terrel Seltzer; based on ideas by Seltzer, Laureen Chew and Wayne Wang. Ph: Emiko Omori. Ed: Ralph Wikke, and Yoshio Kishi and Stephen Stept. Art: Danny Yung. M: Todd Boekelheide. (Project A Partnership/CIM Productions-Mainline). Rel: floating; first shown London (Screen on the Hill), 13 September 1985. 88 mins. Cert U.

Lauren Chew and Victor Wong in the delightful American-Chinese *Dim Sum – A Little Bit of Heart* (Mainline).

The Doctor and the Devils. At last, poet Dylan Thomas's script of the forties about grave-robbing in the style of

Dr Rock (Timothy Dalton, left) takes a look at his latest acquistion from his cadaver suppliers, the grave-robbing, murderous pair of Fallen and Broom (Jonathan Pryce, right, and Julian Sands, second from right) in Fox's film of the Dylan Thomas screenplay *The Doctor and the Devils*.

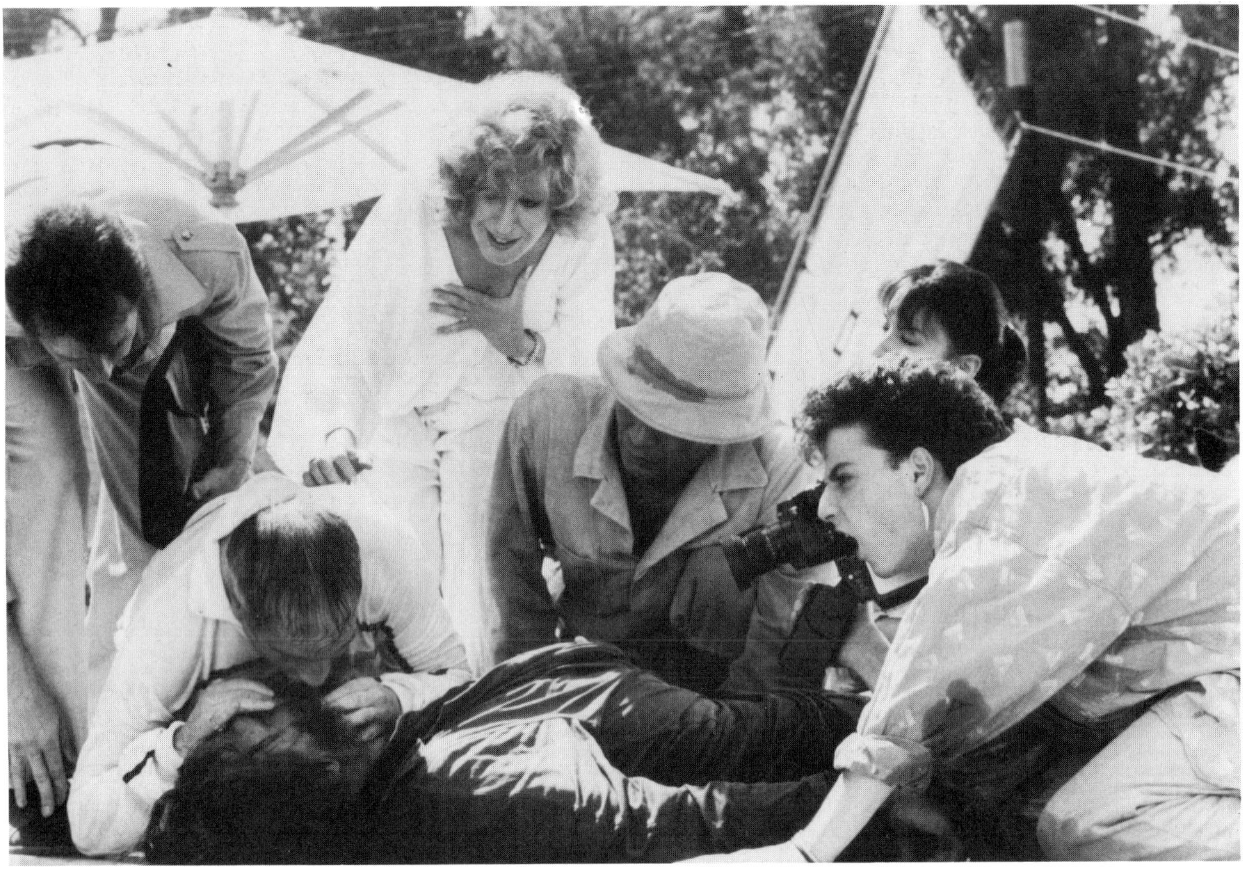

Coathanger tycoon Richard Dreyfuss tries to bring back to life the suicidal tramp (Nick Nolte, left, with canine pal) while his family at the poolside looked on with interest (including wife, Bette Midler, centre, and movie-mad son, Evan Richards) in Paul Mazursky's *Down and Out in Beverly Hills* (UK Film Dist).

Burke and Hare, reaches the screen. (It nearly made it to the studio in 1965 but was postponed and then cancelled.) And a pretty grim business it is, in spite of authentic Thomas touches here and there, with a surfacing of the ethical problem of whether good ends justify bad means. Timothy Dalton is the doctor who illegally pays for cadavers he can't, under the law, obtain, not knowing that the two men he gets them from (Jonathan Pryce and Stephen Rea) make sure of a steady supply by performing a series of brutal murders. Rest of cast: Twiggy, Julian Sands, Phyllis Logan, Lewis Fiander, Beryl Reid, T. P. McKenna, Patrick Stewart, Sian Phillips, Philip Davis, Philip Jackson, Danny Schiller, Bruce Green, Toni Palmer, David Mamber, Nichola McAuliffe, Deidre Costello, Terry Neason, Paul Curran, Merelina Kendall, Dermot Crowley, Sarah Melia, Stephen Yardley, John Horsley, Jack May, Rachel Herbert. Dir: Freddie Francis. Pro: Jonathan Sanger. Ex Pro: Mel Brooks. Screenplay: Ronald Harwood; based on the Dylan Thomas original. Ph: Gerry Turpin and Norman Warwick. Ed: Laurence Mery-Clark. Pro Des: Robert Laing. Art: Brian Ackland-Snow. M: John Morris. (Brooksfilms-Fox-UK Film Dist.) Rel: floating; first shown London (Odeon, Haymarket), 30 May 1986. 93 mins. Cert 18.

Down and Out in Beverly Hills. If your movie-going memory stretches back to 1932 and the marvellous Michel Simon, you'll recall seeing him in this story, filmed then as *Boudu sauvé des eaux* ('Boudu Saved from Drowning'). An uncouth tramp (now Nick Nolte, who's fine in the role), after trying to commit suicide in their private pool, is taken in by a horribly affluent (in this case, Beverly Hills) family, to every member of which he brings a liberating fulfilment to their empty lives, leading to an uproarious, farcical climax and a sadly contrived and *passé* ending. A generally amusing, sharply satirical look at bourgeois America: typical Mazursky, in fact. Rest of cast: Richard Dreyfuss, Bette Midler, Little Richard, Tracy Nelson, Elizabeth Pena, Evan Richards, Mike (dog), Donald F. Muhich, Paul Mazursky, Valerie Curtin, Jack Bruskoff, Geraldine Dreyfuss, Barry Primus, Irene Tsu, Michael Yama, Ranbir Bhai, Felton Perry, Eloy Casados, Michael Greene, Ken Koch, Dorothy Tristan, Raymond Lee. Dir,

Pro and (with Leon Capetanos) Screenplay: Paul Mazursky; based on the French play by René Fauchois. Co-Pro and Pro Des: Pato Guzman. Assoc Pro: Geoffrey Taylor. Ph: Donald McAlpine. Ed: Richard Halsey. M: Andy Summers. (Touchstone Films [Walt Disney] in assoc with Silver Screen Partners II–UK Film Dist.) Rel: 13 June 1986. 103 mins. Cert 15.

Dreamchild. British film about Alice – Mrs Alice Hargreaves *née* Liddell, a wonderful performance by Coral Browne – for whom The Revd Charles Dodgson, under the pen-name of Lewis Carroll, wrote the famous 'Wonderland' stories. During a trip to New York at the age of 80 (and dying) to accept an honorary degree from Columbia University during the Lewis Carroll Centenary celebrations she suddenly realizes the full import of the shy writer's ambiguous adoration of her youthful charms. Unfortunately, awkward construction and abrupt transitions work against the best parts of the film. Rest of cast: Ian Holm (as Carroll), Amelia Shankley (the young Alice), Peter Gallagher, Caris Corfman, Nicola Cowper, Jane Asher, Imogen Boorman, Emma King, Rupert Wainwright, Roger Ashton-Griffiths, James Wilby, Shane Rimmer, Peter Whitman, Ken Campbell, William Hootkins, Jeffrey Chiswick, Pat Starr, Johnny M., Alan Sherman, Danny Brainin, Sam Douglas, Peter Banks, Derek Hoxby, Rob Berglas, Ron Travis, Thomasine Heiner, Olivier Pierce, Steve Whitmire, Tony Mansell. Creatures: Ron Mueck (Gryphon), Steve Whitmire, Karen Prell, Michael Sundin, Big Mick; voices by Fulton Mackay, Alan Bennett, Julie Walters, Ken Campbell, Tony Haygarth, Frank Middlemass. Dir: Gavin Millar. Pro: Rick McCallum and Kenith Trodd. Ex Pro (with Verity Lambert) and Screenplay: Dennis Potter. Pro Assoc: Bob Mercer. Pro Ex: Graham Easton. Pro Sup: Donald Toms. Pro Co-Ord: Jill Bender. 'Alice in Wonderland' characters designed and played by Jim Henson's 'Creature Shop'. Ph: Billy Williams. Ed: Angus Newton. Art: Len Huntingford and Marianne Ford. Pro Des: Roger Hall. M: Stanley Myers. (Pennies in Heaven in assoc with Thorn EMI Screen Entertainment–Thorn EMI) Rel: floating. 94 mins. Cert PG.

Alice (Amelia Shankley) with *Alice in Wonderland* author Lewis Carroll (Ian Holm) in Thorn EMI's *Dreamchild*. Inset, the grown-up, and grown old, *Wonderland* inspirer (Coral Browne, giving a brilliant performance) arrives in America to take a major part in the author's centenary celebrations.

Echo Park. Pleasant little film about life for the less lucky and less favoured in Los Angeles, seen through the life-styles of a trio of strugglers: a would-be actress, a young pizza man and another young man obsessed with body building. With each helping the others, the trio become a family, all of them still hoping for personal fruition of the Great American Dream. Cast: Susan Dey, Tom Hulce, Michael Bowen, Christopher Walker, Shirley Jo Finney, Heinrich Schweiger, Richard Marin, John Paragon, Cassandra Peterson, Timothy Carey, Martin Suppan, Robert H. Shafer, Dorothy Dells, Yana Nirvana, Paul Anselmo, Jesse Atagon, Robert Cabral, Stephen Gaines, Peter Drain, Top Jimmy, John Pochna, Dee

Pizza delivery man and aspiring song-writer Tom Hulce moves into *Echo Park* (Miracle Films).

Cooper, Douglas M. Ford, Fred Leaf, Mary Thompson, Anne Marie Bates, Jason Mayall, Renée Le Ballister, Michael Marloe, Jim Smith, Skip O'Brien, Biff Yeager, Jackie Easton Toelle, Bob Moss, Doug Knott, James Helppi, Patricia Tippo, Max Thumpower, Dana Collins, Penny Harris, Merrill Ward. Dir: Robert Dornhelm. Pro: Walter Shenson. Pro Co-Ord: Victor Korger. Screenplay: Michael Ventura. Ph: Karl Kofner. Ed: Ingrid Koller. Art: Bernt Capra. M: Davis Ricketts. (Sascha-Wien Films–Miracle Films) Rel: floating; first shown London (several Cannon cinemas), 14 March 1986. 92 mins. Cert 15.

The Emerald Forest. If only half of what goes on in this generally excellent production were true – and it claims, after all, to be based on fact – one is forced to polish up that old truism that 'fact is stranger than fiction'. For here, indeed, it *is*. The story concerns a young white boy stolen by a seldom-glimpsed tribe of Amazon Indians and brought up by them in the jungle to be a warrior. At which point, ten years after the kidnap, the ever-hopeful father stumbles on his lad in the undergrowth and the young man, through recurrent dreams of his childhood, recognizes him. Dad, in fact, joins his son in fighting another, more warlike, tribe who have stolen the 'Invisible' tribe's remarkably shapely and pretty women to sell them into the white man's brothel. The film also carries a Friends-of-the-Earth warning that by greedily plundering the riches of the rainforests man is diminishing the efficiency of one of the world's great lungs. A beautifully photographed and always fascinating movie, from a director with the eye of an artist. Cast: Powers Boothe, Meg Foster, William Rodriquez, Yara Vaneau, Estée Chandler, Charley Boorman, Dira Paes, Eduardo Conde, Ariel Coelho, Peter Marinker, Mario Borges, Atilia Iorio, Babriel Archanjo, Gracindo Junior, Arthur Muhlenberg, Chico Terto, Rui Polonah and members of the 'Invisible' and 'Fierce' tribes. Dir and Pro: John Boorman. Ex Pro: Edgar F. Gross. Co-Pro: Michael Dryhurst. Screenplay: Rospo Pallenberg. Ph; Philippe Rousselot. 2nd Unit Ph: Lucio Kodato. Ed: Ian Crafford. Pro Des: Simon Holland. M: Junior Homrich with Brian Gasgoigne. (Embassy-Rank Film Dist.). Rel: 15 November 1985. 113 mins. Cert 15.

The Empty Table – Shokutaku no Naiie. Long, sedately paced, consistently interesting modern Japanese drama about a middle-class electronics executive whose hard exterior covers feelings he finds impossible to express. His determined refusal to be responsible for his family brings him into opposition with conventional ethics, finally driving his wife to suicide. and helping his left-wing son to decide to join his more militant, airplane-hijacking companions when they fly out to exile. Beautifully acted – especially by Tasuya Nakadai as the conscience-stricken but uncompromising father – and altogether something of a minor screen classic. Rest of cast: Mayumi Ogawa, Kiichi Nakai, Takayuki Takemoto, Kie Nakai, Shima Iwashita, Shinobu Ohtake, Azusa Mano, etc. Dir

Right and below, father (Powers Boothe) and jungle-bred son (Charley Boorman) face up to danger in John Boorman's *The Emerald Forest* (Embassy–Rank Film Dist.).

and Screenplay: Masaki Kobayashi; from an original story by Fumiko Enji. Pro: Genshiro Kawamoto. Ph: Kozo Okazaki. Ed: Nobuo Ogawa. Art: Shigemasa Toda. M: Toru Takemitsu. (Electric Pictures) Rel: floating; first shown London (Academy), 13 February 1986. 143 mins. Cert PG.

Erendira. Gabriel Garcia Marquez's own adaptation of his novel *Innocent Erendira*, a strange story of a young girl driven into prostitution by her wicked old grandmother. The latter waxes financially fat on the proceeds of the girl's highly paid favours, until along comes handsome young Ulysses to touch the girl's heart and try to free her from her bondage by dispatching the wicked old crone – not, he finds, an easy task. A black and mysterious French/Mexican/West German co-production. Cast: Irene Papas, Claudia Ohana, Michael Lonsdale, Oliver Wehe, Rufus and Blanca Guerra. Dir: Ruy Guerra. Pro: Alain Queffelean. Screenplay: Gabriel Garcia Marquez; based on his novels *Innocent Erendira* and *100 Years of Solitude*. Ph: Denys Clerval. M: Maurice Lecoeuv. (ICA) Rel: floating; first shown London (ICA), 30 May 1986. 103 mins. No cert.

Matt Dillon as *The Flamingo Kid*, the lad who learns true values the easy way at the Beach Club in this Palace Pictures release. The lovely lady sharing the surf with the 'Kid' is Molly McCarthy.

Fire Festival. Visually captivating Japanese film from Mitsuo Yanagimachi which is otherwise a little difficult for the Westerner, in view of its concern with a man's mystical relationship with the goddess of his neighbouring mountain, at the rear of a little southern Japanese port. The festival of the title is fierily fascinating. Cast includes Kinya Kitaoji, Kiwako Taichi, Ryota Nakamoto, Norihei, Rikiyah Yasuoka. Dir: Mitsuo Yanigimachi. Pro: Kazuo Shimizu. Screenplay: Kenji Nakagami. Ph: Masaki Tamura. Ed: Sachiko Yamaji. Art: Takeo Kimura. M: Toru Takemitsu. (Recorded Releasing Co) Rel: floating; first shown London (ICA) 3 January 1986. 120 mins. No cert.

The Flamingo Kid. In complete contrast to those repellent movies about sex-obsessed, coarse and crude youngsters, this charming, realistic and very entertaining story of a nice Brooklyn teenager growing up and learning a lot about life, through his summer vacation job at a Long Island beach club, stands out by a pleasing mile. With plenty of good performances, especially by Matt Dillon as the lad, Hector Elizondo as his plumber father and Richard Crenna as his mentor and teacher of the final lesson. Rest of cast: Molly McCarthy, Martha Gehman, Jessica Walter, Carole R. Davis, Janet Jones, Brian McNamara, Fisher Stevens, Leon Robinson, Bronson Pinchot, Frank Campanella, Richard Stahl, Joe Grifasi, Ron McLarty, Seth Allen, Irving Metzman, Adam Klugman, Ray Roderick, Googy Gress, Sharon Thomas, The Barbarian Brothers, Christopher Chadman, Martin Chatinover, Lisa Beth Ross, Laurie Stratford, Steven Weber, Eric Douglas, Marisa Tomei, Tracy Reiner, Kristina Kossi, Bobbie Joe Burke, Leslie S. Sachs, Michael Mahon, Lee Morey, Jillian Scharf, Carol Williard, Richard Buck, Bradley Kane, Lauren Costa, Linda Costa, Peter Costa, Scott Marshall, Blake Brocksmith, Steve Whitting, Freddy Frogs, Lee Steele, Beth Noreen Einhorn, Bo Sabato, Frances Peach, Jack Danny Foster, John Turturro, Mark Strait, Mike Markowitz, Kathi Marshall, Novella Nelson, David Berry, Mark Kaplan, George Blumenthal, Mel Allen. Dir: Garry Marshall. Pro: Michael Phillips. Ex in charge of Pro: Herb Jellinek. Assoc Pro: Nick Abdo. Screenplay: Neal and Gerry Marshall. Ph: James A. Contner. Ed: Priscilla Nedd. Pro Des: Lawrence Miller. Art: Duke Durfee. More than a score of musical numbers by various composers, sung and played by various artists and groups. (Mercury Entertainment Productions–ABC Motion Pictures-Palace Pictures.) Rel: floating; first shown London (Classic, Chelsea, etc.) 18 October 1985. 91 mins. Cert 15.

Flesh and Blood. Lavishly funded, comic-strip-style, all-stops-full-out, American–Dutch film of feuds, fury, lust, love, the plague and generally riotous behaviour in medieval Europe, with quite a bit of nudity from Jennifer Jason Leigh. Rest of Cast: Tom Burlinson, Jack Thompson, Rutger Hauer, Fernando Hillbeck, Susan Tyrrell, Ronald Lacey, Brion James, John Dennis Johnston, Simon Andrew, Bruno Kirby, Kitty Courbois, Marina Saura, Hans Veerman, Jake Wood, Hector Alterio, Blanca Marsillach, Nancy Cartwright, Jorge Bosso, Mario de Baros, Ida Bons, Jaime Segura, Bettina Brenner, Siobhan Hayes, Susan Beresford, Monica Luccetti. Dir: Paul Verhoeven. Pro: Gys Versluys. Assoc Pro: Jose Vicuna. Screenplay: Verhoeven and Gerard Soeteman; based on the latter's story. Ph: Jan de Bont. Ed: Ine Schenkkan. Art: Felix Murcia. M: Basil Poledouris. (Riverside Pictures–Orion Impala Pro (Amsterdam)–Rank Film Dist.) Rel: floating. 127 mins. Cert 18.

Fletch. The tale may often have been told before on the screen, but seldom more amusingly than here: Chevy Chase is at his light-comedian best as an investigative Los Angeles reporter whose enquiries into a beach-centred drugs racket are suddenly interrupted when he is offered $50,000 to murder a man – by the would-be victim! He accepts, then starts his own investigation into the strange commission, coming up against crooked businessmen and even-more-crooked cops, as well as a very pretty lady . . . and there is quite a quota of laughs along the crooked way. Rest of cast: Joe Don Baker, Dana Wheeler Nicholson, Richard Libertini, Tim Matheson, M. Emmet Walsh, George Wendt, Kenneth Mars, Geena Davis, Bill Henderson, William Traylor, George Wyner, Tony Longo, Larry Flash Jenkins, Ralph Seymour, James Avery, Reid Cruickshanks, Bruce French, Burton Gilliam, David Harper, Chick Hearn, Alison La Placa, Joe Praml, William Sanderson, Penny Santon, Robert Sorrells, Beau Starr, Nico de Silva, Peggy Doyle, Rick Garcia, Grace Gaynor, Freeman King, Loraine Shields, Bill Sorrells, Arnold Turner, Kareem Abdul-Jabbar, Roger Ammann, Mary Battilana, Henry (Hank) Bleeker, Donald Chaffin, Darren Dublin, Kristine M. Gossman, Irene Olga López, Merv Maruyama. Dir: Michael Ritchie. Pro: Alan Greisman and Peter Douglas. Assoc Pro: Gordon A. Webb. Screenplay: Andrew Bergman; based on the novel by Gregory McDonald. Ph: Fred Schuler. Ed: Richard A. Harris. Pro Des: Boris Leven. Art: Todd Hallowell. M: Harold Faltermeyer. (Universal–UIP). Rel: 27 September 1985. 99 mins. Cert PG.

Uneasy Dana Wheeler Nicholson and amusing investigative journalist Chevy Chase take cover in *Fletch* (Universal–UIP).

Forbidden. Sober, West German/British co-produced drama based on the true story of the German countess, Nina von Halder (Jacqueline Bisset), who kept her Jewish lover (Jürgen Prohnow) hidden in her Berlin flat right through the war (subsequently marrying him), with all the alarms, excursions and escapes this involved – more especially as, even unknown to him, she was working through the Swedish Church for the Resistance. Eschewing melodrama, and all the more convincing because of that. Rest of cast: Irene Worth, Peter Vaughan, Robert Dietl, Avis Bunnage, Malcolm Kaye, George Tryphon, Annie Leon, Amanda Cannings, Osman Ragheb, Guntbert Warns, Herta Schwarz, Ulli Kinalzik, Gerhard Frey, Erich Will, Bernd Vollbrecht, Chris Kurbjuhn, Friedhelm Lehmann, Susanne Bonasewicz, Michael Traynor, Hartmutt Volle, Klaus Münster, Dagmar Cassens-Dunton, Rolf Marnitz, Horst D. Scheel. Dir: Anthony Page. Pro: Mark Forstater, Ex Pro: Gerald I. Isenberg. Co-Ex Pro: Fritz Butenstedt and Herbert G. Kloiber. Co-Pro: Hans Brockman. Assoc Pro: Ingrid Windisch. Screenplay: Leonard Gross; based on his novel *The Last Jews in Berlin*. Ph: Wolfgang Treu. Ed: Thomas Schwalm. Pro Des: Toni Ludi. M: Tangerine Dream. (Mark Forstater Pro/Clasart Film und Fernseh Productions GmbH/Anthea Films GmbH and Stella Films GmbH-Odyssey–Enterprise Films) Rel: floating; first shown London (Cannon, Baker Street), 28 February 1986. 114 mins. Cert PG.

Friday the 13th – A New Beginning. With the previous four 'Fridays' (including the misnamed *Final Chapter*, No. 4) having taken something close to $60 million at box-offices worldwide, it was hardly likely that the producers would stop there, even if the blood-spattered formula is now getting a bit tattered around the edges. But it seems that the customers like the killings, the grislier the better, though it is becoming evident that the writers are beginning to run out of macabre new ideas. Cast: John Shepard, Melanie Kinnaman, Shavar Ross, Richard Young, Carol Lacatell, Vernon Washington, Dominic Brascia, Tiffany Helm, Debbisue Voorhees, John Robert Dixon, Ron Sloan, Marco St John, Juliette Cummins, John Robert Dixon, Jerry

William Ragsdale and Amanda Bearse have every reason to look scared in Columbia's *Fright Night*, during which pretty Miss Bearse changes into a formidably fanged female vampire (inset).

Pavlon, Caskey Swaim, Mark Venturini, Anthony Barrile, Richard Lineback, Corey Feldman, Suzanne Bateman, Todd Bryant, Curtis Conaway, Bob de Simone, Jere Fields, Ric Mancini, M. N. Nunez Jr, Corey Parker, Rebecca Wood-Sharkey, Sonny Shields, Ed Shinstine, Chuck Wells, Dick Wieand. Dir:Danny Steinmann. Pro: Tim Silver. Ex Pro: Fran Mancuso Jr. Screenplay: Steinmann, Martin Kitrosser and David Cohen. Ph: Stephen L. Posey. Ed: Bruce Green. Pro Des: Robert Howland. M: Harry Manfredini. (Paramount–UIP) Rel: 13 September 1985. 92 mins. Cert 18.

Fright Night. Tom Holland's debut as writer–director shows him as a film-maker to watch out for. Here he drags the old and tired vampire legend into modern times and imbues it with plenty of the old traditional horror, but adds enough deft touches of wit, humour and imagination to give the whole thing a new life. Cast: Chris Sarandon, William Ragsdale, Amanda Bearse, Roddy McDowall, Stephen Geoffreys, Jonathan Stark, Dorothy Fielding, Art J. Evans, Stewart Stern, Nick Savage, Ernie Holmes, Heidi Sorenson, Irina Irvine, Robert Corff, Pamela Brown, Chris Hendrie, Prince A. Hughes. Dir and Screenplay: Tom Holland. Pro: Herb Jaffe. Assoc Pro: Jerry A. Baerwitz. Ph: Jan Kiesser. Ed: Kent Beyda. Pro Des: John de Cuir Jr. M: Brad Fiedel. (Vistar Films–Columbia) Rel: floating; first shown London (Warner), 11 April 1986.

The Frog Prince. Conventional, and wholly credible, youthful romance set in Paris in the 'sixties, lusciously and lovingly photographed by Clive Tickner. It concerns an English teenager at the Sorbonne, living with a French family in the suburbs (wonderfully observed), who is hesitant about committing herself to an ardent young French architectural student who wants a physical as well as a romantic dalliance. It is all the more remarkable in that the film, though British-made, is entirely French in character, nuances and spirit. Beautiful performances by Jane Snowden as Jenny, the girl, and handsome young Alexandre Sterling as the boy, with memorable support from Jacqueline Doyen as Madame and Raoul Delfosse as Monsieur Peroche, the couple with whom the girl is staying. There is also a no less impressive performance by Diane Blackburn as Jenny's high-spirited friend. Rest of cast: Jeanne Herviale, Françoise Brion, Pierre Vernier, Oystein Wiik, Françoise Tricottet, Jean-Marc Barr, Arabella Weir, Lucy Durham-Matthews, Marc André Brunet, Brigitte Chamarande, Caterine Berraine, Olivier Achard, Martine Ferrière, André Dumas, Michelle Gleizer, Paul Yvon Colpin, Hugette Faget, Bernard Roselli. Dir and Screenplay: Brian Gilbert; from a story by Posy Simmonds. Pro: Iain Smith. Ex Pro: David Puttnam. Ph: Clive Tickner. Ed: Jim Clark. Pro Des: Anton Furst. M: Enya Ni Bhraonain. (Enigma / Warner - Goldcrest - Warner) Rel: floating: first shown London (Warner) 15 October 1985. 90 mins. Cert 15.

Jane Snowden and Alexandre Sterling in *The Frog Prince*, a British film (Goldcrest-Warner) sadly undervalued by the critics. Right, Diana Blackburn was delightful as the couple's exuberant friend, with equally entertaining support from Jacqueline Doyen and Raoul Delfosse.

The Fruits of Passion. The final film work of Japanese writer, poet and stage and film director Shuji Terayama. Based on the novel which carried on 'the story of O', it shows the decadent English Sir Stephen indulging his voyeuristic and perverted passion with the girl who loves him, O, by installing her in a Hong Kong brothel. Presented in a vaguely poetic pornographic style it leaves nothing, visually, to the imagination while suggesting all sorts of psychological and intellectual underpinnings – but whether these exist or not must be decided by the individual. Klaus Kinsky at his most unlovely as 'Sir' and lovely Isabelle Illiers is his unfortunate sex object. Rest of cast: Arielle Dombasle, 'Peter', Keiko Niitaka, Sayoko Yamacuchi, Hitomi Takahashi, Miyuki Ono, Akiko Suetsugu, Yuka Kamebuchi, Kenichi Nakamura, Takeshi Wakamatsu; and the voices of narrator Georges Wilson and, as Death, Maria Meriko. Dir and Screenplay: Shuji Terayama; based on the novel *Return to the Château* by Pauline Réage. Pro: Anatole Dauman and Hiroko Govaers. Ph: Tatsuo Suzuki. Ed: Henri Colpi. M: J. A. Seazer. Assoc Pro: Jacques-Henri Barratier and Philippe D'Argila. (Argos Films, Paris/ Terayama Production, Tokyo-New Realm) Rel: floating; first shown London (ICA and Electric Screen), 30 August 1985. 83 mins. No cert.

The Girl in the Picture. In the footsteps of *Gregory's Girl* – with the same star, too: John Gordon Sinclair, now a few years older but still playing the shy, inarticulate romancer – this modest, low-budget comedy is full of lovely little touches of wit and insight as it follows Gordon Sinclair (as a professional photographer in Glasgow) and several other very human characters during a few milestone weeks in their lives: a small treasure of British cinema. Rest of cast: Gregor Fisher, Caroline

John Gordon-Sinclair looks a little scared when Joyce Deans turns into a siren in the Rank-released British comedy *The Girl in the Picture*.

Guthrie, David McKay, Irina Brook, Paul Young, Simone Lahbib, Joyce Deans, Katy Hale, John Christie, Valerie and Wendy the Holloway Twins, Benny Young, Walter Carr, William Elliott, Rikki Fulton, Jonathan Watson, Sarah Wishart, Kirstie Anderson, Mairi Wallace, Naomi Leslie, Helen Pike, Ray Jeffries. Dir and Screenplay: Cary Parker. Pro: Paddy Higson. Assoc Pro: Alan J. Wands. Ph: Dick Pope. Ed: Bert Elles. Pro Des: Jemma Jackson. M: Ron Geesin. (Antonine Pro/in assoc with National Film Finance Corp–Rank Film Dist.) Rel: floating; first shown London (several Cannon cinemas), 28 March 1986. 91 mins. Cert 15.

Girls Just Want to Have Fun. Routine youth-aimed musical about some Chicago high-school kids; more especially it concerns one girl student whose burning ambition is to become a dancer in a pop/dance TV series. The physical energy displayed by the cast is almost frightening! (But if you like a spot of analysis you'll find hardly one of the characters morally unflawed.) Cast: Sarah Jessica Parker, Lee Montgomery, Morgan Woodward, Jonathan Silverman, Helen Hunt, Holly Gagnier, Ed Lauter, Shannen Doherty, Biff Yeager, Ian Giatti, Margaret Howell, Terence McGovern, Richard Blade, Kristi Somers, Lee Arnone, Shaun Bryant, Charene Cathleen, Mark Caso, Deanna Claire, Candace Daly, Olive Dunbar, Stuart Fratkin, Larry Gelman, Valerie Grear, Noreen Hennessy, Steve La Chance, Mika, Phineas Newborn III, Jim Ruttman, Sharon Shayne, Susan Styles. Dir: Alan Metter. Pro: Chuck Russell. Ex Pro: Stuart Cornfield. Assoc Pro: Robert F. Lyons. Screenplay: Amy Spies. Ph: Thomas Ackerman. Sup Ed: David Rawlins. Ed: Lorenzo DeStefano. Pro Des: Jeffrey Staggs. Art: Christopher Amy. M Sup: Don Perry. Original Score: Thomas Newman. Pro Assoc: Rachel Talalay. Pro Co-Ord: Mary McLaglen. (Polygram-Miracle Films) Rel: 2 August 1985. 87 mins. Cert PG.

Goodbye, New York! Lively, homespun Israeli film – a debut for writer–director–producer–actor Amos Kollek (son of the mayor of Jerusalem) – which attempts, with variable success to combine comedy with travelogue. It tells the story of a young New Yorker, fleeing from a faithless husband, who oversleeps on the flight to her Paris-dream destination. She ends up in Israel without money but with the luck to meet a helpful part-time cabbie who, while keeping his desire for her under control, shows her something of the country. A stand-out performance by

Jokey trio: Sarah Jessica Parker, Shannen Doherty and Helen Hunt illustrate the *Girls Just Want to Have Fun* title (Polygram–Miracle).

showcased Julie Hagerty and a nice one from Kollek as the cabbie. Rest of cast: David Topaz, Aviva Ger, Shmuel Shiloh, Jennifer Babtist, Christopher Goutman, Hanan Goldblat, Mosku Alkalay, Yaacov Ben Sira, Chaim Banai, Irit Bem Zur, Chaim Girafi, Bella Ben David, Moshe Ishkassit, Lasha Rosenberg, Ali Reed, Danny Segev, Reuven Dayan, Yoel Liba, etc. Dir, Pro and Screenplay: Amos Kollek. Assoc Pro: Mary Jane Cahill. Ph: Amnon Salomon. Ed: Alan Heim. No art credits. M: Michael Abene. (Kole/Hill Pro–Blue Dolphin Films) Rel: floating; first shown London (ABC Fulham Road and Golders Green), 6 June 1986. 90 mins. Cert 15.

The Goonies. If this doesn't qualify as the noisiest film of the year it cannot be far short of that distinction, with everyone shrieking or shouting so much, and often so unintelligibly, that the few sub-titles might have been considerably extended to advantage. The sort of thing that the British Children's Film Foundation used to do so well on a comparatively tiny budget, it is about some youngsters who, finding an old pirate map, go off on a treasure hunt, an adventure complicated by their involuntary involvement with a gang of escaped criminals, who join in the search for the priceless loot and scare the kids more than the macabre skeleton crew they meet along the spooky underground way. Maybe the kids will not mind the noise. Cast: Sean Astin, Josh Brolin, Jeff Cohen, Corey Feldman, Kerri Green, Martha Plimpton, Ke Huy Quan, John Matuszak, Robert Davi, Joe Pantoliano, Anne Ramsey, Lupe Ontiveros, Mary Ellen Trainor, Keith Walker, Curtis Hanson, Steve Antin, Paul Tuerpe, George Robotham, Charles McDaniel, Elaine Cohen McMahon, Michael Paul Chan, George Nicholas McLean, Bill Bradley, Jeb Adams, Eric Briant Wells, Gene Ross, Max Segar, Hewton Dennis Arnold, Jack O'Leary, Patrick Cameron, Erwin Harvey, Ted Grossman. Dir: Richard Donner. Pro: Donner and Harvey Bernhard. Ex Pro: Steven Spielberg, Frank Marshall and Kathleen Kennedy. Screenplay: Chris Columbus; from a Spielberg story. Ph: Nick McLean. Ed: Michael Kahn. Pro Des: J. Michael Riva. Art: Rick Carter. M: Dave Grusin. (Warner) Rel: 29 November 1985. 114 mins. Cert PG.

Casual cabbie Amos Kollek and penniless passenger Julie Hagerty discuss the situation on the boulder-strewn borders of the Dead Sea in Blue Dolphin's *Goodbye, New York.*

The treasure-hunting children (left to right, Josh Brolin, Ke Huy Quan, Corey Feldman and Sean Astin) make a grim discovery in *The Goonies* (Warner).

Gulag. Chilling – literally as well as figuratively – British film about an American athlete and sports reporter (David Keith) who, while covering a Soviet sports event becomes the unfortunate pawn in a piece of nasty Soviet propaganda, and is forcefully and cleverly persuaded to admit he is a CIA agent (which he is not). Instead of

Malcolm McDowell (centre) and David Keith (right) prepare to face the bitter conditions of a snowy Soviet *Gulag* in the Miracle British film of that title.

thereby gaining the freedom promised, he is packed off to an awful Arctic labour camp where he suffers privation until, along with a self-confessed British spy (Malcolm McDowell), he makes a dramatic escape across the snow to safety in Norway. A bitter, no-holds-barred comment on the Soviet system, sometimes a bit hard to take. Rest of cast: David Suchet, Warren Clarke, Nancy Paul, Brian Pettifer, Shane Rimmer, Bruce Boa, Eugene Lipinski. George Pravda, John McEnery, Alexei Jawdokimov, Daniel Wozniak, Angela Pleasance, Ray Jewers, Bogan Kominowski, Barrie Houghton, Forbes Collins, Stuart Milligan, Mark Malicz, Dallas Adams, Bibbs Ekkel. Dir: Roger Young. Pro: Andrew Adelson. Ex Pro: James Retter and Dan Gordon. Sup Pro: Barry Steinberg. Assoc Pro: Frederick Muller. Screenplay: Dan Gordon; from a story by Gordon, Raphael Shauli and Yehpusha Ben-Porat. Ph: Kelvin Pike. Ed: John Jympson. Pro Des: Keith Wilson. M: Elmer Bernstein. (Heron Home Entertainment–Lorimar–Miracle Films.) Rel: floating; first shown London (ABC, Shaftesbury Avenue and Edgware Road), 18 October 1985. 119 mins. Cert 15.

Hail Mary – Je Vous Salue, Marie. A typical Jean-Luc Godard movie. A formless, erratic and obtuse relating of the biblical virgin birth story, set against a modern background and with Mary as a nubile teenager who works in her dad's petrol station. Provocative and pretentious; sexually titillating, with plenty of views of Mary's bare body. Cast: Myriem Roussel, Thierry Rode, Philippe Lacoste, Manon Andersen, Juliette Binoche, Malachi Jara Kohan, Dick, Johann Leysen, Anne Gauthier. Dir and Screenplay: Jean-Luc Godard. Ph: Jean-Bernard Menoud and Jacques Firmann. No other credits listed. (JLG Films/Pegasus/Sara Films/SSR/Channel 4–The Other Cinema) Rel: floating; first shown London (Metro 1), 11 October 1985. 111 mins. Cert 18.

Heartbreakers. Technically excellent movie about some exasperatingly useless and weak characters high in sexual appetite but low in morals. The story concerns an artist obsessed with painting sexual bondage pictures, his factory-owning pal and their women, and the artist's inability even to remain faithful to friendship. A withering look at the mores of Los Angeles society. Cast: Peter Coyote, Nick Mancuso, Carole Laure, Max Gail, James Laurenson, Carol Wayne, Jamie Rose, Kathryn Harrold, George Morfogen, Jerry Hardin, Henry Sanders, Walter Olkewicz, Terry Wills, Annie O'Neill, Michelle Davison, Claire Malis, Carmen Argenziano, Adele Corey, Tina Chappel, Justin Leir, Scott Wade, Alfonse Ruggiero, Howard Shatsky. Dir and Screenplay: Bobby Roth. Pro: Roth and Bob Weis. Ex Pro: Lee Muhl, Harry Cooper and Joseph Franck. Assoc Pro: Cass Coty. Ph: Michael Ballhaus. Ed: John Carnochan. M: Tangerine Dream. (Jethro Films–Rank Film Dist.) Rel: floating; first shown London (Cannon, Tottenham Court Road and ICA), 11 April 1986. 99 mins. Cert 18.

He Died with His Eyes Open – On ne Meurt que Deux Fois. A (very) near miss from Jacques Deray: an intriguing, subtle but never quite brilliant French detection yarn lifted several notches above the average by Michel Serrault's performance as the sincere, dedicated and very lonely cop investigating the brutal murder of a concert pianist, and finding the deceased's mistress (Charlotte Rampling) physically fascinating and mentally puzzling. However, the incest part of the puzzle results in a weak ending. Rest of cast: Xavier Duluc, Elisabeth Depardieu, Gerard Darmon, Jean-Pierre Bacri, Jean Leuvrais, Jean-Paul Roussillon, Riton Liebman, Julie Jezequel. Dir: Jacques Deray. Pro: Norbert Saada. Screenplay: Michele Audiard; based on the novel by Robin Cook. Ph: Jean Penzer. Ed: Henri Lanoe. Art: François de Lamothe. M: Claude Bolling. (Swanie Pro/TSI Films–Cannon Film Dist.) Rel: floating; first shown London (Cannon Première), 16 May 1986. 106 mins. Cert 18.

Henson's Place. A fascinating documentary about the creator of the Muppets, Jim Henson, from his early college experiments to today's elaborate

Peter Coyote as the kinky artist Blue and Carol Wayne as a willing model in Orion/Rank's *Heartbreakers*.

movies and TV series. Plenty of fun, with interviews with 'people' such as Miss Piggy, and a helpful commentary by that remarkable frog, Kermit. (Tri-Star) Rel: floating; first shown London (ICA), 8 February 1986. 50 mins. Cert U.

The Hitcher. Technically excellent – photography, moody score, art direction, etc. – but otherwise routine and contrived killer-diller, which teaches the lesson: do not pick up hitch-hikers along the road if you value your life. Neatly spaced car chases, crashes and bloody murders, with C. Thomas Howell as the picker-up, Rutger Hauer as the psycho who is given a lift and Jennifer Jason Leigh obviously tossed in to give the murder and mayhem a modicum of romance. Rest of cast: Jeffrey de Munn, John Jackson, Billy Greenbush, Armin Shimerman, Eugene Davis, Jon Van Ness, Henry Darrow, Tony Epper, Tom Spratley, Colin Campbell. Dir: Robert Harmon. Pro: David Bombyk and Kip Ohman. Ex Pro: Edward S. Feldman and Charles R. Meeker. Co-Pro: Paul Lewis. Screenplay: Eric Red. Ph: John Seale. Ed: Frank J. Urioste. Pro Des: Dennis Gassner. M: Mark Isham. (HBO Pictures in assoc with Silver Screen Partners–Tri-Star) Rel: 16 May 1986. 97 mins. Cert 18.

The Holcroft Covenant. A thriller (not to be taken too seriously) about an SS General's successful New York architect son (Michael Caine), who is suddenly told that his father (who died in Hitler's bunker) had turned against his master and amassed a vast fortune which he wanted his son to use to try to make some amends for Nazi crimes. And from then on it is go, go go . . . with lots of treachery, thrills, confusion and surprises. Rest of cast: Anthony Andrews, Victoria Tennant, Lilli Palmer, Mario Adorf, Michael Lonsdale, Bernard Hepton, Richard Munch, Carl Rigg, André Penvern, Andrew Bradford, Shane Rimmer, Alexander Kerst, Michael Wolf, Hugo Bower, Michael Balfour, Therita Olivera De Sera, Guntberg Warns, Paul Humpoletz, Tom Deineinger, Keith Edwards, Andrea Browne, Shelley Thompson, Eva Adam, Jorge Trees, Tim Condren. Dir: John Frankenheimer. Pro: Edie and Ely Landau. Ex Pro: Mort Abrahams. Assoc Pro: Tom Sachs. Co-Pro: Otto Plaschkes. Screenplay: George Axelrod, Edward Anhalt and John Hopkins; from the novel by Robert Ludlum. Ph: Gerry Fisher. Ed: Ralph Sheldon. Pro Des: Peter Mullins. M: Stanislas. (Thorn EMI) Rel: floating; first shown London (Cinegate and ABC Edgware Road), 20 September 1985. 112 mins. Cert 15.

House. It's large, it's haunted and it is bequeathed to a writer of horror tales by his aunt who has died by hanging – all familiar, pretty daft and doesn't achieve its 'humorous' object (it was billed as a 'horror comedy'). Well, they apparently lapped it up in the US, where it rose to dizzy box-office heights and initially drew in more than $2 million a day – which again confirms that critics and public don't always see eye to eye. Cast: William Katt, George Wendt, Richard Moll, Kay Lenz, Mary Stavin, Michael Ensign, Erik Silver, Mark Silver, Susan French, Alan Autry, Steven Williams, Jim Calvert, Mindy Sterling, Jayson Kane, Billy Beck, Bill McLean, Steve Susskind, John Young, Dwier Brown, Joey Green, Steven Nichols, Donald Willis, Ronn Carroll, Robert Joseph, Curt Wilmot, Ron Wright, Renée Lillian, Peter Pitossky, Elizabeth Barrington, Jerry Marin, Felix Silla. Dir: Steve Miner. Pro: Sean S. Cunningham. Assoc Pro: Patrick Markey. Screenplay: Ethan Wiley; from a story by Fred Dekker. Ph: Mac Ahlberg. Ed: Michael N. Knue. Pro Des: Gregg Fonseca. M: Harry Manfredini. (Cunningham–Entertainment Film Dist.) Rel: floating; first shown London (Leicester Square Theatre and Odeon, Marble Arch), 20 June 1986. 93 mins. Cert 15.

Hypothesis of the Stolen Painting – L'Hypothèse du Tableau Volé. Raul Ruiz's 1978 'intellectual thriller' only now, thanks to the ICA, reaching the British screen. This pseudo-documentary about a forgotten painter (named as the mysterious artist Tonnère) offers audiences, through its examination of his work and the various clues it contains, an opportunity to solve the mystery at the heart of the matter. It is described as 'a dazzling intellectual jigsaw puzzle and do-it-yourself whodunit'. Well, maybe . . . Cast: Jean Rougeul, Gabriel Gason, Chantal Palay, Jean Reno. Dir and Screenplay: Raul Ruiz; based on an idea by Pierre Klossowski. Ph: Sacha Vierney. M: Jorge Arriagada. (ICA/BFI) Rel: floating; first shown London (ICA), 28 August 1985. In black-and-white. 67 mins. No cert.

Impulse. Minor thriller (released in the United States in 1984) which takes a dim view of human nature, with its story about a nice young couple who return to the wife's hometown when her mother blows her brains out (but lives!) and find it a pretty unhealthy place. Cast: Tim Matheson, Meg Tilly, Hume Cronyn, John Karlen, Bill Pax-

Meg Tilly as the young doctor who returns with new husband to her home town to find that Things – and People – Ain't What They Used to Be in Odyssey's *Impulse*.

ton, Amy Stryker, Claude Earl Jones, Robert Wightman, Lorinne Vozoff, Peter Jason, Abigail Booraem, Mary Celio, Jack T. Collis, Christian Crane, Chuck Dorsett, Christian Giannini, Anne Haney, Bernard Kuby, Darren Muir, Svi Peters, Dawn Eisler Smith, Adam Baumgarten, Leonard Burns, Dan Danforth, Holgie Forrester, Allan Graf, Gary Kirk, Richard E. Norlie, Thomas J. Saubder, Hugo L. Stranger, Sherri Stoner, Janet Sassoon, dancers of the San Franscisco Ballet Co. Dir: Graham Baker. Pro: Tim Zinneman. Ex Pro: Herb Jellinek. Screenplay: Bert Davis and Don Carlos Dunaway. Ph: Thomas del Ruth. Ed: David Holden. Pro Des: Jack Collins. M: Paul Chihara. (ABC Pictures–Odyssey) Rel: floating; first shown London, 14 March 1986. Cert 18.

The Inheritance – Eredità Ferramonti. Italian film based on a strong story about a family whose greed for cash and power, and their sexual desire, brings about death, destruction and the family's downfall. Real 'mellerdrammer', but with fine performances by the always reliable Anthony Quinn, and Dominique Sanda, who won the Cannes Film Festival's 'Best Actress' prize for her role as the scheming little siren. Rest of cast: Fabio Testi, Luigi Proietti, Adriana Asti, Paolo Bonacelli. Rosella Rusconi, Harold Bromley, Silvia Cerio, Maria Russo, Simone Santo, Rosanna Di Lorenzo, Carlo Palmucci. Dir: Mauro Bolognini. Pro: Gianni Hecht Lucari. Ex Pro: Alfredo Mirabile. Screenplay: Ugo Pirro and Sergio Bazzini; based on the novel by G. C. Chelli. Ph: Ennio Guarnieri. Ed: Nino Baragli. Pro Des: Luigi Scaccianoce. M: Ennio Morricone. (Flag Productions–Topart) Rel: floating; first shown London (Tottenham Court Road and Chelsea Classics, Odeon, Kensington and Cinecenta), 11 October 1985. 102 mins. Cert 18.

Michael Emil (the Professor – Einstein?) watches movie star Theresa Russell (the Actress – Marilyn Monroe?) explain the theory of relativity in simple terms in *Insignificance* (Palace Pictures).

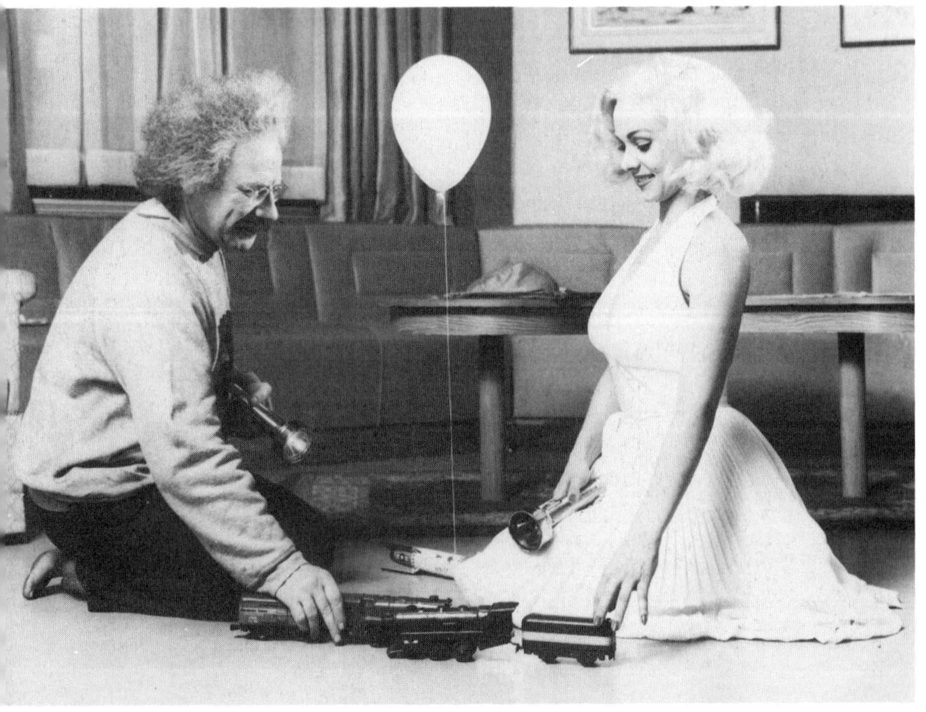

Insignificance. Though some are said to have discovered greater philosophical meaning in this superficially simple and amusing 'comedy' than was ever intended, it does have some claim to hidden depths. The story concerns a film star (a Marilyn Monroe look- and sound-alike), an Einstein-ish professor called to New York to give evidence in the infamous 'Reds-under-the-bed' senatorial inquisition, a simple baseball player (the girl's husband, about to get the marital boot) and a US senator, all of whom, one sticky-hot summer's night in 1953, become deeply if ephemerally involved with each other. Theresa Russell gives a stunning performance as the glamour-girl star, and gets plenty of sterling support from the other players: Tony Curtis (the senator), Michael Emil (the professor), Gary Busey (the ballplayer) and Will Sampson (the Muskogee Indian elevator attendant who likes to reach the roof to see the dawn come up over New York). One of the funniest sequences in the movie is where the star, with a few odd toys, explains the theory of relativity to the professor, while in return he reveals to her the beauty of his legs . . . that says it all. Though set in New York and concerning only American characters, the film is, in fact, British-made. Rest of cast: Patrick Kilpatrick, Ian O'Connell, George Holmes, Richard Davidson, Mitchell Greenberg, Raynor Scheine, Jude Ciccolella, Lou Hirsch, Ray Charleson, Joel Cutrara, Raymond Barry, John Stamford, Desiree Eramus, David Lambert, Cassie Stuart, Miachell Dunsmoor, Daniel Benzali, R. J. Bell, Shinobu Kanai, David Montague. Dir: Nicolas Roeg. Pro: Jeremy Thomas. Ex Pro: Alexander Stuart. Assoc Pro: Joyce Herlihy. Screenplay: Terry Johnson; based on his stage play. Ph: Peter Hannan, Ed: Tony Lawson. Pro Des: David Brockhurst. M: Stanley Myers. (Zenith Productions in assoc with The Recorded Picture Co-Palace Pictures) Rel: 9 August 1985. 105 mins. Cert 15.

Intimate Strangers. Odd, sort of DIY movie about two squatters – a mother and her teenage son – who find their home a mixed blessing . . . but it is all more shadowy and ambiguous than that. Cast: Irene Marot, Colin Smith, Irene Sutcliffe, Anthony Colin. Dir: Robert Smith. Ph: John Davies. (Frontroom Productions) Rel: floating; first shown London (ICA), 11 March 1986. 45 mins. No cert.

Invasion USA. Action pot-boiler with all the stops pulled out. Quite a bit of nastiness emerges from this story about a retired American agent returning to (violent) harness when his old Russian foe blows up his quiet Everglades home and his Indian pal and then proceeds with his plan to land a mercenary army in the United States to strike fear, disaster and death. But it so happens that Chuck Norris plays the American agent-army (he co-wrote the script too,

Fleeing from two-machine-gun-wielding hero Chuck Norris (right), the villains pick up a pretty hostage in Cannon's *Invasion USA*.

it appears), so the Reds don't get too far before being decimated and their leader given his come-uppance. Rest of cast: Richard Lynch, Melissa Prophet, Alex Colon, Eddie Jones, John DeVries, James O'Sullivan, Billy Drago, Jaime Sanchez, Dehl Berti, Alexander Zale, Shane McCamey, Stephen Markle, Martin Shakar, James Pax, Nick Ramus, Bernie McInerney, Lorraine Morin, Marilyn Romero, Anthony Marciona, Michael Carmine, Mario Ernesto Sanchez, Amanda Graham, etc. Dir: Joseph Zito. Pro: Menahem Golan and Yoram Globus. Pro Ex: Christopher Pearce. Pro Assoc: Rob Roda. Pro Sup (2nd unit): Stephen Traxler. Pro Co-Ord: Susan Felditt and Caroline St Clair-Gandy. Screenplay: James Bruner and Chuck Norris; from a story by Aaron Norris and Bruner. Ph: Joao Fernandes. Ed: Daniel Loewenthal and Scott Vickrey. Assoc Ed: Vanessa Procopio and Richard King. Pro Des: Ladislav Wilheim. M: Jay Chattaway. (Cannon Films–Cannon) Rel: floating; first shown London (Prince Charles), 15 November 1985. 107 mins. Cert 18.

Jagged Edge. Murder mystery with strong romantic strings attached, which is so wizardly woven – *did* he kill his wealthy wife for his position and her money? – that it's easy to imagine that not every viewer will be able to keep up with the final savage twists and comprehend who the killer and what the motive were. But the film consistently holds you, especially the courtroom scenes. Cast: Jeff Bridges, Glenn Close, Maria Mayenzet, Peter Coyote, Dave Austin, Richard Partlow, Lance Henriksen, William Allen Young, Ben Hammer, James Karen, Sanford Jensen, Woody Eney, Al Ruscio, Sharon Hanian, Sarah Cunningham, Ann Walker, Bruce French, Brandon Call, Christina Hutter, John Furlong, Karen Wonnell, James Winker, Sharon Madden, Guy Boyd, Phyllis Applegate, Robert Loggia, Michael Dorn, John Clark, Louis Giambalvo, John Dehner, David Wiley, Leigh Taylor-Young, Jay Crimp, Mike Mitchell, Diane Erickson, Marshall Colt, Walter Brooke, Karen Austin, Bill Gratton, Joyce Shank, Dean Webber, John X. Heart, Brenda Huggins, Richard Marion, Edwina Moore, Sue Rihr, Suzanne Lodge, Judith Siegfried, Sally Train,

Lady lawyer Glenn Close defends handsome client Jeff Bridges on a wife-murder charge in Columbia's *Jagged Edge*.

Romancing the Stone pair Michael Douglas and Kathleen Turner (with Danny DeVito) encountering more dangerous adventures, this time in the Middle East, in the 20th Century–Fox sequel *The Jewel of the Nile.*

Abigail Van Alyn, Terry Wills, Biff Yeager. Dir: Richard Marquand. Pro: Martin Ransohoff. Assoc Pro: Michele St Hilaire. Screenplay: Joe Eszterhas. Ph: Matthew F. Leonetti. Ed: Sean Barton and Conrad Buff. Pro Des: Gene Callahan. M: John Barry. (Columbia Delphi IV–Columbia). Rel: 12 April 1986. 108 mins. Cert 18.

Young charmer Meredith Salenger makes another effort to track down her lumberjacking dad in Disney's *The Journey of Natty Gann.*

The Jewel of the Nile. Like nearly every sequel, this follow-up to the wildly successful *Romancing the Stone* never quite reaches the impact of the original, but it is still fast, often furious, sometimes genuinely funny and nicely acted, with the *Stone* co-stars, Michael Douglas and Kathleen Turner, becoming involved in a Middle Eastern potentate's plot to seize power. Rest of cast: Danny DeVito, Spiros Focas, Avner Eisenberg, Paul David Magid, Howard J. Patterson, Randall Edwin Nelson, Samuel Rose Williams, Timothy Daniel Furst, Hamid Fillali, Holland Taylor, Guy Cuevas, Peter de Palma, Mark Daly Richards, Sadeke Colobanane, Hyacinthe N'Iaye, Daniel Peacock, Benyahim Ahed, Alaoui Hassan, Makoula Ahme. Dir: Lewis Teague. Pro: Michael Douglas. Co-Pro: Joel Douglas and Jack Brodsky. 2nd Unit Dir: Glenn Randall. Screenplay: Mark Rosenthal and Lawrence Konner. Ph: Jan DeBont. Ed: Michael Ellis and Peter Boita. Pro Des: Richard Dawkind and Terry Knight. Art: Leslie Tompkins and Damien Lanfranchi. M: Jack Nitzsche. (The Stone Group–Fox–UK Film Dist.) Rel: 2 May 1986. 106 mins. Cert PG.

The Journey of Natty Gann. More or less routine boy-and-dog story except that, in this case, it is a girl and a faithful, friendly wolf. There's plenty of fine scenery, and the impressive young (14-year-old) Meredith Salenger casts her spell over the entire movie. Set at the time of the Great Depression, it's the story of a girl's journey from Chicago, after running away from her guardian, to her father's lumber camp far away, up in the High Country. Rest of cast: John Cusack, Ray Wise, Lainie Kazan, Scatman Crothers, Barry Miller, Verna Bloom, Bruce M. Fischer, John Finnegan, Jack Rader, Matthew Faison, Jordan Pratt, Zachary Ansley, Campbell Lane, Max Trumpower, Doug MacLeod, Gary Chalk, Dwight McFee, Peter Anderson, Corliss M. Smith Jr, Hagan Beggs, Ian Black, Ray Michal, Clint Rowe, Frank C. Turner, Jack Ackroyd, Grant Heslov, Gary Riley, Scott Andersen, Ian Tracey, Jennifer Michas, Wally Marsh, Kaye Grieve, Hannah Cutrona, Gabrielle Rose, Marie Klingenberg, Stephen E. Miller, Robert Clothier, Don Davis, Alex Diakun, Tom Heaton, Harvey M. Miller, Sheelah Megill, Jeff Ramsey,

David (Richard Gere) is wedded to Michal (Cherie Lunghi), the daughter of the tragic King Saul (Edward Woodward, seen between them) in Paramount–UIP's generally serious biblical epic *King David*.

Gary Hendrickson, Wally Beeton, Doug Boyd, Bryan Couture, Al MacIntosh, Lorne La Riviere, Bob Storms. Dir: Jeremy Kagan. Pro: Mike Lobell. Assoc Pro and Screenplay: Jeanne Rosenberg. Pro Co-Ord: Linda Sheehy and Cathy Howard. Co-Assoc Pro: Les Kimber. Ph: Dick Bush. Ed: David Holder and Steven Rosenblum. Pro Des: Paul Sylbert. Art: Michael S. Bolton. M: James Horner. (Walt Disney Pro in assoc with Silver Screen Partners II/Lobell Bergman Pro–UK Film Dist.) Rel: 7 February 1986. 101 mins. Cert PG.

King David. Australian-in-Hollywood director Bruce Beresford brings to the screen in spectacular style, and with less than the usual carelessness in such movies of the past, a colourful, eventful (so eventful that if you don't know your Bible it gets a bit confusing) chapter of ancient history. It tells the stories of King Saul, the prophet Samuel, David and his brothers, and great pal Jonathan, and the blood and thunder that fills the pages of the Old Testament. Better than most but still not as absorbing on film as it is on page. Cast: Richard Gere, Edward Woodward, Alice Krige, Denis Quilley, Niall Buggy, Cherie Lunghi, Hurd Hatfield, Jack Klaff, John Castle, Tim Woodward, David Keyser, Ian Sears, Simon Dutton, Jean-Marc Barr, Arthur Whybrow, Christopher Malcolm, Valentine Pelka, Ned Vucovic, Michael Mueller, James Coombs, Mark Drewry, John Gabriel, Gina Bellman, John Hallam, James Lister, Jason Carter, John Barrard, Peter Frye, David Graham, Genevieve Allenbury, Ishia Bennison, Jenny Lipman, David George, Anton Alexander, Marino Mase, Luigi Montefiori, Roberto Renna, Lorenzo Piani, Massimo Sarchielli, Aiche Nana, Shimon Avidan, Nicholas Van Der Weide. Dir: Bruce Beresford. Pro: Martin Elfand. Assoc Pro: Charles Orme. 2nd Unit Dir: David Tomblin. Screenplay: Andrew Birkin, and James Costigan; from the latter's story based on the Books of Samuel 1 and 2, Chronicles 1 and the Psalms of David. Ph: Donald McAlpine. Ed: William Anderson. Pro Des: Ken Adam. M: Carl Davis. (Paramount-UIP) Rel: floating; First shown London (Odeon, Haymarket) 20 June 1986. 104 mins. Cert PG.

King Solomon's Mines. It would be difficult – the fallibility of memory being what it is – to classify in terms of merit this fourth screen version of Rider Haggard's classic adventure story (previous films in 1937, 1950 and, as *Watusi*, 1959), but certainly this one has been modelled along modern *Indiana Jones* lines, with a frantic pace, plenty of incredible stunts and quite a bit of good clean fun. Great white hunter Allan Quatermain (Richard Chamberlain) is hired by Sharon Stone to find and rescue her archaeologist dad from the clutches of the unholy German–Turkish alliance of Herbert Lom and John Rhys-Davies. Rest of cast: Ken Gampu, June Buthelezi, Bernard Archard, Sam Williams, Shai K. Ophir, Fideliis Che A, Mick Lesley,

The local warriors take a tight grip on Richard (Quatermain) Chamberlain in the Golan–Globus Cannon re-make of Rider Haggard's classic African adventure story *King Solomon's Mines*. Inset, heroine Sharon Stone also takes a firm grip of things.

Vincent Van Der Byl, Bob Greer, Oliver Tengende, Neville Thomas, Bishop McThurzen, Isiah Murert, Rocky Green, Calvin Johns, Isaac Mabhikwa, Innocent Choga, Brian Kagure, Stanley Norris, Anna Ditano, Andrew Whaley. Dir: J. Lee Thompson. Pro: Menahem Golan and Yoram Globus. Assoc Pro: Ronny Yacov. Pro Assoc: Avi Lerner. Pro Sup: John Stodel. Pro Co-Ord: Naomi Mayberg. Screenplay: Gene Quintano and James R. Silke; based on the novel by H. Rider Haggard. Ph: Alex Phillips. Ed: John Shirley. Pro Des: Luciano Spadoni. Art: Leonardo Coen Cagli. M: Jerry Goldsmith. (Cannon Pro–Cannon Dist.) Rel: floating; first shown London (Prince Charles and Classic, Haymarket), 20 December 1986. 100 mins. Cert PG.

Kiss of the Spider Woman. Intriguing and certainly controversial Brazilian/American co-production based on an unusual book: the story of a couple of cell-mates in a South American jail – one overtly homosexual (William Hurt; to some a painful, to others a brilliant performance) and the other a 'straight', politically active journalist (Raul Julia) – and their increasingly close friendship. Inset in the film are sequences from two films which the former has written and the stories of which he relates to his pal. Technically assured and one of the more unusual, interesting and, arguably, better movies of its period. Rest of cast: Sonia Braga, Jose Lewgoy, Milton Goncalves, Miriam Pires, Nuno Leal Maia, Fernando Torres, Patricio Bisso, Herson Capri, Denise Dummont, Nildo Parente, Antonio Petrin, Wilson Grey, Miguel Falabella, Walter Breda, Luis Guilherme, Walmer Barros, Luis Serra, Ana Maria Braga, Benjamin Cattan, Oswaldo Barreto, Sergio Bright, Claudio Curi, Pericles Campos, Edmilson Santos, Walter Vicca, Kenichi Kaneko, Geogers Schlesinger, Carlos Fariello, Frederico Botelho, Silvio Band, Paulo Ludmer, Elvira Bisso. Dir: Hector Babenco. Pro: David Weisman. Ex Pro: Francisco Ramalho Jr. Screenplay: Leonard Schrader; based on the book by Manuel Puig. Ph: Rodolfo Sanchez. Ed: Mauro Alice. Art: Clovis Bueno. M: John Neschling in assoc with Nando Carneiro. (HB

The Knight (Rutgen Hauer) and the young man (Matthew Broderick) who helps him break the spell cast on the Fair Lady (Michelle Pfeiffer), who (inset) is saved from death by the old Friar (Leo McKern) in *Ladyhawke* (Fox–Warner).

Filmes (Sao Paulo) in assoc with Sugarloaf Films, Inc. (Los Angeles), for Island Alive in assoc with Films Dallas–Palace Pictures) Rel: floating; first shown London (Lumière, Screen-on-the-Hill and Gate, Notting Hill), 16 January 1986. 121 mins. Cert 15.

Ladyhawke. A lavishly produced, handsomely mounted fairy story, beautifully photographed in Italy, mainly in and around some marvellously well-preserved and endlessly fascinating old castles. Based on an ancient legend that is known in many parts of Europe, it concerns a handsome knight and his lovely lady who suffer under a spell – cast upon them by an evil bishop with a passion for the lady – by which they are transformed into wolf and hawk respectively, one by night and the other by day. As they are never human at the same time, it is a frustrating situation for the lovers, which is eventually overcome by a conscience-stricken old friar and a very lively young lad. As usual with this kind of movie, the strength of the piece lies in its visual splendours, and its weakness in the dialogue. Cast: Matthew Broderick (the boy), Rutger Hauer (knight), Michelle Pfeiffer (lady), Leo McKern (friar), John Wood, Ken Hutchison, Alfred Molina, Giancarlo Prete, Loris Loddi, Alessandro Serra, Charles Borromel, Massimo Sarchielli, Nicolina Papetti, Russell Kase, Don Hudson, Gregory Snegoff, Gaetano Russo, Rod Dana, Stefano Horowitz, Paul Tuerpe, Venantino Venantini, Marcus Berensford, Valerie O'Brien, Nana Cecchi. Dir: Richard Donner. Pro: Donner and Lauren Shuler. Ex Pro: Harvey Bernhard. Screenplay: Edward Khmara, Michael Thomas and Tom Mankiewicz; based on Khmara's story. Ph: Vittorio Storaro. Ed: Stuart Baird. Pro Des: Wolf Kroeger. Art: Giovanni Natalucci and Ken Court. M: Andrew Powell. (Fox/Warner) Rel: 23 August 1985. 115 mins. Cert PG.

Lady Jane. Another superior, if slightly stodgy, British film, presenting a fairly dark period of British history, when after the death of Henry VIII the Catholic and Protestant factions fought to wrest the throne for their chosen nominees. At the death of Henry's young son Edward VII, the (at least initially) unwilling 15-year-old Lady Jane Grey was, in an ill-managed coup, proclaimed queen; but her reign lasted just nine days, before the Catholic faction deposed her and substituted the boy king's elder sister Mary. And so Mary – somewhat reluctantly and only because of, it is suggested here, gentle blackmail by Spain – sent Jane and her young husband to the block. A tragic story, beautifully and convincingly presented and performed which is marvellously attractive to the eye, with an ending that is tearfully moving. Cast: Helena Bonham Carter, Cary Elwes, John Wood, Michael Hordern, Jill Bennett, Jane Lapotaire, Sarah Kestelman, Patrick Stewart, Warren Saire, Joss Ackland, Ian Hogg, Lee Montague, Richard Vernon, David Waller, Richard Johnson, Pip Torrens, Matthew Guinness, Guy Henry, Andrew Bicknell, Clyde Pollitt, Morgan Sheppard, Zelah Clarke, Laura Clipsham, Janet Henfrey, Brian Poyser, Phillip Voss, Robert Putt, Stewart Harwood, Carole Hayman, Richard Moore, Michael Goldie, Denyse Alexander, Gabor Vernon, Robin Martin Oliver, Nicky Croydon, John Abbott, Jeannette Fox, Alison Woodgate, Philippa Luce, Eliza Kern, Krzysia Bialeska, Cryss Jean Healey, Adele Anderson, Anna Gilbert. Dir: Trevor Nunn. Pro: Peter Snell. Assoc Pro: Ted Lloyd. Screenplay: David Edgar; from a story by Chris Bryant. Ph: Douglas Slocombe. Ed: Anne V. Coates. Pro Des: Alan Cameron. M: Stephen Oliver. (Paramount–UIP) Rel: floating; first shown London (ABC, Shaftesbury Avenue), 29 May 1986. 141 mins. Cert PG.

Helena Bonham Carter as the tragic young queen and Cary Elwes as her husband enjoy a fleeting moment of happiness in Paramount/UIP's page of English history, *Lady Jane*.

Lamb. A superior British film with a religious theme, which sombrely and sadly tells the story of a naïve young priest at an Irish reform school: needing to fill the psychological gap created

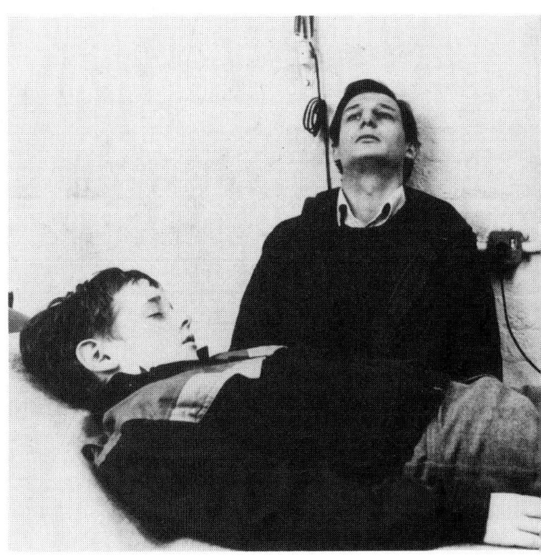

Liam Neeson as the young priest of the title role and Hugh O'Conor as the reform-school fugitive he helps in Cannon's British-made *Lamb*.

by the death of his beloved father, he takes off with a 14-year-old epileptic pupil who, unconsciously, needs a father himself. The duo are soon on the run but escape long enough to achieve a degree of mutual fulfilment before they come to the inevitable and tragic finish to their odyssey. Flawed by the anti-religious angle but still fascinating and moving. Cast: Liam Neeson, Hugh O'Conor, Ian Bannen, Ronan Wilmot, Frances Tomelty, Dudley Sutton, Denis Carey, David Gorry, Stuart O'Connor, Harry Towb, Eileen Kennally, Andrew Pickering, Ian McElhinney, Bernadette McKenna, Jessica Saunders, Robert Hamilton, Roger Booth, Marjie Lawrence, Nicola Wright, Freddie Stuart, Roy Glascock, Al Ashton, Doreen Keogh, Nick Dunning, Nigel Humphries, Tony Wredden, Larrington Walker, Walter McMonagle, Colum Convey, Emmer Gillespie. Dir: Colin Gregg. Pro: Neil Zeiger. Ex Pro: Al Burgess. Assoc Pro: Martin Proctor. Pro Co-Ord: Faye Perkins. Screenplay: Bernard MacLaverty; based on his novel. Ph: Mike Garfath. Ed: Peter Delfgou. Pro Des: Austen Spriggs. Art: Val Wolstenholme. M: Van Morrison. (Flickers Pro and Limehouse Pictures in assoc with Channel 4–Cannon) Rel: floating; first shown London (Cannon Première), 6 June 1986. 110 mins. Cert 15.

The Last Dragon. Hailed as the first kung-fu musical (that is, if your kind of music is of the breakdance variety), this is a mixture of martial arts, combat, videos and goonish comedy. The ingredients don't seem to match up too well, though young people who like rock music will probably find it all quite acceptable. Cast: Taimak, Vanity, Chris Murney, Julius J. Carry III, Faith Prince, Leo O'Brien, Mike Starr, Jim Moody, Glen Eaton, Keshia Knight, Jamal Mason, B. J. Barie, Sarita Allen, Jacqui Smith, Jodi Moccia, Sal Russo, Chazz Palminteri, Frank Renzulli, Torrance Mathis, André Brown, etc. Dir: Michael Schultz. Pro: Rupert Hitzig. Ex Pro: Berry Gordy. Assoc Pro: Joseph Caracciolo. Screenplay: Louis Venosta. Ph: James A. Contner. Ed: Christopher Holmes. Pro Des: Peter Larkin. Art: William Barclay. M: Misha Segal; with additional music by Willie Hutch and Norman Whitfield. (Motown Pro–Tri Star/Delphi III) Rel: 12 July 1986. 109 mins. Cert 15.

Last Night at the Alamo. Low-budget, 1983 Texas film set in a Houston bar due to be demolished: a review of some of the varied characters who frequent the place. Almost claustrophobic in atmosphere, low-keyed in lighting (in black-and-white) and with plenty of four-letter words sprinkled throughout the script. Cast: Sonny Davis, Lou Perry, Steve Matilla, Tina Hubbard, Doris Hargrave, J. Michael Hammond, Amanda Lamar. Dir: Eagle Pennell. Pro and Ed: Pennell and Kim Henkel. Screenplay: Henkel. Ph: Brian Huberman and Eric Edwards. Art: Fletcher Mackay. M: Chuck Pinnell and Wayne Bell. (Alamo Films Acton Screen) Rel: floating; first shown London (ICA), 4 April 1986. 80 mins. No cert.

Julius J. Carry III as the Shōgun of Harlem with his gang of fighters in the 'first kung-fu musical', *The Last Dragon* (Motown Tri-Star).

Legend. Spectacular fairy tale, borrowing from classic themes, about peasant hero Jack and his pretty princess to whom he shows the unicorns, so bringing about a disaster. They are trapped by the Devil (a marvellously macabre creation), who emasculates them and plans to bring about a world of darkness and devilry after he weds the princess. This horrid future is thwarted by the hero, his elfin pals and the sun's reflection in a mirror! Technically quite stunning and just the thing for the Christmas holidays, providing the youngsters can face the horrid Devil without having nightmares later. Cast: Tom Cruise, Mia Sara, Tim Curry, David Bennent, Alice Playten, Billy Barty, Cork Hubbert, Peter O'Farrell, Kiran Shah, Annabelle Lanyon, Robert Picardo, Tina Martin, Ian Longmuir, Mike Crane, Liz Gilbert, Eddie Powell. Dir: Ridley Scott. Pro: Arnon Milchan. Co-Pro: Tim Hampton. Pro Sup: Hugh Harlowe. Screenplay: William Hjortsberg. Ph: Alex Thomson. Ed: Terry Rawlings. Pro Des: Assheton Gordon. M: Jerry Goldsmith. (in US, Universal; in Britain, Fox) Rel: 13 December 1985. 94 mins. Cert PG.

The Legend of Billie Jean. Played by Helen Slater, she's the leader of a gang of young outlaws in a vaguely *Bonnie and Clyde* story, which embraces attempted rape, accidental wounding, kidnapping and sundry other frills. Rest of cast: Keith Gordon, Christian Slater, Richard Bradford, Peter Coyote, Martha Gehman, Yeardley Smith, Dean Stockwell, Barry Tubb, Mona Fuktz, John M. Jackson, Rodney Rincon, Caroline Williams, Rudy Young, Bobby Fite, Kim Valentine, Robby Jones, Janey Smalley, Charles Redd, Joshua Butts, Ray Hanna, Tony Slowik, Celia Newman, B. J. Thompson, Steve Uzzell, Robert Scott Kate, Jim Miller, Lauren Hartman, Rod Pilloud, John Wolfshohl, David Lee Morgan, Barbara Durham, Cass Gabriel, Thomas M. Jarrett, Forrest Patton, Antony Peraino, Kenneth Beall, Robert Wassell, Sage Parker, John Edson, Cathleen Sutherland, Angela Churchill, Stephanie Shook, Sharon-Marie Stoler, Peter Bonanno, Sharon

The pretty princess (Mia Sara) meets the unicorns, and so sparks off all the trouble that occurs in Fox's *Legend*. Inset, Tim Curry in his remarkable 'Devil' make-up.

Holmin, Joy Swan, Kathryn Childers, Al Geanano, Sonya Robbins. Dir: Matthew Robbins. Pro: Rob Cohen. Ex Pro: Jon Peters and Peter Guber. Screenplay: Mark Rosenthal and Lawrence Konner. Ph: Jeffrey L. Kimball. Ed: Cynia Scheider. Pro Des: Ted Haworth. M: Craig Safan. (Tri-Star/ Delphi III–Columbia) Rel: floating; first shown London (Cannon, Piccadilly), 2 May 1986. 95 mins. Cert 15.

A Letter to Brezhnev. A few subtitles might have helped with the wholly

It was a vintage period for British films and none was more that than Palace Pictures's *A Letter to Brezhnev*, the story of a Liverpool 'scallie' (Alexanda Pigg) who is determined to continue her one-night – innocent – romance with a Soviet sailor (Peter Firth), and actually persuades Brezhnev to send her an air ticket for the USSR.

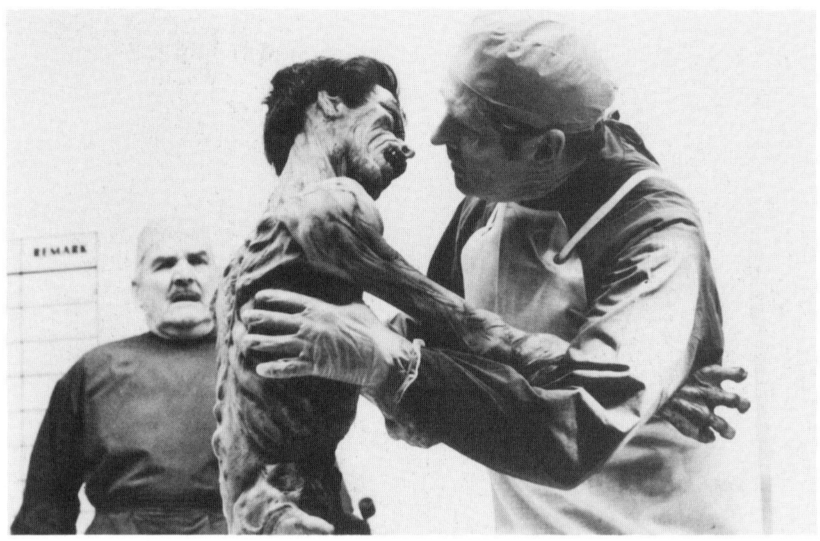

A couple of contrasting embraces in Cannon's *Lifeforce*: the first between reluctant doctor and other-world alien patient and the second, no less deadly, between passionate lovers Steve Railsback and Mathilda May.

authentic dialogue of this Liverpudlian comedy about a couple of girl-friends who pick up and spend the night (in one case, Elaine, wholly innocently; in the other, Teresa, very tiringly physically) with a couple of Soviet sailors. And when the ship sails the next morning Elaine is desperately in love and determined to follow her star to the USSR. This she does, with the help of Premier Brezhnev's complimentary air tickets, against all family and other opposition, right up to British F.O. levels. Raw and real, amusing and, on occasion, moving, with extremely impressive performances by the two young 'scallies' – Alexandra Pigg and Margi Clarke – as well as a creditable one by Peter Firth as the Red tar. Rest of cast: Alfred Molina, Tracy Lea, Susan Dempsey, Ted Wood, Carl Chase, Robbie Dee, Sharon Power, Syd Newman, Eddie Ross, Wendy Votel, Jeanette Votel, Mandy Walsh, Angela Clarke, Joey Kay, Frank Clarke, Paul Beringer, Ken Campbell, Neil Cunningham, John Carr. Dir: Chris Bernard. Pro: Janet Goddard. Co-Pro: Caroline Spack. Screenplay: Frank Clarke. Ph: Bruce McGowan. Ed: Lesley Walker. Pro Co-Ord: Chriss Kerr. Assoc Pro: Paul Lister. M: Alan Gill. (Clarke/Bernard Pro–Yeardream/Film Four International/Palace Pro/Palace Pictures) Rel: 8 November 1985. 95 mins. Cert 15.

Lifeforce. Lavish, obviously very expensive science-fiction horror thriller about some bloodsucking extraterrestrial creatures in human guise (including an irresistibly sexy young woman – played by beautiful newcomer Mathilda May). Their vampire act spreads so rapidly through a London in which the burning buildings gleam on the piles of lifeforced Londoners that, unless the hero can do something quickly (which he does), the whole city will be atomized. Laughably incredible, of course, with lots of amusing dialogue and plenty of thrills and chills. Rest of cast: Steve Railsback, Peter Firth, Frank Finlay, Patrick Stewart, Michael Gothard, Nicholas Ball, Aubrey Morris, Nancy Paul, John Hallam, John Keegan, Christopher Jagger, Bill Malin, Jerome Willis, Derek Benfield, John Woodnutt, James Forbes-Robertson, Peter Porteous, Katherine Schofield, Owen Holder, Jamie Roberts, Russell Sommers, Patrick Connor, Sidney Kean, Paul Cooper, Chris Sullivan, Milton Cadman, Rupert Baker, Gary Hildreth, Edward Evans, Nicholas Donnelly, Peter Lovstrom, Julian Firth, Carl Rigg, Elizabeth Morton, Geoffrey Frederick, David English, Emma Jacobs, Michael John Paliotti, Brian Carroll, Richard Oldfield, Christopher Barr, Burnell Tucker, Thom Booker, Michael Fitzpatrick,

Two of the crooks go into action (Arliss Howard, left, and Robert Duvall) on their lightship refuge in the Rank release *The Lightship*.

Richard Sharpe, John Golightly, William Lindsay, David Beckett, Sydney Livingstone, Ken Parry, John Edmunds, Haydn Wood, Adrian Hedley, Corrine Bougaard, Cal McCrystal, Bob Goody, Paul Anthony-Barber, Kristine Landon-Smith. Dir: Tobe Hooper. Pro: Menahem Golan and Yoram Globus. Assoc Pro: Michael Kagan. Pro Co-Ord: Marlene Butland. Screenplay: Dan O'Bannon and Don Jakoby; based on the novel *The Space Vampires* by Colin Wilson. Ph: Alan Hume. Ed: John Grover. Pro Des: John Graysmark. M: Henry Mancini. (Golan/Globus Productions–Cannon Group) Rel: 1 November 1985. 101 mins. Cert 18.

The Lightship. Lightweight thriller about a trio of fleeing crooks who, when their craft breaks down, take refuge in a lightship captained by Klaus Maria Brandauer, who is at odds with the sulky young son he has brought on board. After settling the family feud, he tries – but finally fails – to keep everything on an even keel as the tension between crew and criminals mounts to the final, inevitable violence. Rest of cast: Robert Duvall, Tom Bower, Robert Costanzo, Badja Djola, William Forsythe, Arliss Howard, Michael Lyndon, Tim Phillips. Dir: Jerzy Skolimowski. Pro: Moritz Borman and Bill Benenson. Ex Pro: Rainer Soehnlein. Screenplay: William Mai and David Taylor; based on the novel by Siegfried Lenz. Ph: Charly Steinberger. Ed: Barry Vince and Scott Hancock. Art: Holger Gross. M: Stanley Myers. (CBS–Rank Film Dist.) Rel: floating; first shown London (Odeon Haymarket) 25 April, 1986. 89 mins. Cert 15.

The Little Drummer Girl. This adaptation of John Le Carré's highly topical thriller about Israeli and Palestinian espionage and terrorism, in which neither side emerges with credit, is too long, too confusingly complicated and, in some roles, too superficially acted. The film does show the large financial investment in it as it moves rapidly between Britain, Greece, West Germany, Israel and the Lebanon. Diane Keaton (below her best) is the shrill Arab-supporting actress who becomes an Israeli agent, but Klaus Kinski walks away with the acting honours as the Israeli counter-espionage chief. Rest of cast: Yorgo Voyagis, Sami

Diane Keaton as the actress who takes up arms and becomes a terrorist in the John Le Carré thriller *The Little Drummer Girl* (Warner).

Frey, Michael Cristofer, David Suchet, Eli Danker, Ben Levine, Jonathan Sagalle, Shlomit Hagoel, Juliano Mer, Danni Roth, Sabi Dorr, Doran Nesher, Smadar Brener, Shoshi Marciano, Phillip Moog, Avi Keiddar, David Shalit, Dor Zweigenbom, Anna Massey, Thorley Walters, Julian Firth, Simon Osman, Albert Moses, Ben Robertson, David Cornwell (John Le Carré), Sebastian Graham Jones, Gawn Grainger, Michael Graham Cox, Illona Linthwaite, Irene Marot, Bill Nighy, Dee Sadler, Melanie Kilburn, Rowena Cooper, Peter Capell, Sasi Saad, Heinz Weiss, Rolf Becker, Ori Levy, Moti Shirin, Robert Pereno, Kerstin De Ahna, Yasein Shawaf, Suhiel Haddad, Dana Wheeler-Nicholson, Mohammed Kassas, Johnny Arbid, Mohammed Ali Badarni, Mahmoud Abu Elkhair, Jeff Lester, Paul Prosper, Adib Jashan, René Kolldehoff, Shimon Finkel, Elisabeth Neumann-Viertel, Yossi Werzansky, Aviva Joel, Noam Almaz, Dieter Augustin, Max Schillinger. Dir: George Roy Hill. Pro: Robert L. Crawford. Ex Pro: Patrick Kelly. Screenplay: Loring Mandel; based on the novel by John Le Carré. Ph: Wolfgang Treu. Ed: William Reynolds. Pro Des: Henry Bumstead. M: Dave Grusin. (Pan Arts–Warner) Rel: 5 July 1985. 130 mins. Cert 15.

Lorca and the Outlaws. Minor spacemen science fiction movie which, though British, was made in Australia with a mostly Aussie cast. About a confrontation on the planet Ordessa, in the year 2084, between bad guys and good guys, humans *v* cop androids. Cast: John Tarrant, Donogh Rees, Deep Roy, Cassandra Webb, Ralph Cotterill, Hugh Keays-Byrne, Joy Smithers, Tyler Coppin, James Syeelle. Dir and (with Matthew Jacobs) Screenplay: Roger Christian. Pro: Michael Guest. Ex Pro: Charles Aperia and Guy Collins. Ph: John Metcalfe. Ed: Derek Trigg. Pro Des: Owen Williams. M: Tony Banks. (Lorca Film Pro–VTC and Rediffusion) Rel: 23 May 1986. 100 mins. Cert PG.

Lord of the Dance. Two years in the making, this French–West German–Swiss co-production is a documentary record of the 'Tibetan Tantric Buddist ceremony of initiates' transformation into the god Garwang Tojay-chenpo, Lord of the Dance'. The preparation, devotions and the ceremony itself were photographed in the Thubten Choling Monastery on the side of Mount Everest. Certainly a unique achievement. Dir and Screenplay: Richard Kohn. Pro: Christopher Gierke. Ph: Jorg Jeshel. (ICA) Rel: floating; first shown London (ICA), 14 June 1986. 113 mins. No cert.

Lost in America. Chuckly little American comedy about a married couple who, on the eve of a move to up-market status – and a new half-million-dollar house – on the strength of the husband's anticipated promotion at an advertising agency, have to change plans when he is demoted instead. After the husband throws up his job and persuades his rather jaded wife to do the same, the couple set off on a trans-America trip which he describes in advance as being something 'like *Easy Rider* with a nest-egg'. Cast: Albert Brooks, Julie Hagerty, Garry Marshall, Art Frankel, Michael Green, Tom Tarpey, Ernie Brown, Maggie Roswell, Charles Boswell, Donald Gibb, Raynold Gideon, Hans Wagner, Ann Brown, Brandy Rubin, Sylvia Farrell, Tina Kincaid, Robert Hughes, John Di Fusco, Michael Cornelison, Radu Gavor, J. C. Reade, Pat Garrison, Byron Tong, Gayle Lanza, Zeke Manners, Ben Manners, Mark Sydney, David Katz, Raul Flores, Herb Nanas, Joey Coleman. Dir: Albert Brooks. Pro: Marty Katz. Ex Pro: Herb Nanas. Screenplay: Brooks and Monica Johnson. Ph: Eric Saarinen. Ed: David Finfer. Pro Des: Richard Sawyer. M: Arthur B. Rubenstein. (David Geffen Co–Warner) Rel: floating; first shown London (Warner), 22 November 1985. 91 mins. Cert 15.

Incestuously inclined father (Matt Clark) and disgusted daughter (Jamie Lee Curtis) in the ICA release *Love Letters*, which looked at a typical love affair from the Other Woman's angle.

Love Letters. Competent, strongly female-angled (both direction and writing) but fairly routine story of an affair between a happily married family man and the girl who takes his fancy, all seen from the point of view of the 'other woman'. Cast: Jamie Lee Curtis, James Keach, Amy Madigan, Bud Cort, Matt Clark, Bonnie Bartlett, Phil Coccioletti, Shelby Leverington, Rance Howard, Betsy Toll, Sally Kirkland, Brian Wood, Michael Villella, Jeff Doucette, Larry Cedar, Lyman Ward, Emma Chapman, Scott Henderson, Robin Thomas, Michelle Cundey. Dir and Screenplay: Amy Jones. Pro: Roger Corman. Ex Pro: Mel Pearl and Don Levin. Assoc Pro: Charles Skouras III.

Lainie Kazan and Tab Hunter find fun in Paul Bartel's rough and ready western *Lust in the Dust*, in which the third star (right) was the ample Divine.

Mel Gibson and the children who play an important part in the third *'Mad Max'* film *Beyond Thunderdome*, the best yet action thriller in this successful Australian series released by Warner. Inset, the striking Tina Turner as 'Queen' Aunty Entity.

Ph: Alec Hirschfield. Ed: Wendy Greene. Art: Jeannine Oppewall. M: Ralph Jones. (ICA Projects) Rel: floating; first shown London (Cannon cinemas, Tottenham Court Road and Panton Street), 9 May 1986. 94 mins. Cert 18.

Lust in the Dust. Paul Bartel (who made that black, bizarre and literally none-too-tasty comedy *Eating Raoul* – which he took a year of weekends to make) was at the helm of this equally rough send-up of a western, which some may find tasteless, but others hilarious. It concerns Tab Hunter's search for a buried treasure of gold. And his 'lady' companion is ample transvestite Divine. Rest of cast: Lainie Kazan, Geoffrey Lewis, Henry Silva, Cesar Romero, Gina Gallego, Nedra Volz, Courtney Gains, Pedro Gonzalez-Gonzalez, Woody Strode, Daniel Frishman, Al Cantu, Ernie Shinagawa, Clinton S. Doran, Pit Ginsburgh, Dir: Paul Bartel. Pro: Allan Glaser and Tab Hunter. Ex Pro: James C.Katz. Screenplay: Philip John Taylor. Ph: Paul Lohmann. Ed: Alan Toomayan. Pro Des: Walter Pickette. M: Peter Matz. (Fox Run Pro–New World Pictures–Columbia) Rel: floating; first shown London (Classic Tottenham Court Road and Times Centa), 29 November 1985. 81 mins. Cert 15.

Mad Max: Beyond Thunderdome. Very few film 'series' become better as they go along, but the Australian 'Mad Max' series has kept its high comic-strip appeal. In this, the third Max movie (the most lavish and expensively produced of the trio), set in some post-holocaust period, the pace is fast and furious, the tongue-in-cheek fun plentiful, the violence considerable, the invention – as well as the borrowing from other movies – continuous and the technical brilliance (including a notable musical score and remarkable photography) highly impressive. Max (again played by Mel Gibson), entering Bartertown in search of his stolen camel train, finds himself fighting a fantastic duel to the death. He is then sent out into the desert to die, but survives, thanks to a colony of kids that he leads back to confront the Bartertown Queen (Tina Turner) and her evil cohorts. And the end . . . well, it makes sure that *MM4* will follow. Rest of cast: Bruce Spence, Adam Cockburn, Frank Thring, Angelo Rossitto, Paul Larsson, Angry Anderson, Robert Grubb, George Spartels, Edwin Hodgeman, Bob Hornery, Andrew Oh, Ollie Hall, Susan Leonard, Ray Turnbull, Lee Rice, Robert Simper, Brian Ellison, Gerard Armstrong, Max Worrall, Virginia Wark, Geeling, Helen Buday, Mark Spain, Mark Kounnas, Rod Zuanic, Justine Clarke, Shane Tickner, Toni Allaylis, James Wingrove, Adam Scougall, Tom Jennings, Gerrt D'Angelo, Travis Latter, Miguel Lopez, Paul Daniel, Tushka Hose, Emily Stocker, Sandie Lillingston, Adam Willits, Ben Chesterman, Liam Nikkenen, Dan Chesterman, Christopher Norton, Katharine Cullen, Heilan Robertson, Gabriel Dilworth, Hugh Sands, Rebekah Elmaloglou, Marion Sands, Shari Flood, Kate

Tatar, Rachael Graham, Pega Williams, Emma Howard, Tarah Williams, Joanna McCarroll, Daniel Willits, Toby Messiter, Tonya Wright, Charlie Kenney, Amanda Nikkenen, Flynn Kenney, Luke Panic, William Manning, James Robertson, Adam McCready, Sally Morton. Dir: George Miller and George Ogilvie. Pro: Miller. Co-Pro: Doug Mitchell and Terry Hays. Ex in charge of Pro: Su Armstrong. Assoc Pro: Steve Amedroz and Marcus D'Arcy. Screenplay: Hayes and Miller. Ph: Dean Semler. Ed: Richard Francis-Bruce. Pro Des: Graham 'Grace' Walker. Art: Ann Browning. M: Maurice Jarre. (Warner) Rel: 18 October 1985. 107 mins. Cert 15.

Defence lawyer Fred Thompson and his client Sissy Spacek fight for integrity against the crooked political machine in Thorn-EMI's *Marie – a True Story:* both gave outstanding performances.

The Man with Two Brains. Hit-and-miss science-fiction lark about a certain Dr Hfuhrnhurr (Steve Martin) who, finding his wife (Kathleen Turner) isn't quite the girl he thought she was (in fact, her idea of fun is to induce fatal heart attacks in her hubbies so she can get her greedy little hands on their cash), then falls in love with the brain (of Sissy Spacek) kept in the laboratory of his nutty pal Dr Necessiter (David Warner). To say more would give the comedy game away. Final balance sheet: hits and misses come out about equal. Rest of cast: Paul Benedict, Richard Brestoff, James Cromwell, George Furth, Peter Hobbs. Dir: Carl Reiner. Pro: David V. Picker and William E. McEuen. Screenplay: Reiner, Steve Martin and George Gipe. Ph: Michael Chapman. Ed: Bud Molin. Pro Des: Polly Platt. Art: Mark Mansbridge. M: Joel Goldsmith. (Aspen Film Soc–McEuen/Picker–Warner) Rel: floating; first shown London (Scala and ICA), 2 May 1986. 93 mins. Cert 15.

Marie. Familiar, but this time apparently true, story of one honest citizen (a brave single mother with three kids) who, unable to compromise with crime in high places, takes on the full might of crooked politicians and even the state governor. And against all odds, fights them in the courts to unexpected victory. And how apt that such a Capra-ish story should be produced by Frank Capra Jr! A wonderful performance by Sissy Spacek as the small voice of integrity finally silencing the loud voices of corruption. Rest of cast: Jeff Daniels, Keith Szarabajka, Lisa Banes, Graham Beckel, John Cullum, Lisa Foster, Morgan Freeman, Vince Irizarry, John-Michael Maas, Colin Wilcox Paxton, Fred Thompson, Trey Wilson, Robert Benson, Dawn Carmen, Shane Wexel, Don Hood, Michael Moran, Clarence Felder, Charles Kahlenberg, Joe Sun, R. Picket Bugg, etc. Dir: Roger Donaldson. Ex Pro: Frank Capra Jr. Ex in charge of Pro: Elliot Schick. Screenplay: John Briley; based on the book *Marie: A True Story* by Peter Maas. Ph: Chris Menges. Art: Ronald Foreman. Ed: Neil Travis. M: no credit listed. (Dino de Laurentiis–Thorn EMI) Rel: floating; first shown London (ABC, Shaftesbury Avenue), 25 April 1986. 111 mins. Cert 15.

Below and inset, director/interviewer Maximilian Schell at work on his feature documentary about Marlene Dietrich, *Marlene*, released by Electric Screen Pictures.

Marlene. An illuminating documentary about La Dietrich, compiled from some 15 hours of taped interviews with the then 84-year-old star at her Paris apartment, made by Maximilian Schell. He plays a major role in the way his artful questions bring out some fascinating comments from a lady who never pulls a punch or forgoes a sharp critical comment, but who has also always insisted that her private life is her own and nothing to do with her professional image. Her insistence that she will not be photogaphed now made it difficult for Schell, but he overcomes that hurdle quite neatly. Dir: Schell. Script: Schell and Meir Dohnal. Ph: Ivan Slapeta. Ed: Heidi

Cher as the mother of a boy (Eric Stoltz) disfigured by a rare disease in Peter Bogdanovich's *Mask*, said to be based on a true story (Universal–UIP).

Genee and Dagmar Hirtz (Zev Braun/ Karel Dirka–Oko Film–Blue Dolphin Films) Rel: floating; first shown London (Electric Screen), 7 February 1986. 94 mins. Cert PG.

Mask. The true story of Rocky Dennis (played by Eric Stoltz), a young American who was stricken by a very rare disease which deformed his face and finally killed him at the age of 16, though he was mentally untouched and very bright until the end. A sometimes moving story of personal courage as the lad tries to lead a more-or-less normal existence in spite of the revulsion that his deformity induces in others, and despite his homelife, comprising a gang of motorbike roughnecks and his hard-swearing, promiscuous mother, played by Cher. Rest of cast: Sam Elliott, Estelle Getty, Richard Dysart, Laura Dern, Nicole Mercurio, Harry Carey Jr, Dennis Burkley, Laurence Monoson, Ben Piazza, Alexandra Powers, L. Craig King, Kelly Minter, Joe Unger, Todd Allen, Howard Hirdler, Jeannie Dimter Barton, Steven James, Cathy Arden, Andrew Robinson, Ivan J. Rado, Anna Hamilton Phelan, Wayne Grace, Nick Cassavetes, Les Dudek, Jo-El Sonnier, Rebecca Sharkey, Paige Matthews, Patricia Pelham, Gale Ricketts, Stan Ross, Scott Willardsen, Marsha Warfield, Allison Roth, David Scott Milton, Creed Bratton, L. Charles Taylor, Rummel Mor, Barry Tubb, Norman Kaplan, Marilyn Hamilton, Anna Thea, Louis Waldon, Toni Sawyer, Lou Felder, Christopher Rydell, Beth McKinley, Jill Whitlow. Dir: Peter Bogdanovich. Pro: Martin Starger. Co-Pro: Howard Alston. Assoc Pro: George Morfogen and Peggy Robertson. Screenplay: Anna Hamilton Phelan. Ph: Laszlo Kovacs. Sup Ed: Eva Gardos. Ed: Barbara Ford. Art: Norman Newberry. M: 21 rock numbers performed by various soloists and groups. (Univeral–UIP) Rel: 5 July 1985. 120 mins. Cert 15.

Matter of Heart. Something of a triumph for director Mark Whitney, in that he manages to make his film of such a non-visual and difficult subject – the life and work of the psychiatrist Carl Jung – both informative and interesting. A neat blend of two recorded interviews with the Master and various interviews with those who knew and, in many cases, learned from him. Dir, Ph and Ed: Mark Whitney. Pro: Michael Whitney. Ex Pro: George Wagner. Pro Assoc: Janet Anderson. Screenplay: Suzanne Wagner. M: John Adams, (Jung Institute of Los Angeles–Cinegate) Rel: floating; first shown London (Gate, Bloomsbury), 16 May 1985. 105 mins. Cert U.

Below, one of the year's most original and memorable (and possibly one of the least commercially successful, I would guess) was Warner's *Mishima: A Life in Four Chapters*, an intricate story of the last day in the life of the warrior-poet-politician of the title, played by Ken Ogata (right).

Mishima: A Life in Four Chapters. A remarkable and memorable movie, not always easy to understand and follow in its intricacies. It tells the story of the last day in the life of the famous Japanese poet, novelist, film and stage director/actor and right-wing political extremist of the title. In 1970, Mis-

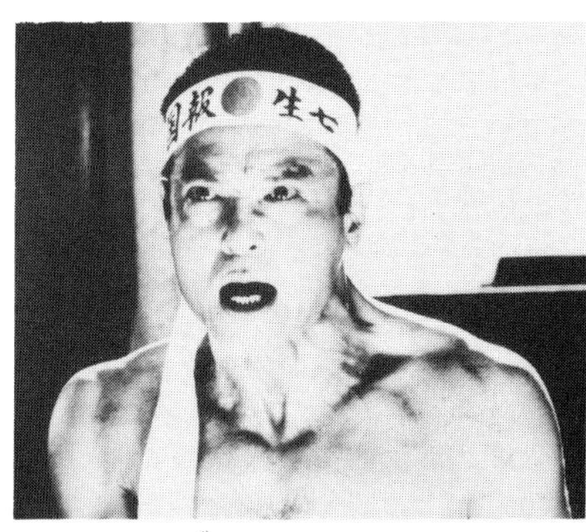

hima, with a few select followers, entered a Tokyo military establishment and, with a general as hostage, barricaded themselves in while Mishima delivered an impassioned plea to a not-very-receptive audience of soldiers, asking for the restoration of the old regime and of veneration of the Emperor; subsequently (as always planned) he committed ritual suicide. Spread throughout the four chapters (which are also based, in part, on Mishima's autobiographical novels) are black-and-white flashback sequences. And woven into the film is the characteristically Japanese love of beauty allied to a fascination with death, and the yearning of a man of letters to be a leader in violent action. And this only explores some of the many, often almost hidden threads in a 'difficult', intelligent and highly individualistic movie, which, above all, in spite of the horror of ritualistic suicide, leaves a haunting impression of great stylistic, melancholy beauty. And a final quote from the film: 'Mishima is acknowledged to have been a real person but his acts have been fictionalised by writers. Other persons and events in the film are fictitious.' Casts: ('25 Nov. 1970') Ken Ogato, Mashayuki Shionoya, Hiroshi Mikama, Yunya Fukuda, Shigeto Tachihara, Junkichi Orimoto; ('Flashbacks') Naoko Otani, Go Riju, Masato Aizawa, Yuki Nagahara, Kyuzo Kobayashi, Yuki Kitazume, Haruko Kato; ('Temple of the Golden Pavilion') Yasosuke Bando, Hisako Manda, Naomi Oki, Miki Takakura, Imari Tsuji, Koichi Sato; ('Kyoko's House') Kenji Sawada, Reisen Lee, Setsuko Karasuma, Tadanori Yokoo, Yasuaki Kurata, Mitsuru Hirata; ('Runaway Horses') Toskiyuki Nagashima, Hiroshi Ida, Jun Negami. Ryo Ikebe. Additional cast: Toshio Hosokawa, Hideo Fukuhara, Yosuke Mizuno, Eimei Ezumi, Minoru Hodaka, Shoichiro Sakata, Alan Mark Poul, Ren Ebata, Yasuhiro Arai, Fumio Mizushima, Shinji Miura, Yuichi Saito, Sachiko Akagi, Tsutomu Harada, Mami Okamoto, Atsushi Takayama, Kimiko Ito, Kojira Oka, Tatsuya Hiragaki, Shinichi Nosaka, Sachiko Hidari. Dir: Paul Schrader. Pro: Mata Yamamoto and Tom Luddy. Ex Pro: George Lucas and Francis Coppola. Assoc Pro: Leonard and Chieko Schrader and Alan Mark Poul. Screenplay: Paul and Leonard Schrader; with Japanese script by Chieko Schrader; scenario conceived in collaboration with Jun Shiragi. Ph: John Bailey. Pro Des: Eiko Ishioka. Ex Art Dir: Kuzuo Takenaka. Ed: Michael Chandler. M: Phillip Glass. (Zoetrope Studios/Filmlink International/Lucas Film Ltd–Warner) Rel: floating; first shown London (Lumière and Electric Screen), 31 October 1985. 121 mins. Cert 15.

Mixed Blood – Cocain. Gang warfare between Puerto Rican and Brazilian youngsters battling for control of the drug traffic on New York's East Side. Oddly tossed into the off-putting violence and mayhem is some comic business centred on the 'Lady' running the little Brazilian beauties. Cast: Marilla Pera, Richard Ulacia, Geraldine Smith, Rodney Harvey, Alvaro and William Rodriguez, Eduardo Gonzalez, Steven Garcia, Edwina Ebron, Andres Castillo, Peter Cruz, Richard Garcia, Emanuelle La Salle, John Leguizamo, Julian Lun Pen, Joselyn Marcano, Ralph Martinez, Christian de Faris, Daniel Martinez, Angel David, Pedro Sanchez, Fabio Urena, Bobby Martinez, Christian De Firis, Richardo Caimares, Anthony Freire, Roberto Santano, William Martinez, John Curet, Isaac Manga, Roland Otero, Arturo, Carlos and John Rodriguez, Abdel Saez, A. W. H. Smith, etc. Dir and Screenplay: Paul Morrissey. Pro: Antoine Gannage and Steven Fierberg. Ex Pro: Alain Sarde. Assoc Pro: Mark Slater. Pro Co-Ord: Susie Prestine. Ph: Stefan Zapasnik and Steven Fierberg. Ed: Scott Vickrey. Art: Stephen McCabe. M: Andy Hernandez. (Sara Films–Mainline) Rel: floating; first shown London (Cannon Cinemas, Panton Street and Oxford Street), 18 April 1986. 97 mins. Cert 18.

The Money Pit. Hysteria-paced farce, with some vague resemblance to the 1948 comedy *Mr Blandings Builds His Dream House* – which *was* funny – about a young couple who fall in love with a house beyond their slight means but find, on closer acquaintance, that they have purchased a disaster area. Tom Hanks' and Shelley Long's performances must have nearly done them a mischief, and Mr Hanks' has certainly done his voice no good at all. Yet there *was* some laughter to be heard at the press show . . . Rest of cast: Alexander Godunov, Maureen Stapleton, Joe Mantaegna, Philip Bosco, Josh Mostel, Takov Smirnoff, Carmine Caridi, Brian Backer, Billy Lombardo, Mia Dillon, John Van Dreelen, Douglas Watson, Lucille Dobrin, Tetchie Agbayani, Radu Gavor, Grisha Dimant, Lutz Rath, Joel Balin, Wendell Pierce, Susan Browning, Henry Baker, Mary Louise Wilson, Irving Metzman, Mike Russo, Joe Ponazecki, Michael Hyde, Mike Starr, Frankie Faison, Jake Steinfeld, Matthew Cowles, Nestor Serrano, Michael Jeter, Afemo Omilami, Bruno Iannone, Ron Foster, Alan Altschuld, Tzi Ma, Cindy Brooks, Leslie West, 'The Fabulous Heavyweights', 'White

Increasingly fraught owner of his dream house Tom Hanks sees his dream becoming a nightmare in Amblin–UIP's *The Money Pit*, as builder Philip Bosco gets to work on restoration.

Romantic municipal gardener *Mr Love* (Barry Jackson) gets some good advice from his pal Theo (Maurice Denham) in the delightful British (Warner) comedy. Inset, Mr Love and loving cinema usherette Julia Deakin.

Lion', Robey. Dir: Richard Benjamin. Pro: Frank Marshall, Kathleen Kennedy and Art Levinson. Ex Pro: Steven Spielberg and David Giler. Screenplay: Giler. Ph: Gordon Willis. Pro Des: Patrizia von Brandenstein. M: Michel Colombier. (Amblin Entertainment–Spielberg– Universal–UIP) Rel: floating; first shown London (Plaza), 27 June 1986. 91 mins. Cert PG.

The Mothers of Plaza de Mayo – Las Madres. American documentary about the Argentinian mothers of people who have 'disappeared' following state activity and who now meet each Thursday in Buenos Aires' Plaza de Mayo to protest against the brutalities of the military *junta*. Dir: Susana Munoz and Lourdes Portillo. (First Run Features–Contemporary) Rel: floating; first shown London (Everyman), 20 June 1986. 64 mins. No cert.

Mr Love. Minor British comedy set in Southport and concerning the strange affair of the municipal gardener who became a legend – and how! After a lifetime with a frigid frau, he decides to cut loose sexually, but fails for various reasons until just before the car smash that kills him, leaving his girl-friend unharmed. When she and all the women he has helped in various ways turn up at his funeral, the myth of his sexual prowess is born. The uproariously funny scene in which he and the usherette of the cinema where he works as part-time projectionist (incidentally, this sequence was filmed at the oldest surviving cinema still in use) take over the star parts in *Casablanca* when the projector fails, would alone make this a memorable movie. Lovely performances from all concerned, especially Barry Jackson (as Mr Love), Maurice Denham (his eccentric pal) and Julie Deakin (the ambitious would-be actress). Rest of cast: Christina Collier, Helen Cotterill, Linda Marlowe, Kay Stonham, Margaret Tyzack, Marcia Warren, Janine Roberts, Donal McCann, Tony Melody, Patsy Byrne, Robert Bridges, Jacki Piper, Alan Starkey, Lill Roughly, Tina Simmons, John Joyce, David Atkins, George Malpas, Chris Jury, James Benson, Jeremy Swift. Dir: Roy Battersby. Pro: Susan Richards and Robin Douet. Ex Pro: David Puttnam, Screenplay: Kenneth Eastaugh. Ph: Clive Tickner. Ed: Alan J. Cumner-Price. Pro Des: Adrienne Atkinson. M: Willy Russell. (Enigma/Goldcrest-Warner) Rel: floating; first shown London (Warner), 21 February 1986. 91 mins. Cert 15.

Mrs Soffel. For her American debut, Aussie director Gillian Armstrong (of *My Brilliant Career* fame) used the true story of a Pittsburgh prison warden's wife who, in 1901, helped two condemned prisoners to escape. She then joined them in their flight, giving up her home, husband and four children for a short time with her murderer lover as the two try to make their wintry way to Canada. Well enough made and acted but somehow lacking the final touch that could have made a good film into an outstanding one. Cast: Diane Keaton, Mel Gibson, Matthew Modine, Edward Herrmann, Trini Alvarado, Jennie Dundas, Danny Corkill,

Matthew Modin (left), Diane Keaton and Mel Gibson were the stars of Australian director Gillian Armstrong's first American movie, *Mrs Soffel* (MGM/UA–UIP).

Harley Cross, Terry O'Quinn, Pippa Pearthree, William Youmans, Maury Chaykin, Joyce Ebert, John W. Carroll, Dana Wheeler-Nicholson, Wayne Robson, Les Rubie, Paula Trueman, David and Douglas Huckvale, Ralph Zeldin, Nancy Chesney, Samantha Follows, Katie McCombs, Linda Cabler, Eric Hebert, Alar Aedma, Tom Harvey, Jack Jessop, Lou Pitoscia, John Dee, William Duell, Len Doncheff, David Fox, Fred Booker, Valerie Buhagiar, Jane Foster, Phillip Craig, John Innes, Norma Dell'Agnese, Al Kozlik, Derek Keurvorst, Kay Hawtrey, Brian Young, Frank Adamson, Don Granberry, Gerald Tucker, Heather Graham, Linda Carola, George Belskey, Marushka Stankova, James Bradford, Charles Jolliffe, Rodger Barton, Jack Mather, Lee-Max Walton, Sean Sullivan, Warren Van Evera, Clay Pollett, Chris Cummings, Dan Lett, Don McManus, Dorothy Phelan, Walter Massey. Dir: Gillian Armstrong. Pro: Edgar J. Scherick, Scott Rudin and David A. Nicksay. Assoc Pro: Dennis Jones. Screenplay: Ron Nyswaner. Ph: Russell Boyd, Peter Norman and Darwin Dean. Ed: Nicholas Beauman. Pro Des: Luciana Arrughi. Art: Roy Forge Smith. M: Mark Isham. (MGM–UIP) Rel: floating; first shown London (Plaza), 27 June 1985. 111 mins. Cert PG.

The Muppets Take Manhattan. Delightful Muppet entertainment for all the family, with those now internationally familiar figures such as Kermit the Frog and Miss Piggy, finding Broadway success with their musical show. Stunningly clever, as muppets and people perform together: marvellous magic! The Muppets: Jim Henson, Frank Oz, Dave Goeltz, Steve Whitmire, Richard Hunt, Jerry Nelson. Feature players: Juliana Donald, Lonny Price, Louis Zorich. Cameos: Art Carney, James Coco, Dabney Coleman, Gregory Hines, Linda Lavin, Joan Rivers, Elliot Gould, Liza Minnelli, Brooke Shields, Frances Bergen, John Landis, The Hon Edward I. Koch, Vincent Sardi. Additional Muppet performers: Kathryn Mullen, Karen Prell, Brian Muehl, Bruce Edward Hall, J. J. Kroupa, David Rudman, Melissa Whitmire, Michael Earl Davis, Glenngo King, Tim de Haas, Cheryl Bartholow, Martin P. Robinson. And supporting cast of human performers. Dir: Frank Oz. Pro: David Lazer. Ex Pro: Jim Henson. Screenplay: Oz, Tom Patchett and Jay Tarses. Ph: Robert Paynter. Ed: Evan Lottman. Pro Des: Stephen Hendrickson. M (plus lyrics): Jeff Moss. M: (score): Ralph Burns. (Tri-Star) Rel: floating; first shown in London (ICA), 15 February 1986. 94 mins. Cert U.

Creator of those marvellous puppets, Jim Henson with one of his most popular stars, Kermit the Frog, in Tri-Star's *The Muppets Take Manhattan.*

My Beautiful Laundrette. Not the least intriguing of the many fascinating angles to this British film is that, had it been written by anyone other than a Pakistani (which Hanif Kureishi is), this story about a group of Asians living in South London would have caused a major uproar about racism, both in and out of Parliament. The characters presented are, with one exception (and he's a gentle drunk) variously ruthlessly ambitious, not adverse to dope-smuggling, irreligious, foul-mouthed, homosexual, wife cheating and, in fact, are at best rather likeable rogues. The story primarily concerns a young ambitious, Cockney-speaking Pakistani (Gordon Warnecke), whose mysteriously rich businessman uncle (Saeed Jaffrey in a delightful performance) sets him up in the laundrette business. He gives him a rundown place to manage, which the nephew quickly converts into a sort of up-market cleaning establishment with the help of his white, former National Front pal and lover (Daniel Day-Lewis). All the Pakistanis seem to share a strong love–hate relationship with their adopted country. You could say that this controversial, obviously made-for-TV film, is a damped-down, potential political firework. Rest of cast: Roshan Seth, Derrick Branche, Shirley Ann Field, Rita Wolf, Souad Faress, Richard Graham, Winston Graham, Dudley Thomas, Garry Cooper, Charu Bala Choksi, Persis Maravala, Nisha Kapur, Neil Cunningham, Walter Donohue, Gurdial Sira, Stephen Marcus, Dawn Archibald, Jonathan Moore, Gerard Horan, Ram John Holder, Bhasker, Ayub Khan Din, Dulice

White boy Daniel Day-Lewis and Pakistani lad Gordon Warnecke as the (very) intimate pals and business partners in the Mainline Pictures release of the splendid British film *My Beautiful Laundrette*. Right, Shirley Ann Field and Saeed Jaffrey both contributed telling performances.

Leicier, Badi Uzzaman, Chris Pitt, Kerryann White, Colin Campbell, Sheila Chitnis. Dir: Stephen Frears. Pro: Sarah Radclyffe and Tim Bevan. Screenplay: Hanif Kureishi. Ph: Oliver Stapleton. Ed: Mick Audsley. Pro Des: Hugo Luczye Wyhowski. M: Ludus Tonalis. (Working Title/SAF Productions for Channel 4–Mainline Pictures) Rel: floating; first shown London (Screen-on-the-Hill and Metro), 16 November 1985. 97 mins. Cert 15.

My First Wife. Yet another outstanding, very personal film from Australia. Paul (*Man of Flowers*) Cox's almost painfully intimate and wonderfully perceptive movie about a marital crisis points to the way in which the sexual roles are changing within marriage, with the female becoming the stronger partner. And within this story is a passionate plea for more tolerance and understanding between partners, and an illustration of the tragic way their behaviour can affect their children. Beautiful performances, an unusually literate script and a wonderful soundtrack make this one of the most distinguished movies of its period. The film was duly honoured by the Australian Film industry in 1984, receiving awards for 'Best Director', 'Best Screenplay' and 'Best Actor' (John Hargreaves). Rest of cast: Wendy Hughes, Lucy Angwin, David Cameron, Anna Jemison, Charles Tingwell, Betty Lucas, Robin Lovejoy, Lucy Uralov, Xenia Groutas, Jon Finlayson, Julia Blake, Ron Falk, Reg Roddick, Renée Geyer, Sabrina Lorenz, Christopher Holligan, Linden Wilkinson, Tony Llewellyn-Jones, Symonetta Dennis, Jentah Sobott, Neela Dey, Marlene Grech, Rex Callahan, Terry Rodman, Jay Mannering, Ian Mumby, Bianca Russel; the Quartet: Hartley Newnham,

Husband John (John Hargreaves, centre, with parents-in-law Charles Tingwell and Betty Lucas) and his wife (Wendy Hughes, right) in Paul Cox's outstanding Australian production *My First Wife* (Artificial Eye).

Heather Langenkamp finds she is sharing her bathtub with something most unpleasant in Wes Craven's thriller *A Nightmare on Elm Street* (Palace Pictures).

Nehama Patkin, Megan Garner, Patrick Nolan; members of the Tudor Choristers (dir David Carolane). Dir and (with Bob Ellis) Screenplay and (with Jane Ballantyne) Pro: Paul Cox. Assoc Pro: Tony Llewellyn-Jones. Ph: Yuri Sokol. Ed: Tim Lewis. Art: Asher Bilu. M: Carl Orff and Christoph Willibald Gluck. (Made with the assistance of Film Victoria–Artificial Eye) Rel: floating; first shown London (Lumière and Chelsea Cinema), 1 August 1985. 97 mins. Cert 15.

The Mystery of Alexina – Mystère Alexina (The Alexina Mystery in USA). Well-made French reconstruction of a bizarre but true 18th-century case. A man's birth certificate, earliest upbringing and schooling all were based on his being female; however, when he seduced his pretty neighbour at the convent school for young ladies which he attended, he was finally revealed for what he was. This confirmation of his true gender comes too late: his early years condemn him to a twilight existence which ends with suicide. Cast: Philippe Vullemin, Valérie Stroh, Véronique Silver, Bernard Freyd, Marianne Basler, Pierre Vial, Philippe Clévenot, Isabelle Gruault, Lucienne Harmon, Michel Amphoux, Claude Bouchery, Oliver Sabran, Vincent Pinel, Anne Cornaly, Paul Descombes. Dir and Pro: René Féret. Screenplay: Féret and Jean Gruault; based on the *Memoirs of Adelaide Herculine Barbin.* Ph: Bernard Zitzermann. Ed: Ariane Boeglin. Art: George Stoll. M: Anne-Marie Deschamps. (Cinéastes Assoc/TF1 Films–Electric Pictures) Rel: floating; first shown London (Everyman, 23 May 1986. 83 mins. No cert.

A Nightmare on Elm Street. Interesting and promisingly original supernatural thriller about a killer with knives on his fingers who haunts the dreams of some Los Angeles teenagers and then emerges into reality to carry out a series of killings. The way in which dreams and reality are mixed into one spine-chilling whole is disturbingly brilliant. The reason for this haunting finally emerges from history, for a child-killer in the district had been effectively dealt with by the local vigilantes. Cast: John Saxon, Ronee Blakley, Heather Langenkamp, Amanda Wyss, Nick Corri, Johnny Depp, Robert Englund, Charles Fleischer, Joseph Whipp, Lin Shaye, Joe Unger, Mimi Meyer-Craven, Jack Shea, Ed Call, Sandy Lipton, David Andrews, Jeffrey Levine, Donna Woodrum, Shaskawnee Hall, Carole Pritkin, Brian Reise, Jason Adams, Don Hannah, Leslie Hoffman, Paul Grenier. Dir and Screenplay: Wes Craven. Pro: Robert Shaye. Ex Pro: Stanley Dudelson and Joseph Wolf. Co-Pro: Sara Risher. Ph: Jacques Haitkin. Ed: Rick Shaine. Pro Des: Greg Fonseca. M: Charles Bernstein. (New Line/Media Home Entertainment/Smart Egg Pictures–Palace Pictures) Rel: 27 September 1985. 92 mins. Cert 18.

9½ Weeks. Overlong, slow and pornish picture of physical obsession, not helped by the two unsympathetic leading characters: obsessed, Kim Basinger; and obsessor, Mickey Rourke (doesn't he like or can't he afford a razor?). A pale shadow of *Last Tango in Paris*. Rest of cast: Margaret Whitton,

The dangerous, increasingly obsessive passion between Kim Basinger and Mickey Rourke that lasts for *9½ Weeks* in the Palace Pictures release of that title.

David Margulies, Christine Baranski, Karen Young, William de Acutis, Dwight Weist, Roderick Cook, Victor Truro, Justine Johnston, Cintia Cruz, Kim Chan, Lee Lai Sing, Rudolph Willrich, Helen Hanft, Michael P. Moran, Raynor Scheine, Olek Krupa, Michael Margotta, Julian Beck, John P. Connolly, Cassandra Danz, Beata Jachulski, Peter Pagan, Terri Perri, Charles Malota, Daniel E. Amrich, Salvatore Sciangula, Ellen Barber, Kim Michel, Jeff Severson, Dan Lauria, Corey Parker, Joe Maruzzo, Tom Traino, Corvova Choy Lee, Ethel Ayler, Elisabeth Senn, Gittan Goding, David Everard, Luther Rucker, Joey Silvera, Petina Cole, Marry Clayton, Kim Issacson, Sarah Kernochan, David Tabor. Dir: Adrian Lyne. Pro: Anthony Rufus Isaacs and Zalman King. Ex Pro: Keith Barish and Frank Konigsberg. Co-Ex Pro: Richard Northcott. Ex in charge of Pro: R. E. Relyea. Assoc Pro: Steven D. Reuther and Stephen J. Ross. Screenplay: Patricia Knop, Zalman King and Sarah Kernochan; based on the novel by Elizabeth McNeill. Ph: Peter Biziou. Ed: Caroline Biggerstaff and Tom Rolf. Pro Des: Ken Davis. Art: Linda Conaway-Pavsloe. M: Jack Nitzsche. (Producers Sales Org./Sidney Kimmel–Palace Pictures) Rel: 6 June 1986. 116 mins. Cert 18.

Nineteen Nineteen. Obviously made for the small screen (and more suitable for that medium), this intimate, chamber piece concerns two ex-patients of Sigmund Freud (Vienna, 1919) who meet in the city in 1970 and discuss their psychological problems, and what might have been: she a father-hating, sadly unfulfilled lesbian, and he a man who desires women that he cannot love but cannot desire the woman that he does love – a fictional extension of a factual base. A thoughtful, intelligent movie graced by the two magnificent performances of Paul Scofield and Maria Schell. Rest of cast: Frank Finlay (the voice of Freud), Diana Quick, Clare Higgins, Colin Firth, Sandra Berkin, Jacqueline Dankworth, Alan Tilvern, Christopher Lahr, Bridget Amies, Christine Hargreaves, Ronald Nunnery, Willy Bowman, Annet Peters, Keith Kraushaar, Norman Chancer. Dir: Hugh Brody. Pro: Nita Amy. Ex Pro: Peter Sainsbury. Screenplay: Brody and Michael Ignatieff. Ph: Ivan Strasburg. Ed: David Gladwell. Art: Caroline Amies. M: Brian Gascoigne. (BFI in assoc with Channel 4 Television) Rel: floating; first shown London (Curzon, Mayfair), 6 December 1985. 99 mins. Cert 15.

Two outstanding performances, from Paul Scofield and Maria Schell, as ex-patients of (the heard but not seen) Sigmund Freud in the BFI film *Nineteen Nineteen.*

No Surrender. A, by turns, funny, bleak, black, cruel and, more than once, downright off-putting minor-budgeted British film bristling with new and promising talent. Set on the seamier side of Liverpool, it is mainly –

Ex-Ulster terrorist Billy (Ray McAnally) with his unwelcome guest (on-the-run Norman – Mark Mulholland) in Palace Pictures' *No Surrender.* Inset, Michael Angelis as the new manager of seedy Liverpool nightclub who finds more than he bargained for during his first night on duty.

though not entirely – about the fiercely divided Irish factions of the city, seen in a story about the newly appointed manager of a seedy nightclub who arrives to find his predecessor being tortured in the backroom by the club's gangster boss, and has to face up to the deliberate triple booking of the club to Catholic, Protestant and far-gone geriatric groups. A mixed bag of a movie, with good and bad well shaken together to produce at least a very interesting example of low-budget moviemaking. Fine performances by Michael Angelish as the tyro manager and Mark Mulholland as the ex-terrorist forced to hide – and then murder – an old comrade on the run. In view of some of the dialogue, subtitles would have been an asset! The film won the critics' award at the 1985 Toronto Film Festival. Rest of cast: Avis Bunnage, James Ellis, Tom Georgeson, Bernard Hill, Ray McAnally, Joanne Whalley, J. G. Devlin, Vince Earl, Ken Jones, Michael Ripper, Marjorie Sudell, Joan Turner, Richard Alexander, Pamela Austin, Ina Clough, Paul Codman, Paul Connor, Elvis Costello, James Culshaw, Gabrielle Daye, David Doyle, Lovette Edwards, Gerry Fogarty, Harry Goodier, Eric Granville, Robert Hamilton, Ian Hart, Gerard Hely, Joey Kaye, Vera Kelly, Phil Kernot, Al Kossy, Penny Leatherbarrow, Stephen Lloyd, Joe McGann, Mark McGann, Johnny Mallon, Ron Metcalf, Bill Moores, Robert Nield, Doc O'Brien, Steve O'Connor, Peter Price, Christopher Quinn, Helen Rhodes, Linus Roache, Tony Rohr, Tommy Ryan, Andrew Schofield, Tony Scoggo, Mabel Seward, Georgina Smith, Arthur Spreckley, Mike Starke, Frank Vincent, Eileen Walsh, Harry Webster, Gerry White, Dean Williams, Peter Wilson. Dir: Peter Smith. Pro: Mamoun Hassan. Ex Pro: Michael Peacock. Assoc Pro: Clive Reed. Screenplay: Alan Bleasdale. Ph: Mick Coulter. Ed: Rodney Holland. Sup Ed: Kevin Brownlow. Pro Des: Andrew Mollo. M: Daryl Runswick (song: 'We're Gonna Die', music and lyrics by Andrew Schofield). (Dumbarton Films in assoc with National Film Finance Corp, Film Four International and William Johnston/Ronald Lillie Lauron International Inc.–Palace Pictures) Rel: floating; first shown London (Odeon, Haymarket), 28 March 1986. 104 mins. Cert 15.

The Official Version – La Historia Oficial. Made in Buenos Aires in three months (April–June 1984), this Argentinian political drama deals with the infamous baby racket during the time of the military *junta*, whereby the babies born to pregnant 'vanished' women were sold off to supporters of the army dictatorship. In this case, a mother begins to suspect that her adopted baby, beloved by her increasingly worried businessman husband (as he sees the régime ending), is one of these children and sets out to find the bitter truth. All is boldly and accusingly spelt out in sometimes highly dramatic terms. Cast: Héctor Alterio, Norma Aleandro, Hugo Arana, Guillermo Battaglia, Chela Ruiz, Patricio Contreras, Anibal Morixe, Maria Luisa Robledo, Jorge Petraglia, Analia Castro, Chunchuna Villafane, Daniel Lago, Augusto Larreta, Laura Palmucci, Leal Rey, Floria Bloise. Dir: Luis Puenzo. Pro: Marecelo Pineyro. Screenplay: Puenzo and Aida Bortnik. Ph: Félix Monti. Ed: Juan Carlo Macias. Art: Abel Facello. M: Atilio Stampone (song: 'In the County I Don't Remember', by Maria Elena Walsh). (Virgin Films) Rel: floating; first shown London (Curzon, West End), 20 September 1985. 112 mins. Cert 15.

Orion's Belt – Orion's Belte. The most expensive Norwegian film to date turns out to be a first-rate thriller with a sting in the tail, revealing the ruthlessness of national and international diplomacy (that 'sting' having quite a bit in common with the British film *Defence of the Realm*). It is about a trio of tough characters who, when a storm sends their ship off course, stumble on to a secret Soviet station on a Norwegian island. Two are killed by the Soviets; the third makes his way through the wastelands to home, and is then whisked off to Oslo and the authorities, who make dead certain that the story shall not leak out. Cast: Helge Jordal, Sverre Anker Ousdal, Hans Ola Sørlie, Kjersti Holmen, Vidar Sandem, Nils Johnson, Jon Eikimo, Johan Sverre, Jan Harstad, Holger Vistisen, Erik Øksnes, Bjørg Telstad, John Ousland, Jarl E. Goli. Tor Stokke, Jarl Staernes, Knut Ørvig, Steve Plytas, Steiner Danielsen, Eli Lundaas, etc. Dir: Ola Solum. Pro: Dag Alveberg and Petter Borgli. Screenplay: Richard Harris; based on the book by Jon Michelet. Ph: Harald Paalgard. Ed: Bjørn Breigutu. Pro Des: Harald Egede-Nissen. M: Geir Bøhren and Bent Aserud. (Filmeffekt a/S Pro–Enterprise Pictures) Rel: floating; first shown London (Cannon Classics, Tottenham Court Road and Chelsea), 10 January 1986. 92 mins. Cert 15.

The Outcasts. Strange mixture of reality and fantasy in a well-handled Irish film about a widower and his three daughters in 19th-century Ireland, one of the trio imagining herself to be a witch but is shocked when a wandering fiddler initiates her into his 'otherworld'. Cast: Mary Ryan, Mick Lally, Don Foley, Tom Jordan, Cyril Cusack, Brenda Scallon, Bairbre ni Chaoimh, Mairtin O'Flathearta, Brendan Ellis, Gillian Hackett, Hilary Reynolds, Donal O'Kelly, James Shanahan, Paul Bennett. Dir and Screenplay: Robert Wynne-Simmons. Pro: Tony Dollard (manager). Ph: Seamus Corcoran. Ed: Arthur Keating. Pro Des: Bertram Tyrer. M: Stephen Cooney. (Tolmyax Co. with assistance of Bord Scannan na hEireann and Channel 4–Cinegate) Rel: floating; first shown London (Gate, Bloomsbury), 3 October 1985. 100 mins. Cert 15.

Out of Africa. Long, lovely and decidedly leisurely adaptation of a true and romantically unhappy story about a rich Danish lady (Meryl Streep) who marries a Swedish count (Klaus Maria Brandauer) – her money for his title – and accompanies him to Kenya to set up a coffee plantation there and, without his help (all that he gives her is his friendship and syphilis), makes it a success. Then comes romance with a white hunter played by Robert Redford – who gives the film much of its strength and reality as well as its sad ending. Rest of cast: Michael Kitchen, Malick Bowens, Joseph Thiaka, Stephen Kinyanjui, Michael Gough, Suzanna Hamilton, Rachel Kempson, Graham Crowden, Leslie Phillips, Shane Rimmer, Mike Bugara, Job Seda, Mohammed Umar, Donal McCann, Kenneth Mason, Tristram Jellinek, Stephen Grimes, Annabel Maule, Benny Young, Sbish Trzebinski, Allaudin Qureshi, Niven Boyd, Iman, Peter Strong, Abdullah Sunado, Amanda Parkin, Muriel Gross, Ann Palmer, Keith Pearson. Dir and Pro:

Meryl Streep as the Danish lady who starts a coffee plantation in Africa and, on becoming successful, grows to love the country and its people in Mirage/UIP's seven-Oscar-winning *Out of Africa*. Right, Robert Redford as the lover who will not be tied down.

Sydney Pollack. Co-Pro: Terence Clegg. Ex Pro: Kim Jorgensen. Assoc Pro: Judith Thurman and Anna Cataldi. Screenplay: Kurt Luedtke; based on *Out of Africa* and other writings by Isak Dinesen (Karen Blixen), *Isak Dinesen: The Life of a Storyteller* by Judith Thurman and *Silence Will Speak* by Errol Trzebinski. Ph: David Watkin. Ed: Fredric and William Steinkamp, Pembroke Herring and Sheldon Kahn. Pro Des: Stephen Grimes. M: John Barry. (Mirage–Universal–UIP) Rel: 21 March 1986. 161½mins. Cert PG.

Out of Order – Abwärts. Brilliantly sustained West German suspense thriller with a clever (if fairly incredible) story of what happens when a lift containing four people stops midway between floors and the night watchman fails to notice the breakdown lights flashing on his board. This causes all variety of tensions, physical struggles and thrills as the two younger men – foolishly – attempt to make repairs to the cage themselves, while the older man and the girl become terrified onlookers. Cast: Renée Soutendijk, Götz George, Wolfgang Kieling, Hannes Jaenicke, Kurt Raab, Jan Groth, Claus Wennemann, Ralph Richter, Ekmekyemez Firdevs, Hans Schwöfler. Dir and Screenplay: Carl Schenkel (additional dialogue by Frank Göhre); based on the book by Wilhelm Heynes. Pro: Thomas Schüly and Matthias Deyle. Ph: Jacques Steyn. Ed: Norbert Herzner. Art: Toni Lüdi. M: Jacques Zwart. (Laura Film/Mutoskop Film/ Maran Film/Dieter Geissler Filmproduktions–Virgin Films) Rel: floating; first shown London (Cannon, Panton Street), 28 February 1986. 88 mins. Cert 15.

Pale Rider. A welcome, and first-class, return to the recently neglected western, with director–producer–star Clint Eastwood combining the classic *Shane* formula with that of the *Man with No Name*, and getting the mixture just right. Eastwood plays the mysterious lone rider who interrupts his journey across the prairie long enough to aid a community of gold-miners fighting off ruthless land-grabbers and their hired killers. When he's killed off the baddies in a classic showdown (against incredible odds), it's back to the saddle in spite of the two grieving ladies he leaves behind. Lovely stuff – though the fine camera work does occasionally get too dark for comfort. Rest of cast: Michael Moriarty (a fine performance), Carrie Snodgress, Christopher Penn, Richard Dysart, Sydney Penny, Richard Kiel, Doug McGrath, John Russell, Charles Hallahan, Marvin J. McIntyre, Fran Ryan, Richard Hamilton, Graham Paul, Chuck Lafont, Jeffrey Weissman, Allen Keller, Tom Oglesby, Herman Poppe, Kathleen Wygle, Terrence Evans, Jim Hitson, Loren Adkins, Tom Friedkin, S. A. Griffin, Jack Radosta, Robert Winley, Billy Drago, Jeffrey Josephson, John Dennis Johnston, Lloyd Nelson, Jay K. Fishburn, George Orrison, Milton Murrill, Mike Munsey, Keith Dillin, Wayne Van

Left, quick-on-the-draw stranger, the *Pale Rider* (Clint Eastwood), sends the villain stumbling to his death in the Malpaso–Warner western film of that title. Above, a less violent scene with Michael Moriarty and Sydney Penny.

Horne, Fritz Manes, Glenn Wright. Dir and Pro: Clint Eastwood. Ex Pro: Fritz Manes. Assoc Pro: David Valdes. Screenplay: Michael Butler and Dennis Shryack. Ph: Bruce Surtees. Ed: Joel Cox. Pro Des: Edward Carfagno. M: Lennie Niehaus. (Malpaso–Warner) Rel: 4 October 1985. 115 mins. Cert 15.

Parade of the Planets – Parad Playnet. Strange little Soviet film with a quite unfathomable but fascinatingly dream-like story about a group of part-time soldiers who, when 'killed' during manoeuvres, wander off to find a town of lovely ladies, a deserted island, another town of sleepy old people . . . All very odd but endlessly intriguing. Cast: Oleg Borisov, Pyotr Zaichenko, Sergei Shakurov, Alexei Zharkov, Sergei Nikonenko, Alexander Pashutin. Dir: Vadim Abdashitov. Screenplay: Alexander Mindadze. Ph: Vladimir Shevisik. Art: Alexander Tolkachev. M: Vyacheslav Ganelin. (Mosfilm–The Other Cinema) Rel: floating; first shown London (Metro), 24 April 1986. 97 mins. No cert.

The Patsy – L'Addition. Grim and, at times, brutal French movie about a young actor who becomes involved with a pretty girl thief (who has taste – she only pinches caviar from supermarkets!) which leads to a punch-up with the cops and a short prison term. Innocently involved with an attempted jailbreak, he becomes the victim of a sadistic prison officer and finally has to commit murder to save his own life. Faced with the result, he uses his acting ability to escape, with the girl (who has fallen in love with him), to a dubious future on the run. Cast: Richard Berry, Richard Bohringer, Victoria Abril, Farid Chopel, Fabrice Eberhard, Daniel Sarky, Simon Reggiani, Jacques Sereys, Riton Liebman, Luc Florian. Dir: Denis Amar. Pro: Norbert Saada. Ex Pro: Pierre Tatischeff and Norbert Chalon. Screenplay: Amar, Jean-Pierre Bastid and Jean Curtelin. Ph: Robert Fraisse. Ed: Jacques Witta. Art: Serge Douy. M: Jean-Claude Petit. (Swanie Pro/TFI Film Pro/UGT–Top 1 Co-Pro–Cannon/Gala) Rel: floating; first shown London (Berkeley and Arts, Chelsea), 2 August 1985. 87 mins. Cert 18.

Peppermint Freedom – Peppermint Frieden. A subtle anti-war film from West Germany, which presents post-war history as seen through the eyes of a small girl, whose fears, fantasies and deep desire for peace reflect her interest and that of her small friends in the withheld and strange world of adults. Cast: Peter Fonda, Saskia Tyroller, Hans Brenner, Hans Peter Korff, Cleo Kretschmer, Elisabeth Neumann–Viertel, Gesine Strempel, Konstantin Wecker, Sigi Zimmerschied, Robby Spitz, Ute Hofinger, Beate Rose, Hubert Käser, Markus Reisinger, Ernst Klünner, Monika Fuchs, Christine Lang, Stephen Koerfer, Gideon Bachmann, Veronika von Quast, Cornelia Maué, Rolf Walter, Markus Weber, Sascha Kohmann, Gérard Samaan, Franz Tyroller, Traudi Müller–Nowotny, Michael Böger, Herta-Friedl Henckl, Günter Trober, Ronny Lang, etc. Dir and Screenplay: Marianne S. W. Rosenbaum. Ex Pro: Monica Aubele. Ph: Alfred Tichawsky. Ed: Gérard Samaan. M: Konstantin Wecker. (Nourfilm–The Other Cinema) Rel: floating; first shown London (Metro 1), 10 January 1986. 100 mins. Cert PG.

Perfect. John Travolta as a less than convincing *Rolling Stone* investigative reporter who, while preparing a far from complimentary story about the American health club boom, falls in love with aerobics teacher (Jamie Lee Curtis) and alters the tone of his highly critical piece, only for his editor (chubby, real life *Rolling Stone* editor, Jann Wenner) to thwart him and publish the original piece, which almost – but of course, not quite – ruins the romance! Overlong and, between the suggestive aerobic rock numbers, too slow and meandering as it wanders off into a complicated sub-plot. And either some of the cast missed their elocution lessons that week or the sound department were having an off-day; either way, some of the dialogue is hard to understand. Rest of cast: John Napierala, Ramey Ellis, Alma Beltran, Perla Walter, Gina Morelli, Stefan Gierasch, Anne De Salvo, Philippe Delgrange, Tom Schiller, Paul Kent, Murphy Dunne, Kenneth Welsh, Michael Laskin, Robert Stark, Laurie Burton, Ann Travolta, Nanette Pattee-Francini, Robin Samuel, Robert Parr, Rosalind Ingledew, Chelsea Field, Dan Lewk, Laraine Newman, Marilu Henner, Mathew Reed, Andrea Adams, Kurek Ashley, Paul Barresi, Leslie Borkin, Candy Ann Brown, Brent Carlton, Eileen Finney, Christian Letelier, Donna Perkins, Jill Schachne, Kai Maxwell, Kevin Boyle, Frank Cavestani, Brian Maguire, Elaine Perkins, Marlene Cramer, Bob Henry, Rick Avery, Chere Bryson, Carly Simon, Roger Menache, Charlene Jones, John Wesley, Mario Marin, Lee Nicholl, Stacy Bayne, Tracy Bayne, David Paymer, Julie Fulton, Ken Silk, Jim Vanko, Murphy Cross, Laura Owens, Beth Herzhaft, Anson Downes, Renée Tetro, Ronnie Claire Edwards, Joan Edwards, Sam Travolta, Clarke Wilson, Kim Connell, Kim Isaacson, Wendy Shawn, Dan Peterson, Doug Campbell, Gregory Hormel, Daniel Dayan, Annick Romain, Steven Solberg, Susan Burritt, John M. Kelly, Bruce Savin, Jean Lubin. Dir and Pro: James Bridges. Ex Pro: Kim Kurumada. Co-Pro: Jack Larson. Assoc Pro: Joan Edwards. Screenplay: Bridges and Aaron Latham; based on the latter's feature in *Rolling Stone*. Ph: Gordon Willis. Ed: Jeff Gourson. Pro Des: Michael Haller. Art: Lynda Paradise. M: Ralph Burton (score); Becky Manusco (supervisor). (Columbia) Rel: 13 September 1985. 120 mins. Cert 15.

Pigs. Minor Irish film originally shown at the 1984 London Film Festival and only now, in 1986, surfacing for a limited public run. A series of character sketches of a few diverse squatters (young drug-pusher, black pimp, gay jailbird and another fugitive from society who is off his trolley) living in a house in Dublin. And some promising talent is involved. Cast: Jimmy Brennan, George Shane, Maurice O'Donoghue, Liam Halligam, Kewsi Kay, Joan Harpur, etc. Dir: Cathal Black. Pro: David Collins. Ex Pro: Kevin Moriarty. Screenplay: Jimmy Brennan. Ph: Thaddeus O'Sullivan. Ed: Se Merry. Art: Frank Conway. M: Roger Doyle. (Samson Films/Irish Film Board–Ritzy) Rel: floating; first shown London (Ritzy), 20 March 1986. 79 mins. No cert.

The Pleasure – Il Piacere. In this case, the (Italian) pleasure is all erotic, understandably so since it is directed and photographed by Aristide Massaccesi, who was responsible for a lot of the spin-off *Emmanuelle* films. It all – the nudity, titillation and traumas – happens in 'thirties Venice. Cast: Steve Wyler, Laura Gemser, Isabelle Andrea Guzon, Marco Mattioli, Lillie Carati, Dagmar Lassander. Dir (under the name of Joe D'Amato) and Ph: Aristide Massaccesi. Pro Sup: Donatella Donati. Screenplay: H. S. Zweitag and Clyde Anderson. Ed: Franco Alessandri. Art: Italo Focacci. M: Cluster. (Filmirage–Elephant Entertainment) Rel: floating; first shown London (several Cannon cinemas), 2 May 1986. 91 mins. Cert 18.

Investigative reporter John Travolta discusses his assignment with his photographer (Anne De Salvo) and his 'Rolling Stone' boss (Jann Wenner – the journal's actual editor, left) in *Perfect* (Columbia).

Plenty. A very angry and pessimistic view of Britain past, present and future, presented by David Hare (in a screen adaptation of his stage play) and projected through the central character: an utterly selfish, bitter, destructive and, finally, mentally unstable young woman, who had her finest hour as a member of the French Resistance, and whose dreams of a postwar heaven are

Meryl Streep embarrasses her diplomat husband Charles Dance (second from left) and their guests, including the urbane F.O. boss (John Gielgud) in the RKO Radio/Thorn EMI release *Plenty*.

smashed by postwar reality. The episodic story isn't always that easy to follow or even understand – a minus to be set against a very big plus of some wonderful performances (especially by Meryl Streep in the central role, and John Gielgud as the urbane but acid-tongued F.O. boss), polished production and some fine dialogue. Rest of cast: André Maranne, Sam Neill, Charles Dance, Tracey Ullman, Ian Wallace, Sting, Bert Kwouk, Pik Sen Lim, Ian McKellen, Tristram Jellinek, Peter Forbes-Robertson, Hugh de Vernier, James Taylor, Andy de la Tour, Hugh Laurie, Mitch Davies, Christopher Fairbank, Lindsay Ingram, Richard Hope, Roddy Maud-Roxby, Andrew Seear, Roger Rowland, John Kidd, James Snell, Michael Johnson, Bernard Brown, Rupert Vansittart, Beth Morris, Geoffrey Larder, Tim Seely, Jasper Jacob, Karen Lewis, Nicholas Frankau, Clare McIntyre, Ali Refaie, William Hoyland, Roger Ashton-Griffiths, Jeffry Wickham, Alexander John, Matthew Guinness, John Rees, Lyndon Brook, Joan Blackham, John Serret, Terry Lightfoot and his band. Dir: Fred Schepisi. Pro: Edward R. Pressman and Joseph Papp. Ex Pro: Mark Seiler. Screenplay: David Hare; based on his stage play. Assoc. Pro: Roy Stevens. Ph: Ian Baker. Ed: Peter Honess. Pro Des: Richard MacDonald. M: Bruce Smeaton. (RKO Pictures–Thorn EMI) Rel: 7 March 1986. 124 mins. Cert 15.

Police. An oddball cops-and-crooks movie from France which kicks off at a great pace with the hectic, fairly rough and certainly tough routine of a Paris police station, and then winds down as it drifts into the personal psychological problems and romance of one cop with a crook's mistress. And though the picture on the screen shows the difficulties they had with the story and script, there's plenty left to keep one attentive. A typical strong, rough-diamond performance by Gerard Depardieu as the hard-shelled, soft-centred detective. Rest of cast: Sophie Marceau, Richard Anconina, Pascale Rocard, Sandrine Bonnaire, Frank Karoui, Jonathan Leina, Jacques Mathou, Bernard Fuzellier, Meaachou Bentahar, Mohamed Ayari, Abdel Kader Touati, Jamil Bouarada, Bechir Idani, Sylvain Maupu, Alain Artur, Remi Carpentier, Taya Ouzrout, Jocelyn Persillet, Lofti Chouaiekh, Kadija Smaali, Maaike Jansen, Catherine le Nevez, Didier Creste, Yann Dedet, Gil Noir, Miguelle Monthieux, Antonio Cauchoix, Germaine Lièvre, Marie-Josephe Dunand, Dimitri Melsan, Henri Plesse, Driss Kadiri, Maurice Coussonneaux, Gerard Dauzat, Frederic Fabre, Philippe Loffredo, François Pancrazi, Alain Payen, Artus de Penguern, Frank Saillour, Dir: Maurice Pialat. Pro: Emmanuel Schlumberger. Pro Dir: Jean-Claude Bourlat. Screenplay: Pialat, Catherine Breillat, Sylvie Danton and Jacques Fieschi; based on an idea by Breillat. Ph: Luciano Tovoli. Ed: Yann Dedet, Helene Viard and Nathalie Letrosne. Art: Constantin Mejinsky. M: Henryk Mikolaj Gorecki. (Gaumont/TFI–Artificial Eye) Rel: floating; first shown London (Lumière, Renoir and Cannon, Chelsea), 13 June 1986. 113 mins. Cert 15.

Police Academy II: Their First Assignment. After earning something in the region of £30 million for its makers, *Police Academy* inevitably inspired this sequel, which almost as inevitably, is well below the original in most departments. Best asset of *PAII* is cast-newcomer Art Metrano as the cop 'lootenant' who hardly endears himself to his men as they fight the local punk gangs. Rest of cast: Steve Guttenberg, Bubba Smith, David Graf, Michael Winslow, Bruce Mahler, Marion Ramsey, Colleen Camp, Howard Hesseman, George Gaynes, Bob Goldthwait, Julie Brown, Peter van Norden, Tim Kazurinsky, Ed Herlihy, Sandy Ward, Lance Kinsey, Christopher Jackson, Church Ortiz, George R. Robertson, Arthur Batanides, Jackie Joseph, Andrew Paris, Monica Parker, Kenji Shintani, Jennifer Darling, Lucy Lee Flippin, Jason Hervey, Diana Bellamy, Julie Paris, Debra Dusay, Jim Boyce, Tim Haldeman, Bert Williams, Pamela Matteson, Bufort L. McClerkins Jr, Conrad Hurtt, William Yamadera, Morris Beers. Dir: Jerry Paris. Pro: Paul Maslansky. Ed Pro: John Goldwyn. Co Pro: Leonard Kroll. Screenplay: Barry Blaustein and David Sheffield. Ph: James Crabe. Ed: Bob Wyman. Pro Des: Trevor Williams. M: Robert Folk. (Ladd Co–Warner) Rel: 19 July 1985. 87 mins. Cert PG.

Porky's Revenge. With the two previous *Porky* films having made more than $70 million in the US, it wasn't likely that the recipe would be greatly altered for this third one, though repetition makes for less impact. It concerns a plot by Angel High School scholars (*sic*) to avenge their previous humiliation by Porky, and carrying it out in the same crude, rude way they do everything else at this hardly esteemed seat of learning. Cast: Dan Monahan, Wyatt Knight, Tony Ganios, Mark Herrier, Kaki Hunter, Scott Colomby, Nancy Parsons, Chuck Mitchell. Dir: James Komack. Pro: Robert L. Rose. Ex Pro: Melvin Simon and Milton Goldstein. Screenplay: Ziggy Steinberg. Ph: Robert Jessop. Ed: John W. Wheeler. Pro Des: Peter Wooley. M: Dave Edmonds. (Astral–Fox) Rel: 5 July 1985. 91 mins. Cert 18.

The Princess – Adj Kiraly Katonat! A generally joyless, overlong Hungarian film (made, suitably enough, in black-and-white) about a 16-year-old provincial school-leaver who leaves her foster-parents to take up a job – hard, monotonous and ill-paid – in a Budapest textile mill, taking the opportunity to visit her real and obviously uncaring mother (a disastrous confrontation). Becoming pregnant, the girl is raped by two of her lover's friends and has a state abortion. Taking her girlfriend's unwanted baby, she cares for the child with fierce, instinctive maternal joy – until the true mother turns up and, breaking her promise, demands the return of the child. This film was the winner of the Golden Camera Award at Cannes and the Golden Leopard/Grand Prix at Locarno, both in 1982. Cast: Erika Ozsda, Andrea Szendrei, Denes Diczhazy, Arpad Toth, Juli Nyako, Lajos Soltis. Dir: Pal Erdöss. Screenplay: István Kardos. Ph: Lajos Koltai, Ferenc Pap and Gabor Szabo. No other credits listed. (Mafilm–Tarasulas Studio, Budapest) Rel: floating; first shown London (Gate, Bloomsbury), 11 July 1985. 113 mins. Cert 18.

Prizzi's Honor. John Huston's brilliant variation on the *Godfather* theme, giving it a touch of bitter black comedy and ornamenting it with some outstanding performances, notably by Jack Nicholson as the Mafia Prizzi family's top hit man, and Kathleen Turner as the girl he falls violently in love with, marries and then finds she is in the same line of murderous business as

Left, Jack Nicholson and Kathleen Turner, the loving married couple employed to kill each other by the Godfathers (above, left to right Robert Loggia, Lee Richardson and William Hickey), in John Huston's *Prizzi's Honor* (Rank Film Dist.).

himself, and, moreover, has been hired to murder him! The Prizzi 'family' itself would give the Borgias a good run for their money when it comes to sheer, callous villainy. Even if the film didn't become quite the most commercially successful of its year, it is certainly one of the artistically best. Rest of cast: Robert Loggia, John Randolph, William Hickey, Lee Richardson, Michael Lombard, Anjelica Huston, George Santopietro, Lawrence Tierney, C. C. H. Pounder, Ann Selepegno, Vic Polizos, Dick O'Neill, Sully Boyar, Antonia Vasquez, Tomasino Baratta, John Calvani, Murray Staff, Joseph Ruskin, Ray Serra, Seth Allen, Dominic Barto, Teddi Siddall, Tom Signorelli, Raymond Iannicelli, Stanley Tucci, Themi Sapountzakis, Debra Kelly, Scott Campbell, Beth Raines, Michael Sabin, Michael Tuck, Michael Fischetti, Kenneth Cervi, Marlene Williams, Joe Copmar, Eramus Alfano, Peter D'Arcy, Thomas Lomonaco, Bill Brecht, Enzo Citarelli, Theodore Theoharous, John Codiglia, Henty Fehren, Alexandra Ivanoff, Skip O'Brien, J. L. Arland, Reuban Gonzalez, Luis Accinelli, Danielle Frederick. Dir: John Huston. Pro: John Foreman. Ex in charge of Pro: Herb Jellinek, Pro Assoc: Laila Nabulsi. Pro Ex: D. L. Judd II. Screenplay: Richard Condon and Janet Roach; based on the former's novel. Ph: Andrzej Bartkowiak. Ed: Rudi and Kaja Fehr. Pro Des: Dennis Washington. M: Alex North. (ABC Motion Pictures–Rank Film Dist.) Rel: 15 November 1985. 129 mins. Cert 15.

The Protector. Sizzling all-out action film from Golden Harvest's Hong Kong studios, with plenty of chances for Jackie Chan to show lots of box-office promise with his athletic and acrobatic powers and sense of fun. Rest of cast: Danny Aiello, Roy Chiao, Victor Arnold, Kim Bass, Richard Clarke, Saun Ellis, Ronan O'Casey, Bill Wallace. Dir and Screenplay: James Glickenhaus. Pro: David Chan. Ex Pro: Raymond Chow. Ph: Mark Irwin. Ed: Evan Lottman. Art: W. F. De Seta and Oliver Wong. M: Ken Thorne. (Golden Harvest–Warner) Rel: 13 June 1986. 95 mins. Cert 18.

Pumping Iron II: The Women. George Butler's follow-up to his first *Pumping Iron* documentary about body-building, the movie that launched strongman Schwarzenegger to stardom. Now Butler takes a look at female body-worshippers and manages to make a merry movie out of the cult. Cast: Lori Bowen, Carla Dunlap, Bev Francis, Rachel McLish, Kris Alexander, Lydia Cheng, Steve Michalik, Steve Weinberger, Randy Rice, Tina Plakinger. Dir and Pro: George Butler. Ex Pro: Bernard Heng and Lawrence Chong. Co-ord Pro: John Hoffman. Co-Pro: Craig Berry. Screenplay: Butler and Charles Gaines; based on their book *Pumping Iron II: The Unprecedented Women*. Ph: Dyanna Taylor. Ed: Paul Barnes, Susan Crutcher and Jane Curson. M: David McHugh and Michael Montes. (Cinecom International/Pumping Iron/ White Mountain films in assoc with Gym Tech USA–Bat Belle Productions–Blue Dolphin Films) Rel: floating; first shown London (Classics, Oxford Street and Charing Cross Road), 29 November 1985. 107 mins. No cert.

The Purple Rose of Cairo. Easily the cleverest and most consistently witty, and funny of Woody Allen's movies to date, without any hint of the self-indulgence and intellectual pretentiousness which crept into some of his past productions. A celluloid film star falls in love with one of his most fervent fans, and steps out of the screen into the auditorium to woo her – to the consternation and confusion of the other actors on the screen (not to men-

Milo O'Shea, Deborah Rush, John Wood and on-and-off-screen hero Edward Herrman peer out of the picture at the audience in Woody Allen's comedy *The Purple Rose of Cairo* (Orion–Rank). And in this other scene (inset) mixing celluloid and real-life characters you may spot yesteryear's star Van Johnson (second from left).

tion the cinema's manager), who are left to stand around arguing and waiting for his return so that they can carry on with the movie! It's a totally unexpected and unique 'strike', which sends the movie moguls into a panic in case the revolt spreads to other cinemas and other films. A mad situation, handled with both wit and skill in the writing and directing, and a mental agility which makes sense out of nonsense. Jeff Daniels is superb in the twin roles of the celluloid figure with a mind of his own and the actor who created him, who sees his *alter ego* ruining his chances of stepping up to stardom. These are matched by Mia Farrow's performance as the fan who, literally, steps into the picture. A major comedy movie gem. Rest of cast: Danny Aiello, Irving Metzman, Stephanie Farrow, David Kieserman, Elaine Grollman, Victoria Zussin, Mark Hammond, Wade Barnes, Joseph G. Graham, Don Quigley, Maurice Brenner, Paul Herman, Rick Petrucelli, Peter Castellotti, Milton Seaman, Mimi Weddell, Tom Degidon, Mary Hedahl, Ed Herrmann, John Wood, Deborah Rush, Van Johnson (how good to see him on the screen again), Zoe Caldwell, Eugene Anthony, Ebb Miller, Karen Akers, Annie Jo Edwards, Milo O'Shea, Peter McRobbie, Camille Saviola, Juliana Donald, Dianne Wiest, Margaret Thompson, George Hamlin, Helen Hanft, Leo Postrel, Helen Miller, George Martin, Crystal Field, Ken Champin, Robert Trebor, Benjamin Rayson, Jean Shevlin, Albert S. Bennett, Martha Sherrill, Gretchen MacLane, Edwin Bordo, Andrew Murphy, Thomas Kubiak, Alexander Cohen, John Rothman, Raymond Serra, George J. Manos, David Tice, James Lynch, Sydney Blake, Michael Tucker, Peter Von Berg, David Weber, Glenne Headley, Willie Tjan, Lela Ivey, Drinda La Lumia, Loretta Tupper. Dir and Screenplay: Woody Allen. Pro: Robert Greenhut. Ex Pro: Charles H. Joffe. Assoc Pro: Michael Peyser and Gail Sicilia. Ph: Gordon Willis, Ed: Susan E. Morse. Pro Des: Stuart Wertzel. Art: Edward Pisoni. M: Dick Hyman. (Jack Rollins and Charles H. Joffe/ Orion–Rank Film Dist.) Rel: 30 July 1985. 82 mins. Cert PG.

Queen Kelly. A sparkling new (monochrome) print of the incompleted 1928 silent movie which marked the climax and end of Erich von Stroheim's controversial directing career, the opening reels showing him for the great master that he was, and the later ones his weaknesses. It concerns a mad German queen (Seena Owen), her princely husband-to-be (Walter Byron) and the little convent girl (Gloria Swanson) who loses her panties, her innocence and her heart to him in that order. This is the most complete version (and the nearest to Stroheim's scenario) of the several that have been shown (or constructed but not shown generally) through the years, and includes various amounts of footage – sometimes quite considerable – that have been discovered from time to time, though this 'final' print represents less than a third of the movie that Stroheim had planned. A remarkable and fascinating glimpse of the art of the silent film, and the brilliance of the director. Rest of cast: Madge Hunt, Florence Gibson, Tully Marshall, Wilhelm von Brincken, Wilson Benge, Sidney Bracey. Dir and Screenplay: Erich von Stroheim. Pro: Gloria Swanson. Ph: Gordon Pollock and Paul Ivano. Ed: Viola Lawrence. Art: Harold Miles. M: Adolph Tandler. (Kino International–Contemporary) Rel: floating; first shown London (Everyman), 20 September 1985. 99 mins. Cert PG.

The Quiet Earth. Another film from New Zealand which indicates that that country is now following closely behind Australia as a producer of superior movies: an imaginative, technically highly polished and assured film about a scientific experiment that goes horribly wrong, leaving one of those who had been involved in it thinking he is the last man left on Earth (though in fact another man and a woman turn up later), with all material things having remained intact. The obvious holes in this yarn have been expertly papered over by the excellent direction and first-rate performances. Cast: Bruno Lawrence, Alison Routledge, Peter Smith, Anzac Wallace, Norman Fletcher, Tom Hyde. Dir: Geoff Murphy. Pro: Don Reynolds and Sam Pillsbury. Screenplay: Pillsbury, Bill Baer and Bruno Lawrence; based on the novel by Craig Harrison. Ph: James Bartle. Ed: Michael Horton. Pro Des: Josephine Ford. Art: Rick Kofoed. M: John Charles. (Cinepro/Pillsbury Film Pro-Cannon) Rel: floating; first shown London (Première and Cannon, Oxford Street), 7 February 1986. 91 mins. Cert 15.

Sylvester Stallone as the one-man army, with pretty helpmate Julie Nickson, fighting the jungle and some nasty Vietnamese in *Rambo – First Blood Part II* (Thorn EMI).

Rambo – First Blood Part II. Continuation of the hectic life story of one-man-army Rambo, the fighting machine honed in the Vietnam war. This time, after his brush with the civil

Gloria Swanson and Walter Byron as the lovers in the 1928 movie *Queen Kelly*, revived with a sparkling new print for a 1985 re-release by Contemporary Films.

Bruno Lawrence comes to terms with the apparent fact he's the only human being left on earth in Cannon's imaginative movie from New Zealand, *The Quiet Earth*.

authorities leading to (in *First Blood*) a hard-labour sentence, he is offered a free pardon if he'll return, undercover, to Vietnam and search out the true answer to the legend (which does, in fact, exist in the US) that GI POWs are still held, hidden deep in the jungles. With arrows unlimited, a serrated shark's-tooth knife and various weapons salvaged from his dead enemies, plus a body impervious to burning, torture, electric shocks and all else, Rambo makes the myth reality and brings back the living proof in a stolen Soviet helicopter. All very brutal, bloody, body-strewn and incredible – but exciting enough to make the movie a great moneyspinner. But it leaves a nasty after-taste. Cast: Sylvester Stallone, Richard Crenna, Julie Nickson, Charles Napier, Steven Berkoff, Martin Kove, Andy Wood, George Kee Cheung, William Ghent, Vojo Goric, Dana Lee, Baoan Coleman, Steve Williams, Don Collins, Chris Grant, John Sterlini, Alain Hocquenghem, William Rothlein, Tony Munafo, Tom Gehrke. Dir: George P. Cosmatos. Pro: Buzz Feitshans. Ex Pro: Mario Kassar and Andre Vajna. Assoc Pro: Mel Dellar. Screenplay: Sylvester Stallone and James Cameron; from a story by Kevin Jarre, based on the characters created by David Morrell. Ph: Jack Cardiff. Ed: Mark Goldblatt and Mark Helfrich. Pro Des: Bill Kenney. M: Jerry Goldsmith. (Carolco–Thorn EMI) Rel: 30 July 1985. 96 mins. Cert 15.

A thrilling moment in the many-thrilled Australian movie *Razorback* (Thorn–EMI) which featured, among other things, a man-eating porker!

Ran. Visually gorgeous, stunningly stylish Kurosawa adaptation (and modification) of Shakespeare's *King Lear*, with a magnificent performance by Tatsuya Nakadai as Lord Ichimonji (Lear), whose decision to pass his crown to his eldest son on his 70th birthday leads to fraternal warring and double crossing which sends the old chap off his rocker and makes a large dent in the local population figures. The considerable battle scenes are among the finest of their kind ever staged for the screen. Among the fine supporting cast, Mieko Harada is memorable as the ruthless revenge-seeking Lady Kaeda who triggers off the bloodshed. A wonderfully photographed movie of classic proportions. Rest of cast: Satoshi Terao, Jinpachi Nezu, Daisuke Ryu, Peter, Hisashi Igawa, Masayuke Yui, Yoshiko Miyazaki, Akira Terao, Takeshi Nomura, etc. Dir: Akira Kurosawa. Pro: Matso Hara and Serge Silberman. Ex Pro: Katsumi Furukawa. Assoc Pro: Mataso Hara and Serge Silberman. dear little old lady (Katharine Hep- Masato Ide. Ph: Takao Saito and Masaharu Ueda. Ed: no credit. Pro Des: Yoshiro and Shinobu Muraki. M: Toru Takemitsu. (Franco-Japanese Co-Production/Greenwich Films SA/ Herald Act Inc./Nippon Herald Films Inc., Tokyo–Virgin Films) Rel: floating; first shown London (Curzon, West End, Gate and Screen-on-the-Hill), 7 March 1986. 160 mins. Cert 15. (*See also* entry for *A.K.*)

Tasia Valenza and Mario Van Peebles framed by Richie Abanes (left), Eriq la Salle and Melvin Plowden ('Fats', on right) in *Rappin'* a film featuring a new craze (Cannon).

Rappin'. A sort of follow-up to the same company's *Breakin' 1* and *2*, this quite sweet and often mildly amusing fairy-tale is set among a harmonic ethnic mixture living happily in a kind of Disney-ish ghetto in Pittsburgh where everything but the film stock is black and white, with the villains of any colour double-dyed and the heroes of all races a sparkling, snow-white. All about the whirlwind careers of two ex-jailbirds who, reformed by their incarceration, clean up their district, send the villains packing, win a recording contract, and girl, and squeeze in some trendyish 'rappin' interludes along the way. Cast: Mario Van Peebles, Tasia Valenza, Charles Flohe, Eriq La Salle, Kadeem Hardison, Richie Abanes, Leo O'Brien, Melvin Plowden, Harry Goz, Rony Clanton, Rutanya Alda, Edye Byrde, Ruth Jaroslow, Michael Esihos, Anthony Bishop, Fredric Mao, Brandi Freund, Debra Greenfield, David Butler, Scott Peck, Clayton Hill, Joe Schad, Joe Marmo, William Mott, Tommy Ross, Harry Scanlon, Anthony Bradberry, Don Brockett, Thomas Clint Clutter, Carl Fred Robinson. Dir: Joel Silberg. Pro: Menahem Golan and Yoram Globus. Pro Ex: Christopher

Pearce. Assoc Pro: Jeff Silver. Pro Co-Ord: Paula Connelly. Screenplay: Robert Litz and Adam Friedman. Ph: David Gurfinkel. Ed: Andy Horvitch and Bert Glatstein (additional editing: Daniel Wetherbee). Pro Des: Steve Miller. (Cannon Films–Cannon Film Dist.) Rel: floating; first shown London (Classic, Oxford Street) 23 August 1985. 92 mins. Cert PG.

Razorback. Australian horror/thriller about a man-eating pig, its victims and its ultimate fate of being sliced into rashers. Plenty of side-issues, such as the brutality of kangeroo-killing, the sad end of an animal rights campaigner and plenty of other murderous activity – all adding up to an unusual, off-putting picture of the less attractive side of Aussie life. Cast: Gregory Harrison, Arkie Whiteley, Bill Kerr, Chris Haywood, David Argue, Judy Morris, John Howard, John Ewart, Don Smith, Mervyn Drake, Redmond Phillips, Alan Beecher, Peter Schwartz, Beth Child, Rick Kennedy, Chris Hession, Brian Adams, Jinx Lootens, Angus Malone, Peter Boswell, Don Lane. Dir: Russell Mulcahy. Pro: Hal McElroy. Assoc Pro: Tim Sanders. Pro Co-Ord: Fiona McConaghy. Screenplay: Everett de Roche; based on the novel by Peter Brennan. Ph: Dean Semler. Ed: William Anderson. Pro Des: Bryce Walmsley. Art: Neil Angwin. M: Iva Davies. (Western Film Productions/UAA Film Presentation–Thorn EMI) Rel: 26 July 1985. 95 mins. Cert 18.

Re-Animator. Wryly funny, horrifically bloody, over-the-top thriller about the (on film) familiar potty scientist – in this case a young one – who, having succeeded in bringing a dead cat back to life, tries his serum, successfully, on a cadaver, only to find that he's got a killer on his hands. And the fun really begins when a severed head, which he has brought back to life, starts to make a play for a pretty damsel . . . ! Surely no need to go on? Cast: Jeffrey Combs, Bruce Abbott, Barbara Crampton, David Gale, Robert Sampson, Gerry Black, Carolyn Purdy-Gordon, Peter Kent, Barbara Pieters, Ian Patrick Williams, Bunny Summers, Al Berry, Derek Pendleton, Gene Scherer, James Ellis, James Earl Cathay, Hans Jonnason, Greg Rose, Annyce Holzman, Velvet Debois, Lawrence Lowe, Robert Holcomb, Mike Filloon, Greg Reid,

A 'restricted area', but that's about the only restriction in the Entertainment-released *Re-Animator*, which mixed a certain kind of comedy with lots of bloodcurdling and blood-letting activity.

Jack Draheim, Robert Pitzele, Kim Deitch, Stephen Kienzle, Lillian Avery, Grace Keller, Ed Brummett, Peter Martin, Jerry Thomas, Steve Frakes, Michael Muscal, Tom Reeves, Bruce Curtis, Bob Johnnene, Greg Robbins, Robert Veilleuz, Timothy White, Linda Adams, Donna Wilkie, Walter Sims, Donna Matson, Alana Anderson, Carol Thomas, Janice Sims, Donald Olsen, Eric Gartner, Frederic Gartner, Lavonda Lawson, Kevin Copeland, Teddy Haggarty, Ed Haggerty, Jeffrey Comstock, Carrie Shear, Ricky Woodard, Cathy Yuzna, Marta Goodfellow, Darryl Dick, Anna Coates, Lisa Girolami, Terri Lynn, Steve Knudsen, Stuart Dennis, Sara Curtis. Dir: Stuart Gordon. Pro: Brian Yuzna. Ex Pro: Michael Avery and Bruce Curtis. Assoc Pro: Bob Greenberg and Charles Donald Storey. Pro Ex: Dennis Murphy. Pro Co-Ord: Misty Carey. Screenplay: Dennis Paoli, W. J. Norris and Stuart Gordon; based on the story 'Herbert West – The Re-Animator' by H. P. Lovecraft. Ph: Mac Ahlberg and Stephen Sealy. Ed: Lee Percy. Art: R. A. Burns and Charles Nixon. M: Richard Band. (Re-Animator Productions–Entertainment) Rel: floating; first shown London (Odeon, Kensington, and Screen-on-the-Green), 17 January 1986. 84 mins. Cert 18.

Red Sonja. No, not the US/USSR espionage tale that the title might lead you to expect, but an often amusing fairy-tale about macho heroes and lovely ladies in distress. Arnold Schwarzenegger (the world's strongest man!) insists on helping the not-always-welcoming lady in red (Brigitte Nielsen) as she sets out to recover the magic talisman – so powerful it could end the world – from the hands of its present owner, the Evil Queen, and so achieve the double of saving the world and avenging her wronged sister . . . and it's actually quite good fun. Rest of cast: Sandahl Bergman, Paul Smith, Ernie Reyes Jr, Ronald Lacey, Pat Roach, Terry Richards, Janet Agren, Donna Osterbuhr, Lara Naszinsky, Hans Meyer, Francesca Romana Coluzzi, Stefano Mioni, Tutte Lemkow, Kiyoshi Yamazaki, Tad Horino. Dir: Richard Fleischer. Pro: Christian Ferry. Ex Pro: A. M. Lieberman. Assoc Pro: José Lopez Ropero. Screenplay: Clive Exton and George MacDonald Fraser; based on the stories of Robert E. Howard. Ph: Giuseppe Rotunno. Ed: Frank J. Urioste. Pro Des: Danilo Donati. Art: Giovanni Giovagnoni. M: Ennio Morricone. (MGM/UA–EMI) Rel: floating; first shown London (Film Centre), 18 October 1985). 88 mins. Cert PG.

Left, Remo (Fred Ward) dodges his murderous pursuers at the top of the Statue of Liberty in the Orion–Rank release *Remo – Unarmed and Dangerous* – in which Joel Grey (above) as a Korean mystic gives a remarkable performance.

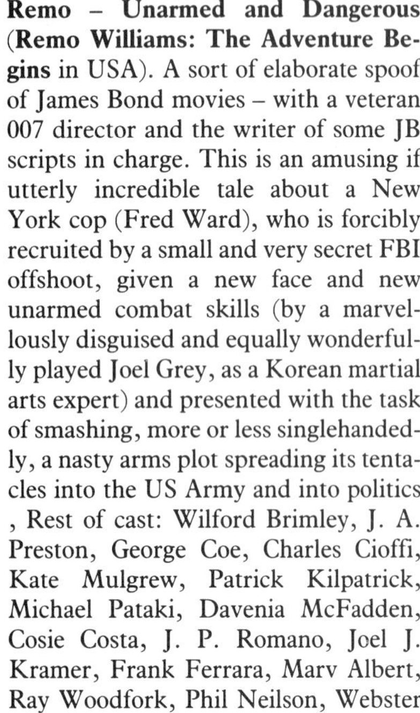

Remo – Unarmed and Dangerous (Remo Williams: The Adventure Begins in USA). A sort of elaborate spoof of James Bond movies – with a veteran 007 director and the writer of some JB scripts in charge. This is an amusing if utterly incredible tale about a New York cop (Fred Ward), who is forcibly recruited by a small and very secret FBI offshoot, given a new face and new unarmed combat skills (by a marvellously disguised and equally wonderfully played Joel Grey, as a Korean martial arts expert) and presented with the task of smashing, more or less singlehandedly, a nasty arms plot spreading its tentacles into the US Army and into politics , Rest of cast: Wilford Brimley, J. A. Preston, George Coe, Charles Cioffi, Kate Mulgrew, Patrick Kilpatrick, Michael Pataki, Davenia McFadden, Cosie Costa, J. P. Romano, Joel J. Kramer, Frank Ferrara, Marv Albert, Ray Woodfork, Phil Neilson, Webster Whinery, Frank Simpson, Dodi Kenan, Reginald Veljohnson, Jon Polito, Gene LeBell, Michael M. Ryan, Jeff Allin, Will Jeffries, Sebastian Ligarde, Roger Chudney, Duane B. Clark. John Christianson, Phil Culotta, Tom McBride, Andrew MacMillan, Wendy Gazelle, Suzy Snyder, William Hickey. Dir: Guy Hamilton. Pro: Larry Spiegel. Co-Pro: Judy Goldstein. Ex Pro: Dick Clark and Mel Bergman. Screenplay: Christopher Wood; based on *The Destroyer* series by Richard Sapir and Warren Murphy. Ph: Andrew Laszlo. Ed: Mark Melnick. Pro Des: Jackson De Govia. M: Graig Safan. (Orion–Rank Dist). Rel: 16 May 1986. 99 mins. Cert 15.

Restless Natives. Uneven comedy from Scotland with a rather weak story (but prize-winning script), based on the unlikely premise that American tourists visiting north of the border would be so tickled by a couple of youths on a motorbike in fancy dress who hold up coaches and steal the occupants' cash that they would flock to be fleeced in ever greater numbers! The Rob Roy-ish highwaymen are a couple of not-so-bright Edinburgh lads. And there needs to be total suspension of disbelief for audiences to try to swallow the climax. Cast: Vincent Friell and Joe Mullaney (the two lads), Bernard Hill, Ann Scott-Jones, Rachel Boyd, Iain McColl, Mel Smith, Bryan Forbes, Nanette Newman, Lawrie MacNicol, Neville Watchurst, Dave Anderson, Eiji Kusuhara, Sabu Kimura, Michael Stroud, Ed Bishop, Teri Lally, Ned Beatty, Robert Urquhart, Derek Starr, Peter Pringle, Laura Smith, Robin Brown, Irene Sunters, Frances Lonergan, Karen McCrary, Jean Faulds, Sally Kinghorn, Andrew Brown, Sharon MacKenzie, 'Big D', Jim Boyce, Margaret Robertson, Victoria Rutherford.

Two modern motor-cycle highwaymen (Vincent Friell and Joe Mullaney) escape the police net in the British comedy *Restless Natives* (Thorn–EMI) and then sit down (inset) to ponder their next move.

Dir: Michael Hoffman. Pro: Rick Stevenson. Ex Pro: Mark Bentley. Screenplay: Ninian Dunnett. Co-Pro: Andy Paterson. Assoc Pro: Paddy Higson. Ph: Oliver Stapleton. Ed: Sean Barton. Pro Des: Adrienne Atkinson. Art: Andy Harris. M: Stuart Adamson, performed by Big Country. (Oxford Film Co–Thorn EMI Screen Entertainment) Restricted rel: 5 July 1985. 89 mins. Cert PG.

The Return of the Living Dead. Presumably to be accepted as a horror movie spoof, and the outrageous 'preface' – 'The events portrayed in this film are all true. The names are real names or real people . . . – offers the clue. However, the film in spite of some witty asides and funny, over-the-top touches, is a pretty revolting business about a group of people fending off hordes of dead 'things' which, through a spillage of some mysterious military embalming fluid, rise from their graves eager for their only possible sustenance . . . living brains! Some foul language and nudity are tossed in for good measure. But the 'final solution' (after cops and soldiers have been chewed up by the dozen) means there can hardly be a sequel . . . or can there? Cast: Clu Gulager, James Karen, Don Calda, Thom Mathews, Beverly Randolph, John Philbin, Jewel Shepard, Miguel Nunez, Brian Peck, Linnea Quigley, Mark Venturini, Jonathan Terry, Cathleen Cordell, Drew Geighan, James Dalesandro, John Durbin, David Bond, Bob Libman, John Stuart West, Michael Crabtree, Ed Krieger, Robert Craighead, Paul Cloud, Derrick Brice, Leigh Drake, Terrence M. Houlihan, Allan Trautman, Robert Bennett, Jerome 'Daniels' Coleman, Cherry David. Dir and Screenplay: Dan O'Bannon; based on story by Rudy Ricci, John Russo and Russell Streiner. Pro: Tom Fox. Co-Pro: Graham Henderson. Ex Pro: John Daly and Derek Gibson. Ph: Jules Brenner. Ed: Robert Gordon. Pro Des: William Stout. Art: Robert Howland. M: Matt Clifford. (Hemdale/Fox Films/Tartan Films–

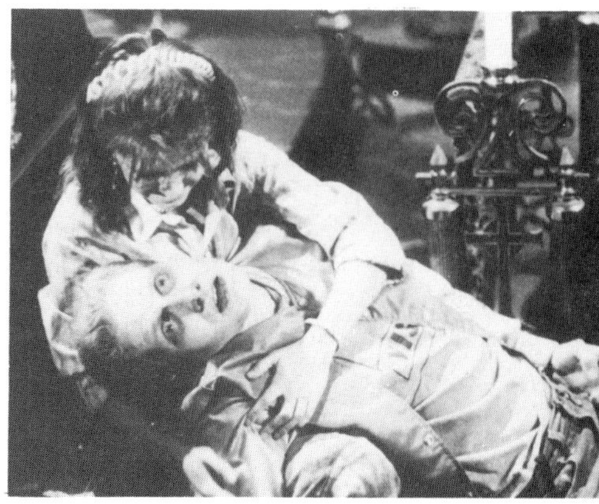

Tina (Beverly Randolph) doesn't care much for the look of her boyfriend (Thom Mathews) in the Blue Dolphin release *The Return of the Living Dead*.

Blue Dolphin) Rel: floating; first shown London (Several Cannon Cinemas), 21 March 1986. 91 mins. Cert 18.

Return to Oz. This 'return' to L. Frank Baum's magical land bears little relationship to the 1939 *The Wizard of Oz*, with its lack of infectious gaiety, humour and hummable musical num-

Above and inset, Fairuza Balk as Dorothy in *Return to Oz* (Walt Disney). Under her arm, her pet hen Bellina and, escorting her, tubby tin man Tik Tok.

bers, as well as its obvious lack of the brilliant young personality of the late Judy Garland as Dorothy (although it should be said that *Return to Oz* sticks far more closely to the original). Against that, however, this follow-up, with its – now broken – Yellow Brick Road leading to the – now ruined – Emerald City, has the marvellous effects and the electronic wizardry that were lacking in the original excursion into the magical world of Oz. The new Oz movie leaves one stunned by the advances made by the special-effects department with all its modern magic. And though not Judy, little Fairuza Balk makes a charming if rather serious Dorothy. Rest of cast: Nicol Williamson, Jean Marsh, Piper Laurie, Matt Clark, Michael Sundin, Tim Rose, Sean Barrett (plus voice), Mark Wilson, Denis Bryer (plus voice), Brian Henson (plus voice), Stewart Larange, Lyle Conway (plus voice), Steve Norrington, Justin Case, John Alexander, Deep Roy, Susan Dacre, Geoff Felix, David Greenaway, Swee Lim, Emma Ridley, Sophie Ward, Fiona Victory, Pons Maar, Rachel Ashton, Robbie Barnett, Ailsa Berk, Peter Elliot, Roger Ennals, Michele Hine, Mark Hopkins, Colin Skeaping, Ken Stevens, Philip Tan, Robert Thirtle, Bruce Boa, Nicola Roche, Cheryl Brown, Alison Lynn, Sarah White, Tansy. Dir: Walter Murch. Pro: Paul Maslansky. Ex Pro: Gary Kurtz. Ex in charge of Pro: Bruce Sharman. Assoc Pro: Colin Michael Kitchen. Screenplay: Murch and Gill Dennis; based on the novels *The Land of Oz* and *Ozma of Oz* by L. Frank Baum. Ph: David Watkin. Ed: Leslie Hodgson. Pro Des: Norman Reynolds. Art: Charles Bishop (Sup) and Fred Hole. M: David Shire. (Walt Disney in assoc with Silver Screen Partners II) Rel: 26 July 1985. 110 mins. Cert U.

Revolution. Well, everyone can make mistakes, but how sad to see Hugh Hudson, the director of that British screen classic *Chariots of Fire*, perpetrating such a big one as this overblown, indifferently scripted, historical 'epic' about the Brits losing America – though you won't learn much about that event from this confusing and (in several star cases) indifferently acted movie. The only ones to triumph are those who staged the impressive battle scenes – a contrast to the glum episodes about a man (Al Pacino) and his son (Dexter Fletcher) caught up in the struggle. And it's not pleasant to have to say all this. Rest of cast: Donald Sutherland, Nastassja Kinski, Joan Plowright, Dave King, Steven Berkoff, John Wells, Annie Lennox, Dexter Fletcher, Sid Owen, Richard O'Brien, Paul Brooke, Eric Milota, Felicity Dean, Jo Anna Lee, Cheryl Miller, Harry Ditson, Rebecca Calder, Theresa Boden, Jesse Birdsall, Cameron Johann, Danny Potts, William Marlow, Stefan Gryff, Frank Windsor, Skeeter Vaughan, Larry Sellers, Graham Greene, Denis Lacroix, Joseph Running Fox, Harold Pacheco, John Patrick, Malcolm Terris, Steve Kligerman, Adrian Rawlins, Manning Redwood, Kate Hardie, Richard Hicks, Tristram Jellinek, Lex Van Delden, Matthew Sim, Jonathon Adams, Robbie Coltrane, Brendan Conroy, Paul Humpoletz. Dir: Hugh Hudson. Pro: Irwin Winkler. Ex Pro: Chris Burt. Screenplay: Robert Dillon. Ph: Bernard Lutic. Ed: Stuart Baird. Pro Des: Assheton Gorton. Art: Malcolm Middleton and John Bunker. M: John Corigliano. (Warner/Goldcrest/Viking–Warner Bros) Rel: floating; first shown London (Warner), 31 January 1986. 125 mins. Cert PG.

Rocky 4. For the fans of *Rocky* and star Sylvester Stallone, this fourth episode in the life and career of the perky pugilist will probably be so welcome they won't notice or even care that there are some pretty obvious threadbare patches in this story of the American bruiser who always comes from behind, and against virtually impossible odds, to walk away, limping

One of the superbly staged battle sequences that were the best thing about Goldcrest/ Warner's *Revolution*, in which the Yanks beat the Brits. Inset, reluctant recruit Al Pacino and rebellious belle Nastassja Kinski.

perhaps, with the title. This time its a Soviet masterman who gets his stars-and-stripes slugging lesson. A really bruising business. Rest of cast: Talia Shire, Burt Young, Carl Weathers, Brigitte Nielsen, Tony Burton, Michael Pataki, Dolph Lundgren, R. J. Adams, Al Dandiero, Dominic Barto, Daniel Brown, James Brown, Rose Mary Campos, Jack Carpenter, Mark Deealessandro, Marty Denkin, Lou Filippo, James 'Cannonball' Green, Dean Hammond, Rocky Krakoff, Sergei Levin, Anthony Maffatone, Sylvia Meals, Dwayne McGee, Stu Nathan, Leroy Neiman, George Pipaski, George Rogan, Barry Tompkins, Warner Wolf, Robert Doornick, Richard

American pugilist Rocky (Sylvester Stallone) takes a winning swing at his more favoured Russian opponent (Dolph Lundgren) in the UIP release of MGM/UA's *Rocky 4*.

The lovers (Julian Sands and Helena Bonham Carter) about to clinch their romance in the Merchant–Ivory/Goldcrest film of E. M. Forster's *A Room With a View*, which included some magnificent performances by (right) Denholm Elliott (i), Daniel Day-Lewis (ii) and Maggie Smith (iii).

Blum, Gerald Berns, Ray Glanzmann, Julie Inouye, Patrick Pankhurst, Jean Thoreau, Jim Bullock, Frank D'Annibale, Rose Dursy, Rick Kelley, Craig Schaefer, Jeff Austin, Leslie Morris, Bob Giovane, Julio Herzer, George Spaventa, Rolf Williams, Jim Hodge. Dir and Screenplay: Sylvester Stallone. Pro: Robert Chartoff and Irwin Winkler. Ex Pro: James D. Brubaker and Arthur Chobanian. Ph: Bill Butler. Ed: Don Zimmerman, and John W. Wheeler. Pro Des: Bill Kenney. M: Vince Di Cola, with themes from *Rocky* by Bill Conti. (MGM/UA–UIP) Rel: 24 January 1986. 91 mins. Cert PG.

A Room with a View. From the opening titles, accompanied by a soaring Puccini aria, this intelligent adaptation of the E. M. Forster novel is a marvellous example of civilized cinema, with its near-perfect blending of superb performances, lovingly photographed Florentine backgrounds, sympathetic direction and consistent good taste. It is, of course, about an unusual love affair between two strong-minded and convention-defying characters who don't fit into their period – the early 1900s. Quibbles? The lovely music sometimes becomes too intrusive, and perhaps the two leading players might have shown more passion. But these criticisms don't lessen by a jot the impact of this shining example of the true art of moviemaking. Cast: Maggie Smith, Helena Bonham Carter, Denholm Elliott, Julian Sands, Daniel Day-Lewis, Simon Callow, Judi Dench, Rosemary Leach, Rupert Graves, Patrick Godfrey, Fabia Drake, Joan Henley, Maria Britneva, Amanda Walker, Peter Cellier, Mia Fothergill, Patricia Lawrence, Mirio Guidelli, Matyelock Gibbs, Kitty Aldridge, Freddy Korner, Elizabeth Marangoni, Lucca Rossi, Isabella Celani, Luigi de Fiori. Dir: James Ivory. Pro: Ismail Merchant. Assoc Pro: Paul Bradley and Peter Marangoni. Pro Co-Ord: Caroline Hill. Screenplay: Ruth Prawer Jhabvala. Ph: Tony Pierce-Roberts. Ed: Humphrey Dixon. Pro Des: Gianni Quaranta and Brian Ackland-Snow. M: Richard Robbins. (Merchant Ivory Productions/A Goldcrest film in assoc with National Film Finance Corp–Curzon Film Dist.) Rel: floating; first shown London (Curzon, Mayfair), 11 April 1986. 120 mins. Cert PG.

Below right, Santa Claus David Huddlestone drives his sleigh, powered by eight flying reindeer, across the Manhattan skyline in the Salkinds' *Santa Claus: The Movie*. Below, John Lithgow as the scene-stealing villain and a view of Santa's workshop (Rank Film Dist.).

Runaway Train. Unrelentingly brutal, express-tempoed, well-acted (in context), old-fashioned, all-action thriller (but with unending new-fashioned foul language) about a couple of convicts (the old lag making his third break and determined it shall be his last; the young one a simple, voluble tagger-on) and a girl on board a runaway train in a snow-misted, savagely cold Alaskan winter. As it rushes to its doom, the increasingly fraught people in the control room try to prevent the impending disaster. It is based on a script by the Japanese master moviemaker, Akira Kurosawa. The film is dedicated to Rick Holley, the helicopter pilot who died during the stunt filming. Cast: Jon Voight, Eric Roberts, Rebecca de Mornay, Kyle T. Heffner, John P. Ryan, T. K. Carter, Kenneth McMillan, Stacey Pickren, Walter Wyatt, Edward Bunker, Reid Cruikshanks, Michael Lee Gogin, John Bloom, Norton E. Warden, John Otrin, Norman Alexander Gibbs, Dennis Ott, Don Pugsley, John Fountain, Wally Rose, Daniel Trejo, Big Yank, Tom 'Tiny' Lister, Dana Belgrade, Diane Erickson, Larry John Meyers, Don McLaughlin, Vladimir Bibic, William Tregoe Jr, Loren James, Obie Weeks, John Clay Scott, Robert M. Klempner, Carmen Filpi, Phillip Earl, Tom Keenan, Tony Epper, Jerry Brainum, Duey Thomasick. Dir: Andrei Konchalovsky. Pro: Menahem Golan and Yoram Globus. Ex Pro: Robert Whitmore, Henry Weinstein and Robert A. Goldston. Assoc Pro: Mati Raz. Stunt Co-ordinator: Loren Janes, Ex in charge of Pro: Sue Baden-Powell. 2nd Unit Dir: Max Kleben. Screenplay: Djordje Milicevic, Paul Zindel and Edward Bunker; based on an original screenplay by Akira Kurosawa. Ph: Alan Hume. Ed: Henry Richardson. Pro Des: Stephen Marsh. M: Trevor Jones. (Cannon) Rel: floating; first shown London (Warner), 27 June 1986. 111 mins. Cert 18.

Santa Claus: The Movie. The Salkinds, who brought moviegoers that flying hero and heroine 'Superman' and 'Supergirl', now at fabulous expense bring them an eight-reindeer-powered flying sledge and an aerial Father Christmas. Slow-starting, this Christmassy fanasy (which always looks like a Disney cartoon with live performers) gets faster-paced and more amusing as it goes along and even becomes involving. David Huddlestone makes a large, cosily plump Santa who lives with his

hard-working elves at the North Pole preparing the presents that will be distributed the following Christmas Eve. However it is John Lithgow as the – ultimately – flying villain who steals the show and gets the chuckles. And how nice to see that rare 'U' certificate. Rest of cast: Dudley Moore (as an inventive elf), Burgess Meredith, Judy Cornwell, Jeffrey Kramer, Christian Fitzpatrick, Carrie Keiheim, John Barrard, Anthony O'Donnell, Peter O'Farrell, Tim Stern, Christopher Ryan, Dickie Arnold, Don Estelle, Melvyn Hayes, Aimée Delamain, Dorothea Phillips, John Hallam, Judith Morse, Jerry Harte, Paul Aspland, Sally Cranfield, Michael Drew, Walter Goodman, John Cassady, Ronald Fernee, Michael Ross. Dir: Jeannot Szwarc. Pro: Ilya Salkind and Pierre Spengler. Assoc Pro: Robert Simmonds. Pro Ex: Pauline Coutelene. Pro Sup: Vincent Winter. Screenplay: David Newman; based on a story by David and Leslie Newman. Ph: Arthur Ibbetson. Ed: Peter Hollywood, Pro Des: Anthony Pratt. Sup Art Dir: Tim Hutchinson. M: Henry Mancini. (Salkind Productions–Rank Film Dist.) Rel: 29 November 1985. 108 mins. Cert U.

The Scorpion – De Schorpioen. From the Dutch director of the intriguing *Girl with Red Hair*, made a few years back, comes this highly competent if cold thriller about a truck driver who is caught up in a web of crookery by his boss. The driver agrees to take part in a passport plot but then changes his mind and, in spite of some very 'heavy' dissuasion, starts to investigate why his truck has been burned out and the driver, who was mistaken for himself, murdered. At the end, both he and his girl are more 'complete people'. Fine atmosphere, very good performances and superb photography finally outweigh the greyly etched characters. Cast: Peter Tuinman, Monique Van der Ven, Adrian Brine, Henk van Ulsen, Rima Melati, Huub Stapel, Senne Rouffaer, Marijke Veugelers, Walter Kous, Edwin de Vries, Teddy Schaank, Frank Van Oostmerssen, Willem Alkemade, Roldjah Matulessy, René Van Paridon, Ico de Kruiter, Iketut Sunesa, Joop Van Der Donk, Frits Kampinga, Sam Tjioe, Hans Holtkamp, Hans Kerckhoffs, Albert Abspoel, Loes Luca, Diane Lensink, Willem Van Rinsum, Marc Krone, Willem Bogaard, Ernst Zwaan, Tizar Purbaya. Dir: Ben Verbong. Pro: Chris Brouwer and Haig Balian. Screenplay: Verbong and Pieter de Vos. Ph: Theo Van De Sande. Ed: Ton de Graaf. Art: Dorus Vanderlinden. M: Nicola Piovani; songs performed by Brenda Lee. (Movie Film Productions–Thorn EMI Classics) Rel: floating; first shown London (Cannon cinemas), 7 February 1986. 101 mins. Cert 18.

He-Man and She-Ra are the unbeatable brother and sister combination in the animated Braveworld/Miracle family feature *The Secret of the Sword.*

Screwballs 2: Loose Screws. Poor (Canadian) follow-up to the not-too-exciting *S1* original: about a feverishly sex-obsessed bunch of routine, less-than-brilliant pupils at Beaver High School. And the only visible lesson here is for the movie's makers! Cast: Brian Genesse, Lance Van Der Kolk, Alan Deveau, Jason Warren, Annie McCauley, Karen Wood, Liz Green, Mike McDonald, Cyd Belliveau, Deborah Loban, Carolyn Tweedle, Stephanie Sulik, Terrea Oster, Wayne Fleming, Cindy Fidler, etc. Dir: Rafal Zielinski. Pro: Maurice Smith. Screenplay: Michael Cory. Ph: Robin Miller. Ed: Stephan Fanfara. Pro Des: Judith Lee. M: Fred Mollin. (Maurice Smith Pro/Concord Pictures–Avatar) Rel: 19 July 1985. 92 mins. Cert 18.

The Secret of the Sword. Animated feature aimed at the family trade – more especially the kiddies – about the adventures of He-Man and his twin sister She-Ra. It was in September 1983 that the heroic figure of He-Man was introduced to TV audiences in the United States, since when he's become the top-rated children's series in syndication, with 36 countries now taking the TV series. With the voices of: John Erwin, Melandy Britt, George Dicenzo, Linda Gary, Ericka Scheimer, Erik Gunden, Alan Oppenheimer. Dir: Ed Friedman, Lou Kachivas, Marsch Lamore, Bill Reed and Gwen Wetzler. Pro: Arthur H. Nadel. Ex Pro: Lou Scheimer. Screenplay: Larry Ditillo and Robert Forward. (Filmation–Braveworld–Miracle) Rel: 27 March 1986. 91 mins. Cert U.

Sex Mission – Seksmisja. Jokey little Polish film from a (comparatively) new director (Juliusz Machulski) which somehow fairly successfully manages to mix science-fiction with broad comedy, overlaid with a rather more serious criticism of female chauvinism, dictatorships of all kinds and other political and sexual hiccups of modern society. The story, with its wryly amusing twists and turns, concerns a couple of modern Rip Van Winkles who awake to find that women are ruling the world and have dispensed, figuratively and literally, with the male phallus . . . or have they? (See twist in the tail!) Cast: Olgierd Lukaszewicz, Jerzy Stuhr, Bożena Stryjkówna, Bogusława Pawelec, Hanna Stankówna, Beata Tyszkiewicz, etc. Dir: Juliusz

Machulski. Pro: Andrezej Soltysik. Screenplay: Machulski, Jolanta Hartwig and Pavel Hajny. Ph: Jerzy Lukaszewicz. Ed: Miroslawa Garlicka. Art: Janus Sosnowski. M: Henry Kuzniak. (Zespoly Filmowe/Kadr Film Unit–Cinegate). Rel: floating; first shown London (Gate, Notting Hill), 22 August 1985. 128 mins. Cert 15.

Shadey. Commendably original, offbeat and pretty surrealistic, this British black comedy twists and turns and persistently non-conforms so often that it is difficult to say more than the story is about a young man whose desire it is to have a sex change operation; to raise the money for it, he is tempted into becoming involved with a small experimental MI5 cell. A crazy tale sprinkled with laughter and ambiguity, and very well played, too: all amounting to one of the year's most 'different' movies. Cast: Anthony Sher, Billie Whitelaw, Patrick Macnee, Leslie Ash, Bernard Hepton, Larry Lamb, Katherine Helmond, Jon Cartwright, Jesse Birdsall, Olivier Pierre, Stephen Persuad, Basil Henson, Madhav Sharma, Susan Engel, Jan Myerson, Peter Kelly, Gillian de Tourville, Andrew Bradford, Jenny Runacre, Jonathan Scott-Taylor, Melody Howe, Simon Prebble, Zabu, Rita Keegan, Zohra Segal, Bill Bingham, Jonathan Perkins, Silver Spurs (pop group). Dir: Philip Saville. Pro: Otto Plaschkes. Screenplay: Snoo Wilson. Ph: Roger Deakins. Ed: Chris Kelly, Pro Des: Norman Garwood. (Mainline Pictures) Rel: floating; first shown London (Screen-on-the-Hill and ABC, Fulham Road), 2 May 1986. 106 mins. Cert 15.

Antony Sher as he is (i) and as he wants to be (ii) in Mainline's release of the eccentric but commendably imaginative British black and surrealistic comedy *Shadey*.

Shaker Run. Minor carobatics caper movie from New Zealand about two down-at-heel American stunt drivers (Cliff Robertson and Leif Garrett) involved in a feature-length chase with scientist Lisa Harrow as passenger and the nasty, ruthless NZ Secret Service as pursuers. Wanted (also by the CIA, equally ruthless): the deadly virus in the boot. And after causing multi-mayhem among pursuers, both car and human, the trio finally and literally take-off into the blue! Rest of cast: Shane Briant, Peter Hayden, Peter Rowell, Bruce Philips, Ian Mune, Fiona Samuels, Deirdre O'Connor, Mat Lees, Daniel Gillion. Dir: Bruce Morrison. Pro: Larry Parr and Igor Kantor. Pro Co-Ord; Chloe Smith. Ex Pro: Henry Fownes. Screenplay: Morrison, Fownes and James Kouf Jr. Ed: Ken Zemke and Bob Richardson. Ph: Kevin Hayward. Pro Des: Ron Highfield. M: Stephen McCurdy. (Mirage/Aviscom Pro in assoc with Laurelwoods Pro–Miracle Films) Rel: floating; first shown London (Cannon, Charing Cross Road), 28 February 1986. 89 mins. Cert 15.

The kind of car-crashing action which was offered as the main attraction of New Zealand's all-action *Shaker Run*, released in Britain by Miracle Films.

She'll Be Wearing Pink Pyjamas. Reminiscent in some ways of Losey's *Steaming*, this is a far less serious story about another group of women – in this

A wind-swept Julie Walters struggles along the survival course in the British comedy *She'll Be Wearing Pink Pyjamas*, and made it all seem worth while.

case, an octet undergoing the first female Outward Bound survival course in the Lake District – and their exchange of confidences as they sweat and strain their way over the course. And it's another triumph for Julie (*Educating Rita*) Walters, who puts most of the other women and their problems into the shade as she takes hold of the film and finally makes it her own. Rest of cast: Anthony Higgins, Jane Evers, Janet Henfrey, Paula Jacobs, Penelope Nice, Maureen O'Brien, Alyson Spiro, Jane Wood, Pauline Yates, Bill Lund, Paul Butterworth, Nicky Putnam, Paul Atkinson, Gail Herring. Dir: John Goldschmidt. Pro: Tara Prem and Adrian Hughes. Assoc Pro: David McFarlane. Screenplay: Eva Hardy. Ph: Clive Tickner. Ed: Richard Key. Pro Des: Colin Pocock. M: John du Prez. (Pink Pyjama Pro/Film Four International–Virgin Films) Restricted rel: 14 June 1985. 90 mins. Cert 15.

Silverado. Large-scale western which, mixing classic themes with a modern treatment, should – and certainly deserves to – revive the more recently flagging fortunes of this great cinema genre. It's a vastly entertaining, if awfully noisy (musically and otherwise), saddle-and-spurs piece about four drifters who come together in Silverado where, miraculously revived after near-death, they effectively shoot the town free of the evil men who control it. Wonderfully photographed, spectacular New Mexico backgrounds, fine, full-blooded performances (Scott Glenn as the classic hero; Brian Dennehy as the classic villain) and lots of violent (if commendably visually bloodless) action and the occasional rich chuckle. Rest of cast: Kevin Kline, Kevin Costner, Danny Glover, Marvin J. McIntyre, Brad Williams, Sheb Wooley, John Kasdan, John Cleese, Todd Allen, Kenny Call, Bill Thurman, Meg Kasdan, Dick Durock, Gene Hartline, Autry Ward, Jacob Kasdan, Rosanna Arquette, Rusty Meyers, Zeke Davidson, Lois Geary, James Gammon, Troy Ward, Roy McAdams, Linda Hunt, Jeff Goldblum, Ray Baker, Joe Seneca, Lynn Whitfield, Jeff Fahey, Patricia Gaul, Amanda Wyss, Earl Hindman, Tom Brown, Jim Haynie, Richard Jenkins, Jerry Biggs, Sam Gauny, Ken Farmer, Bill McIn-

Shades of the 'Seven Samurai': left to right, Rusty Meyers, Danny Glover, Kevin Kline and Scott Glenn as the four drifters who come together to rid the town of its strangleholding villains in Columbia's classically constructed western *Silverado*. And (inset) surprise, surprise, the local sheriff turns out to be John (*Fawlty Towers*) Cleese!

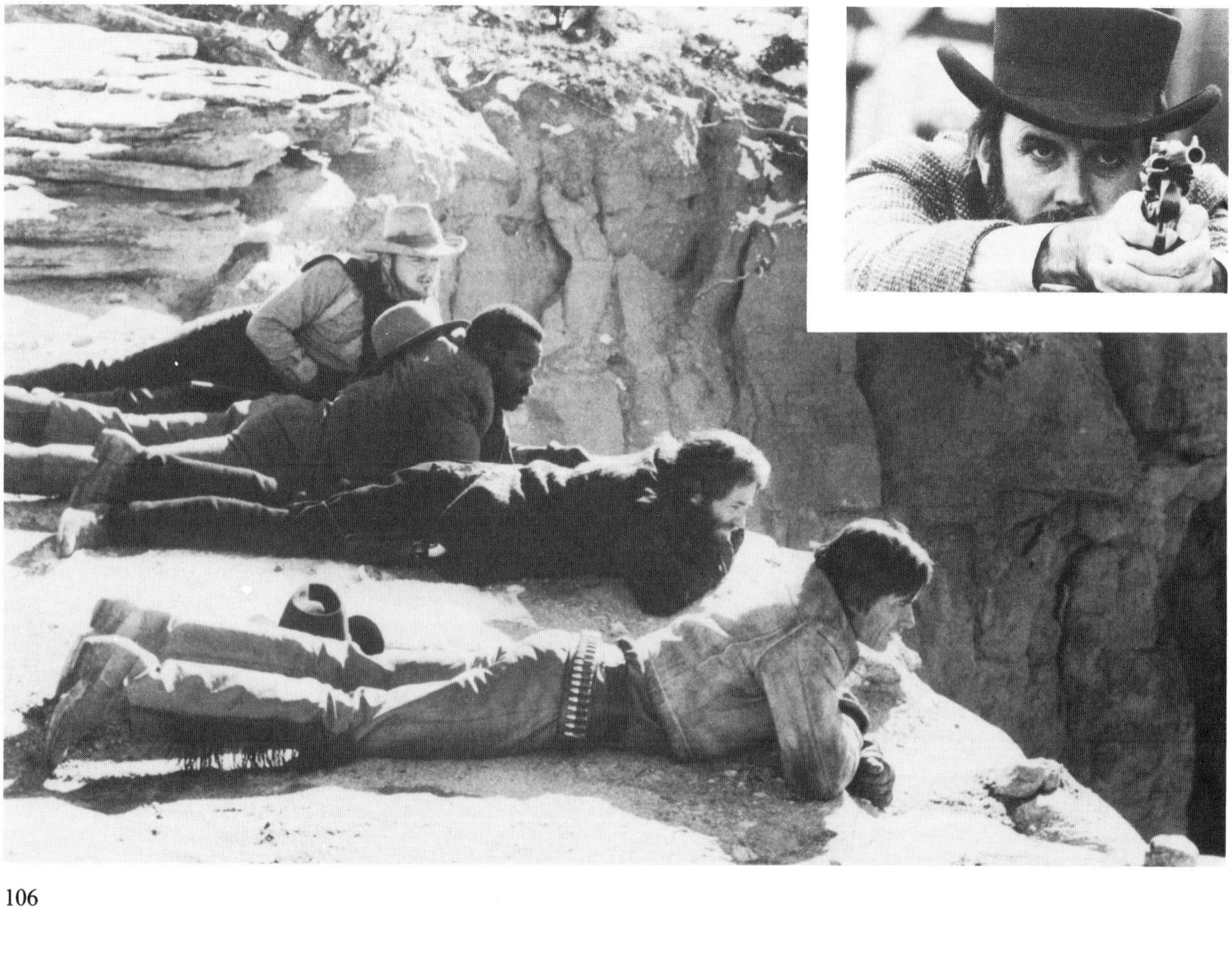

Above left, Chevy Chase and Dan Aykroyd (right) as two inept secret agents in the Warner comedy *Spies Like Us*. Above, aptly named Vanessa Angel, as the amenable crew-woman of a Russian rocket, about to take off.

tosh, Charles Seybert, Jane Beauchamp, Jerry Block, Ben Zeller, Pepe Serna, Ted White, Ross Loney, Walter Scott, Bob Terhune. Dir and Pro: Lawrence Kasdan. Ex Pro: Charles Okun and Michael Grillo. Assoc Pro: Mark Kasdan. Screenplay: Lawrence and Mark Kasdan. Ph: John Bailey. Ed: Carol Littleton. Pro Des: Ida Random. M: Bruce Broughton. (Columbia–Delphi IV in co-operation with The American Humane Assoc–Columbia) Rel: 10 January 1986. 133 mins. Cert PG.

Silver Bullet. Another minor horror addition, in which the residents of the little town of Tarker's Mill suddenly find a *thing* in their midst and realize that it wasn't a train that severed the head from the body of that railway worker! They have to stand up to all sorts of horrors before a silver bullet, which happens to be lying around, finishes off the werewolf – and a prominent local citizen. Cast: Gary Busey, Corey Haim, Megan Follows, Everett McGill, Terry O'Quinn, Robin Groves, Leon Russom, Bill Smitrovich, Joe Wright, Kent Broadhust, Heather Simmons, James A. Baffico. Dir: Daniel Attias. Pro: Martha Schumacher. Assoc Pro: John M. Eckert. Screenplay: Stephen King: based on his story 'Cycle of the Werewolf'. Ph: Armando Nannuzzi. Ed: Daniel Lowenthal. Pro Des: Giorgi Postiglione. M: Jay Chattaway. (Dino de Laurentiis–Cannon) Rel: 20 June 1986. 95 mins. Cert 18.

Six Nix Hicks Pix. A package of six films made by young British moviemakers who 'refuse to be bound by the restrictions of narrow regionalism, or by the tradition of British naturalist drama'. The films are: (1) *The Discovery of Gravity* by Gerry Feeney; (2) *Maelstrom* by Nigel Grierson; (3) *Wings of Death* by Nicola Bruce and Mike Coulson; (4) *Sins of the Father* by Harry Hook; (5) *Killing Time* by Christopher O'Reilly; (6) *The Life of Their Own* by Roger Parsons. (ICA) Rel: floating; first shown London (ICA Cinémathèque), 2 June 1986. 189 mins. No cert.

Slumber Party Massacre. The victims: a party of basketball-playing girls at the house of one of the team giving the party of the title. The killer? That would be telling. Very black and bloody comedy with some neat dialogue and nice female performances. Cast: Michele Michaels, Robin Stille, Michael Villela, etc. Dir and Pro: Amy Jones. Ex Pro: Roger Corman. Screenplay: Rita Mae Brown. Ph: Steve Posey. M: Ralph Jones. (Enterprise Pictures) Rel: floating; first shown London (ICA), 16 May 1986. 78 mins. Cert 18.

Spies Like Us. Though there are a number of good gags and some witty lines, this is not as funny a comedy as it might have been, considering its two comic stars, Chevy Chase and Dan Aykroyd, and it is marred by the occasional needless vulgarity. The duo play a couple of inept, would-be espionage agents who are overjoyed when their ambition seems fulfilled with their call-up to undertake a special mission – not knowing they have been selected because they are regarded by their bosses as suitably expendable decoys. Rest of cast: Steve Forrest, Donna Dixon, Bruce Davison, William Prince, Bernie Casey, Tom Hatten, Charles McKeown, Derek Meddings, Ray Harryhausen, Robert Paynter, Terry Gilliam, Gusti Bogok, Stephen Hoye, Ronald Reagan, Jim Staahl, James Daughton, Tony Cyrus, Mart Stewart, Sean Daniel, Jeff Harding, Heidi Sorenson, Margo Random, Douglas Lambert, Frank Oz, Christopher Malcolm, Terrance Conder, Matt Frewer, Guardial Sira, Joel Coen, Martin Brest, Sam Raimi, Michael Apted, B. B. King, Larry Cohen, Rico Ross, Richard Sharpe, Stuart Milligan, Sally Anlauf, Costa Gavras, Seva Novgorodtsev, John Daveikis, Laurence Bilzerian, Richard Kruk, Sergei Rousakov, Bjarne Thomsen, Garrick Donbrovski, Svetlana Plotnikova, Vanessa Angel, Heather Henson, Erin Folsey, Bob Swaim, Dir: John Landis. Pro: Brian Grazer and George Foley Jr. Ex Pro: Bernie Brillstein. Assoc Pro: Sam Wil-

Ernie (Keith Gordon) can see heaven on his specially adapted television screen but all his invited friends can see is *Static*, in the Blue Dolphin release of that title.

liams and Leslie Belzberg. Screenplay: Dan Aykroyd, Lowell Ganz and Babaloo Mandel. Ph: Robert Paynter. Ed: Malcolm Campbell. Pro Des: Peter Murton. M: Elmer Bernstein; title song sung by Paul McCartney. (Warner) Rel: 14 February 1986. 102 mins. Cert PG.

Starchaser – The Legend of Orin. American-Korean 3–D science-fiction cartoon feature which isn't particularly enhanced by stereoscopy, although it does use the process with commendable restraint. Its *Star Wars*-like story is chock-a-block full of incident and moves at a smart pace, and is generally superior to the average of the type, even though the technical quality is not beyond reproach. Hero Orin defeats the underground robots, who have enslaved the humans, and makes the earth a reasonable place to live in again. Voices of: Joe Colligan (Orin), Carmen Argenziano, Noelle North, Anthony Delongis, Les Tremayne, etc. Dir and Pro: Steven Hahn. Animation Dir: Mitch Rechon and Jang-Gil Kim. Ex Pro: Thomas Coleman and Michael Rosenblatt. Assoc Pro: Daniel Pia and Christine Danzo. Pro Sup: Young Chol Choi and Kim Soon Min. Assoc Dir: John Sparey. Screenplay: Jeffrey Scott. Ph Sup: Charles Flekal. Ed: D. W. Ernst. M: Andrew Belling. (Coleman Rosenblatt–Entertainment) Rel: floating; first shown London (Cannon, Oxford Street), 23 May 1986. 100 mins. Cert PG.

Hero Orin and Dagg flee from a Zygon patrol airplane in Entertainment's animated feature release, *Starchaser – The Legend of Orin.*

Static. Witty and original film which tells – with constant allusion to modern American mores and culture – a story about a young inventor who claims he has invented a TV set which can look into heaven and will thus bring about a quiet revolution (enabling the 'world to be happy, not sad'). However, when the machine is unveiled, the screen shows just a picture of static which only the young inventor can see as life beyond the pearly gates. The tongue-in-cheek comedy ends with a sudden, unexpected bang as the mood switches to deadly drama. A film full of directorial–screenplay promise from Mark Romanek. It could be termed a small, slightly flawed masterpiece. Cast: Keith Gordon, Amanda Plummer, Bob Gunton, Barton Heyman, Lily Knight, Jane Hoffman, Reathel Bean, Kitty Mei-Mei Chen, Joel Krehbeil, Eugene Lee, Jack Murakami, Mike Murakami, Uma Ridenhour, Janice Abbott, Tamma Allgood, Tito Larriva, Chalo Quintana, Tony Marsico, Dean Winans, Mary Hunka, Paul Stucky, David Pape, Art Louisignau, Nancy Helin, Mark Bork, Gary Petersen, Mark Gordon, Dave Donham, Dane Kocjan, Robby Bunch, Beth Durell, Barbara Glenn Gordon, Michael Conner, Danny Stefan, Ronald Pearson, James Paul White, Bill Bass. Dir and (with Keith Gordon) Screenplay: Mark Romanek. Pro: Amy Ness. Ex Pro: Julio Caro. Assoc Pro: Nancy Israel. Ph: Jeff Jur. Ed: Emily Paine. Pro Des: Cynthia Sowder. M: rock numbers. (Blue Dolphin) Rel: floating; first shown London (Chelsea Cannon and Electric), 13 June 1986. 88 mins. Cert 15.

St Elmo's Fire. The film takes its title from the bar where a group of students spend much of their time. All told, these Washington (DC) High School graduates are a pretty alienating bunch; the story is tied to their emergence into the world of adults, and having some misgivings about it. Cast: Rob Lowe, Demi Moore, Andrew McCarthy, Judd Nelson, Ally Sheeds, Emilio Estevez,

Mare Winningham, Martin Balsam, Jon Cutler, Joyce Van Patten, Andie MacDowell, Jenny Wright, Blake Clark, Matthew Laurance, Gina Hecht, Anna Maria Horsford, James Carrington, Kaaren Lee, Nora Meerbaum, Don Moss, Whip Hubley, Michele Winding, Jim Turner, Maria Machado, Judy Kain, Seth Jaffe, Jeffrey Lampert, Elizabeth Arlen, Scott Nemes, Bernadette Birkett, V. J. Issac, D. R. Miller, Jamison Anders, Cindi Dietrich, David L. Baker, Daniel Eden, Laurel Page, Thom Bierdz, J. T. Solomon, The New Breed Band. Dir: Joel Schumacher. Pro: Lauren Shuler. Ex Pro: Ned Tanen and Bernard Schwartz. Screenplay: Schumacher and Carl Kurlander. Ph: Stephen H. Burum. Ed: Richard Marks. Art: William Sandell. M: David Foster. (Columbia Delphi IV–Columbia) Rel: floating; first shown London (Plaza), 1 November 1985. 108 mins. Cert 15.

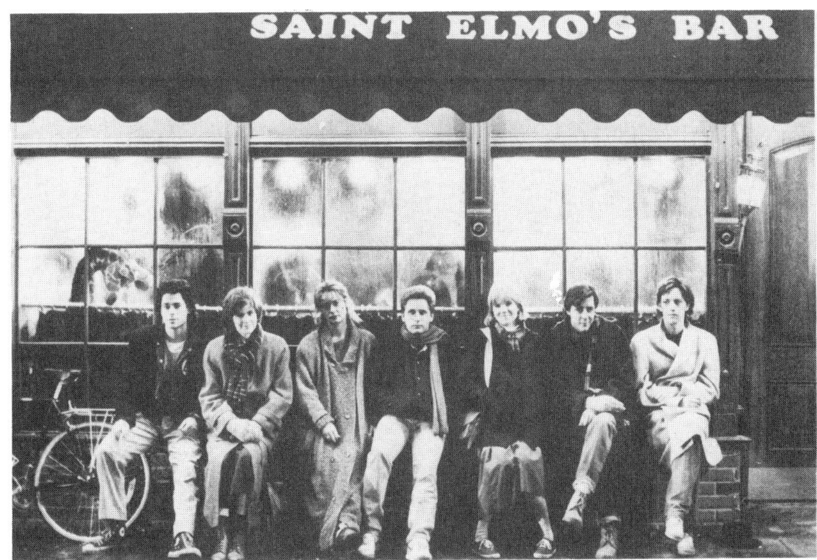

Left to right: Rob Lowe, Ally Sheedy, Demi Moore, Emilio Estevez, Mare Winningham, Judd Nelson and Andrew McCarthy as the tightly knit college student group who make their leisure headquarters the bar which gives this Columbia release its title, *St Elmo's Fire*.

Streetwalking. This low-budget Roger Corman production is a thriller set on the shadier side of New York where a prostitute is pursued with evil intent by her psychopathic pimp during a nightmare night of murder and mayhem. Cast: Melissa Leo, Dale Midkiff, Antonio Fargas, Julie Newmar, etc. Dir: Joan Freeman. Pro: Robert Alden. Ex Pro: Roger Corman. Screenplay: Alden and Freeman. Ph: Steven Fierberg. Ed: John Adams and Patrick Rand. (ICA/ Enterprise Pictures) Rel: floating; first shown London (ICA), 16 May 1986. 85 mins. No cert.

Streetwise. Grim, depressing but generally impressively well-made documentary about teenage drifters and social outcasts in Seattle. Some of them tell their own gloomy stories, with the overall suggestion (now the common excuse) that their march to the figurative scaffold and other hardly less unpleasant ends is the fault of the Family and of Society at large. A highly competent celluloid social document which gained an Oscar nomination. Featuring real characters such as 'Tiny', 'Rat' and 'Shadow', etc. Dir and Ph: Martin Bell. Pro: Cheryl McCall. Ex Pro: Angelika T. Saleh and Connie and Willy Nelson. Ed: Nancy Baker. (Mainline) Rel: floating; first shown London (Screen-on-the-Green), 14 February 1986. 90 mins. Cert 18.

The Stuff. A modest, well-made thriller with a science-fiction base, satirical elements and increasingly farcical leanings as it relates the story of the finding of a mysterious 'stuff' bubbling out of the earth, which is irresistible (when packaged and sold by ruthless big business characters) but kills from within. Targets include fast food, martial arts nuts and advertising agencies. Grand performances by Michael Morison as an industrial saboteur and Paul Sorvino as the military menace. Rest of cast: Andrea Marcovicci, Garrett Morris, Scott Bloom, Danny Aiello, James Dixon, Alexander Scourby, Russell Nype, Gene O'Neill, Cathy Schultz, Jim Dukas, Peter Hock, Colette Blonigan, Frank Telfer, Brian Bloom, Marilyn Staley, Beth Teagarden, Ann Dane, Rutanya Alda, David Snell, Edward Power, Broke Adams, Tammy Grimes, Clara Peller, Laurence Landon, Abe Vigoda. Dir, Ex Pro and Screenplay: Larry Cohen. Pro: Paul Kurta. Assoc Pro: Barry Shils. Ph: Paul Glickman. Ed: Armond Lebowitz. Art: Marleen Marta and George Stoll. M: no credit

Dire results of eating *The* (delicious) *Stuff* in the Recorded Releasing thriller of that title which suggests that not all nice things are good for you!

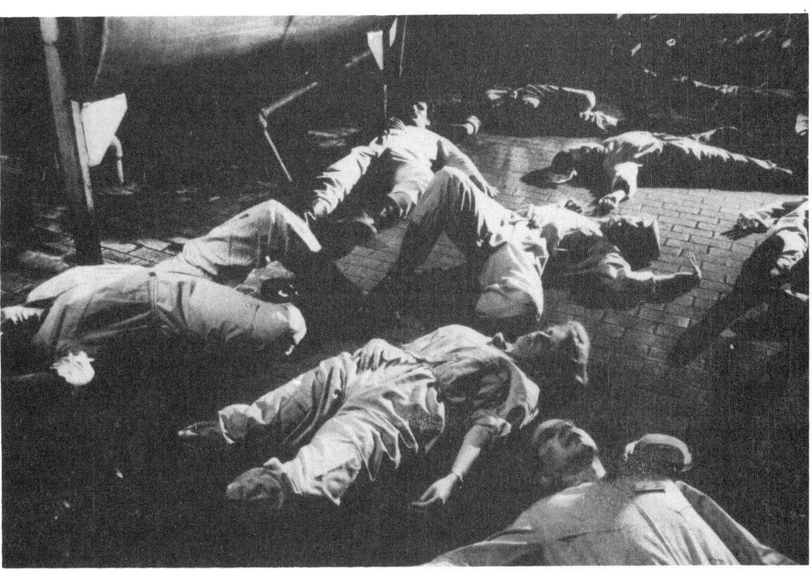

listed. (Largo Pro–Recorded Releasing) Rel: floating; first shown London (Prince Charles), 18 April 1986. 87 mins. Cert 15.

Suburbia. Rather unlikeable film about a group of youthful San Fernando Valley squatters who steal food, are often violent and appear to be completely aimless and useless . . . and, of course, it is the parents who once more get the blame for their indefensible behaviour. Played for the most part by amateurs. Cast: Timothy O'Brien, Grant Miner, 'Flea' Michael Bayer, Bill Coyne, Andrew Pece, Chris Pederson, Wade Walston, Dee Waldron, Jennifer Clay, Maggie Ehrig, Christina Beck, André Boutilier, Robert Peyton, Jeff Prettyman, Donald V. Allen, Joe Battenberg, Dorlinda Griffin, Robert Griffin, Donna La Manna, Julie Winchester, John McCormack, Gavin Courtney, Robert A. Van Senus, Larry Wiley, Marlena Brause, Ron Hugo, Barbara Doyle, Jerry Madison, Barbara Benhan, James Harrison, Ed Mertens, Ray Lawrence, Gil Christner, J. Dinan Myrtrtus, Rick Jewett. Dir and Screenplay: Penelope Spheeris. Pro: Bert Dragin. Ph: Timothy Suhrstedt. Ed: Ross Albert. Art: Randy Moore. M: Alex Gibson. (Roger Corman/New Horizon–ICA) Rel: floating; first shown London (Screen-on-the-Green), 28 June 1985. 94 mins. Cert 18.

Subway. France's 26-year-old Luc Bresson (whose first film *Le Dernier Combat* revealed a highly original directing talent) is here, in his second effort, happily playing trains with the Paris Métro, weaving a script around his original inspiration, which is loosely constructed, often amusing, sometimes exciting and, in spite of the occasional lapse, never dull. It's a comedy drama about an eccentric character who repays an invitation to a rich girl's party by dynamiting her safe. He then takes refuge in the Underground, where he is helped by a roller-skating, purse-snatching pal and is pursued indefatigably if unsuccessfully by the *flics*, led by a weary, coffee-swilling superintendent. And though not everyone is going to find the strange mixture to their taste, there can be no denying the talent, imagination and control over the medium displayed by the young writer-director. Cast: Isabelle Adjani, Christopher Lambert, Richard Bohringer, Michel Galabru, Jean-Hughes Anglade, Jean-Pierre Bacri, Jean Bouise, Pierre-Ange Le Pogam, Jean Reno, Arthur Simms, Constantin Alexandrov, Jean-Claude Lecas, Eric Serra, Benoit Regent, Alain Guillard, Christian Gomba, Jean-Michel Castanie, Isabelle Sadoyan, Jimmy Blanche, Michel d'Oz, Marie Vincent, Pierre Carrive, Michel Montarey, Patrick Perez, Guy Laporte, Eric Proville, Francis Lemonnier, Dominique Hennequin, Vincent Skimenti, François Ruggieri, Magali Guidasci, Roselyne Brunet, Bernard Pollak, Brigitte Chanerande, Arnold Walter, Jacky Jakubowicz, Jean-Luc Miesch. Dir: Luc Bresson. Pro: Bresson and François Ruggieri. Pro Sup: Edith Colnel and Gisele Thenaisie. Screenplay: Bresson, Pierre Jolivet, Alain le Henry, Marc Perrier and Sophie Schmit. Ph: Carlo Varini. Ed: Schmit. Art: Alexandre Trauner. M: Eric Serra, Ricky Lee Jones and Corinne Marieneau. (Les Films du Loup/TSF Production Gaumont/TFI Films–Artificial Eye) Rel: floating; first shown London (Lumière and Chelsea Cinema), 5 September 1985. 104 mins. Cert 15.

A Summer at Grandpa's – Dongd on De Jiaql. Delightful little film from Taiwan about a couple of youngsters spending their vacation in a village in which their grand-dad is the local medico, contrasting their own town life with the quiet existence of the countryside. An artistic triumph which deserves, but is unlikely to get, a large commercial reward. But it *is* significant in showing the sophisticated moviemaking talent which exists in some of the most unexpected places. Apparently this was the star attraction of the Asia-Pacific Film Festival in Tokyo in June 1985. Cast: Koo Chuen, Mei Fong, Wang Chi-kwang, Lin Hsiao-ling, etc. Dir: Hou Hsiao-hsien, Pro: Chang Hwa-kun. Screenplay: Chu Tien-Wen. Ph: Chen Kwen-hou. Ed: Liao Ching-song. M: Edward Yang. (Marble Road Films–BFI) Rel: floating; first shown London (NFT), February 1986. 103 mins. No cert.

The Supergrass. The debut feature production of a company of comedians who began their careers in a small 'alternative' cabaret in Soho and go under the name of The Comic Strip. And their first film turns out to be a more or less routine, essentially British comedy that contains quite a lot of fun as well as some quite needless dips into appalling bad taste. It's about a moronic character who boasts of his connection with the drug-smuggling racket in order to impress his girl-friend, and is then overheard by the cops (a somewhat unlikely lot) who take his dream-world as reality. The two strands become interlocked when some real dope-runners arrive on the small seaside-town scene. Cast: Adrian Edmondson,

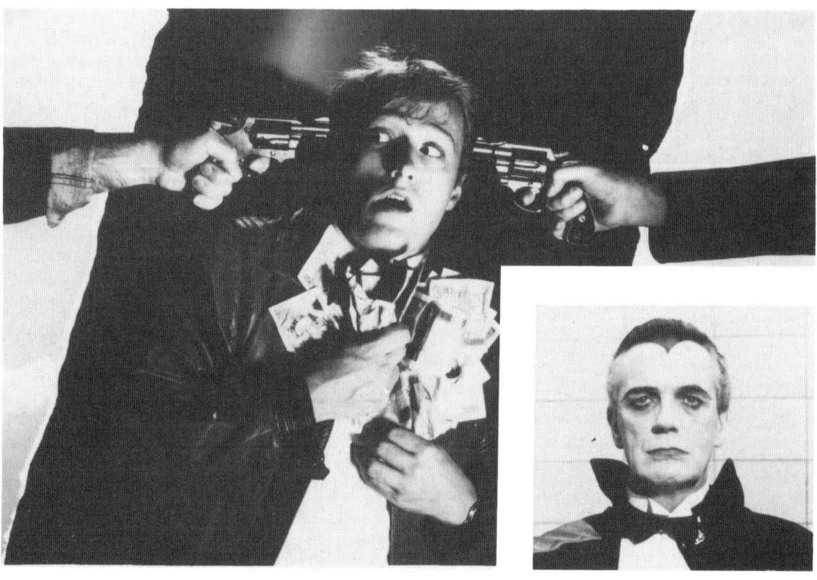

Dim-wit Dennis (Adrian Edmondson) discovers that finders are not aways keepers in the first production by the British Comic Strip team, *The Supergrass* (Recorded Releasing). Inset, direct from *Crossroads*, Ronald Allen in a contrastingly devilish role!

Jennifer Saunders, Peter Richardson, Dawn French, Keith Allen, Nigel Planer, Robbie Coltrane, Danny Peacock, Ronald Allen, Alexei Sayle, Michael Elphick, Patrick Durkin, Marika Rivera, Rita Treisman, Neil Cunningham, Michael White, David Beard, Zoe Clarke, Joanna Crickmay, Kim Pappas. Dir: Peter Richardson. Pro: Elaine Taylor. Ex Pro: Michael White. Pro Co-Ord: Rachel Krish. Screenplay: Richardson and Pete Richens. Ph: John Metcalfe. Ed: Geoff Hogg. Art: Niki Wateridge. M: Keith Tippett and Working Week Big Band. (Comic Strip/Recorded Releasing Co–Miracle Films) Rel: 7 November 1985. 105 mins. Cert 15.

The Sure Thing. The old-fashioned idea that love is more important in life than lust is at the heart of this nicer-than-usual film about American youth. He's a lad who finds that the prim little miss he's crossed off his list of possible lays is the only one for him, while she finds herself unexpectedly attracted to him and the fun he brings into her life. Cast: John Cusack, Daphne Zuniga, Anthony Edwards, Boyd Gaines, Tim Robbins, Lisa Jane Persky, Viveca Lindfors, Nicollette Sheridan, Larry Hankin, Fran Ryan, George Memmoli, Sunshine Parker, Teresa Baxter, Joshua Cadman, Carmen Filpi, Gary Goodrow, Bobby Marcucci, Rosalind Moreland, Julie Ow, John Putch, Marcie Reibel, Tracey Reiner, Amy Resnick, Kristal Richards, Christopher Rydell, Robert Snively, Frantz Turner, Danielle von Zerneck, Noelle Williams, Richard Hamilton, Jimmy Baron. Dir: Rob Reiner. Pro: Roger Birnbaum. Co-Pro: Andrew Scheinman. Ex Pro: Henry Winkler. Screenplay: Steven L. Bloom and Jonathan Roberts. Ph: Robert Elswit. Ed: Robert Leighton. Pro Des: Lilly Kilvert. M: Tom Scott. (Embassy–Films Associates/Monument Pictures–Rank Film Dist.) Rel: 17 January 1986. 94 mins. Cert 15.

John Cusack takes a drink with a few pals in the Rank release *The Sure Thing*, a modern movie with an old-fashioned heart – and moral.

Sweet Dreams. Biopic about country-and-western singer Patsy Cline, who rose to star status from small-town obscurity in the 1950s and died in a

Jessica Lange, scoring heavily as country-and-western star Patsy Cline in Thorn EMI's biopic *Sweet Dreams*. Inset, marrying her unsatisfactory husband, played by Ed Harris.

Eleanor David, as real-life character Sylvia Ashton-Warner, the Australian outback teacher who had her own controversial ideas about educating children and fought for them, in *Sylvia* (Enterprise Pictures).

plane crash at the peak of her career. The movie concentrates on her stormy personal life with her macho, anti-hero hubbie, giving Jessica Lange the opportunity for a stand-out performance in the role. Recordings of the real Cline were used for the stage sequences. Rest of cast: Ed Harris, Ann Wedgeworth, David Clennon, James Staley, Gary Basabara, John Goodman, P. J. Soles, Caitlin Kelch, Terri Gardner, Robert L. Dasch, Courtney Parker, Colton Edwards, Holly Filler, Bruce Kirby, Jerry Haynes, Kenneth White, Stonewall Jackson, Jake T. Robinson, Boxcar Willie, Tony Frank, Charlie Walker, Frank Knapp Jr, Richard J. Kidney, Jack Slater, Missy Proulx, Aleda Pope, Carlton Cuse, John E. Davis, John Walter Davis, Toni Sawyer, Robert Rothwell, Patricia Allison, Patsy's Band, Kracker Band. Dir: Karel Reisz. Pro: Bernard Schwartz. Co-Pro: Charles Mulvehill. Screenplay: Robert Getchell. Ph: Robbie Greenberg. Ed: Malcolm Cooke. Pro Des: Albert Brenner. M: Charles Gross. (Thorn EMI) Rel: 7 March 1986. 114 mins. Cert 15.

Sylvia. Introduced by the real 'Sylvia' (Sylvia Ashton-Warner), this New Zealand feature is the true story, set in the 'thirties, of a teacher at a remote village school comprising a majority of Maori children, who introduces her own unconventional methods and falls foul of the authorities who, to defeat her, go to the extent of 'accidentally' burning her workbooks. Eventually she moves on, to write an apparently famous book on education. All shown in a low-profile, solid manner which is consistently interesting even if it never approaches the excitement one feels is contained somewhere in the subject, and in the woman. A very sound performance in the title role by Eleanor David, with good support from: Nigel Terry, Tom Wilkinson, Mary Regan, Martyn Sanderson, Terence Cooper, David Letch, Sarah Peirse, etc. Dir: Michael Firth, Pro: Firth and Don Reynolds. Screenplay: Firth, Michele Quill and F. Fairfax; based on the books *Teacher* and *I Passed This Way* by Sylvia Ashton-Warner. Ph: Ian Paul. Ed: Michael Horton. Pro Des: Gary Hansen. Art: Kirsten Shouler. M: Leonard Rosenman. (Southern Light Pictures/Cinepro Productions, New Zealand–MGM/UA Classics–Enterprise Pictures) Rel: floating; first shown London (Curzon, West End), 26 July 1985. 98 mins. Cert PG.

A Taste of Water – De Smaak Van Water. Low-key, sombre and intense Dutch film about a social worker who, in spite of his own warnings of the dangers to his young assistant, becomes too personally involved with a crazy young girl in his care, leaving his home and wife to live with her, and finally suffering greatly through his well-intentioned obsession. Among the awards the film has won is the 1982 Golden Lion at the Venice Festival. Cast: Gerard Thoolen, Dorijn Curvers, Joop Admiral, Hans Van Tongeren, Olga Zuiderhoek, Moniek Toebosch, Standa Bares, Ab Abspoel, Rene Groothoff, Jean Pierre Plooij, Bram Van Der Vlugt, Roeland Radier, Elsje Scherjon, Omar El Jout, Hans Veerman, Frans Faassen, Jaap Hoogstra, Peer Macini, Johan Vigeveno, Robert Ouwerkerk. Dir and (with Dirk Ayelt Kooiman) Screenplay: Orlow Seunke. Pro: Jan Musch, Orlow Seunke and Tijs Tinbergen. Ph: Albert Van Der Wildt. Ed: Seunke and Tom Erisman. Art: Dorus Van Der Linden. M: Maarten Koopman. (Maya Films–Cinegate) Rel: floating; first shown London (Gate, Bloomsbury), 4 July 1985. 100 mins. Cert 15.

Teen Wolf. Michael J. Fox (who made quite an impact with his *Back to the Future* performance) as the lad who finds he can change virtually at will and

Michael J. Fox, who made a big hit as the lad who finds he can change into 'wolf' at the drop of a hat in the amusing Entertainment release *Teen Wolf*.

at a moment's notice into a furry-handed, red-eyed, wolfish character, and by this little touch of magic gets the girls as well as the goals that take his disastrous basketball team from the bottom to the top of the table. Nicely made minor-league stuff, with some good laughs and witty lines. Rest of cast: James Hampton, Scott Paulin, Susan Ursitti, Jerry Levine, Jim MacKrell, Lorie Griffin, Mark Arnold, Matt Adler, Mark Holton, Jay Tarses, Elizabeth Gorcey, Malanie Manos, Doug Savant, Charles Zucker, Harvey Vernon, Clare Peck, Gregory Itzin, Doris Hess, Troy Evans, Lynda Wiesmeier, Rod Kageyama, Carl Steven, Richard Brooks, Rick Domeier, Brian Sheehan, Jat Footlik, Richard Baker, Fred Nelson, Tanna Herr, Kris Hagerty, Mark L. Flowers, Larry B. Daugherty. Dir: Rod Daniel. Pro: Mark Levinson and Scott Rosenfelt. Ex Pro: Thomas Coleman and Michael Rosenblatt. Screenplay and Assoc Pro: Joseph Loeb III and Matthew Weisman. Ph: Tim Suhrstedt. Ed: Lois Freeman-Fox. Set Decorator: Rosemary Brandenberg (no other art credits shown). M: Miles Goodman (Wolfkill Pro–Entertainment Releasing) Rel: 14 February 1986. 92 mins. Cert PG.

That's Dancing. Compilation feature of famous terpsichorean extracts from musical films of the past and near present, such as Fred Astaire's 'I Won't Dance', the Nicholas Brothers' amazingly agile number from *Down Argentine Way, The Red Shoes* ballet, Nureyev and Fonteyn from *An Evening with the Royal Ballet*, Ray Bolger and Judy Garland singing and dancing 'If I Only Had a Brain' from *The Wizard of Oz* – and much, so much more. Dir: Jack Haley Jr. Pro: David Niven Jr. Ex Pro: Gene Kelly. Assoc Pro: Bud Friedgen. Pro Assoc: Jan Walchko. Screenplay: Jack Haley. (MGM–UIP) Rel: floating; first shown London (Classics), 31 May 1985. 104 mins. Cert U.

Thunder Alley. Not the war film you might expect from the title but a routine, minor story about a rock band's rise to renown in spite of a few hiccups along the way. Cast: Roger Wilson, Jill Schoelen, Scott McGinnis, Cynthia Eilbacher, Clancy Brown, Leif Garrett. Dir and Screenplay: J. S. Cardone. Pro: William R. Ewing. Ex Pro: Menahem Golan and Yoram Globus. Ph: Karen Grossman. Ed: Daniel Wetherbee. Art: Pal Tagliaferro. M: Ken Topolsky. (Cannon) Rel: 9 May 1986. 111 mins. Cert PG.

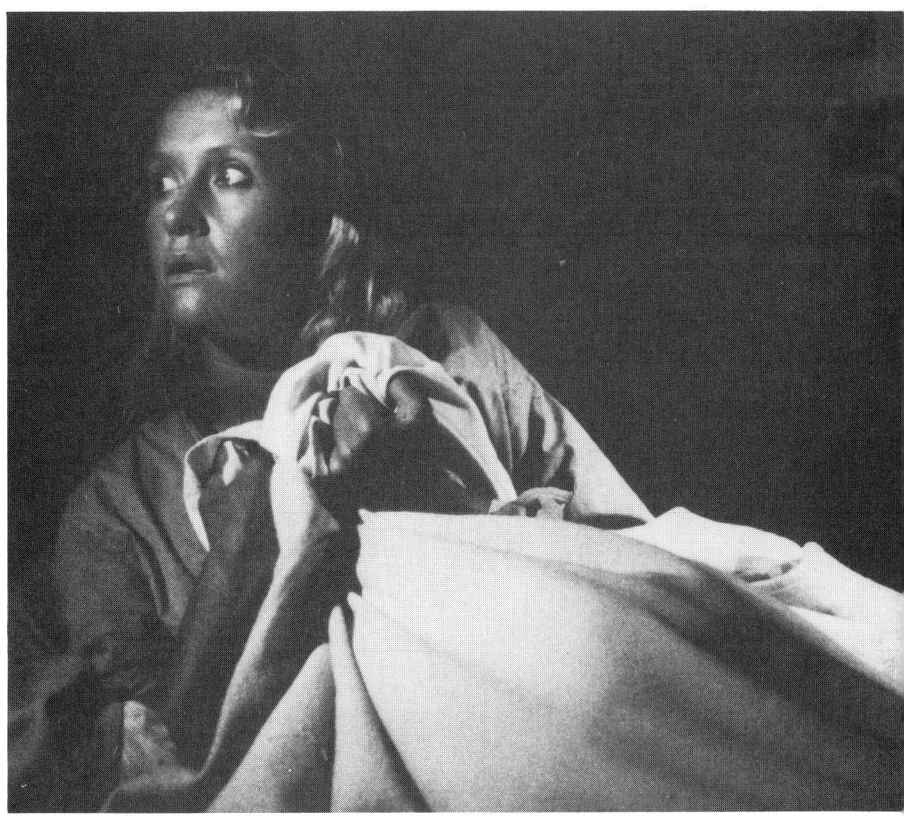

Annie Whittle, isolated and alone, senses danger in the night in *Trial Run* (Miracle Films), an excellent thriller from New Zealand.

To Live and Die in L.A. Superficially brilliantly achieved, but in a number of ways marred, William Friedkin's film of the *French Connection* genre is a crime thriller about a somewhat (to say the very least) unconventional undercover cop's grim tracking down of the counterfeiting killer of his erstwhile partner. The quest leads him into and through the shadiest side of Los Angeles; to the constant use of some of the most foul language to be heard on the screen; to the murder of innocents; to the casual (*sic*) treatment of the opposite sex; and to a classic re-hash of the old car-chase sequence. Cast: William L. Petersen, Willem Dafoe, John Pankow, Debra Feuer, John Turturro, Darlanne Fluegel, Dean Stockwell, Steve James, Robert Downey, Michael Greene, Christopher Allport, Jack Hoar, Val de Vargas, Dwier Brown, Michael Chong, Jackelyn Giroux, Michael Zand, Bobby Bass, Dar Allen Robinson, Anne Betancourt, Katherine M. Louie, Edward Harrell, Gilbert Espinoza, John Petievich, Zarco Petievich, Rick Dalton, Richard Lane, Jack Cota, Shirley J. White, Gerald H. Brownlee, David M. DuFriend, Ruben Garcia, Joe Duran, Buford McClerkins. Gregg Dandridge, Donny Williams, Ernest Hart Jr, Thomas F. Duffy, Gerald Petievich, Mark Gash, Pat McGroarty, Brian Bradley, Jean Leaves. Dir and (with Gerald Petievich) Screenplay: William Friedkin; based on the novel by Petievich. Pro: Irving H. Levin. Ex Pro: Samuel Schulman. Co-Pro, Sup Ed and 2nd Unit Dir: Bud Smith. Ph: Robby Muller. Ed: Scott Smith. Pro Des: Lilly Kilvery. Art: Buddy Cone. M: Wang Chung. (New Century Pro/SLM Inc.–MGM/UA–UIP) Rel: 6 June 1986. 116 mins. Cert 18.

Trial Run. A very promising writing–directing debut by New Zealander Melanie Read with this fascinating and cleverly worked thriller which requires greater than usual intuitive perceptiveness in order to make head or tail of the

1986 Oscar-winning Geraldine Page giving the performance of a lifetime in Mainline's moving and beautifully moulded movie *The Trip to Bountiful.*

plot's resolution. It concerns a 35-year-old housewife, mother, professional photographer and amateur long-distance runner who, during her combined efforts to make a photographic study of some rare penguins and train for her forthcoming marathon, has an uncomfortable sojourn at a lonely cabin where things go bump and snarl in the night. A nice performance by popular singer–composer Annie Whittle in the leading role. Rest of cast: Judith Gibson, Christopher Broun, Philippa Mayne, Martyn Sanderson, Lee Grant, Frances Edmond, Roy (the dog), Teresa Woodham, Allison Roe, Karen Sims, Maggie Eyre, Margaret Blay. Dir and Screenplay: Melanie Read. Pro: Don Reynolds. Assoc Pro: Alain Hunter. Ph: Allen Guilford. Ed: Finola Dwyer. Pro Des: Judith Crozier. Art: Kirsten Shouler. M: Jan Preston. (Cinema & Television Productions, with assoc of New Zealand Film Comm–Miracle) Rel: floating; first shown London (Classic, Oxford Street), 26 July 1985. 90 mins. Cert 15.

The Trip to Bountiful. Geraldine Page giving the performance of a lifetime – and winning the 1986 'Best Actress' Oscar for it – as an old lady, living an unhappy and frustrating existence with her weak son and shrewish daughter-in-law in Houston, who yearns for and finally returns to the now wrecked house in the deserted town where she lived her happy childhood. A marvellously evocative film delicately conceived and realized; a celluloid gem of no mean worth. Rest of cast: John Heard, Carlin Glynn, Richard Bradford, Rebecca de Mornay, Kevin Cooney, Mary Kay Mars, Norman Bennett, Harvey Lewis, Kirk Sisco, Dave Tanner, Gil Glasgow, Jerry Nelson, Wezz Tildon, Peggy Ann Byers, David Romo. Dir: Peter Masterton. Pro: Sterling Wegenen and Horton Foote. Ex Pro: Sam Grogg and George Yaneff. Screenplay: Foote; based on his play. Ph: Fred Murphy. Ed: Jay Freund. Pro Des: Neil Spisak. Art: Philip Lamb. M: J. A. C. Redford. (Film Dallas and Bountiful Film Partners–Mainline Pictures) Rel: floating; first shown London (Screen-on-the-Hill and Odeon, Kensington), 6 June 1986. 106 mins. Cert U.

Troll. All about the horrid little Trollies who take over a large 'Frisco house and one of the families living there, planning to spread themselves outwards . . . Though pretty ludicrous, quite a lot of style has gone into the production, making the non-Trollish sequences easy to watch. Cast: Noah Hathaway, Michael Moriarty, Shelley Hack, Jenny Beck, Sonny Bono, Phil Fondacaro, Brad Hall, Anne Lockhart, Julia Louis-Dreyfus, Gary Sandy, June Lockhart. Dir: John Buechler. Pro: Albert Band. Ex Pro: Charles Band. Screenplay: Ed Naha. Ph: Romano Albani. Ed: Lee Percy. M: Richard Band. (Band–Cannon) Rel: 13 June 1986. 86 mins. Cert 15.

Tuff Turf. Yet another youth-aimed American movie concerning some high school kids who have formed a criminal gang, The Tuffs, and use the charms of a lovely member to lure rich men into their brutal, thieving grasp. Cast: James Spader, Kim Richards, Paul Mones, Matt Clark, Claudette Nevins, Olivia Barash, Robert Downey, Panchito Gomez, Michael Wyle, Catya Sassoon, Frank McCarthy, Art Evans, Herb Mitchell, Ceil Cabot, Donald Fullilove, Vivian Brown, Bill Beyers, Jered Barclay, Lou Fant, Gene Pietragallo, Donna Fuller, Evonne Kezios, Cheryl Ann Clark, Matt Gavin, Chas McCann, W. J. Bergman, John Berry Jr, Rick Braun, Mark Campbell, J.R. Coile, Peter Freiberger, Andrew Kastner, Jack Mack. Dir: Fritz Kiersch. Pro: Donald P. Borchers. Co-Pro: Pat Kehoe. Assoc Pro: Bob Manning. Pro

The brothers Lynch (Timothy Hutton, right, and bureaucracy victim Robert Urich) in the crusading drama *Turk 182!* (20th Century–Fox).

Co-Ord: Patricia Swenson. Screenplay: Jette Rinck. Ph: Willy Kurant. Ed: Marc Grossman. Assoc Ed: Joe Woo Jr. Art: Craig Stearns. M: Jonathan Elias. (New World Pictures–Blue Dolphin) Rel: floating; first shown London (Classic, Oxford Street), 6 December 1985. 112 mins. Cert 18.

Turk 182! Though essentially American down to its final sprocket hole, this crusading drama with neat comedy touches should appeal to everyone for its searchlight on the evils and weaknesses of civic bureaucracy. These are seen here through the refusal of the mayor and officers of a city to meet their obligation of granting a pension to a heroic fireman who, when off duty, had been severely injured while trying to rescue a child from a fire. His outraged brother, taking on the city – and, more especially, its corrupt mayor – fights for a citizen's rights and, by brain rather than crude brawn, wins out in the end – with Frank Capra looking over his shoulder? A strong, human story decorated by some fine performances, notably by Timothy Hutton as the crusader, Robert Urich as the victim brother, and Robert Culp as the mayor. Rest of cast: Kim Cattrall, Darren McGavin, Steven Keats, Peter Boyle, Paul Sorvino, Thomas Quinn, Norman Parker, Dick O'Neill, James S. Tolkan, Maury Chaykin, Richard Zobel, David Wohl, Lou Griscuolo. Dir: Bob Clark. Pro: Ted Field and René Dupont. Ex Pro: Peter Samuelson and Robert Cort. Screenplay: James Gregory Kingston and John and Denis Hamill; based on the former's novel. Ph: Reginald H. Morris. Ed: Stan Cole. Pro Des: Harry Pottle. Art: Paul Eads. M: Paul Zaza. Assoc Pro: Gary Goch. (Fox) Rel: 13 September 1985. 96 mins. Cert 15.

Turtle Diary. Though apparently infuriating to some who have read the book on which it is based, to others this is a small, essentially British classic about a trio of initially unrelated characters – a shy and nervous children's author (Glenda Jackson), a bookseller's assistant who has a failed life behind him (Ben Kingsley) and a very human zoo attendant (Michael Gambon) – who combine in a plot to steal several 30-year-old turtles from their prison-zoo and release them into the sea off the Devon coast. Fine, simple direction, marvellous performances and plenty of Harold Pinter wit in the script make this a brilliant all-round achievement and easily one of the best, if less ambitious, British movies of the year. Rest of cast: Richard Johnson, Rosemary Leach, Eleanor Bron, Harriet Walter, Jeroen Krabbe, Nigel Hawthorn, Michael Aldridge, Rom Anderson, Tony Melody, Gary Olsen, Peter Capaldi, Harold Pinter, Barbara Rosenblat, Chuck Julian. Dir: John Irvin. Pro: Richard Johnson. Ex Pro: Peter Snell. Pro Sup: Christabel Albery. Screenplay: Harold Pinter; based on the novel by Russell Hoban. Ph: Peter Hannan. Ed: Peter Tanner. Pro Des: Leo Austin. Art: Judith Ariadne Lang and Diane Danklefsen. M: Geoffrey Burgon. (United British Artists/Britannic Pro for CBS Productions–Rank Film Dist.) Rel: floating; first shown London (Curzon, West End), 1 December 1985. 96 mins. Cert PG.

The three plotters – zoo-keeper Michael Gambon, author Glenda Jackson and bookseller Ben Kingsley – drink a toast to themselves after stealing the giant tortoises from the zoo and freeing them into the South Coast seas in the delightful Rank-released comedy *Turtle Diary*.

The Ultimate Solution of Grace Quigley (also shown as **Grace Quigley**). Chuckly black comedy built around the controversial theme of euthanasia. A dear little old lady (Katharine Hepburn, at 76 still going skilfully, if a little shakily, strong) blackmails a professional hit-man (Nick Nolte) into helping some of her lonely old friends painlessly into a better world; this strange relationship develops into a sort

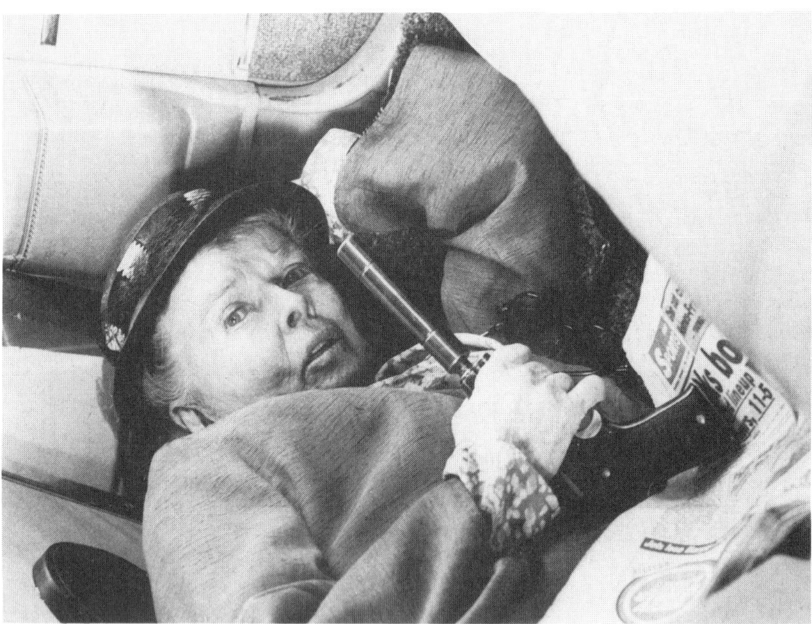

Miss Quigley (Katharine Hepburn) finds herself in a tight corner as she takes shelter from the hit-man (Nick Nolte) in *The Ultimate Solution of Grace Quigley* (Cannon).

of mother-and-son affection. Rest of cast: Elizabeth Wilson, Chip Zien, Kit le Fever, William Duell, Walter Abel, Frances Pole, Truman Gaige, Paula Trueman, Christopher Murney, William Cain, Howard Sherman, Jill Eikenberry, Michael Charters, Christopher Charters, Harris Laskawy, Carl Low, Lucy Saroyan, Isabella Hoopes, Dortha Duckworth, Nicholas Kepros, Denny Dillon, Michael P. Moran, Vincent Harta. Dir: Anthony Harvey. Pro: Menahem Golan and Yoram Globus. Ex Pro: A. Martin and Adrienne Zweiback. Assoc Pro: Christopher Pearce. Screenplay: A. Martin Zweiback. Ph: Larry Pizer. Ed: Robert Reitano. Pro Des: Gary Weist. Art: Jack Blackman. M: John Addison. (Cannon/Northbrook-Cannon) Rel: floating; first shown London (Classic, Haymarket), 21 June 1985. 95 mins. Cert 15.

Ursula and Glenys. Strange little movie about two sisters, long parted, who are brought together again by their father. In the discussions that ensue, their hidden pasts are brought to life. Cast: Brid Brennan, Gaylie Runcimen, Ric Morgan, Joe and Kieran Davies. Dir: John Davies. Screenplay: Davies, and members of the cast. Ph: Robert Smith. (Frontroom Productions/ICA) Rel: floating; first shown London (ICA), 11 March 1986. 56 mins. No cert.

Vagabonde – Sans Toit ni Loi. Fascinating Agnès Varda film which starts with the discovery of a young girl who has frozen to death in a ditch and goes on to investigate what has led up to her demise, revealing her as a homeless, rootless drifter with no moral sense or motivation and always bound for total disaster. A tale told without sympathy or any attempt to blame the girl's hopeless situation on anyone but herself. Cast: Sandrine Bonnaire, Macha Meril, Stephane Freiss, Laurence Cortadellas, Martha Jarnias, Yolande Moreau, Joel Fosse, Patrick Lepeczynski, Yahiaoui Assouna. Dir and Screenplay: Agnès Varda. Ph: Patrick Blossier. Ed: Varda and Patricia Mazuy. M: Joanna Druzdowiecz. (Cine Tamaris/Films A2 in assoc with French Ministry of Culture and Channel 4–Electric Pictures) Rel: floating; first shown London (Minema and Renoir), 9 May 1986. 107 mins. Cert 18.

A View to a Kill. Though the 007 film formula is still virtually a millionaire-maker, it is becoming a bit frayed around the edges, with obvious difficulties in finding new angles, new thrills and gimmicks and the essential touch of novelty. James Bond – as cheerfully careless about personal safety as ever, and as amorous, too – is up against a psychopathic billionaire from East Germany who plans to corner the computer market by wiping out the opposition. And it all gets a bit confusing at times. But despite that, the mixture is still good enough to ring all the bells in the cinema box-offices. Varied performances from Roger Moore (as casually good as ever), Christopher Walken (too light for a Bond villain), Grace Jones (with nothing much to do except scowl), Tanya Roberts, Patrick MacNee, Patrick Bachau, David Yip, Fiona Fullerton, Manning Redwood, Alison Doody, Willoughby Gray, Desmond Llewelyn, Robert Brown, Lois Maxwell, Walter Gotell, Geoffrey Keen, Jean Rougerie, Daniel Benzali, Albert Simono, Bogdan Kominowski, Papillon Soo Soo, Mary Stavin, Dominique Risbourg, Carole Ashby, Anthony Chin, Lucien Jerome, Joe Flood, Gérard Bühr, Dolph Lundgren, Tony Sibbald, Bill Ackridge, Ron Tarr, Taylor McAuley, Peter Ensor, Seva Novgorodtsev. Dir: John Glen. Pro: Albert Broccoli and Michael G. Wilson. Assoc Pro: Thomas Pevsner. 2nd Unit Dir and Ph: Arthur Wooster. Screenplay: Wilson and Richard Maibaum. Ph: Alan Hume. Ski sequences Dir and Ph: Willy Bogner. Ed: Peter Davies. Pro Des: Peter Lamont. M: John Barry (Title song by Barry and Duran Duran, performed by the latter). (MGM/UA–UIP) Rel: 19 July 1985. 131 mins. Cert PG.

Volunteers. In 1962, a rich Yale graduate who is a fugitive from his gambling debts take the place of a genuine member of the Peace Corps, goes to Asia and gives plenty of umbrage when he starts a bit of bridge-building, complicated by Communists, black marketeers and others. It is, quote, a 'comedy'! Cast: Tom Hanks, John Candy, Rita Wilson, Tim Thomerson, Gedde Watanabe, George Plimpton, Ernest Harada, etc. Dir: Nicholas Meyer. Pro: Richard Shepherd and Walter F. Parkes. Screenplay: Ken Levine and David Isaacs; based on a story by Keith Critchlow. Ph: Ric Waite. Ed: Ronald Roose and Steven Polivka. Pro Des: James Schoppe and Delia Castaneda. M: James Horner. (HBO in assoc with Silver Screen Partners–Tri-Star) Rel: 18 April 1986. 107 mins. Cert 15.

Weird Science. Routine American movie aimed at the young end of the market, about a couple of teenagers who can't pluck up the courage to lay

siege to the girls they would like to know more about. With the help of an old Frankenstein film video, a Barbie doll and dad's home computer, they create a very lively and forthright young lady (pretty Kelly le Brock, one of the best things in the film) who helps them overcome their shyness and into their girls' arms. Rest of cast: Anthony Michael Hall, Alan Mitchell-Smith, Bill Paxton, Suzanne Snyder, Judie Aronson, Robert Downey, Robert Rusler, Vernon Wells, Britt Leach, Barbara Lang, Michael Berryman, Ivor Barry, Anne Bernadette Coyle, Suzy J. Kellems, John Kapelos, Fred D. Scott, Vince Monroe Townsend, Chino Williams, Jill Whitlow, Theodocia Goodrich, Wally Ward, Johnny Timko, Mikul Robins, Darren Harris, Babette Props, Michael Cramer, Todd Hoffman, D'Mitch Davis, Mary Steelsmith, Robin Frohman, Alison Carole Lowe, Kym Malin, Jennifer Balgobin, Jeff Jensen, Prince A. Hughes, Rick le Fevor, Rock Walker, Joe Gieb, Kevin Thompson, Doug MacHugh, Pamela Gordon. Dir and Screenplay: John Hughes. Pro: Joel Silver. Assoc Pro: Jane Vickerilla. Ph: Matthew F. Leonetti. Ed: Mark Warner, Christopher Lebenzon and Scott Wallace. Pro Des: John W. Corso. Art: James Allen. M: Ira Newborn. (Universal–UIP) Rel: 1 Nov 1985. 92 mins. Cert 15.

Roger (007) Moore flanked by Lois Maxwell (Miss Moneypenny), Desmond Llewelyn (as 'Q' – centre), Patrick MacNee and Robert Brown (as 'M' – right) in the James Bond opus *A View to Kill* (MGM/UA–UIP). Right, 007 gets down to the fizzy-wizzy with glamour girl Tanya Roberts.

When Father Was Away on Business – Otac na Sluzbenom Nutu. From Yugoslavia, a highly diverting comedy with a serious theme. Here, a view of a family reflects life in general in that country during the uneasy and difficult period following Tito's break with Stalin (1948–52). The events of the film are seen through the eyes of a small boy who gradually comes to realize that the so-called 'business trip' of his father, a cheerful lecher, is really a politically punitive stay in a labour camp, although he is in fact totally innocent. The family is brilliantly portrayed, and the film won the 1985 Cannes Film Festival *Palme d'Or* Award. Cast: Miki Manojlovic (the father), Moreno D. E. Bartolli (the younger son), Mirjana Karanovic (the long-suffering wife), Pavle Vujisic, Mustafa Nadarevic, Miraa Furlan, Fredrag Lakovic-Pepi, Slobodan Aligrudic, Davor Dumovic, Amer Kapettanovic, Aleksandar Dzordzev, Eva Ras, etc. Dir: Emir Kusturica. Pro: Mirza Pasic. Ex Pro: Vera Milic-Jolie. Screenplay: Abdulah Sidran. Scenarist: Pedrag Lukovac. Ph: Vilko Filac. Ed: Andrija Zafranovic. Pro Des: Predrag Lukovan. M: Zoran Simjanovic. ('Forum' Sarajevo–Cannon/Gala) Rel: floating; first shown London (Cannon Film Centre), 22 November 1985. 135 mins. Cert 18.

When We Were Young – Kak Molody My Byli. A Soviet equivalent of the current series of American films which have looked back lovingly to the not-too-distant past – in this case, to youngsters growing up in the USSR of

Wife (Isabella Rossellini) and ballet-star husband (Mikhail Baryshnikov) in the arms of the KGB (Jerzy Skolimowski, right) in Columbia's *White Nights* – the Royal Film Performance selection for 1986. Inset, dancers of two very different kinds, ballet (Baryshnikov) and tap (Gregory Hines), rehearse and plan their escape together.

the late 'fifties. A curious, puzzling telling by the director, whose efforts at originality somewhat rebound on him. Cast: Taras Denisenko, Elena Shkurpelo, N. Sharolapova, A. Pashutin, A. Sviridovsky, A. Lukyanenko. M. Kokshenov, etc. Dir and Screenplay: Mikhail Belikov. Pro: A. Vishnyevsky and N. Fedyuk. Ph: Vasily Trushkovsky. Ed: N. Akaemovoi. Art: A. Levchenko. M: Y. Vinnik and Chopin, Gershwin, etc. (Dovzhenko Studio–The Other Cinema) Rel: floating; first shown London (Metro), 28 March 1986. 90 mins. No cert.

Where Is Parsival? Critical reaction to this Cannes-shown British film varied between 'surprisingly diverting entertainment' and 'summery frolic' to *Variety*'s 'ludicrous beyond belief' and '. . . makes one wonder how it got made.' So you pays your money and makes your own judgement. It's a frenetic farce about Parsival, a nutty inventor, who lives in a castle with a bunch of equally odd nuts. But don't expect any sort of traditional story – there just isn't one. Cast: Tony Curtis, Cassandra Domenica, Erik Estrada, Peter Lawford, Ron Moody, Donald Pleasence, Orson Welles, Christopher Chaplin, Nancy Roberts, Vladel Sheybal, Ava Lazar, Jay Benedict, Edward Burnham, Anthony Dawson, Victoria Burgoyne, Stuart Latham, Simon Cloquet, David Baxt, Peter Poll, Sally Cranfield, Christian Artemis, Pamela Trigg, Arthur Beatty. Dir: Henri Helman. Pro: Daniel Carrillo. Ex Pro: Terence Young. Pro Sup: Vincent Winter. Screenplay: Berta Dominguez. Ph: Norman Langley. Ed: Russ Lloyd and Peter Hollywood. Pro Des: Malcolm Stone. Art: Lucy Richardson. M: Hubert Rostaing and Ivan Jullien. (Slenderline–Rank) Rel: floating; first shown London (Scene), 19 July 1985. 87 mins. Cert 15.

White Nights. Though misguidedly trying to be too many things at once – classical-and-pop musical, international thriller and racial romance – this out-of-the-rut movie emerges with considerable credit, deserving to have been chosen for the 1986 Royal Film Performance. It's about a Russian ballet star (a remarkable dramatic and balletic performance by ex-Kirov star Mikhail Baryshnikov) who had, some years before, defected to the United States. Unfortunately, he is a passenger in a New York–Tokyo airplane which, through malfunction, is forced to crash-land at a Soviet military airport, where the dancer is arrested as a criminal. 'Encouraged' to return to the Soviet ballet company by the KGB, the dancer plans – along with a black American tap-dancing star (Gregory Hines) who defected to the Soviet Union but is now unhappy with his lot, and the latter's Russian interpreter wife (Isabella Rossellini, Ingrid Bergman's daughter) – to escape from his comfortable detention and regain his freedom by way of a heart-stopping dangerous flight through Moscow to the US Embassy. Rest of cast: Jerzy Skolimowski, Helen Mirren, Geraldine Page, John Glover, Stefan Gryff, William Hootkins, Shane Rimmer, Florence Faure, David Savile, Ian Liston, Benny Young, Hilary Drake, Megumi Shimanuki, Daniel Benzali, Maria Werlander, Galina Pomerantzeva, Sergei Rousakov, Alexander Naumov, Maryam D'Abo, Mark Sinden, Josephine Buchan, Helene Denbey, Susannah Morley, Elisa Tornqvist, Jiri Stanislav, Edward Ochagavia, Marc Michalsky, Michael Petrovich, Andreas Markos. Dir and (with William S. Gilmore) Pro: Taylor Hackford. Assoc Pro: Bill Borden. Ex Sup: Stuart Benjamin. Screenplay: James Goldman and Eric Hughes; based on a story by the former. Ph: David Watkin. Ed: Fredric and William Steinkamp. Pro Des: Philip Harrison. Choreographer: Twyla Tharp; 'Le Jeune Homme et la Mort' chor. by Roland Petit. M (score): Michael Colombier. (New Visions Pro–Columbia) Rel: 18 April 1986. 136 mins. Cert PG.

The Wind – Finye. A rare opportunity to see an example of a modern African movie: Souleymane Cisse's more or less one-man Mali production (1982) about a romance, frowned on by the families, between a former chieftain's grandson (who fails his exams because he has no status in his society) and a girl (whose success has been purchased by her repressive military-governor dad) and their joining with other restless and unhappy students in a fight against inequality. And all presented with sympathy and no lack of humour. Cast: Fousseyni Sissoko, Goundo Guisse, Balla Moussa Keita, Ismaila Sarr, Oumou Diarra, etc. Dir, Pro and Screenplay: Souleymane Cisse. Ph: Etienne Carton de Grammont. Ed: André Davanture. Art: Malick Guisse. M: Radio Mogadiscio, Pierre Gorse and Malinese folk music. (BFI) Rel: floating; first shown London (ICA), 4 October 1985. 100 mins. No cert.

A Woman or Two – Une Femme ou Deux. Gérard Depardieu as a French archaeologist who falls in love with a 2 million-year-old female he has dug up, but eventually decides that the charms of lovely American advertising executive Sigourney Weaver are to be preferred. Lightly amusing, typically Gallic comedy-farce. Rest of cast: Ruth Westheimer, Michel Aumont, Zabou, Jean-Pierre Bisson, Yann Babilée, Maurice Barrier, Robert Blumenfeld, Michael Goldman, Adrian Howard, Tanis Vallely, Jean-Quentin Chatelain, Axel Bogousslavsky, André Julien, Jean-Paul Muel, Jean-François Perrier, André Haber, Philippe Dehesdien, Mathé Souverbie, Philippe Desboeuf, Janet Aldrich, Dion Anderson, Seth Allen, Kyle Scott Jackson, Dir: Daniel Vigne. Pro: Michel Choquet. Ex Pro: Philippe Dussart. Screenplay: Vigne and Elizabeth Rappeneau. Ph: Carlo Varini. Ed: Marie-Josèphe Yoyotte. Art: Jean-Pierre Kohut Svelko. M: Kevin Mulligan, Evert Verhees and Toots Thielemans. (Virgin Films) Rel: floating; first shown London (Cannon, Tottenham Court Road), 13 June 1986. 97 mins. Cert 15.

The Woman Who Married Clark Gable. A half-hour short based on the idea that the cinema has the power to affect the emotions and even the lives of some members of the audience. This is presented, not always sufficiently clearly, through the story of a married couple of mixed religious belief (he a British Protestant, she a fervent Irish Catholic) and the manner in which their marriage is changed, at least temporarily, by the wife's fascination with Clark Gable's performance in the film *San Francisco*. Nice performances by Bob Hoskins and Brenda Fricker. Rest of cast: Peter Caffery, Eamon Kelly, Maeve Germaine, Jill Doyle, Helen Roche, Anto Nolan, Bobby Lepla, Eugene Kavanagh, Paul McCarthy. Dir: Thaddeus O'Sullivan. Pro: Sally Hope and David Collins. Ex Pro: Michael Algar (Irish Film Board). Screenplay: Andrew Pattman; based on a short story by Sean O'Faolain. Ph: Jack Conroy. Ed: J. Patrick Duffner. Art: Frank Conway. M: John Buckley. (Bord Scannan na hEireann/Brook Films/Channel 4) Rel: 8 November 1985. 28 mins. Cert 15.

Bob Hoskins and Brenda Fricker as the married couple who suffer from different religious beliefs – and the power of the cinema! – in the Irish Film Board's half-hour movie bound for Channel 4 *The Woman Who Married Clark Gable.*

Year of the Dragon. Michael Cimino's first movie since his ill-fated *Heaven's Gate* is an interesting but flawed thriller which, although rich and impressive in detail and with some superb cinematic sequences, never quite ties the bundle into an outstanding whole. The key figure in the mayhem is a much-decorated (and, almost, too-dedicated) New York 'Pollack' cop who decides personally to take on and clean up the city's closed and secretive Chinatown, and by his violent methods annoys his bosses almost as much as he infuriates his big-time drug-trafficking Chinese opponents. (And the large Vietnam chip on his shoulder must surely alienate some of his audience as much as it alienates his wife and mistress.) Spectacular and intermittently fast-paced – and, on occasion, very bloody – with dialogue peppered with those familiar four-letter words, it is nevertheless visually lavish and exciting. Cast:

Dedicated cleaner-upper cop Mickey Rourke shoots his way out of a tight corner in Michael (*Heaven's Gate*) Cimino's Columbia release *Year of the Dragon*. Inset, New York's Chinatown bosses discuss the situation his advent has created.

Mickey Rourke, John Lone, Ariane, Ray Barry, Lenny Termo, Eddie Jones, Caroline Kava, Joey Chin, Mr Lee, Victor Wong, Pao Han Lin, Rosang, K. Dock Yip, Dennis Dun, Way Dong Woo, Jimmy Sun, Daniel Davin, Mark Hamner, Jack Kehler, Steven Chen, Paul Scaglione, Joseph Bonaventura, Jilly Rizzo, Tony Lip, Fabia Drake, Tisa Chang, Gerald Orange, Fan Mui Sang, Yukio Yamamoto, Doreen Chan, Harry Yip, Dermot McNamara, Dr Vallo Benjamin, Myra Chen, Rev. Julian Szumilo, George Kodisch, Bruce Kennedy, Geoffrey Lee, John Sparks; supporting cast of (mostly) American-Chinese. Dir: Michael Cimino. Pro: Dino de Laurentiis. Ex in charge of Pro: Fred Caruso. Screenplay: Oliver Stone and Cimino; based on the novel by Robert Daley. Ph: Alex Thompson. Ed: Françoise Bonnot. Pro Des: Wolf Kroeger. Art: Vicki Paul. M: David Mansfield. (De Laurentiis Corp for MGM/UA–Thorn EMI) Rel: 7 February 1986. 134 mins. Cert 18.

Year of the Quiet Sun – Rok Spokojnego Slonka. Highly impressive, very

The young master-sleuth-to-be (Nicholas Rowe) and the future Doctor Watson (Alan Cox) discuss a case – or something! – against a suitable background of fog, gas lamps and hansom cabs in UIP's *Young Sherlock Holmes*.

moving and memorable Polish–American–West German co-production from Krzysztof Zanussi, which quite deservedly won the 1984 Venice Film Festival's premier Golden Lion Award. It is the sad, low-toned love story of an American soldier – the sole survivor of a death camp who stays on in a Polish town to work for an organization investigating atrocities – and a local war-widow eking out a living with her invalid mother. Unable to converse, they still manage to communicate their increasing love for each other, but fate (a little puzzlingly) prevents a happy ending. Beautifully acted by Scott Wilson (soldier), Maja Komorowska (widow) and Hanna Skarzanka (mother). Rest of cast: Ewa Dalkowska, Vadim Glowna, Daniel Webb, Zbigniew Zapasiewicz, Tadeus Bradecki, Jerzy Nowak, Jerzy Stuhr, etc. Dir and Screenplay: Krzysztof Zanussi. Ex Pro: Michal Szczerbic and Michael Boehme. Pro Con: Zbigniew Dobrowolski. Ph: Slawomir Idziak. Ed: Marek Denys. Art: Janusz Sosnowski. M: Wojciech Kilar. (Film Polski/Tor Film, Warsaw/ Teleculture, Munich/Regina Ziegler Filmproduction. Berlin–Blue Dolphin Films) Rel: floating; first shown London (ICA), 21 February 1986. 106 mins. Cert 15.

Guisje Van Tilborgh as the lady with hat, trumpet and book but nought else (in *A Zed and Two Noughts*).

Young Sherlock Holmes and the Pyramid of Fear. Though having little in common with Conan Doyle's classic detective stories, except for the names of the two major characters, this Spielberg production is quite a lot of fun in its supposition as to what might have occurred if Mr Holmes and Dr Watson had met as students and had then carried out a little investigation of a less-than-cerebral kind! What emerges as the film's strongest point are the brilliant effects, contributed by George Lucas's Industrial Light and Magic set-up. Nice performances, too, by Nicholas Rowe as the embryo super-sleuth, Alan Cox as his young pal and Sophie Ward as the female angle. But to suppose that young Sherlock perfected the flying machine isn't very logical, is it? If he had done, he would surely never have gone on to play his lonely fiddle in Baker Street! Rest of cast: Anthony Higgins, Susan Fleetwood, Freddie Jones, Nigel Stock, Roger Ashton-Griffiths, Earl Rhodes, Brian Oulton, Patrick Newell, Donald Eccles, Matthew Ryan, Matthew Blakstad, Jonathan Lacey, Walter Sparrow, Nadim Sawalha, Roger Brierley, Vivienne Chandler, Lockwood West, John Scott Martin, George Malpas, Willoughby Goddard, Michael Cule, Ralph Tabakin, Nancy Nevinson, Michael Hordern (as voice of the older Watson). Dir: Barry Levinson. Pro: Mark Johnson. Ex Pro: Steven Spielberg, Frank Marshall and Kathleen Kennedy. Assoc Pro: Harry Benn. Screenplay: Chris Columbus. Ph: Stephen Goldblatt. Ed: Stu Linder. Pro Des: Norman Reynolds. Art: Fred Hole, Charles Bishop and Dave Carson. Special effects: Industrial Light and Magic (supervisor: Kit West). M: Bruce Broughton. (Spielberg/Amblin Entertainment in assoc with Henry Winkler and Roger Birnbaum–Paramount–UIP) Rel: 21 March 1986. 109 mins. Cert PG.

A Zed and Two Noughts. Indulgently overlong, consistently stylish, beautifully photographed, idiosyncratic and wilfully 'difficult' British movie from Peter (*Draughtsman's Contract*) Greenaway, which attempts to cover many subjects, more especially the concept of symmetry. A film which will almost certainly delight the highbrows as much as it will confuse, irritate and possibly alienate movie-goers from the likes of the Old Kent Road and Steeple Bumstead. Its meandering, convoluted and never-really-clear story – with, some may find, unpleasant undercurrents – concerns two brothers – Siamese twins – who become attracted to the one-legged woman (who eventually has her other leg removed for the sake of symmetry) who drove the car which killed their wives, and – jointly – go to bed with her, beget twins (which she apparently gives to a legless man) and then commit a carefully planned, patterned suicide which is an artistic failure. And there's plenty of significance to be sniffed out from all this. Yet, in spite of its irritations, it is a highly original, intelligent and consistently fascinating work. Cast: Andrea Ferreol,

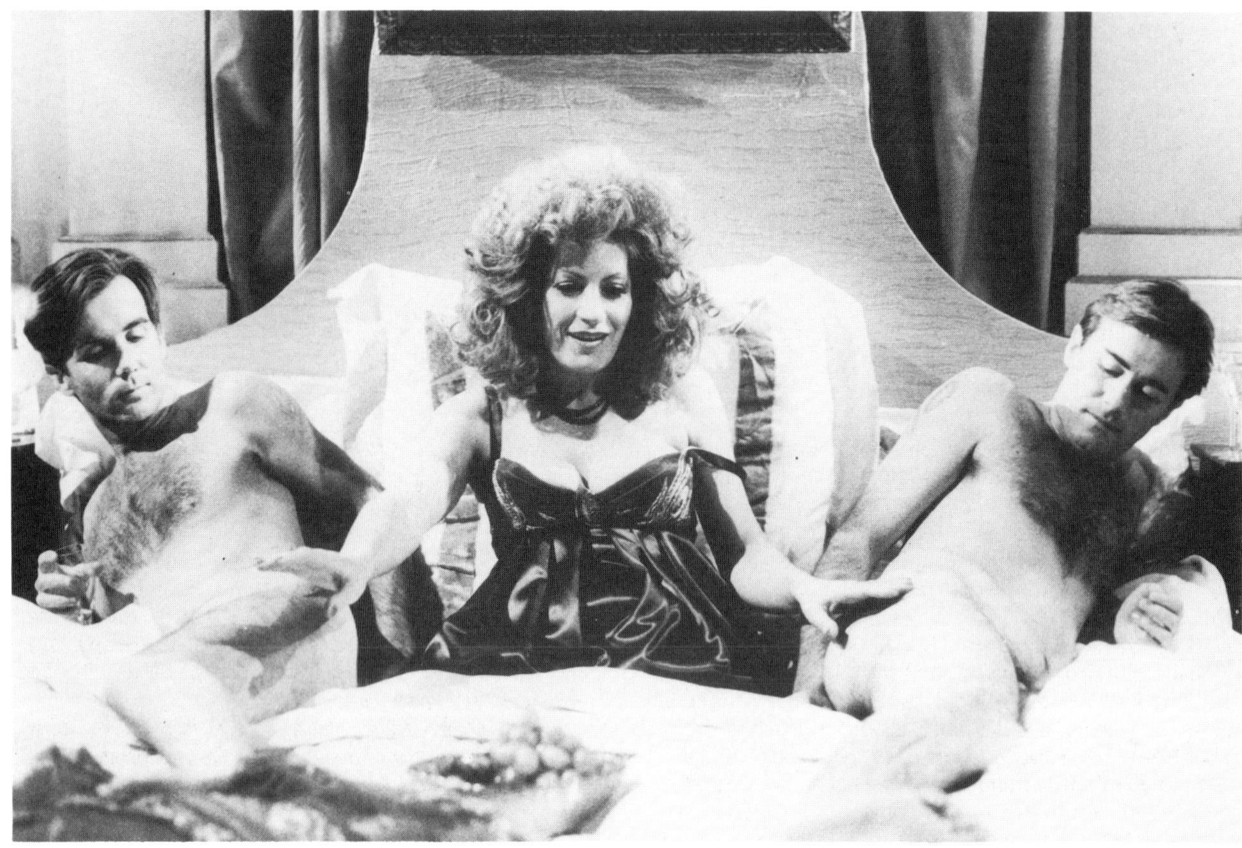

Andrea Ferreol as the one-legged lady who lures twins Brian and Eric Deacon into her bed, as a result of which she eventually bears them identical twin sons, in the BFI film *A Zed and Two Noughts*, released by Artificial Eye.

Brian Deacon, Eric Deacon, Frances Barber, Joss Ackland, Jim Davidson, Agnes Brulet, Guisje Van Tilborgh, Gerard Thoolen, Ken Campbell, Wolf Kahler, Geoffrey Palmer. Dir and Screenplay: Peter Greenaway. Pro: Peter Sainsbury and Kees Kasander. Ph: Sacha Vierny. Ed: John Wilson. Pro Des: Ben Van Os and Jan Roelfs. M: Michael Nyman ('The Teddy Bears' Picnic' and 'An Elephant Never Forgets' performed by Henry Hall's BBC Dance Orchestra.) (BFI/Allart's Enterprise/Artificial Eye Pro/ Film Four International–Artificial Eye) Rel: floating; first shown London (Lumière), 5 December 1985. 115 mins. Cert 18.

Zina. British production which probes into the life and psychology of Leon Trotsky's daughter, who is generally believed to have committed suicide in Berlin in 1931. The story is told with a clever and remarkably smooth mix of reconstruction and historical fact, dream sequences and interviews with a psychoanalyst, all presented to flesh out the portrait and taking precedence over the politics which are still an important part of the study. Obviously of limited appeal, but intelligent, imaginative and well worth while. Cast: Domiziana Giordano, Ian McKellen, Philip Madoc, Rom Anderson, Micha Bergese, Gabrielle Della, Paul Geoffrey, William Hootkins, Leonie Mellinger, Maureen O'Brien, Dominique Pinon, Tusse Silberg, George Yiasoumi, Georges Levantis, Jeff Teare, Eleanor Greet. Dir, Pro and (with Terry James) Screenplay: Ken McMullen. Ex Pro: Andrew Lee, Penny Corke, Adrian Munsey and Paul Levinson. Ph (in black-and-white and colour): Bryan Loftus. Ed: Robert Hargreaves. Pro Des: Paul Cheetham. M: David Cunningham, Barry Guard and Simon Heyworth. (TSI/Looseyard–Virgin) Rel: floating; first shown London (Gate, Notting Hill and Metro), 1 May 1986. 93 mins. Cert 15.

Zone Troopers. A war film, set in Italy in 1944, with science-fiction trimmings. The 'Iron Sergeant', his two men, and a war correspondent, trapped behind German lines, are eventually helped to escape by the spaceship sent to rescue a crashed spacecraft pilot who, as well as the Americans, has been captured. Made on a very modest budget, this equally modest little movie is quite good fun, with some neat performances and a nice sense of humour. Cast: Tim Thomerson, Timothy Van Patten, Art La Fleur, Biff Manard, William Paulson, Peter Boom, Max Turilli, Eugene Brell, John Leamer, Bruce McGuire, Alviero Martin, Mike Manderville, Archille Brunini, Ole Jorgensen, Peter Hintz, Joshua McDonald, Anita Zagaria. Dir: Danny Bilson. Pro: Paul de Meo. Ex Pro: Charles Band. Assoc Pro: Debra Dion. Pro Ex: Roberto Bessi and Dennis Murphy. Screenplay: Bilson and de Meo. Ph: Mac Ahlberg. Ed: Ted Nicolaou. Pro Des: P. D. Foreman. M: Richard Band. (Altar Pro/Empire Pictures–Entertainment) Rel: floating; first shown London (Cannon, Panton Street, 28 February 1986. 86 mins. Cert 15.

Video Releases

ANTHONY HAYWARD

Feature films are becoming increasingly available on low-priced video cassettes in Britain. This trend was initiated in late 1985 by Prestwich Holdings, which launched the 'Video Collection' label, selling classic films, music cassettes and children's material through branches of the Woolworth/Woolco chain – for only £6.99. In its first year, the Video Collection's 'Movie Greats' releases included Fred Astaire and Ginger Rogers in *Flying Down to Rio* and *The Gay Divorcée*, the Marx Brothers and a young Marilyn Monroe in *Love Happy*, and the Alfred Hitchcock classics *Notorious* and *Spellbound*. The label's first modern feature film, also at £6.99, was *The Amityville Horror*.

Heron Home Entertainment and PolyGram Video followed the move towards budget-priced features with their own video label, 'Channel 5', selling cassettes through specialist dealers and chain stores. Channel 5's releases – costing less than £10.00 – have included *Citizen Kane, An American Werewolf in London* and *Sophie's Choice*.

In the full-price video market, the big success of the past year has been *Rambo – First Blood Part II*, first in the United States, then in Britain, where there were 45,000 advance orders for the cassette. Other major successes were the Christmas releases *Beverly Hills Cop*, *Gremlins* and *Ghostbusters*, each with an advance order of about 40,000 in Britain.

The peak year for video cassette sales was 1983 when, according to the British Videogram Association, about £90 million of business was done by distributors. By the end of 1985, however, sales were down for the second consecutive year – but only slightly less than in 1984, thanks to a massive boost in the last three months of the year. On the other hand, cassette rentals continued to increase in 1985 and video retailers' revenues rose.

The American video industry has reason for optimism following a study that forecast a five-fold increase in business, to $20 billion, by 1995. The report, by Wilkofsky Gruen Associates, predicted that 85 per cent of homes would have video recorders by 1995, with one-quarter of a television's use being devoted to the watching of videos. Another report, this time from the Electronic Industries Association, estimated that 45,000 video recorders were sold every day over the 1985 Christmas holiday period. In fact, video is becoming such big business in the United States that many people were predicting that its revenue would overtake that of cinema box-offices by the end of 1986.

July 1985

All of Me (Thorn EMI)
The Arrangement (Warner)
Avenging Angel (RCA/Columbia)

The Bastard (CIC)
Blume in Love (Warner)
Boggy Creek II . . . And the Legend Continues (Screentime/PolyGram)
The Bostonians (Embassy)
Buster and Billy (RCA/Columbia)

Cheerleaders' Wild Weekend (Thorn EMI)
Chocky (Thorn EMI)
Codename: Foxfire – Slay It Again, Sam (CIC)
The Cold Room (Heron)
Common-Law Cabin (VideoSpace/PVG)
The Cradle Will Fall (re-release; Careyvision)

Deceptions (Embassy)
The Dirty Dozen – Next Mission (MGM/UA)
Draw (PolyGram)

Flight of the Cougar (MGM/UA)

Give My Regards to Broad Street (CBS/Fox)
Greyfriars Bobby (Walt Disney)

Harem Holiday (MGM/UA)
Hell Squad (Guild)
Hennessy (Rank)
Heroes (CIC)
The Hunting Instinct (Walt Disney)

I Married a Centerfold (Precision)
The Immoral Mr Teas (VideoSpace/PVG)
The Imposter (Ariel)

The Joy of Sex (CIC)

The Karate Kid (RCA/Columbia)

A Little Romance (Warner)
Live a Little, Love a Little (MGM/UA)
Love, Honor and Obey (Warner)

Manhattan (Warner)
Man, Woman and Child (RCA/Columbia)
Marco Polo (RCA/Columbia)
Modern Romance (RCA/Columbia)

National Lampoon's *Movie Madness* (Warner)

One Deadly Summer (Guild)

Praying Mantis (Careyvision)
Prime Suspect (Heron)

Raging Bull (Warner)
The Razor's Edge (RCA/Columbia)
Romantic Comedy (Warner)

Scream for Help (Heron)
The Seduction (re-release; Heron)
Stay Away Joe (MGM/UA)

The Three Lives of Thomasina (Walt Disney)
The Trouble with Girls (MGM/UA)

Under the Rainbow (Warner)

August 1985

Across 10th Street (Warner)

Bank Shot (Warner)

Calendar Girl Murders (CBS/Fox)
Chiefs (Heron)
The Chinese Boxer (Thorn EMI)
Christopher Columbus (Heron)
City Heat (Warner)
Concrete Beat (Embassy)
The Corsican Brothers (Rank)

Deep in My Heart (MGM/UA)
Disaster on the Coastliner (Heron)

Electra Glide in Blue (Warner)

Flashpoint (Thorn EMI)
French Postcards (CIC)

The Grey Fox (Palace)

Heavenly Bodies (CBS/Fox)

Jekyll and Hyde . . . Together Again (CIC)

The Key (Embassy)

Midnight Madness (Walt Disney)
Mike's Murder (Warner)
Mikey and Nicky (PolyGram)
Misunderstood (Odyssey)
Murder at the World Series (Heron)
Mussolini and I (Embassy)

Not My Kid (Precision)
The Nude Bomb (CIC)

Places in the Heart (CBS/Fox)
The Pope of Greenwich Village (Warner)
A Private Function (Thorn EMI)

Report to the Commissioner (Warner)
The Rise and Fall of Legs Diamond (Warner)

Sexpionage (Precision)
Smash Up on Interstate Five (Heron)
Snap (Avatar/CBS/Fox)
Starcrossed (CBS/Fox)

Take This Job and Shove It (re-release; Embassy)
Ten Who Dared (Walt Disney)
Tex (Walt Disney)

Ulzana's Raid (CIC)
The Unsinkable Molly Brown (MGM/UA)

Violent Strangers – Wetherby (Palace)

September 1985

Agatha (Warner)

Bad Manners (CBS/Fox)
Barbarian Queen (Medusa)
The Bawdy Adventures of Tom Jones (CIC)
Bedroom Eyes (CBS/Fox)
Blackout (PolyGram)
Blind Alley (Embassy)
Blood Simple (Palace)
BMX Bandits (Rank)
Body Double (RCA/Columbia)
The Brother from Another Planet (Virgin)
Buck and the Preacher (RCA/Columbia)
The Burning Bed (CBS/Fox)

Caravan of Courage – An Ewok Adventure (CBS/Fox)
Careful, He Might Hear You (IPC/VideoSpace)
Cat Ballou (RCA/Columbia)

East of Eden (Warner)
Escape (Apex)
Executioner (re-release; Apex)

Fast Talking (Embassy)
The Fighting Prince of Donegal (Walt Disney)
Flash and the Firecat (CIC)
Fly Me (Apex)

Follow Me, Boys (Walt Disney)
Fraternity Vacation (PolyGram)
The Fury of Hercules (Precision)

Garbo Talks (Warner)
Giant (Warner)
Goldface (Precision)

Hardbodies (RCA/Columbia)

Impulse (re-release; Apex)

The Killing Fields (Thorn EMI)

Looker (Warner)

MacKenna's Gold (RCA/Columbia)
Malibu Express (CIC)
The Molly Maguires (CIC)
Monkey's Uncle (Walt Disney)
Morons from Outer Space (Thorn EMI)

The New One-Armed Swordsman (Thorn EMI)
Number One (Heron)

Operation Counterspy (Precision)

Parker (Virgin)
Phase IV (CIC)

Razorback (Thorn EMI)
Rebel Without a Cause (Warner)
The River (CIC)

Screwballs 2: Loose Screws (Avatar)
The Shooting Party (Thorn EMI)
Slumber Party Massacre (Thorn EMI)
Star Chasers (Ariel Films/CBS Records)
Striking Back (RCA/Columbia)
Summer Girl (PolyGram)
A Summer to Remember (CIC)

Toby Tyler (Walt Disney)
Tomboy (RCA/Columbia)
The Twist (Thorn EMI)
2010 (MGM/UA)

Until September (Warner)

Wet Gold (Odyssey)
Wheels of Fire (Medusa)
Wild Geese II (Thorn EMI)

October 1985

And Your Name Is Jonah (Heron)

The Bells of St Mary's (Video Collection)
Between the Lines (Heron)
Black Venus (MGM/UA)
Breakdance 2 – Electric Boogaloo (Guild)

Carmen (RCA/Columbia)
Christine (MGM/UA)
City Girls (CBS/Fox)
The Coca-Cola Kid (Palace)
Constance (MGM/UA)
The Cotton Club (Embassy)
Country (Rank)

The Day the Loving Stopped (Heron)
Death Sentence (Guild)
Def Con 4 (CBS/Fox)
Delta Fox (CIC)

Father Goose (Video Collection)
Finders Keepers (CBS/Fox)

Goodbye Franklin High (PolyGram)
The Gypsy Moths (MGM/UA)

Happy Endings (Heron)
Heidi's Song (Rank)
High Noon (Video Collection)
Hot Stuff (RCA/Columbia)

Ike (Heron)
Indiscreet (Video Collection)
Insignificance (Palace)
Invasion of the Body Snatchers (Video Collection)
It's a Wonderful Life (Video Collection)

Juarez (Warner)

Kids Don't Tell (Odyssey)

The Last Remake of Beau Geste (CIC)
The Last Starfighter (Heron)
Leave Yesterday Behind (Heron)
Little Drummer Girl (Warner)
Lois Gibbs and the Love Canal (Heron)

The Man Who Wasn't There (CIC)
The Men (Video Collection)
Micki and Maude (RCA/Columbia)
Missing in Action (Guild)
Mrs Soffel (MGM/UA)

Neighbors (RCA/Columbia)
Never Love a Stranger (Video Collection)
The Nutty Professor (CIC)

The Odessa File (RCA/Columbia)
One Cooks, the Other Doesn't (PolyGram)
Operation Petticoat (Video Collection)

The Parade (Odyssey)
Private Maneuvers (Guild)
Protocol (Warner)

The Quiet Man (Video Collection)

The Rebels (CIC)
Revenge of the Nerds (CBS/Fox)
Rio Grande (Video Collection)
Riot in Cell Block II (Video Collection)

Sands of Iwo Jima (Video Collection)
Screen Test (RCA/Columbia)
The Shadow Box (Heron)
She'll Be Wearing Pink Pyjamas (CBS/Fox)
Sins of the Father (CBS/Fox)
A Small Killing (Heron)
Starman (RCA/Columbia)
Street Hero (Medusa/CBS/Fox)
Swing Shift (Warner)

That Touch of Mink (Video Collection)
Thief of Hearts (CIC)
13 at Dinner (Warner)
Titan Find (PolyGram)
The Trial of Lee Harvey Oswald (Heron)
The Wild Life (CIC)
The Woman in Red (Rank)

Young at Heart (Video Collection)

November 1985

The Amazing Captain Nemo (Warner)

Baby – Secret of the Lost Legend (Rank)
The Beast With Five Fingers (Warner)
Beverly Hills Cop (CIC)
Brazil (Thorn EMI)
The Breakfast Club (CIC)

Camille (Vestron)

Charlie Grant's War (Careyvision)
Choose Me (Odyssey)
A Christmas Story (MGM/UA)
The Courier of Death (RCA/Columbia)
Cover Girl Models (Apex)

Dance with a Stranger (CBS/Fox)
Day of the Animals (Warner)
Death Dimension (Apex)
Don't Open Till Christmas (Vestron)

Enter the Ninja (RCA/Columbia)

Falling in Love (CIC)
Fireback (Apex)

Girls Just Want to Have Fun – The Movie (PolyGram)
The Good Soldier (Granada/PolyGram)
Gremlins (Warner)
The Guardian (Heron)
Gymkata (MGM/UA)

The Hit (CIC)
Hot Moves (Vestron)

The Jigsaw Man (Thorn EMI)

Kicks (CBS/Fox)
Kidnapped (Walt Disney)

The Last Flight of Noah's Ark (Walt Disney)
Love and Larceny (Careyvision)

Mickey's Christmas Carol (Walt Disney)
The Mutations (RCA/Columbia)

The Night They Saved Christmas (Embassy)
Nine Deaths of the Ninja (RCA/Columbia)
Ninja Warriors (Apex)

Old Yeller (re-release; Walt Disney)
On the Air Live with Captain Midnight (CIC)

A Passage to India (Thorn EMI)
Play Misty for Me (CIC)
Prime Risk (Medusa)

Rob Roy (Walt Disney)
Runaway (RCA/Columbia)

School Risk (Medusa)
Silent Madness (Avatar/CBS/Fox)
Songwriter (RCA/Columbia)
Special People (Odyssey)
The Story of Robin Hood (Walt Disney)
Streamers (Medusa)

The Temptress (Apex)
The Terminator (Rank)
Tess (Thorn EMI)
Them (Warner)
Thor the Conqueror (Apex)
Trog (Warner)
Two Fathers' Justice (Embassy)

Wizards of the Lost Kingdom (Medusa)
Women in Cages (Apex)

December 1985

The Adventures of Bullwhip Griffin (Walt Disney)
Alfie (CIC)
Amadeus (Thorn EMI)
A Billion for Boris (Heron)

Candleshoe (re-release; Walt Disney)
Captain Sinbad (MGM/UA)
Chiller (CBS/Fox)
Crazy for You (Warner)

Delivery Boys (PolyGram)
Doin' Time (Virgin)

The Falcon and the Snowman (Rank)
The Flamingo Kid (Palace)
For the Love of It (Heron)

Get Crazy (Heron)
Ghostbusters (RCA/Columbia)

The Hunchback of Notre Dame (Heron)

Inside Man (CBS/Fox)
Into the Night (CIC)

Johnny Dangerously (CBS/Fox)

King Kong (Heron)

Metropolis (Vestron)
The Muppets Take Manhattan (CBS/Fox)

The Neverending Story (Warner)

One Little Indian (re-release; Walt Disney)

Room Service (Heron)

Savage Dawn (PolyGram)
Second Sight: A Love Story (Odyssey)
The Seekers (CIC)
Shall We Dance? (Heron)
Steaming (RCA/Columbia)
Stop Making Sense – The Movie (Palace)
Super Fly TNT (CIC)
Swing Time (Heron)

Teachers (Warner)
The 36th Chamber of Shaolin (Thorn EMI)
Tonka (Walt Disney)
Top Hat (Heron)

Water (Thorn EMI)
Western Fort Apache (Heron)
White City – The Music Movie (Vestron)
The Wild Country (Walt Disney)

January 1986

The Ambassador (Guild)

Billion-Dollar Brain (Warner)

Cut and Run (Medusa/CBS/Fox)

The Defiant Ones (MGM/UA)

The Frog Prince (Warner)

The Guns of Diablo (MGM/UA)
Gus (Walt Disney)

The Horse in the Grey Flannel Suit (Walt Disney)
Hostages (Medusa)
How the West Was Won (MGM/UA)

The Judgement (Ariel/CBS Records)

King of the Grizzlies (Walt Disney)

The Last Dragon (CBS/Fox)
The Late Show (Warner)

The Mackintosh Man (Warner)
Mask (CIC)
Mata Hari (Guild)
The Mean Season (Rank)
Miracle of the White Stallions (Walt Disney)

The Official Version (Virgin)
Pumping Iron II: The Women (Virgin)

Rambo – First Blood Part II (Thorn EMI)
The Roommate (CBS/Fox)

Special Effects (Embassy)
The Swiss Conspiracy (Warner)

Tuff Turf (CBS/Fox)
Turk 182 (CBS/Fox)

February 1986

Birdy (RCA/Columbia)
Bon Voyage (Walt Disney)
Brewster's Millions (CIC)
Buddy Buddy (MGM/UA)

The Chain (Rank)
Cop au Vin (Virgin)

Deadly Intentions (CBS/Fox)
Dealer (MGM/UA)
Déjà Vu (Guild)
Double Trouble (RCA/Columbia)

Ecstasy (MGM/UA)

First Family (Warner)
First Love (CIC)
The Fortune Cookie (Warner)

Gas-s-s-s (RCA/Columbia)
Gulag (Heron)
Gumshoe (RCA/Columbia)

The Holcroft Covenant (Screen Entertainment)
Honey Boy (TransWorld Entertainment)

Light Blast (Medusa)
Love Circles (MGM/UA)
Lust in the Dust (RCA/Columbia)

Night of the Comet (CBS/Fox)

Oh God! You Devil (Warner)

The Party (Warner)
Police Academy II: Their First Assignment (Warner)
Pray for Death (TransWorld Entertainment)

Rafferty and the Gold Dust Twins (Warner)
Rappin' (MGM/UA)
Restless Natives (Screen Entertainment)
Return of the Jedi (CBS/Fox)
Robbery Under Arms (Precision)
Rustler's Rhapsody (CIC)

The Slugger's Wife (RCA/Columbia)
The Strongest Man in the World (Walt Disney)
The Sword of the Valiant (Guild)

Thieves and Robbers (RCA/Columbia)

Up the Military (Medusa)

The Zoo Gang (PolyGram)

March 1986

An American Werewolf in London (Channel 5)
The Amityville Horror (Video Collection)
The Assassination of Trotsky (Channel 5)
The Aviator (Warner)

Bachelor Mother (Video Collection)
Back to Bataan (Video Collection)

Beat the Devil (Video Collection)
The Black Pirate (Apex)
Brannigan (Warner)
Bringing Up Baby (Video Collection)

Cannonball Run II (Channel 5)
The Care Bears Movie (Vestron)
Catholic Boys (Screen Entertainment)
Christiane F (Channel 5)
Citizen Kane (Channel 5)
Cromwell (RCA/Columbia)
Crossfire (Video Collection)

Dark Command (Video Collection)
Deadly Blessing (Channel 5)
Doc Savage (Warner)
Duel in the Sun (Video Collection)

A Fair Wind to Java (Video Collection)
Flying Down to Rio (Video Collection)
Flying Leathernecks (Video Collection)
Flying Tigers (Video Collection)
Foreplay (Medusa/CBS/Fox)
The Forgotten Warrior (Apex)
For the Love of Betty (Apex)
Fort Apache (Channel 5)

The Gay Divorcée (Video Collection)
GI Blues (Channel 5)
Girls, Girls, Girls (Channel 5)
The Grass Is Greener (Video Collection)
Gunga Din (Video Collection)

Hamlet (RCA/Columbia)
Hickey and Boggs (Warner)
High School USA (re-release; Ariel Films/CBS Records)
Huckleberry Fox (Walt Disney)
The Hunchback of Notre Dame (Channel 5)

The Jerusalem File (MGM/UA)

Kimberley Jim (Channel 5)
King Creole (Channel 5)
King Lear (RCA/Columbia)
Kiss of the Spider Woman (Palace Première)

Last Train from Gunhill (Channel 5)
Love Happy (Video Collection)
The Love Pill (Apex)

Macbeth (RCA/Columbia)
The Magnificent Ambersons (Video Collection)
Manson's Certain Fury (Medusa/CBS/Fox)
Mischief (CBS/Fox)
The Moon Spinners (Walt Disney)
Murder My Sweet (Video Collection)
My Favorite Wife (Video Collection)

A Nightmare on Elm Street (CBS/Fox)
Nights of Terror (Apex)
Notorious (Video Collection)
Not Quite Jerusalem (Rank)
Number One (Channel 5)

The Offence (Warner)
One of Our Aircraft Is Missing (Video Collection)
Out of the Blue (Apex)

Paradise Hawaiian Style (Channel 5)
Perfect (RCA/Columbia)
Peter Coyote (ET)
A Piece of the Action (Warner)

The Punch and Judy Man (Screen Entertainment)

Quadrophenia (Channel 5)

Rebecca (Video Collection)
The Rebel (Screen Entertainment)
Red Sonja (Screen Entertainment)
Red Sun (Channel 5)
Rock Baby, Rock It (MMG)
Room at the Top (Video Collection)
Run Like a Thief (Apex)

Scalpel (RCA/Columbia)
Scandalous John (Walt Disney)
Sexual Desires (Apex)
Sinbad the Sailor (Video Collection)
A Soldier's Story (RCA/Columbia)
Spellbound (Video Collection)
The Spiral Staircase (Video Collection)
Stage Door (Video Collection)
Stranger than Paradise (Virgin)
The Supernaturals (Embassy)
Sylvester (RCA/Columbia)

This Is Callan (Channel 5)
Top Hat (Channel 5)
Treasure Island (Video Collection)

Up Your Ladder (Apex)

A View to a Kill (Warner)

The Wake of the Red Witch (Video Collection)

April 1986

Agent on Ice (Medusa)
Alphabet City (CBS/Fox)

Beyond the Walls (Warner)
The Body Snatcher (Video Collection)
The Boys Next Door (CBS/Fox)
The Bride (RCA/Columbia)
Bridge on the River Kwai (RCA/Columbia)

Carefree (Video Collection)
Castle Keep (RCA/Columbia)
Cat's Eye (Thorn EMI)
Chato's Land (Warner)

Deadly Intentions (CBS/Fox)
Dead Man's Folly (Warner)
Desperately Seeking Susan (Rank)

Fear City (Thorn EMI)
Flame of the Barbary Coast (Video Collection)
Force 10 from Navarone (RCA/Columbia)

Guns of Navarone (RCA/Columbia)

The Hunting Party (Warner)

Impulse (Odyssey)
Invasion USA (MGM/UA)

King Boxer (Warner)

Little Treasure (RCA/Columbia)
Love on the Run (RCA/Columbia)

Murder and Number Seventeen (Thorn EMI)
My Beautiful Launderette (Virgin)
My Science Project (Rank)

Number Seventeen/Murder (Thorn EMI)

Orion's Belt (Embassy)

Pale Rider (Warner)
Pimpernel Smith (Video Collection)
Pollyanna (Rank)
Porky's Revenge (CBS/Fox)
Pray TV (RCA/Columbia)

Rage (Warner)
Return of the Gunfighter (MGM/UA)
Return to the 36th Chamber (Warner)

Satire (RCA/Columbia)
The Scalphunters (Warner)
Sergeant Deadhead (RCA/Columbia)
The Shaggy D.A. (Rank)
Shaolin Challenges Ninja (Warner)
The Sisterhood (Medusa)

Vigil (MGM/UA)

The Wrong Arm of the Law (Video Collection)

May 1986

A.K.A. Cassius Clay (Warner)

Best Defense (CIC)
Blind Terror (RCA/Columbia)

Cave Girl (CBS/Fox)
Chase (CBS/Fox)
Cocoon (CBS/Fox)
Code of Silence (Rank)
Cowboy (MGM/UA)
Creepers (Palace Premiere)
Cul de Sac (Stablecane)

The Deep (RCA/Columbia)
The Devil and Miss Jones (Stablecane)

The Emerald Forest (Embassy)
The Evil that Men Do (Channel 5)
Expresso Bongo (Stablecane)
The Eyes of Laura Mars (RCA/Columbia)

False Witness (MGM/UA)
Fists of Steel (Vestron)
Foxtrap (Medusa)

Gloria (RCA/Columbia)

Hot Resort (Guild)
Hot Water (Stablecane)

Investigations of a Citizen Above Suspicion (RCA/Columbia)

King Kong (Channel 5)

L.A. Streetfighters (Guild)
Letter to Brezhnev (Palace)

The McConnell Story (Warner)
Mad Max: Beyond Thunderdome (Warner)
Marathon Man (CIC)
Martin's Day (Warner)
Mass Appeal (CIC)
Massive Retaliation (Vestron)
Mausoleum (Apex)
Miami Supercops (RCA/Columbia)
Mission Kill (Avatar/Screen Entertainment)
Monsieur Hulot's Holiday (Stablecane)

Out of Order (Virgin)

Playtime (Stablecane)
Plenty (Screen Entertainment)
Private Resort (RCA/Columbia)

Repulsion (Stablecane)
Return to Oz (Walt Disney)

St Elmo's Fire (RCA/Columbia)
Scorpion (Screen Entertainment)
Shaker Run (MGM/UA)
Sleep, My Love (Stablecane)
Sophie's Choice (Channel 5)
Spirit of St Louis (Warner)
Springbreak (RCA/Columbia)
Stitches (Medusa)
Swing Time (Channel 5)

Tainted (Avatar/Screen Entertainment)
Three Sovereigns for Sister Sarah (Stablecane)
Thunder Run (Guild)
To Kill a Mocking Bird (CIC)
Trackdown (Warner)
The Train (Warner)
The Trial (Screen Entertainment)

Warbus (Medusa/CBS/Fox)

The Zero Boys (PolyGram)

June 1986

American Dreamer (CBS/Fox)
The Assisi Underground (Guild/Cannon)

The Bay Boy (Rank)
The Best Years of Our Lives (Video Gems)

Car Trouble (Screen Entertainment)
Codename Emerald (MGM/UA)
A Cry for Justice (Virgin)
Cry for Strangers (MGM/UA)

Forbidden (Odyssey)

The Great Kidnapping (Screen Entertainment)

Hired Hand (CIC)
The Hurricane (Video Gems)

An Indecent Obsession (Screen Entertainment)

Ladyhawke (CBS/Fox)

Maria's Lovers (Guild/Cannon)
My Foolish Heart (Video Gems)
My Sister's Keeper (Screen Entertainment)

A Night in Heaven (CBS/Fox)

The Princess and the Pirate (Video Gems)
The Purple Rose of Cairo (Rank)

Raffles (Video Gems)
The Real Glory (Video Gems)
The Rideout Case (PolyGram)

Silence of the Heart (CBS/Fox)
The Supergrass (CBS/Fox)

Takin' It Off (Odyssey)

Up in Arms (Video Gems)

Weird Science (CIC)
The Westerner (Video Gems)

Letter from Hollywood

ANTHONY SLIDE

The Hollywood Museum, about which I wrote so glowingly last year, has closed – the victim of a lack of public support, created by a lack of interest from the Hollywood Chamber of Commerce and by the jealousy of various political factions, all of whom had their own visions of having a Hollywood museum under their control. With the closure of this privately-funded venture, there is little likelihood that the film capital will ever again boast a museum devoted to its history.

Also within the last year, the closure on 3 April 1985 of another landmark – the Brown Derby restaurant, which had been in business on Vine Street since 1929. The Hollywood Brown Derby was the last of the four – the original was located across Wilshire Boulevard from the Ambassador Hotel, and the other two were in Beverly Hills and the Los Feliz district. The Hollywood Brown Derby was particularly famous for the caricatures of film personalities which graced its walls.

Within weeks of the Brown Derby closure, the Masquers Club, a once-popular theatrical social club which had been housed for 58 years in Antonio Moreno's former home at 1765 North Sycamore Avenue in Hollywood, was forced to move to new headquarters at the Variety Arts Center in downtown Los Angeles. The original building was demolished.

On the plus side, the so-called Jesse L. Lasky/Cecil B. De Mille barn, which had originally stood near Hollywood Boulevard and Vine Street, and was the site of the filming by De Mille and Oscar Apfel of *The Squawman* (1914) – erroneously described as Hollywood's first feature film – opened to the public on a new site in the parking lot of the Hollywood Bowl. It is now called the Hollywood Studio Museum, and features an exhibit devoted to the history of the silent film, with particular emphasis on Paramount Pictures, at whose studio the barn had been relocated for many years. Presently, the barn – which is California State Landmark No. 554 and the first state landmark connected with the film industry – is open only on weekends.

Hollywood Heritage, which is sponsoring the Hollywood Studio Museum, is a preservation group, founded by Marian Gibbons. It is also responsible for saving and showing a unique exhibit of Hollywood in miniature, created over 40 years ago by Joe Pellkofer: 45 city blocks containing 450 buildings, all to scale. It is 11 feet wide by 12 feet deep, and is presently on display at the old El Capitan Building, next to the Paramount Theatre and almost opposite Mann's Chinese Theater on Hollywood Boulevard.

Cecil B. De Mille, along with his brother William, father Henry and niece Agnes, were honoured with a major exhibit, 'The De Mille Dynasty', at the Century City shopping centre from November 1985 to April 1986. The exhibit presented an extraordinary collection of artifacts, although, unhappily, many badly captioned – the number of typographical errors was amazing, with even Kevin Brownlow's name misspelled. However, there was enough spectacle and bad taste in design to delight even C.B., with the highspots being Agnes De Mille's childhood garden and the curious entrance – a walk through a darkened room lit by fairylights. Unfortunately, perhaps because of the location, the exhibit seemed to be poorly attended: the Saturday afternoon I was there, not one other visitor was seen touring the display.

The Max Factor Company was

The Max Factor Museum on Highland Avenue in Hollywood.

Cecil B. De Mille directing Fredric March and Elissa Landi in *The Sign of the Cross* (1932).

founded on 2 January 1909, and has been taking care of the make-up needs of Hollywood stars, as well as most American women, ever since. (Interestingly, the first make-up specially for motion-picture use was developed by Max Factor in 1914, and first worn by Henry B. Walthall, leading man in D. W. Griffith's *The Birth of a Nation.*) Max Factor opened his Hollywood salon on Highland Avenue in 1935, and it now features a museum devoted to his work. There is a display of the hairpieces worn by James Stewart, John Wayne and Frank Sinatra; a cosmetic pulverizing machine from the 1904 St Louis Exposition; and classic advertisements for Max Factor products. The Max Factor Beauty museum is open daily, at no charge, from Monday to Saturday.

A couple of blocks away from the Max Factor Beauty museum is the Hollywood Roosevelt Hotel, which has now been completely refurbished and offers a good idea of what it must have looked like during its heyday in the 1930s. Its famed Cinegrill nightclub is open once again, with stars such as Buddy Greco performing there. The hotel was officially reopened on 7 March 1986, with an inaugural toast by Tony Curtis, who plans to be the hotel's first permanent resident (D. W. Griffith was probably the most famous permanent resident of the old hotel).

At the other end of Hollywood Boulevard, on Vine Street, stands the former Huntington Hartford Theater, now renamed the James A. Doolittle Theater, and looking simply hideous, thanks to what its present owners consider to be modern style: walls stripped bare, chandeliers removed and scaffolding added for effect. Here, during November 1985, the American Cinémathèque presented its first film series, a week-long tribute to 'Fifty Years of Film from New York's Museum of Modern Art'.

The American Cinémathèque was the brainchild of Gary Essert, who was co-founder and long-time director of Filmex, and serves as artistic director of the new organization. The plan is to refurbish the Pan Pacific Auditorium, opened in 1935, as a cinémathèque, with three state-of-the-art theatres, a multi-media lab, bookstore, restaurant and exhibition gallery, and a hotel as an ancillary to the complex. The American Cinémathèque was founded in 1981, and surprised everyone, early in 1986, by taking over the running of Filmex, from which Essert had been dismissed a couple of years previously. Ken Wlaschin will stay on as artistic director of the festival, which is in a bad way financially and which has become very lack-lustre under Wlaschin's direction. At the time of writing, it seems unlikely that Los Angeles will enjoy a 1986 Filmex.

The tribute to the Museum of Modern Art included screenings of the restored *Way Down East* (with live orchestral accompaniment), a discussion on film preservation with Robert Gitt (from UCLA Film Archives) and Jon Gartenberg and Peter Williamson (from the museum), and additional screenings at UCLA and the Los Angeles County Museum of Art. The highspot was unquestionably the presentation of the restored wide-screen version of *The Big Trail* (1930), directed by Raoul Walsh and starring John Wayne.

Ivan Mosjoukine in the newly restored *Casanova* (1927).

The American Cinémathèque followed this tribute by organizing a lavish fund-raising 'Moving Picture Ball' on 28 February 1986, at which it honoured Eddie Murphy for his contributions to the cinema. As the size of Murphy's body of work is somewhat on the small side, the award seemed a little precipitous. However, Murphy was a good choice from a box-office point of view, and the evening raised more than $250,000.

An unusual film presentation took place at MGM's Cary Grant Theater on 1 October, 1985. Titled 'Dartmouth in Hollywood', it was a tribute to Dartmouth College alumni who had entered the film industry, including: Walter Wanger, Charles Starrett, Budd Schulberg, Buck Henry, Paul Ford, Meryl Streep, Stan Brakhage, Robert Ryan, Michael Moriarty, and Arthur Hornblow Jr. None of the graduates was present, and the film clips were so dull that many in the audience wondered for what the film industry had to be thankful to Dartmouth . . .

The major retrospective screenings at UCLA in the past year included an impressive tribute to Technicolor, with films including *Becky Sharp* and *The Toll of the Sea* (both restored by Robert Gitt), *Doctor X*, *Follow Thru*, *The Garden of Allah*, *The Trail of the Lonesome Pine*, *The Adventures of Robin Hood*, *Rope* and two from Britain: *Henry V* and *Black Narcissus*. One Los Angeles newspaper, the *LA Weekly*, described the latter as the greatest film ever to come out of England, which even in Hollywood seemed a somewhat outrageous overstatement. During April 1986, UCLA presented an interesting programme honouring the music-hall tradition in musicals and comedies, with a representative sampling of films starring Jessie Matthews, the Crazy Gang, George Formby, Gracie Fields and Max Miller.

To help foster a better relationship between UCLA Film Archives and the Cinémathèque Française, and to build up a collection of French films at UCLA, a group called Cinema 89 was formed. Its first presentation, introduced by Leslie Caron and a boring bunch of French and American bureaucrats, was the restored version ot *Casanova* (1927; also known as *The Loves of Casanova* and *Surrender* in the US), starring Ivan Mosjoukine and directed by Alexander Volkoff. While not the legendary work that the UCLA publicists would have one believe, *Casanova* was an entertaining film, made even more so by the delightful score composed by Georges Delerue, who conducted one of the best orchestras to accompany a silent film that I have yet heard.

The Directors Guild of America celebrated its 50th anniversary with a major, and noisy, afternoon party on 16 January. André de Toth served as a diverting master of ceremonies, introducing the lone survivor of the Guild's founding members, Rouben Mamoulian, who proved, as always, that he knows how to entertain an audience. (Although illness prevented his presence, Mamoulian was honoured, on 7 March 1986, with the Jean Renoir Humanities Award from the Los Angeles Film Teachers Association. In a filmed speech, he said, 'To me, all real art is entertainment. It should carry some excitement with it, so the people who come to see it leave the theatre a little better man and a little better woman – even if it just lasts a week. It's up to you to require, insist on better films, on quality, on something that maintains the dignity of the human being.')

The Directors Guild also hosted, on 2 November 1985, a tribute to Orson Welles, with appearances by, among others, Peter Bogdanovich, Janet Leigh, Dan O'Herlihy, Geraldine Fitzgerald and Norman Lloyd. Barbara Leaming, author of the authorized biography of Welles [see 'Film Books of the Year'], was one of the speakers, but I wonder how many in the audience noticed the quiet presence of Charles Higham, the author of an unauthorized and, one suspects, more honestly accurate biography of the director.

As part of the 50th anniversary celebrations, the Los Angeles County Museum of Art screened a series of films in the presence of their directors – including John Schlesinger, Tony Richardson, Sidney Furie, Martin Ritt, and Ida Lupino. The evenings were surprisingly poorly attended, with only one director, Billy Wilder, garnering a full house. Wilder was also the 1986 recipient of the American Film Institute Life Achievement Award – on 6 March at the Beverly Hilton Hotel. Jack Lemmon served as master of ceremonies, introducing Walter Matthau, Fred MacMurray, Audrey Hepburn, I. A. L. Diamond, Jessica Lange, Carol Burnett, Don Ameche, Whoopi Goldberg, James Stewart, Ginger Rogers and many others. In his speech of thanks, Wilder commented on the films of the present, in which technology has the upper hand: 'Relax, fellow picturemakers. The bigger they get, the more irreplaceable we become. Theirs may be the kingdom, but ours is the power and the glory.'

British Film Year ground to a dreary halt in Los Angeles. The most curious aspect of its celebrations was a party for Susan George, honouring her 20 years in film. Susan George, the star of *Mandingo, Enter the Ninja* and *Venom*? Yes, Susan George! The party was held at the residency of the British Consul in Los Angeles, and there was no one present from British Film Year to explain 'Why Susan George?' On hand for the party were Patrick MacNee, Roddy McDowall, Morgan Fairchild, George's husband Simon MacCorkindale and her co-star from *Mandingo*, Ken Norton.

On 10 January 1986, a special presentation of the British Post Office film stamps was made by the British Consul in Los Angeles, Donald Ballentyne, to the Academy of Motion Picture Arts and Sciences, represented by its president, Robert Wise. Michael Caine and Patricia Hitchcock O'Connell, (whose father, Alfred Hitchcock, is featured on one of the stamps) were present at the ceremony.

Also at the Academy, beginning on 10 February 1985, was an exhibit of stills, collected together by Patricia Warren for her book, *The British Film Collection, 1896–1984*. The photographs were a curiously dull bunch, which perhaps explains why the only celebrities at the opening-night cocktail party were Michael York and Fionnula Flanagan.

Among the other major events at the Academy during 1985–86 were an evening with Shirley Temple, at which the actress received a full-size Oscar to replace the miniature one she received in 1935, and a tribute to Fred Zinnemann, at which the director presented his papers to the Academy's Margaret Herrick Library. The Academy also celebrated the 100th anniversary of Jerome Kern's birth with a slightly pretentious evening, hosted by Arthur Hamilton and Gene Barry on 21 October 1985. Present to sing and play Jerome Kern's music were Johnny Green, Peggy King, Kathryn Grayson, Dudley Moore, Henry Mancini and Lalo Schifrin. The evening was made particularly delightful by the presence, from England, of Elisabeth Welch, who sang 'Smoke Gets in Your Eyes' and 'She Did Just What You'd Do, Too'. Surprisingly, Miss Welch told me that Kern was not her favourite composer; he was easily eclipsed by Ivor Novello and Cole Porter.

The Academy Awards show on 24 March 1986 was arguably the best presentation yet, thanks to producer Stanley Donen and comedian Robin Williams. The musical salute to MGM stars was surprisingly entertaining, but there was a genuine feeling of irritation that Paul Newman had not seen fit to travel from Chicago to attend the Awards

Michael Caine and Academy president Robert Wise with a set of the British Film Year stamps.

Former Academy president Gene Allen presents Shirley Temple with a full-size Oscar to replace the miniature one she received in 1935.

ceremony in person in order to accept his honorary Oscar. If he thought so little of the award, why bother to accept it at all? Compare his behaviour with that of Ann Miller, who performed in *Sugar Babies* on Sunday evening in Florida, took a midnight flight to Los Angeles, rehearsed all day Monday, appeared live that evening and flew back to Florida after the show to appear on stage in *Sugar Babies* on Tuesday.

Naturally the quality of the Awards show was overshadowed by controversy due to the fact that *The Color Purple* did not receive any awards (despite being nominated for 11) and its director, Steven Spielberg, had not even been nominated. After all the fuss, one can only agree with Vincent Canby, writing in the *New York Times*:

> Wouldn't it be a relief if the Academy of Motion Picture Arts and Sciences became a pace-setter for a change, and decided to vote just one award a year to one movie, with the understanding that everybody connected with the film – producer, director, writer(s), actors, cameraman, editor, on down to best boy and unit publicist – would share in the award?

The other two major awards presentations were fairly predictable. As always, there were enough Emmys at the annual Academy of Television Arts and Sciences ceremony on 22 September 1985 to go to most of the television shows on air. The highspot of the evening was an 'imposter' Barry Bremen appearing to accept the award on behalf of *Hill Street Blues*'s Betty Thomas; that of the Golden Globe awards on 26 January 1986, was the presentation of the Cecil B. De Mille Award to Barbara Stanwyck by Kirk Douglas. *Out of Africa* and *Prizzi's Honor* were the big winners here, with both sharing 'Best Motion Picture', and Kathleeen Turner and Whoopi Goldberg and Jack Nicholson and John Voight sharing the awards for 'Best Actress' and 'Best Actor'.

To end on a personal note, memories of Hollywood past were evoked last October, when I hosted a party at my home to celebrate the publication of Esther Ralston's autobiography *Some Day We'll Laugh*. On hand to congratulate Esther were two of her friends from the silent era, Mary Brian and Priscilla Bonner. Esther and Priscilla, along with Margery Wilson (see 'In Memoriam'), Ruth Clifford and others, are interviewees in a documentary film which Jeff Goodman and I are producing on *The Silent Feminists*, the women directors active in the American film industry during the silent era. These pioneering women have been long forgotten, as evidenced by a 24 January 1986 ceremony at which Dorothy Arzner was posthumously honoured with the 1820th star on the 'Hollywood Walk of Fame'. Speakers, such as Lee Grant and Fay Kanin, praised Arzner as Hollywood's first female director, along the way giving her credit (incorrectly) for being the director of Paramount's first talkie and the director who made a star of Katharine Hepburn. As the saying goes in Hollywood, the legend is more important than the fact.

Mary Brian (left) and Priscilla Bonner (right) help Esther Ralston celebrate publication of her autobiography, *Some Day We'll Laugh*.

In Memoriam

Dawn Addams, the English actress who died in mid-1985 at the age of 55, made her movie debut in 1951 in *Night into Morning*. Further roles were in *The Moon Is Blue* and *The Robe* in 1953 and Chaplin's *A King in New York* in 1957. Subsequently she made a number of films in various European countries – the last of which was *The Vault of Horror* in 1973. A pleasing personality, she gained a certain fame by becoming a real live princess through her marriage – in 1954 – to Italy's Prince Vittorio Massimo.

Brian Aherne, the tall, handsome British actor who began his theatrical career when he was 8 years old, died at his American home on 10 February 1986 at the age of 83. After studying architecture at Malvern College, he resumed his stage career at the age of 20, and in the 'twenties made a number of British films, the first of which was *The Eleventh Commandment* in 1924. In 1933, after something of a triumph in *The Constant Nymph*, he was lured to Hollywood for *Song of Songs*, thereafter appearing in such films as *Sylvia Scarlett* (1935), *Beloved Enemy* (1936), and *Juarez* (1939). In the 'forties his career continued with *My Son, My Son, My Sister Eileen* and *Smilin' Through*; and in the 1950s came *Titanic, Prince Valiant* and *The Swan*. His last films prior to his retirement to Vevey in Switzerland were *Susan Slade* in 1961 and *Rosie* in 1967. Married to Joan Fontaine for six years (1939–45), he wrote about this as well as his long career on stage and screen in his autobiography *A Proper Job*, published in 1969.

Evelyn Ankers known to film buffs as 'Queen of the Horror Movies' or, alternatively, 'The Screamer' – died at her Hawaiian home on 28 August 1985 at the age of 67. Born in Chile of British parents, she began her career as a child actress on the London stage, and had a small role in the Korda film *Rembrandt* in 1936. In 1939 she moved to New York and made her stage debut there before going to Hollywood where she became typecast in horror movies including *Hold that Ghost, The Ghost of Frankenstein, The Mad Ghoul, Son of Dracula* and similar features. However, she also appeared in other types of roles, in films such as *Fire over England, Sherlock Holmes and the Voice of Terror, His Butler's Sister, Black Beauty* (in which her husband, British actor Richard Denning, was co-star) and her final commercial movie, *The Texan Meets Calamity Jane*, in 1950 (although ten years later she starred in the Lutheran Church-sponsored film *No Greater Love*). After her 1950 movie she turned to TV work, having done little in any medium for some years. It may come as a surprise to some that she made more than 35 movies during her screen career.

Brian Aherne with Marlene Dietrich.

Patrick Barr, the British actor, died in London on 29 August 1985 at the age of 77. During his stage and screen career of more than half a century, he made a large number of movies including *The Longest Day, Billy Liar, The Blue Lagoon, Saint Joan, The Scarlet Pimpernel* and *The House of Whipcord*. Having trained in India as an engineer, he started his acting career as a film extra, rising to feature player though never reaching anything like major stardom. Quite apart from his considerable stage performances (he made his London debut in 1936 in *The Country Wife*) he enjoyed a good deal of success on TV.

Anne Baxter died on 12 December 1985, a few days after suffering a brain haemorrhage while shopping in New York. She was generally considered seldom to have won the calibre roles which her considerable thespian talents merited, despite the fact that she made some 50 films and gained the reputation of being a conscientious and reliable performer. In particular, she never really achieved the major stardom that her Oscar-winning ('Best Supporting Actress') performance in *The Razor's Edge* in 1946 seemed to suggest was her due. She was still relatively young – only 62 – when she died.

Born in Indiana, Miss Baxter was the granddaughter of one of America's greatest architects, Frank Lloyd Wright, and it was with her family's full support that, at the age of 11, she announced that her future was to be an acting career. After two years training, she arrived on Broadway in *Seen but Not Heard*, subsequently studying under the famous actress Maria Ouspenskaya for two years, during which the equally strong-willed women, young and old, were quite frequently at loggerheads. In 1938, Miss Baxter took to the Broadway stage again, in a couple of flops. Trying Hollywood, she initially found things difficult but after missing out on *Rebecca* (Hitchcock wanted her but producer David O. Selznick thought she looked too young to play opposite Olivier), she was, as a sort of consolation prize, given a seven-year contract by Selznick who, not having anything for her himself, loaned her out to MGM. It was in their *20-Mule Team* that she made her screen debut in 1940. Previously reproved for 'overacting' by Bette Davis in a stage play in which both appeared, it was now the stars of this film, Wallace Beery and Marjorie Main, who made a similar complaint. Star John Barrymore was also critical of her when she played with him in her second movie, *The Great Profile*, but she was improving her technique all the time and had a big success in Jean Renoir's first US film, *Swamp Water* (1941). One of her best performances was in the 1944 production, *Guest in the House*, and among that half century of films in which she appeared were: *The Magnificent Ambersons, Five Graves to Cairo, The Walls of Jericho, All About Eve* (for which she rejected an Oscar nomination for 'Best Supporting Actress'), *The Outcasts of Poker Flat, The Ten Commandments, Cimarron, Chase a Crooked Shadow* and *Mix Me a Person*, both British pictures, *The Summer of the Seventeenth Doll* (Australia; *Season of Passion* in the UK), and her final movie, originally made for television but subsequently given a cinema release in the US, *Little Mo* (1978).

Anne Baxter.

In 1961, Miss Baxter married (for the second time) and lived with husband Randoph Galt for several years in primitive surroundings on a cattle ranch in the Australian outback – an experience she later related in a highly acclaimed book *Intermission: A True Story*, published in 1976. Subsequently, the family (now increased by the births of her second and third daughters) moved to a deserted mining town in New Mexico, where they lived until her divorce in 1967. Throughout the latter part of her life, she made occasional TV appearances, a medium which brought her considerable success – both in TV films and in series. Because of her unique personality, her beauty and the quality of her performances, nobody who ever saw Anne Baxter could forget her.

Marie Bell (real name Marie-Jeanne-Lucie Bellon-Downey) died at Neuilly in France on 15 August 1985 at the age of 84. A familiar name during the flowering of the French cinema, her professional career began when she danced on the English stage when she was only 13, afterwards turning to drama. In 1921 she made her first appearance with the Comédie-Française and soon became known for her impressive performances in the French classics. She continued to act throughout the German occupation, during which she also carried out work for the Resistance for which she was subsequently to be decorated by General de Gaulle. She appeared in some 30 films, starting in 1924 with *Paris*, and is probably best recalled in this country for her outstanding performances in *Le Grand Jeu* in 1934 and Duvivier's star-studded classic *Un Carnet de Bal* in 1937. She made one British film, the comedy *Hotel Paradiso*, in 1966. Her final stage appearance was in 1973 and her last recorded screen part was in *Les Volets Clos* in 1973.

Elisabeth Bergner, the Viennese actress (born Elizabeth Ettel) who had made her home in London since she became a British citizen in 1938, died

Elisabeth Bergner.

there in 12 May 1986 at the age of 85, succumbing to a long-lasting ailment. Miss Bergner made her professional debut in 1919 in Zurich and thereafter remained busily employed in the theatre, usually in minor roles, until she made a big hit in 1924 in Berlin, playing the title role in *Saint Joan*. This was the start of a long international stage career that took her to many European and Scandinavian capitals, and to New York. She made her first – German – film in 1923 (*Der Evangelimann*) and between then and 1932 made a total of eight movies in that country. She had a great success when she made her British stage debut in *Escape Me Never* in 1933 and repeated that triumph three years later in James Barrie's last play *The Boy David*: in his will, Barrie left her the (then) considerable sum of some £7500, with the instructions that 'she gave the best-ever performance in the play'. In 1935 she starred in the film version of *Escape Me Never*, a performance which won for her an Oscar nomination. She made only one American film – *Paris Calling* in 1942 – and most of her filming, including *Dreaming Lips* in 1937 and *Stolen Life* in 1939, was done in either London or Paris. Her last British films were *Cry of the Banshee* in 1970 and *Courier to the Tsar* (1971) and her last film of all was the West German production *The Pedestrian* in 1974.

She was married to the late Dr Paul Czinner, the Budapest-born violinist and child prodigy who was to become doctor of philosophy and literature before turning, from journalism, to film directing. With Miss Bergner as his star, he made several distinguished movies. Elisabeth Bergner had a quite unique style and presence, a kind of fey, shy appeal (which covered an inner strength) to which it was almost impossible not to succumb.

John Boulting, one of the Boulting twins whose techniques were so identical that they took it in turns to direct and produce their films (with no observable difference in style), died at the age of 71 at his Sunningdale, Berkshire home on 17 June 1985. The only time the brothers worked separately was during World War II, when John was with the RAF Film Unit while Roy was attached to the Army Film Unit. A series of shorts in the late 1930s marked the beginning of their cinema careers, and they made their first feature, *Trunk Crime* (*Design for Murder* in the US), in 1939. The following year they made *Pastor Hall* and in 1942 completed *Thunder Rock*. Some of their best work came in the late 'forties and 'fifties with such films as *Brighton Rock* (*Young Scarface* in US), *Seven Days to Noon, The Magic Box, Private's Progress, Lucky Jim* and that uproarious comedy *I'm all Right Jack*, in which Peter Sellers made a big hit.

Louise Brooks, in *Diary of a Lost Girl*.

Marion Byron Breslow, who died in Santa Monica on 5 July 1985 after a long illness, was a star comedienne of the 'twenties and 'thirties, making her screen debut opposite Buster Keaton in his *Steamboat Bill Junior*. She also starred in a number of Hal Roach short comedies, appeared in a succession of features including *Broadway Babes of 1929, Song of the West, The Tenderfoot, Love Me Tonight* and, in 1938, gave her final screen performance, in *Five of a Kind*, with the Dionne quintuplets.

Louise Brooks, one of Hollywood's brightest (shooting) stars, died from a heart attack at her New York home on 8 August 1985; she was 78. It was only quite recently that, after some 45 years away from the showbusiness spotlight and almost forgotten, there was a revival of interest in and appreciation of her almost magical screen presence which began with the 'discovery' and showings of G. W. Pabst's two classic silent films in which she starred: *Pandora's Box* and *Diary of a Lost Girl*.

Born in Kansas in 1906, Brooks became a professional dancer at the age of 15, performing with a company that included Martha Graham. In the early 'twenties, she appeared in *George White's Scandals* in New York, followed by an appearance on the London stage. Back in the States, she performed in two of Ziegfeld's Broadway shows and, in 1925, made her screen debut in *The Street of Forgotten Men*, which resulted in a Paramount contract and ten films within the next couple of years. These included *The American Venus* and the W. C. Fields movie *It's the Old Army Game*, the latter directed by Edward Sutherland whom she married in 1926 (the marriage lasted only two years). After several more pictures, she was loaned to Fox, who starred her in Howard Hawks' *A Girl in Every Port*. It was after seeing this film in Berlin that Pabst caused a sensation by choosing her – in preference to Dietrich and other equally famous stars – for the tragic leading role in his film *Pandora's Box* released in 1929. She was then still only 23 years old. Along with a subsequent film for the great German director – *Diary of a Lost Girl* – this period marked the height of Louise Brooks' career, and it is for these two movies that she has been hailed as one of the greatest stars of the silent cinema.

Back in the United States, however, she faced a furious Paramount whose contract she had casually ignored, and so, unpopular with Hollywood, she went to France to make *Prix de Beauté*. Her attitude towards American film executives, allied to her unpredictability and general independence, made film work increasingly difficult for her to come by, and on her return to the United States, she was only able to land a role in the 1930 two-reel comedy *Windy Riley Goes to Hollywood*, directed by 'William Goodrich', the discredited Fatty Arbuckle who was also finding Hollywood a place of closed doors. During the next ten years, Miss Brooks appeared in a few small roles – some just bit parts – and returned for a while to New York to dance in the town's nighteries. In 1936 she went back to Hollywood to make her last four films, among which were the Buck Jones western *Empty Saddles* and Republic's John Wayne vehicle *Overland Stage Raiders*.

In 1940 she left Hollywood for good, and after a period back in Kansas with her own dance studio she returned to New York to work with a publicity firm and then as a counter-hand at the famous Saks Fifth Avenue store. At about this time, she wrote – and then burnt! – her autobiography, which she called *Naked on My Goat*. Other writing followed, and she began to be published in various magazines, contributing articulate and perceptive articles on Hollywood. In 1979 the *New Yorker* published a profile of her, written by Kenneth Tynan, which resulted in a sudden upsurge of interest in her and her work – and did no harm to her book, *Lulu in Hollywood*, when it was published a few years later.

Small in stature, with her jet-black hair always cut short with a fringe, Louise Brooks in her prime simultaneously exuded a strange and exciting sexual promise and a girlish innocence – although, according to *Variety*, her own somewhat more cerebral appraisal was that her appeal lay in 'movements of thought and soul, transmitted in a kind of intense isolation'. What is unarguable is that Louise Brooks had a strong individuality of character and that almost indefinable quality of which stars are made. Certainly she was one of the most interesting and challenging women of the silent cinema.

Yul Brynner, as seen in *Taras Bulba*.

Yul Brynner, the famous bald-pated, theatrical King of Siam, died on 10 October 1985 from lung cancer, at the age of . . . well, that is in some doubt: certainly Brynner was between his passport age of 65 and the oft-repeated reference book one of 70. In fact, Brynner's birth and early life were always shrouded, possibly deliberately, in mystery. However, it seems that his real name was Taidje Khan and he had a Mongolian father – who changed the family name at some point to Brynner – and a gypsy mother, though here again there appears to be some debate.

Brynner's education was initially, as a schoolboy, in China, later in Paris at the Sorbonne (again the details are vague). Certainly the young man spent some 15 years as a trapeze artist with the Paris Cirque d'Hiver, that career coming to an abrupt end when a bad fall grounded him – indeed, almost crippled him for life. It was at this point that Brynner came to Britain to study theatre under Michael Chekhov and, with the maestro's Chekhov Players, went to New York, making his Broadway debut with the company's *Twelfth Night* in 1941. Following this, Brynner returned to Britain and appeared in a number of London stage productions. Fluent in several languages, during World War II he was recruited by the US Office of War Information to become a radio commentator in French. The war over, Brynner appeared in the 1946 New York production of *Lute Song*; three years later he had the opportunity to work in TV and was soon in great demand.

In 1949, complete with a head of luxurious dark hair, he made his screen debut in the undistinguished *Port of New York*, but it was while he was working as a successful TV director in 1951 that Brynner accepted the male lead in the projected Rodgers and Hammerstein musical *The King and I*. For the next four years he continued to play the role on Broadway, on tour and in the Fox film that brought him the 1956 Oscar for best actor. *The King and I* established him as a movie star, and he went on to make a long succession of films including De Mille's *The Ten Commandments, Anastasia, The Buccaneer, Solomon and Sheba, The Sound and the Fury* and, in 1960, the classic western *The Magnificent Seven*.

After this high point, Brynner's screen career dipped somewhat and though he appeared in many more movies, most of them were undistinguished. However, he did have big personal successes in the twin fantasies *Westworld* (1973) and *Futureworld* (1976) – the same year in which he made his last movie, in Italy, *Gli Indesiderabili*. The previous year Brynner was in a Broadway stage flop called *Home Sweet Homer* (which ran for only one night), but in 1976 a revival of *The King and I* brought him great success in New York, London and on tour, his story thus ending on a happy note.

James Cagney, one of Hollywood's greatest Golden Age stars – who made movie history and was lifted to stardom by squashing a grapefruit into Mae Clarke's face, so becoming the screen's first authentic anti-hero in *The Public Enemy* – died on 30 March 1986, aged 86, at his farm in New York State. The cinema's greatest tough guy and gangster, short, volatile, pugnacious, Cagney was at the same time a superb hoofer, and in the course of his career, he was to prove to have an unexpected versatility.

Born in New York of Irish-Norwegian parentage, Cagney was kept in line, along with his brothers and sisters, by his strict mother. By the time he was 14, and still at school, Cagney had had a series of jobs including spells as a 'bouncer' at a nightclub and as a restaurant waiter. It was also while he was still in his teens that he was runner-up for the New York amateur lightweight boxing championship. After desultorily appearing in some amateur stage shows, Cagney landed a job in the chorus of a professional stage musical but quit after a few weeks. However, he was back on the – this time, Broadway – boards in 1920 in *Pitter-Patter*, where he met Frances Vernon, who soon became his wife and to whom he stayed happily married until his death.

After a spell in vaudeville, the couple went hopefully to Hollywood but, failing to get work there, were soon back in New York. In fact, it wasn't until 1930 and a string of stage successes later that Cagney returned to Hollywood to make his screen debut in *Sinners' Holiday*. After four films within six months for Warner, Cagney was cast in *The Public Enemy* in 1931 and became a star. Realizing his subsequent box-office value to the studio, he launched the first of his many fights over cash with studio boss Jack Warner (who called him 'The Professional Againster'). After three more films – *Taxi, The Crowd Roars* and *Winner Take All* – the star again walked out, only returning after a six-month 'strike', after which he was offered £2000 a week and a limit of four films per year. After a trio of typical tough-guy roles in *Hard to Handle, Picture Snatcher* and *The Mayor of Hell*, Jack Warner allowed him to change his image by putting him into the musical *Footlight Parade* as a dancer. Cagney again switched when he played the law enforcer in *G-Men*, which was to prove one of his biggest successes. More diversity followed: a pugilist in *The Irish in Us*, the part of Bottom in *A Midsummer Night's Dream*.

His running battle with Jack Warner eventually reached suspension and the law courts in 1936. Cagney won the case, but was subsequently blacklisted

James Cagney.

and, after a year's enforced idleness, was glad to make two second-league movies for Grand National. However in 1938 peace (of a sort) was declared, and the star returned to Warners to make *Boy Meets Girl* and the classic *Angels with Dirty Faces* in 1938. The following year saw *Each Dawn I Die* and *The Roaring Twenties*. *The Strawberry Blonde* in 1941 (in which, some claim, he gave one of his best-ever performances) was followed by some fairly indifferent films, but in 1942 he made *Yankee Doodle Dandy*, which won him universal acclaim and an Oscar. Caught up in the anti-Reds furore, Cagney, like many others, had to appear in front of the House Un-American Activities Committee to clear his name. Leaving Warner to make some films in co-operation with his brother, Cagney returned to the Warner banner once more to make the vicious *White Heat* in 1949. The 1950s brought few real successes, although *Love Me or Leave Me* in 1955 saw him back at his best and won him his third Oscar nomination. After *One, Two, Three* in 1961, Cagney retired, and apart from recording a few commentaries and writing his autobiography *Cagney by Cagney* (1975), he remained in retirement for the next 20 years, only returning to the studio to appear in Miloš Forman's *Ragtime* in 1983. Thereafter, he only worked in television. A brilliant natural actor, outstanding dancer and strong personality, Cagney's whole story would fill several volumes.

Yakima Canutt (born Enos Edward Canutt) – the greatest stuntman of them all, and the man who made the work respectable and well paid – died in Hollywood on 24 May 1986, aged 90. After slight schooling, Canutt started work at 12 breaking in horses, and was on the rodeo circuit by the time he was 17, becoming world champion 'all-round cowboy' in 1917. After serving on a minesweeper in World War I, Canutt won the second of his five rodeo championships soon after demobilization. As a result, he began to get offers to perform movie stunts and, in 1924, became an accepted star of westerns, making a large number of silent 'oaters' before the advent of sound put a stop to his career, his voice being unsuitable. He became a full-time stuntman, doubling for such big stars as Wayne, Flynn, Gable and even Roy Rogers, Tex Ritter and Randolph Scott. His own favourite death-defying stunt was in *Stagecoach*, in which he fell between the galloping horses of the coach, and was then dragged along the ground, finally letting the horses trample over his inert body. During his years as a stuntman, involving many hundreds of stunts, he was badly injured on only two occasions: once when he suffered six broken ribs during the filming of *San Francisco*, and once when the stunt went wrong and he punctured a lung while working on *Boom Town*. He also appeared as an actor, usually as a villain, in such films as *Gone with the Wind* and *The Far Horizon*. During the early 1940s he began directing second-feature westerns and graduated to be a second-unit director on some major movies, creating many of the best action sequences ever to be filmed. He was awarded a special Oscar in 1966 for 'creating the profession of stuntman as it exists today and for the development of many safety devices used by stuntmen everywhere.' Incidentally, both his sons are well-known stuntmen.

Adolfo Celi, the Italian heavyweight international actor, died in Sienna of a heart attack on 19 February 1986 at the age of 63. On screen, Celi was known by sight even by those who couldn't easily recall his name. The some 90 films that comprise his career were made and seen all over the world, and include *Von Ryan's Express, The Agony and the Ecstasy, Thunderball, El Greco, Grand Prix, Murders in the Rue Morgue, The Italian Connection* and *Brother Sun, Sister Moon*. Born in Sicily and educated in Rome, Celi also spent some 15 very successful years in Brazil as both actor and director.

James Craig (real name James H. Meador and whose original stage name was James Mead), who died from lung cancer in Santa Ana, California on 28 June 1985 at the age of 73, reached the height of his screen popularity in the 'thirties and 'forties, when he played top roles in such films as *All that Money Can Buy* (an adaptation of *The Devil and Daniel Webster*), which is generally considered to have been his best performance. Thereafter he was almost always doomed to play rugged heroes in routine action movies.

A college football and tennis star, the Nashville-born Craig's performance in a stage presentation of *The Petrified Forest* in 1937 resulted in an offer of a small role in De Mille's *The Buccaneer*. A part in the western serial *Winners of the West* and a number of western features eventually brought him the reward of a star role in the Ginger Rogers film *Kitty Foyle*. A seven-year contract with MGM kept him busy with parts in films such as *The Heavenly Body, Kismet, Our Vines Have Tender Grapes*, and *Boys' Ranch*. His films in the 'fifties and 'sixties included *Drums in the Deep South, Hurricane Smith, Fort Vengeance* and *Fort Utah*. His final movie was *The Doomsday Machine* (1973), after which he went into the real-estate business, finally announcing his retirement from the movies in the early 'eighties.

Broderick Crawford, who died in Rancho Mirage, California, on 26 April 1986 at the age of 74, was one of those reliable actors who, for one reason or another, never seem to get enough of the roles which their talent deserves. However, he did give some memorable performances, including the one in *All the King's Men* – that of a ruthless politician – which brought him both the 1949 Oscar and the New York Critics' accolade as their selected 'Best Actor' of the year. Born William Broderick Crawford, of Philadelphia-based theatrical parents, he appeared with them in vaudeville and did some radio work before making his stage debut – in London – in the unsuccessful *She Loves Me Not*, subsequently making his Broadway debut in the hardly less successful Noel Coward (who recommended him for the role) production *Point Valaine*. It was this performance that led to Samuel Goldwyn signing him up for his 1937 film *Woman Chases Man*. Two years later, Crawford made four films within 12 months, including *Beau Geste*, but these and many other roles that followed were minor and unrewarding, and in 1942 he joined the US Army Air Force, taking part in the famous Battle of the Bulge. Discharged in 1945, he was soon back playing the same kind of support roles, though he did give a memorable performance in *Born Yesterday* in 1950, and again showed his very considerable thespian talent five years later in Fellini's *Il Bidone* ('The Swindle'). But of his 50-odd films, few gave him any real chance to prove his worth. Some of his more recent appearances were in *Terror in the Wax Museum* (1973), *Proof of the Man* (a Japanese film) in 1977 and *The Private Files of J. Edgar Hoover* (in the title role) the following year, and he was last seen in *Harlequin, There Goes the Bride, The Uppercrust* and *Liar's Moon*. In 1974, he returned to the London stage in *That Championship Season*. For four years – from 1955 to 1959 – Crawford appeared with great success in the American TV series *Highway Patrol* and, in recent years, had roles in a number of TV movies.

Derek Farr, born in Chiswick, London and a former schoolmaster, died, of cancer, in his London home, on 22 March 1986. He was 74. He made his theatrical acting debut in 1937 and his first film (*The Outsider*) two years later. After *Spellbound* in 1940 and *Quiet Wedding* in 1941, he spent several years as a lieutenant in the Royal Artillery. His first postwar film was *Quiet Weekend* in 1945. From then on until the early 'seventies, he was kept busy with films such as *Wanted for Murder, The Dam Busters, Thirty Is a Dangerous Age, Cynthia, Murder Without Crime* and *Pope Joan* (in 1972) – the total exceeding 25. In recent years, he appeared in several TV series and also starred in dozens of stage plays.

Frank Faylen, born on one of the old American river steamers (his parents were showboat entertainers), died, aged 79, on 2 August 1985, after a long illness. He joined his parents' act at an early age and worked as clown, acrobat and song-and-dance performer before making his first film, *Bullets or Ballots* in 1936, after which practically every year saw his appearance on the screen until *Funny Girl* in 1968. His finest performance is generally reckoned to be that of the heartless male nurse in *The Lost Weekend*. Among his many other movies were *Grapes of Wrath, The Blue Dahlia, Road to Rio, Francis* and *Gunfight at the OK Corral*. He also appeared successfully in a number of TV series.

Stepin Fetchit (real name Lincoln Theodore Monroe Andrew Perry), who died from heart failure in Woodland Hills, California on 19 November 1985 at the age of 83, was the son of a Jamaican cigar-maker. He started out as a vaudeville performer in 1913 and played a role in a popular minstrel show of the period. Changing his name to (according to Fetchit) that of a racehorse that had once won him money, he made his first film in 1927 – *In Old Kentucky* – and this was followed by about 40 more including *Show Boat, Miracle in Harlem, The Prodigal, Judge Priest, Steamboat 'Round the Bend, The Galloping Ghost, Stand Up and Cheer, Bend of the River, The Sun Shines Bright* and, in 1974, *Amazing Grace*. Two years later he made his last screen appearance in *Won Ton Ton – the Dog that Saved Hollywood*. Having at one time accumulated a $2 million fortune that allowed him to be the owner of 16 cars, including Rolls-Royces, Fetchit was declared bankrupt in 1947, and in the 1960s was converted to the Black Muslim faith, becoming a friend and helpmate of Muhammad Ali.

The character that Stepin Fetchit created and played consistently throughout his film career – that of a whining, lazy, subservient black man – would today cause an uproar of protest for its implied insult to black people. However, this was always strenuously denied by Fetchit, who claimed that he opened the doors of the film studios to other black performers and, indeed, he was honoured a number of times for his work on behalf of black people.

Jane Frazee, who died on 4 September 1985 at the age of 67 from the last of a series of strokes that had struck her down during the past couple of years, will be best remembered for the bubbling, vivacious personality she displayed in a number of musicals she made in the 'forties. Born Mary Jane Freshe, she began her showbusiness career with sister Ruth when she was six, and the two girls continued their joint act until Jane made her movie debut in the 1940 musical *Melody and Moonlight*. Though never achieving major stardom, Jane made some 40 films, including Abbott & Costello's *Rookies* (*Buck Privates* in US), *Hellzapoppin, Kansas City Kitty, Ten Cents a Dance, Calendar Girl, Springtime in the Sierras* and, her last film, made in 1951, *Rhythm Inn*. In 1970 she moved into the estate agency business.

Frank Faylen.

Ruth Gordon (real name Ruth Gordon Jones), actress, playwright and screenwriter, died in her sleep at her Martha's Vineyard home on 28 August 1985, at the age of 88, having worked right up until the end – her final film, *Maxie*, opened in New York just a few weeks after her death. Diminutive (she was under 5 feet tall), dynamic and intelligent, Miss Gordon made her first film, *Camille*, in 1915 and put in a few more appearances on celluloid before devoting herself entirely to the theatre for a quarter of a century. Then she returned to the studios for a few movies – *Spirit of the People* (*Abe Lincoln in Illinois* in US), *Dr Erlich's Magic Bullet* and *Two-Faced Woman* – before moving back to New York for a further period of stage activity. It was not until 1966 that she made another movie – *Inside Daisy Clover* – one that brought her an Oscar nomination for best supporting actress, and this was followed by the winning of the actual award for her 'Manhattan witch' role in *Rosemary's Baby* in 1968. This success brought her plenty of offers, and she had a series of meaty parts – in the crazy black comedy *Harold and Maude* in 1971, *The Big Bus* in 1976, *Boardwalk* in 1979 and one or two other productions. Her second husband was writer-director Garson Kanin, with whom she had a string of hits as a screenwriter, including *Pat and Mike* and *Adam's Rib* (both of which brought Oscar nominations); on her own, she wrote the screenplay for *The Actress* (from her stage play *Years Ago*, which, in turn, was based on her own early experiences of trying to persuade her ex-sea captain father to agree to her making the theatre her profession) and *Rosie!*.

A woman of seemingly tireless energy, she appeared in many TV productions and, in 1979, won an Emmy for her performance in *Taxi*. She also co-wrote with Kanin the successful TV movie *Hardhat and Legs* (shown on British television in August 1984) and was a popular guest on various talk shows. Ruth Gordon also had the distinction of being the first American actress to be invited to join the Old Vic company, with whom she starred in *The Country Wife*.

Sterling Hayden, once hailed by the Paramount publicity department as 'The Most Beautiful Man in the Movies', died in California on 23 May 1986 at the age of 70, after a long fight against cancer. Six-and-a-half-foot-tall Sterling Relyea (some references give his real name as John Hamilton) was 23 before he made his first film test, having earned his living before then from the sea, which he loved deeply and to which he returned periodically throughout his life; having previously voyaged round the world, he won his master's certificate at the age of 22. Signed by Paramount after the test, Hayden played in only two films, – both opposite Madeleine Carroll, whom he married in 1942 – before joining the US Marines, during the war serving with Tito's forces so effectively that he was given the Yugoslav leader's commendation, as well as winning a Silver Star from the Marines. Back to Hollywood in 1947, he made *Blaze of Noon, El Paso* and *Manhandled* before appearing in the 1950 success *The Asphalt Jungle* and giving what many critics judge to be his best performance. Called before the infamous Un-American Activities Committee in 1951, he admitted his former membership of the Communist party (while fighting in Yugoslavia) and gave the names of some of his friends as fellow-travellers – an act which scarred him psychologically for the rest of his life.

During the 'fifties, Hayden made a large number of seldom-better-than-average movies, though he did give superior performances opposite Bette Davis in *The Star* (1953), opposite Joan Crawford in *Johnny Guitar* and in *Crime Wave* (both 1954). But though kept busy Hayden was not happy, and once went on record as saying that 'I always hated acting' – and he had the same hatred for Hollywood generally. Periodically he fled away from the studios and once, defying a court order, took his four children on a sailing trip to Tahiti. He returned to acting in 1964 with a notable performance in Kubrick's *Dr Strangelove* and so began a new career as a character actor, appearing with success in such films as *Sweet Hunters, The Godfather* and *The Long Goodbye* in 1973, which some critics rate as the best of his later screen work.

Rock Hudson, with Kim Novak and Elizabeth Taylor during the filming of *The Mirror Crack'd*.

Other films of his late period include *1900, Winter Kills, Nine to Five, The Outsider, Venom* and *Gas* – a career grand total of 50 films.

Hayden was also a popular TV performer, his last appearance on the small screen being as John Brown in *The Blue and the Gray* in 1982. The following year, he was the subject of an outstanding documentary film, *Pharos of Chaos*, which showed his life in Paris on board a barge. He also wrote two very successful books *Voyage: A Novel of 1896* and his autobiography, *Wanderer*. In later years, Hayden became something of an eccentric, with an enormous beard and affecting a walking stick. Though never liking his profession, Hayden could, when he liked, give a fine performance; when he didn't like, his work could be routine, to say the least.

Rock Hudson, whose death from the disease AIDS on 2 October 1985 at the age of 59 brought him more headline publicity than he had ever had for his acting performances, was the perfect example of the old Hollywood-manufactured star. Roy Scherer (his real name) had been a truck driver and done other odd jobs before his persistent agent got him a film test. During the waiting period, Hudson (who had taken his stepfather's surname, Fitzgerald, but was persuaded to adopt the more virile-sounding name of Rock Hudson) was coached intensively in acting, dancing, singing, fencing and riding, but when it came to his first appearance before the cameras – in Raoul Walsh's *Fighter Squadron* in 1948 – it needed 38 takes before he could say his first line successfully. However, Hudson persevered and, with his good looks and rugged charm, began to get work, improving to the extent that, in 1954, he was given the star role and was a big success in *Magnificent Obsession*. Now one of the most popular players on the Universal payroll, Hudson was actually nominated for an Oscar in 1956 for his performance in *Giant*, and the following year exhibitors voted him 'Star of the Year' in the annual *Motion Picture Herald* poll. In 1959, despite his own misgivings – it appears he never really got over his lack of self-confidence – he switched into comedy opposite Doris Day in *Pillow Talk*, a big enough box-office success for the studio to renew the pairing in *Lover Come Back* and *Send Me No Flowers*. From then on, Universal cast him alternately in dramas and comedies. In the late 'sixties and early 'seventies, however, Hudson struck a bad patch when *Ice Station Zebra* and *Darling Lili*

proved expensive flops. His film career waned, with roles in some quite indifferent movies, but, luckily for him, his television popularity waxed and he had big successes in several TV series and in films for the small screen. One of his last (cinema) films was *The Ambassador* with Robert Mitchum, and his final appearance was in George Stevens' documentary salute to his father, *George Stevens: A Filmmaker's Journey*.

In July 1985, a shocking photograph of a gaunt, emaciated and ill Rock Hudson appeared in the press, setting off rumours about the disease that had so quickly wasted him. However, when Hudson flew to Paris for treatment and then home by specially chartered jet, the true nature of his ailment emerged: he could no longer hide the fact that he was suffering from the killer disease AIDS, and his homosexuality, of which the film colony had been aware for a long time, became public knowledge. He wrote his own final words for a big fund-raising event in Los Angeles for cash to continue medical efforts to combat the disease: 'I am not happy that I have AIDS, but if that is helping others, I can, at least, know that my own misfortune has had some positive worth.' He died a few weeks later.

Isabel Jeans, who died in London on 5 September 1985 at the age of 93, was a relatively late starter, in that she had reached the age of 18 when, without any dramatic training, she made her first appearance on the stage, in a non-speaking role in *Pinkie and the Fairies*. It was not until 1913 that she spoke her first words to an audience. Ten years later, having meanwhile toured America with the Granville Barker company, she made a success in London with the role of Yasmin in *Hassan* (which she took over from Cathleen Nesbitt). Although primarily a stage actress, whose beauty was her original key to success, Isabel Jeans appeared in a number of film productions on both sides of the Atlantic, her first being *The Profligate* in 1917, followed by a role in *Tilly of Bloomsbury* four years later. Thereafter she made the occasional movie appearance, including *Gigi* in 1958, *Heavens Above!* in 1963 and, her last, *The Magic Christian*, in 1969.

John Lodge, who died at the age of 84 on 29 October 1985, was a star whose career followed the same pattern as Ronald Reagan's: a handsome, popular star of the 'thirties, after war service as a US Navy captain he switched to politics and, in 1946, was elected to the US House of Representatives, becoming Governor of Connecticut in 1950 and then serving as US Ambassador to Spain (1955–61), to Argentina (1969–73) and to Switzerland (1979–83), after which he was appointed delegate to the United Nations in 1984. John Lodge made his movie debut in 1933 in *The Woman Accused* and followed that with *Murders in the Zoo, Under the Tonto Rim, Little Women* and – the role which many critics thought was his most rewarding – the star part opposite La Dietrich in Von Sternberg's *The Scarlet Empress*. During the next few years, Lodge commuted regularly between Hollywood, Italy, England and France, making films in all those countries. These included diverse roles, which he always played with authority, in *Koenigsmark* ('The Crimson Dynasty'), *Sensation, Bulldog Drummond at Bay, The Tenth Man, Bank Holiday, Batticuore* and Max Ophuls' *De Mayerling à Sarajevo* ('Mayerling to Sarajevo').

Bessie Love, another of the great stars of the silent screen, died in the London she loved and in which she had lived since 1935, on 26 April 1986 at the age of 87. Born Juanita Horton in Midland, Texas, Miss Love made her screen debut in 1915 while still attending a Los Angeles high school. By the following year, she was starring opposite Douglas Fairbanks (in *Reggie Mixes In*) and William S. Hart (in *The Aryan*), as well as playing in the D. W. Griffith epic *Intolerance* (no one – including Miss Love herself – has been able to confirm the oft-printed credit of her appearance in *The Birth of a Nation*). She was small, pretty and sweet – and that's how the directors of the period inevitably cast her. By 1920 she had amassed a score of starring credits, and went on to appear in John Ford's *The Village Blacksmith* (1922), William Wyler's *Anybody Here Seen Kelly?* and Frank Capra's *The Matinée Idol* (both 1928). Unlike many other silent stars, Miss Love made a triumphant transition to the sound film when she showed her song-and-dance prowess in *The Broadway Melody* and *The Hollywood Revue* (both 1929 movies). But after making a few more films, she retired in

Bessie Love.

1931 and stayed away from the studios for a decade.

Then, living in London, she did accept roles in a couple of British productions: *Atlantic Ferry* in 1941 and *Journey Together* in 1945. It was not until 1954 that she made her next return to the studios in *The Barefoot Contessa*, after which she again appeared regularly in such films as *The Story of Esther Costello* (1957), *The Greengage Summer* (*Loss of Innocence* in the US) and *The Roman Spring of Mrs Stone* (both 1961), *On Her Majesty's Secret Service* (1969), *Sunday Bloody Sunday* (1971) and, more recently, *The Ritz, Lady Chatterley's Lover, Ragtime, Reds, Isadora* and *The Hunger*. She also appeared in a number of London stage presentations and was kept pretty busy by the TV companies. In recent years, she wrote a number of plays, in one of which – *The Homecoming* – she also appeared. During her long career, Bessie Love made more than 120 movies, but somehow, throughout a career that see-sawed regularly, producers found it difficult to give her the roles which offered a challenge to her considerable talent and great versatility.

Gordon MacRae, who died of cancer at the age of 64 on 24 January 1986, will be best recalled as the singing cowboy in the Fox musical *Oklahoma*. A performer since childhood, MacRae won a two-week engagement with the Harry James Orchestra and subsequently worked for two years with the Horace Heidt band. After the war, MacRae made a success in the Broadway revue *Three to Make Ready* and this won him a Warner contract. He made a number of movies for the company, including *The Big Punch* (his screen debut, 1948), *Look for the Silver Lining, Tea for Two, The West Point Story, On Moonlight Bay, Carousel, The Best Things in Life Are Free* and, his last film, *The Pilot* (1979). He made a large number of successful recordings (including 'I've Grown Accustomed to Her Face') and, also appeared regularly on TV. Married twice, one of his daughters by his first marriage, Meredith, has made a number of movies and is a popular TV personality, and his other four offspring have also been involved in showbusiness.

Margo – the actress, dancer and singer whose professional name was somewhat shorter than her real name of Maria Marguerita Guadalupe Teresa Estela Bolado Castilla O'Donnell – died on 17 July 1985 at her California home at the age of 68. Mexican by birth, she went to the United States as a young girl to live with her grandmother and aunt, the singer Carmen Castillo. Taught dancing by Rita Hayworth's father, she made her professional debut at the age of 10 with the famous band of her uncle Xavier Cugat. In 1934 she made her first movie, co-starring with Claude Rains in Hecht and MacArthur's *Crime Without Passion*. Three years later she won the co-starring role in Frank Capra's *Lost Horizon* and, in between successful seasons of dancing on the stage, made a number of films including *A Miracle on Main Street, Winterset, The Falcon in Mexico, Viva Zapata, I'll Cry Tomorrow, From Hell to Texas* and (apparently her last screen appearance) *Who's Got the Action?* in 1962. Married to the Czech actor Francis Lederer from 1937 to 1940, in 1945 she married the actor Eddie Albert; five years later, with him as co-star, she presented her own successful stage revue, and she also made records with him. Latterly, her interests were mainly in the arts and with civic activities – she was appointed the Commissioner of Social Services for Los Angeles in 1974. Her son, Edward Albert (originally Eddie Albert Jr), is also an actor.

Una Merkel, whose bubbling, enlivening personality lit up so many films in which she appeared as supporting actress, died at her Los Angeles home on 2 January 1986, at the age of 82. By then, she had chalked up more than 100 screen appearances. Initially cast as Lillian Gish's sister (because of her similar looks) in a film which was never finished, she subsequently played the star's stand-in in many of Gish's most famous films, including *Way Down East*. She obtained stardom in 1924 with the lead in *The Fifth Horseman* and then switched to the theatre for the next few years, returning to Hollywood and the movies in 1930 to play a role in D. W. Griffith's *Abraham Lincoln*. In the next ten years, she appeared in some 60 films, mostly in supporting roles, including *Command Performance, The Maltese Falcon* (the first, 1931 version), *Daddy Long Legs, 42nd Street, The Merry Widow, Evelyn Prentice, Broadway Melody of 1936, Riff Raff, Born to Dance, Test Pilot* and – one of her most delightful performances – *Destry Rides Again*, in which she had the memorable slugging match with Dietrich. In 1944, she returned to the Broadway stage, subsequently touring in several productions, including Tennessee Williams' *Summer and Smoke*, which provided her with one of her most memorable screen performances when the play was made into a movie in 1961. More recent film roles were in *The Kentuckian* (1955), *The Parent Trap (1961), Summer Magic* (1963), *A Tiger Walks* (1964) and apparently her final screen role, *Spinout* in 1966.

Una Merkel.

Ray Milland (real name Reginald Truscott-Jones; changed initially to Spike Milland, later to Raymond Milland) died of cancer at the age of 81 on 10 March 1986 in Los Angeles. He had appeared in more than 120 films (including a number of TV feature films and cameo appearances) during his long acting career, which began with no fewer than four movies in 1929 (in one of which, *The Informer*, he played a trick shooter). Born in Neath, in South Wales, Milland started his working life, after various, sometimes part-time jobs, by enlisting in the Army, in which he served for three years with the Household Cavalry. It was through the help of film actress Estelle Brody that he broke

Ray Milland, seen with Ryan O'Neal and Meg Munday in *Oliver's Story*.

into films (he always maintained that he entered the acting profession 'more by accident than design') as an extra and small-part player. But after a trip to Hollywood to appear in *The Bachelor Father* (1931), he began to be offered larger roles, journeying back and forth across the Atlantic for alternate British and American productions. He was never idle: in between his acting roles, he was a professional bridge player and a steeplechase jockey! In 1932 he married an American, Muriel Weber, who was also in showbusiness, and two years later decided to make Hollywood his permanent home.

Signing a long-term contract with Paramount, after impressing them with his performance in *Bolero* (1934) with Ginger Rogers and George Raft, Milland was offered as much work as he could handle, generally playing the handsome hero in such films as *The Gilded Lily, Three Smart Girls, Beau Geste* and *Bulldog Drummond Escapes*. He was chosen by Billy Wilder to star, opposite Ginger Rogers, in Wilder's American directing debut with *Arise My Love* and *The Major and the Minor*, but it was when the latter cast him against type as the alcoholic writer in *The Lost Weekend* (1945) that Milland gained his greatest triumph – and a number of important awards, including the year's Oscar for 'Best Actor'. Although he was to appear in scores of films and give an equal amount of very sound performances – especially in Hitchcock's *Dial M for Murder* – he never again quite reached that peak.

Milland produced as well as starred in Jacques Tourneur's 1951 production *Circle of Danger*, and directed himself in several interesting movies such as *A Man Alone, Lisbon* and *Panic in the Year Zero*. After several years when he never entered a studio, he resumed his film career in the 'seventies, but now appeared, for the most part, in unimportant horror pictures such as *The Thing with Two Heads, Terror in the Wax Museum* and *Frogs*. He garnered a great deal of praise for his portrayal of Ryan O'Neal's father in the 1970 weepie *Love Story* (and its sequel *Oliver's Story*), and continued to make films in United States, Canada, Italy and Britain until his final illness. He also worked on TV (for which he produced and directed as well as starred) and video features (the last of which, *The Gold Key*, he completed in April 1985). In spite of his battle against cancer, he was well enough to visit his birthplace in the December of that year. He wrote one book, his autobiography *Wide-Eyed in Babylon*, published in 1974.

Anna Neagle, as seen in *Victoria the Great*.

Dame Anna Neagle (real name Marjorie Robertson), who died on 3 June 1986 at the age of 81 was the generally accepted 'Queen of the British Cinema'. In the film business it was universally acknowledged that, while she may not have been our greatest film actress (though she did give some very good performances and never a bad one), she was certainly the nicest, most sincere, best tempered, most painstaking and reliable – just some of the qualities that made her loved both in and out of her profession. Her teaming with producer (later husband) Herbert Wilcox produced some of Britain's greatest box-office hits of the 'thirties and 'forties. The team made 32 films between 1932 and 1959, among them *Nell Gwyn, Victoria the Great, Sixty Glorious Years, I Live in Grosvenor Square* (*A Yank in London* in US) and *Spring in Park Lane*. Although she made her name in light and, in some cases, musical movies, Dame Anna also starred in a number of serious films such as *Nurse Edith Cavell, They Flew Alone* (called *Wings and the Woman* in the US, the story of pioneer woman aviator Amy Johnson), *The Lady with the Lamp* (the story of Florence Nightingale) and the film in which many think she gave the finest performance of her career, the story of French Resistance heroine *Odette*.

After taking dancing lessons as a child, Dame Anna became a chorus girl in 1925 and remained in the singing–dancing line for the following six years, during which she also appeared in some of the large-scale cabaret bills at the old Trocadero. After bit parts in films, she won a role in *Goodnight, Vienna* (*Magic Night* in US), which was followed by the long string of Wilcox movies. Latterly, though still the darling of the British public, her films declined in value. She produced three films herself: *These Dangerous Years* (1957), *Wonderful Things* (1958) and *The Heart of a Man* (1959). Her last film was *The Lady Is a Square* in 1959. In 1977 Wilcox died, aged 87 (see *Film Review* 1977–8). Dame Anna's successful stage career included runs of almost 500 performances in *The Glorious Days* and more than 2000 performances in *Charlie Girl*. She was created a Dame of the British Empire in 1969.

Lloyd Nolan died from lung cancer at his Los Angeles home on 27 September 1985 at the age of 83 after making more than 70 films. In the many obituaries that followed his death, nearly all the writers credited him with being a better actor than most of his roles allowed him to reveal. San Francisco-born, Nolan studied English at college but opted out when he had the chance to join the Pasadena Playhouse company. After touring, he reached Broadway in a musical as a member of the chorus but later was seen in more important roles and was signed up by Paramount in 1934, appearing in no fewer than four films the following year, including *G-Men*. For the next ten years Nolan was usually cast as a western villain, a gangster, or in other similarly unsympathetic roles, breaking away from this image only with the roles of an FBI agent in *The House on 92nd Street* and the kindly cop in *A Tree Grows in Brooklyn*. Nolan may also be recalled for his performances in *The Lemon Drop Kid* (1951), *Peyton Place* (1957), *Airport* (1970) and *Earthquake* (1974). His final screen appearance appears to have been in the 1986 Woody Allen film *Hannah and Her Sisters*. He also appeared frequently on TV and made a big hit with Diahann Carroll in the series *Julia*.

Lloyd Nolan.

George O'Brien, a highly successful school and college athlete who became known as 'The Chest' because of his impressive physique (he was at one time the heavyweight boxing champion of the US Pacific Fleet), died on 4 September 1985 at the age of 85 at his Oklahoma home, where he had lived in retirement since suffering a stroke some six years previously. Serving in the US forces in both world wars (and again, though in a moviemaking capacity, in the Korean and Vietnam wars) in which he saw considerable action and won numerous medals, O'Brien's introduction to the movie business was as an assistant cameraman, doubling as stuntman, in the Tom Mix westerns of the 'twenties. It came as a surprise when John Ford picked him to be the star of his 1924 film *The Iron Horse*. Among the films which followed were F. W. Murnau's *Sunrise*, in which he co-starred with Janet Gaynor; but in the 'thirties O'Brien specialized almost entirely in western roles, starring in several more John Ford productions as well as other 'oaters' such as *The Lone Star Ranger*, *Riders of the Purple Sage* and *The Gay Caballero*. After World War II O'Brien worked less regularly, although he did appear in two further Ford films, *Fort Apache* and *She Wore a Yellow Ribbon*, and, indeed, the last of the 70 or so films that he made was again for Ford – the latter's *Cheyenne Autumn* in 1964.

Lilli Palmer (real name Lillie Marie Peiser), who died on 27 January 1986 at her home in Los Angeles, aged 71, was a truly international actress, having worked on stage, screen and TV in Germany, France, Austria, Britain, the United States and many other countries during her lifetime. Born in Posen – then Germany, now Poland – she inherited her acting ambition from her Austrian actress mother (her father was a doctor) and attended drama school in Berlin, the city which saw her stage debut in 1932. However, with the coming of Hitler, Lilli Palmer moved to Paris, where she appeared in an operetta staged at the Moulin Rouge. In 1935, she came to Britain, where, in the same year, she made her film debut in *Crime Unlimited* subsequently landing a small role in Hitchcock's *Secret Agent*, and thus beginning what was to become a highly successful screen career which included some 50 films, as well as periodic stage appearances. Some of the best movies in which she appeared include: *Thunder Rock* (1942), *The Gentle Sex* (1943), *The Rake's Progress* (*Notorious Gentleman* in the US; 1945), *Anastasia* (1956), *The Glass Tower* and *Mädchen in Uniform* (both 1958), *And So to Bed* (1963), *Operation Crossbow* (1965), *Murders in the Rue Morgue* (1971) and *The Boys from Brazil* (1978). Her final appearance on the screen was in the 1985 release *The Holcroft Covenant*.

Married to Rex Harrison from 1943 to 1957, shortly after their divorce she married again, to Argentinian actor/writer Carlos Thompson. He encouraged her to paint and write as well as act, and this resulted in some successful shows of her paintings and a highly successful quartet of books: her autobiography *Change Lobsters and Dance* and three novels, *The Red Raven*, *Night Music* and *Face Value* (published posthumously).

Otto Ludwig Preminger, director-producer and sometime actor, died at the age of 79 in New York on 23 April 1986 after a miserable period of ill health, including cancer. Controversial, often caustic-tongued but also sometimes charming (according to some of those who have worked with him; others openly hated him), he enjoyed causing a stir with the subjects of his films and was always ready to welcome a fight, be it with the censor, his bosses or members of his cast.

Born in Vienna (although there is some doubt about the precise location) in 1906 (again some doubt; it may have been a year either way), this son of the Attorney-General of the Austrian Empire initially studied law, graduating from the University of Vienna in 1928, when he could at last indulge his passion for the theatre. Making his acting debut in a Max Reinhardt production of *A Midsummer Night's Dream*, he was soon directing plays and running his own company. Eventually he was invited by Reinhardt to direct at the Josefstadt Theatre in Vienna, where several successes led to his being asked to succeed the maestro. It was around this period that Preminger directed his first film – and the only one he ever did in German – *Die Grosse Liebe*.

In 1935, conscious of the political situation in Europe and aware of what might happen to him as a Jew, Preminger moved to New York, where a very successful re-staging of his Vienna success *Libel* brought him an offer from Darryl Zanuck at Fox to study the work of various Hollywood directors and then, later, direct two minor movies himself. Falling out with his boss, Preminger returned to New York to produce the highly successful stage play *Outward Bound*. Two years later, Preminger was tempted back to the Fox studios where, ironically, he played a Nazi in *The Pied Piper* before directing and playing (another Nazi) in *Margin for Error*. Returning to the studio after war service, Zanuck was furious about the contract the studio had given Preminger, but reluctantly agreed that he should direct *Laura* after the original director had proved unsuitable. The film turned out to be something of a masterpiece, winning Preminger the first of his three Oscar nominations. Now established at Fox, Preminger made ten films for the company within six years, including the completion of Lubitsch's *The Lady in Ermine* when that director died during production.

It was shortly after his confrontation with the censor over *Forever Amber* in 1947 that Preminger bowed out of Fox to set up his own production company, in 1953 making the film version of his highly successful stage production *The Moon Is Blue*, which, harmless as it seems today, led to more fighting with the censor. And still more censorship troubles met his next film, the highly successful *The Man with the Golden Arm*, the first time that the problem of drug addiction had been tackled on the screen. Two films with all-black casts followed: *Carmen Jones*, a qualified success, and *Porgy and Bess*, an unqualified critical and box-office flop. Then came Shaw's *St Joan* with the young and untried Jean Seberg in the title role (a woeful piece of casting which earned Preminger vilification from the critics). But he persisted with Miss Seberg in the far more commercially successful *Bonjour Tristesse*. More headline stories – and critical and commercial success – came in 1959 with the explosive rape and murder story *Anatomy of a Murder*. Several large and expensive productions of varying worth followed, including *Advise and Consent, The Cardinal, In Harm's Way* and the odd, made-in-Britain movie *Bunny Lake Is Missing*. Later films – such as *Skidoo!, Tell Me That You Love Me, Junie Moon, Rosebud* and *Such Good Friends* – were never very good and sometimes pretty bad. The last film he finished (against all financial odds) was his 1979 production of the Graham Greene novel *The Human Factor*, although he had numerous movies planned when increasing ill-health eventually forced him into unwilling inactivity. Because of his bald-pated, saturnine looks and the headline-hitting controversies in which he was involved, Preminger was one of the few film directors whose appearance was familiar to the public.

Director Preminger with Sir Richard Attenborough.

Donna Reed who died from cancer at her Hollywood home on 14 January 1986, aged 64, was a farm-bred girl from Iowa who became her hometown beauty queen, moving to Los Angeles later – to learn shorthand and typing! However, after winning the title of Campus Queen in 1940, no fewer than three Hollywood studios offered her screen tests. In the one for MGM, she appeared with Van Heflin, as a result of which both were signed. Donna's real name was Donna Belle Mullenger, but she made her movie debut as Donna Adams in the 1941 films *The Getaway* and *Shadow of the Thin Man*. She continued to play minor roles for the next few years before winning star status, usually playing the nice, wholesome, girl-next-door. However, in 1953 she was cast very much against type as the prostitute Alma in Fred Zinnemann's

Donna Reed.

From Here to Eternity, for which she won an Oscar as 'Best Supporting Actress'. Despite this, she found a lack of meaty roles, her career declined and, in 1958, she bade farewell to the studios and went into television where her *Donna Reed Show* was a long-running success. She made only two more movie appearances as far as can be ascertained: a cameo role in *Pepe* in 1960 and a major role in the seemingly still unreleased *Yellow-Headed Summer*. Some of her more memorable movies include *Babes on Broadway, The Courtship of Andy Hardy, Calling Dr Gillespie, Mrs Parkington, It's a Wonderful Life, The Last Time I Saw Paris, The Benny Goodman Story* and *The Far Horizons*, but she will probably be best remembered by younger audiences for her relatively brief stint as stand-in for the then-indisposed Barbara Bel Geddes, as 'Miss Ellie' in the international hit TV series *Dallas*.

Kathleen Ryan died, aged 63, in her native city of Dublin on 11 November 1985. Sweet and a little melancholy is the description that springs to mind when one recalls this Irish actress, a star of the British screen in the late 'forties and 'fifties. A former Abbey Theatre actress, her finest film performance was her first, in the classic *Odd Man Out* in 1947. Her other films include *Captain Boycott* (also 1947), *Esther Waters, Christopher Columbus, The Yellow Balloon* and, her only American movie, *Captain Lightfoot* (1955). Her last film was *Sail into Danger* in 1957.

George Savalas, brother of the more famous Telly (*Kojak*) Savalas, who died a victim of leukaemia, aged 58, on 2 October 1985, will best be recalled for his entertaining performances in that TV series. Curly-headed, chubby and cheerful, this former drama coach made his acting debut on radio in *The Dick Powell Theater* series. Although he only appeared in a few movies, they included *Kelly's Heroes, The Greatest Story Ever Told, Johnny Cool, Ghengis Khan* and *The Outfit*.

Simone Signoret (real name Simone Kaminker), one of France's greatest film stars, died from cancer at her Normandy home on 30 September 1985 at the age of 64, shortly after completing a new French TV series called *Music Hall*. Born in Wiesbaden of French parents, Mme Signoret had to leave school to help support her mother and brothers during the German occupation, after her Jewish linguist father had fled to England to join the Free French. It was for additional much needed money that she began her career in films as an extra, quickly making enough of an impression to gain small parts. After the war she moved easily into major roles, including those she did for her husband, director Yves Allégret, in his films, *Les Démons à l'aube, Dédée d'Anvers* and *Manèges*. Other successes of the period include her performances in Tourneur's *L'Impasse des deux anges* and Ophuls' *La Ronde*, when she was often cast as a prostitute or, as later in Becker's *Casque d'or* (*Golden Marie*), as a gangster's moll, a role which incidentally, brought her international acclaim and the London Film Academy's best actress award for 1951. In 1950, she was divorced from Allégret and married Yves Montand, with whom she later co-starred in Rouleau's *Les Sorcières de Salem* (an adaptation of Arthur Miler's *The Crucible*) and Costa-Gavras's *L'Aveu* (*The Confession*). Among the 50 or so movies in which she had roles, some of the most easily recalled will be Carné's *Thérèse Raquin* (*The Adulteress*), Clouzot's *Les Diaboliques*, Buñuel's *La Mort en ce jardin* (*Death in the Garden*), Clément's *Le Jour et l'heure* (*The Day and the Hour*) and Sidney Lumet's *The Deadly Affair* and *The Seagull*. For her

Simone Signoret with Vera Clouzot in *Les Diaboliques*.

performance in the 1958 British film *Room at the Top*, she won the Oscar for best actress and was again nominated for her performance in the American film *Ship of Fools* in 1965. Her other British films were *Against the Wind* in 1948 and *Term of Trial* in 1962, and in 1966 she appeared at London's Royal Court Theatre in the role of Lady Macbeth.

Mme Signoret was well known for her leftish political opinions, which she shared with Montand. She wrote two books of autobiography: *Nostalgia Isn't What It Used to Be* in 1976 and *Le Lendemain, elle était souriante* two years later. Simone Signoret's success as an actress was due to a great extent to her ability to bring her considerable intelligence into every role she essayed.

Howard Da Silva, who died in New York on 16 February 1986, at the age of 76, was best known for his stage work, as actor, director, writer and producer. However, he did make more than 40 films, including *Abe Lincoln in Illinois, Sergeant York, The Lost Weekend, The Blue Dahlia, Two Years Before the Mast, M, David and Lisa, Topkapi*, both the film versions of *The Great Gatsby* (1949 and 1974) and *Garbo Talks*. Blacklisted by Hollywood for refusing to affirm or deny membership in the Communist Party to the infamous 'Reds under the beds' House Un-American Activities Committee, within two years he was starring as well as directing and co-producing the stage version of *The World of Sholem Ash*. Da Silva, who was born Harold Silverblatt and started his working life in the Ohio steel mills, was also a regular TV performer.

Phil Silvers, the American comic actor, died on 1 November 1985 at the age of 73. Though it is for his performances as Sergeant Bilko in the long-running and subsequently much-revived *Phil Silvers Show* that he will be best remembered, Silvers did in fact appear in some 36 feature films. Born Philip Silversmith, in the toughest part of the Bronx, of Russian immigrant parents, he started earning his keep in his early teens by singing and was soon touring in vaudeville. His first contact with films came with a series of Warner two-reelers in the 1930s, but it wasn't until 1939 that he made his first feature, playing – of all things – a priest in *Pride and Prejudice*. He subsequently appeared in *Tom, Dick and Harry, Lady Be Good* and *You're in the Army Now* (all 1941), *Coney Island* (1943), *Cover Girl* (1944) and *A Thousand and One Nights* (1945). However, his real success during that period came in such Broadway stage shows as *High Button Shoes* and *Top Banana*; he repeated his role in the latter in the film version. After a somewhat uneasy start in 1955, *The Phil Silvers Show* (originally called *You'll Never Get Rich*) soared to the top of the American TV ratings and ran for 144 episodes. In later years, Silvers provided a lot of the laugh content in films such as *It's a Mad, Mad, Mad, Mad World* (1963), *A Funny Thing Happened on the Way to the Forum* (1966), *Follow That Camel* (his only British film, made in 1967), *Won Ton Ton – the Dog that Saved Hollywood* (1976) and *Racquet* (1977). In 1972, Silvers won a Tony award for his work in a Broadway revival of *A Funny Thing Happened . . .*, and the same year suffered a stroke that forced him to reduce his activities, though he did appear in a few more movies and periodically on TV. His autobiography *The Laugh Is on Me* was published in 1973.

Gale Sondergaard, the Minnesota-born actress of Danish descent (real name: Edith Holm Sondergaard), died in California after a long illness on 14 August 1985 at the age of 86. She had the distinction of winning, for her very first film performance (in the 1936 adaptation of *Anthony Adverse*), the very first 'best supporting actress' Oscar ever to be presented. The daughter of a professor, Gale Sondergaard started her acting career in college theatricals, subsequently working with several professional companies before making her New York debut in 1923. Five years later she returned to the Broadway boards on a three-year Theater Guild contract. However, it was not until 1934 – and then, it appears, only with some reluctance – that she signed with Columbia Pictures to make *Anthony Adverse*. After that instant success she was soon making one movie after another in quick succession, including *Seventh Heaven, The Life of Emile Zola, Never Say Die, Juarez, The Cat and the Canary, The Mark of Zorro* and the 1940 version of *The Letter*. The following year she moved from Columbia to Universal, for whom she made about two films a year from 1941 to 1947, including *The Black Cat, The Spider Woman, Follow the Boys, Christmas Holiday* and *The Time of Their Lives*. During this period she was also loaned out to other companies for such films as *My Favorite Blonde, Road to Rio, A Night to Remember, Appointment in Berlin* and *Anna and the King of Siam* (which brought her an Oscar nomination). For a considerable period, she was the favourite female screen 'baddie' and was repeatedly cast as a very unlikeable character.

In 1947, along with her director husband Herbert Biberman, she suffered from blacklisting during the McCarthy witch-hunts, and after *East Side, West Side* in 1949 was not to appear in front of the cameras for 20 years. She returned to the screen in 1969 in *Slaves*. Her final film appearance was in 1976 in *The Return of a Man Called Horse*.

Sam Spiegel, who died on 31 December 1985 at the age of 84 during a holiday on a Caribbean island, was one of the world's few authentic independent producers. Always working closely with his directors and writers, at a leisurely pace (it took him four years to make *Lawrence of Arabia*) and with careful costing (he brought in *The Bridge on the River Kwai* for $2.5 million, which in three years grossed $30 million!), Spiegel's list of films includes a majority of big commercial and artistic successes. He never had a real failure. This was partly due to his consistent rule of working with the finest talent he could afford: directors such as David Lean, Orson Welles, Julien Duvivier, Joseph Losey and Lewis Milestone; writers such as Carl Foreman, Ben Hecht, Harold Pinter and James Agee; and some of the finest actors and actresses in the world.

Born in a part of Austria now belonging to Poland, Spiegel took a degree in economics at the University of Vienna, later going to Palestine for a year. He lived in California in 1927, where he worked as a reader for MGM. Moving to Germany, to produce German and French versions of Universal films, he fled that country in 1933 with the advent of Hitler. In Hollywood, under the name of S. P. Eagle, he co-produced Fox's *Tales of Manhattan* and made his solo producing debut in 1946 with *The Stranger*, directed by Welles and co-written by John Huston. Then came *The African Queen*, which won its star

Humphrey Bogart an Oscar and established Spiegel as an outstanding producer. The first time the latter used his own name on a film was in the credits of *On the Waterfront*, which brought Spiegel himself his first Oscar in 1954. Then came the award-laden – including a second Oscar – *Bridge on the River Kwai*, to be followed by *Lawrence of Arabia*, for which Spiegel received his third Oscar. Other films were *The Chase, Night of the Generals, The Happening, Nicholas and Alexandra* and *The Last Tycoon*. At the 1963 Oscar awards ceremony, Spiegel was presented with the Irving Thalberg Memorial Award.

Charles Starrett – probably best recalled for his 66 films as the 'Durango Kid' in the old western series of that title – died on 22 March 1986 at the age of 82. A football star at Dartmouth College in New Hampshire, he made his screen debut when he was picked for a role as an extra in the 1926 Richard Dix film *The Quarterback*. His massive output in a career that spanned 30 years included a period when he was making as many as nine films per year. After playing romantic leads for several years in such films as *The Royal Family of Broadway, Damaged Love, The Mask of Fu Manchu, Our Betters* and *Jungle Bride*, he then moved to Columbia in 1936 to take over from Buck Jones as their top cowboy star. His westerns included *The Pinto Kid, West of Tombstone, Riders of the Lone Star* and *Last Days of Boot Hill*. His last film was *Rough Tough West*, made in 1952.

Robert Stevenson died at the age of 81 on 30 April 1986. Although he was 22 before he saw his first film, when the lights came up at the end of that film he had decided that his future was to be in the celluloid business. When he retired in 1978, he had directed, as well as often having written and sometimes produced, more than 40 movies, the majority of which were so successful that *Variety* dubbed him 'the most commercially successful director of all time'. Born in Buxton, educated at Shrewsbury and Cambridge, he moved steadily up the moviemaking ladder, from script reader, dialogue director, production supervisor to film editor and screenwriter, finally reaching directing in 1932 with *Happy Ever After*. After some dozen British films, Stevenson moved to Hollywood in 1939 to make a hit with his first movie there, *Tom Brown's Schooldays*, and among the successes that followed was, notably, *Jane Eyre* in 1944. In 1956 he accepted an offer from Walt Disney to join his organization, and for the remainder of his career stayed with Disney, making some of the company's greatest moneyspinners including the greatest of all, *Mary Poppins*, which earned some $42 million on its original release in 1964, as well as having won five Oscars, and is still making money today. Others of his 19 Disney movies include *Kidnapped, That Darn Cat, Blackbeard's Ghost, The Love Bug, Bedknobs and Broomsticks, The Island at the Top of the World* and *One of Our Dinosaurs Is Missing*.

Paul Stewart, who died, aged 77, on 17 February 1986, reckoned that, as well as his stage, screen and TV work, he had also appeared in more than 5000 radio shows! Actor and producer in Orson Welles' Mercury Theatre – it was Stewart who produced the famous radio play *War of the Worlds* which caused America to go into a panic – he made his film debut in *Citizen Kane*. His subsequent films – made in between his many radio, stage and TV commitments, – included *Johnny Eager, Twelve O'Clock High, The Bad and the Beautiful, Bite the Bullet, Carbine Williams, The Day of the Locust* and, what appears to have been his final screen appearance, *The Revenge of the Pink Panther* in 1978.

John Sutro, who died in Monte Carlo in mid-June 1985 at the age of 82, was a British producer with a very small output, the high spot of his career being his co-production of the famous Carol Reed film *The Way Ahead*. Sutro's main interests were in the literary world and among his close friends were Graham Greene and Evelyn Waugh. A lawyer by profession (though he never practised), he was something of an eccentric.

Orson Welles, the cinema's so-called 'boy wonder', died, apparently from a heart attack, at his Hollywood home on 10 October 1985 at the age of 70. Because of the obvious limitations of working within the commercial cinema and, in most cases, the artistic restrictions it imposes, Welles – like that other film genius Jacques Tati – was seldom allowed sufficient freedom to express himself in the medium and, sadly, again like Tati, many of the screen masterpieces of which he was capable remained no more than projects.

Actor, director, writer and sometime magician, as well as being a splendid orator with a sonorous voice that was often in demand, George Orson Welles was born in Kenosha, Wisconsin, on 6 May 1915, to a father who was an inventor and a mother who was a concert pianist of celebrated beauty. Welles became identified with genius by the age of 10, by which time he could recite Shakespeare from memory, was writing poems and had had some of his cartoons published. While attending a private school that did not frown on his obsession with the theatre, he staged and acted in a number of productions. At the age of 16, Welles embarked on a painting tour of Ireland, which ended when, by telling seemingly convincing tall stories about his acting ability and achievements, he impressed the management of Dublin's Gate Theatre enough to persuade it to give him roles in and even let him direct some seven productions. For the next few years, the Welles star waxed mightily in the capacities of actor, director and playwright (he had three plays to his credit by the time he was 18). Back in the United States, he founded the Mercury Theater with John Houseman, and now had the opportunity to express himself in diverse theatrical ways. The most famous of these was his radio production of H. G. Wells's *War of the Worlds*, which in 1938 caused something of a national panic when it convinced many listeners that the earth was being invaded by creatures from another world.

Desperate for the cash to put on an ambitious Shakespeare production, Welles at last turned to the movies and, with his first effort, *Citizen Kane*, produced one of the all-time masterpieces of the screen, even though press baron William Randolph Hearst (whom it was said to portray) did his considerable best to keep the finished film away from the public. After a return to the theatre, Welles embarked on his second film, *The Magnificent Ambersons*, which some critics think an even greater achievement than *Citizen Kane*, although its previews were disasters and it was subsequently butchered before being sent out on release. Turned down on health grounds for war service, Welles toured with his *Mercury Wonder Show* (in which he sawed stars such as Marlene Dietrich in half!) and produced, co-wrote and co-starred in another outstanding film, *Journey into Fear*. After his involvement in the fortune-costing – and losing – stage musical *Around the World in 80 Days*, Welles returned to Hollywood to direct and star in *The Stranger* and *The Lady from Shanghai* – the former a routine melodrama, the latter (in part) excitingly original. After making his idiosyncratic *Macbeth* (never likely to be a box-office success), Welles left to act in several European movies, including a notable performance as Harry Lime in *The Third Man*. With the cash that these roles brought him, Welles made his *Othello*, a film that won him the first prize at the 1952 Cannes Festival but did little, subsequently, for his bank balance.

At this time, Welles would accept any sort of role in any sort of movie just for the cash. It was in the theatre that he had a big success with his adaptation of *Moby Dick*. Back again in Hollywood, after a number of radio successes including some BBC series, Welles achieved another artistic milestone in *A Touch of Evil*, the last time he was offered a directorial assignment in the United States. Thereafter he concentrated on acting, notably in John Huston's version of *Moby Dick*. In Europe , he directed Kafka's *The Trial* for the Salkinds, failing to make it either a commercial or an artistic success, but in 1966 his *Chimes at Midnight* (retitled *Falstaff* in the US) won him critical acclaim and a special award at the Cannes Film Festival; as a whole, it was below his best, but in part it was magnificent cinema. Two years later, Welles made the one-hour film *The Immortal Story* for French TV and, seven years after that, produced his witty movie *F for Fake*. Although he did not act again in feature films after *The Voyage of the Damned* in 1976 and *The Muppet Movie* in 1979, Welles was working vigorously on numerous projects for screen, stage and TV at the time of his death.

It is little known that the always-ebullient Welles, while wandering in the wilderness in 1932 after being snubbed by Broadway, actually fought in a Spanish bullring. Another little-known fact about him is that, in 1938 (before

Orson Welles, as seen in *The Third Man*.

Citizen Kane), Welles made a 40-minute movie called *Too Much Johnson* that was never seen by the public, the only known print being destroyed by a fire at his house in 1970.

After praising its 'boy wonder', Hollywood went through various stages of disillusion and distrust of him and his ways (although he never wasted fortunes on his films, as did some other, less gifted but somehow more easily accepted and forgiven moviemakers). Later the movie world allowed itself a somewhat grudging admiration for and then finally, pride in the man who was, without doubt, one of the most gifted of all its writer-director-actors and who, in more ways than one, entirely revolutionized the motion picture.

Dorothea Wieck, Swiss-born and pupil of Max Reinhardt, died in Berlin, aged 78, on 23 February 1986. She was already a star of the German stage when she made her sensational screen success in 1931 in *Mädchen in Uniform*. Lured to Hollywood on the strength of this, she made only a couple of films there – neither a success – before returning to Germany, where she chalked up a total of some 50 movies, few of which were seen outside Europe. A baroness by marriage, she retired from acting in 1976, long after her last film, *Brainwashed* (*The Royal Game* in the UK) in 1960.

Margery Wilson, veteran screen star and director, died, aged 89, at her California home on 21 January 1986. Making her screen debut in her teens in D. W. Griffith's *Intolerance*, she subsequently appeared in a number of films including several in which she played opposite William S. Hart. In 1920 she both directed and starred in *That Something*, and the following year directed a further couple of movies. Retiring from acting, Miss Wilson began a new literary career, producing books on such subjects as deportment, charm, positive thinking and the like, as well as her autobiography, which came out in the 'fifties.

Margery Wilson with Frank Keenan and Jerome Storm in *Bride of Hate*.

The Ten Most Promising Faces of 1986

JAMES CAMERON-WILSON

F. Murray Abraham, a distinguished stage actor with classically menacing looks, sprang on to the Hollywood screen from left field. The most wanted film role of 1984 – Salieri in Miloš Forman's *Amadeus* – had been coveted by every international star worth his salt. Paul Scofield had originated it at the National Theatre, Frank Finlay had played it in London's West End, Ian McKellen had performed it on Broadway. And yet it was an 'unknown' actor from Pittsburgh (born 1939) who nabbed it, made it his own and, in 1984, won the Oscar for 'Best Actor' for it. An imposing figure with a pockmarked face and prominent nose, Abraham would make a fine screen villain, but his starring role opposite Sean Connery in *The Name of the Rose* suggests he is bound for better things. Previous film roles include bits in *They Might Be Giants, The Sunshine Boys, All the President's Men, The Ritz* and *The Big Fix*, and the Mafia hood 'Omar' in Brian De Palma's *Scarface*.

F. Murray Abraham as Salieri in Miloš Forman's *Amadeus*.

Rosanna Arquette became a very big star indeed with her role as the bored housewife-turned-kook who's desperately seeking Susan. The actress had already been around a while, acting in local theatre while still in her teens, and was the inspiration for Toto's 1982 hit song 'Rosanna' (she was then dating Steve Porcaro, on keyboards). Born in New York City, Rosanna was moved around like a chess piece by her parents, living in Chicago, Los Angeles, and, finally, Front Royal, Virginia. Spotted by a casting director in a production of *Metamorphosis* there, she never looked back. First, there was a series of high-calibre TV movies: *Harvest Home*, with Bette Davis; *The Wall*, with Tom Conti; and *The Long Way Home*, with Timothy Hutton. Then she had a bit in the comedy *Gorp*; starred opposite Paul Sorvino in *Off the Wall*; and played a sexy hitch-hiker in Blake Edwards' successful *S.O.B.* However, the role that first caught the attention of critics was in the TV movie *The Executioner's Song*, in which she played the pathetic, vulnerable (and, yes, sexy) Nicole, girl-friend of mass-murderer Gary Gilmore (Tommy Lee Jones). Top-billing followed in John Sayles' *Baby, It's You*, with Vincent Spano and Matthew Modine, and then three more TV movies: *Johnny Belinda, One Cooks, the Other Doesn't* and *The Parade*. She had a starring role opposite Christopher Reeve in *The Aviator*, which crashlanded at the US box-office (and even failed to secure a release in

Rosanna Arquette: *Desperately Seeking Susan.*

the UK), and then had a guest role in Martin Scorsese's highly acclaimed *After Hours*, with Griffin Dunne. Then came *Desperately Seeking Susan*. Dizzy, confused, but eminently believable as a nobody thought to be somebody else by practically everybody, Rosanna strode off with the acting honours, and even managed to steal the limelight from her attention-grabbing co-star Madonna. In truth, the bubbly blonde is as eccentric as the latter, and could play Madonna at her own game any day. A guest role in Lawrence Kasdan's sprawling, epic western *Silverado* largely wasted her talents, a misfortune that should be avoided in Hal Ashby's upcoming thriller, *8 Million Ways to Die*, with Jeff Bridges. Next: an untitled omnibus comedy from John Landis and Joe Dante, with Steve Guttenberg, and the romantic comedy *Nobody's Fool*, co-starring Eric Roberts.

Michael J. Fox, a pint-sized (he's 5 feet 5 inches tall) 23-year-old, certainly deserves the title of 'overnight star'. A newcomer to films, he was chosen to star in Steven Spielberg's *Back to the Future* when the original lead – Eric Stoltz, from *Mask* – was considered unsuitable. The director, Robert Zemeckis, confessed, 'I found myself with a very good actor playing the wrong part.' But unfortunately for Fox (born on 9 June 1961, in Edmonton, Alberta), he was already committed to a TV series – *Family Ties* – and found himself working round the clock on both projects. Still, the effort was worth it. *Family Ties* earned the young actor more fanmail than Elvis Presley had been used to, and *Back to the Future* became the most financially successful film of 1985. Shortly after the film's release, Fox's only other movie – the lycanthropic spoof *Teen Wolf* – was distributed, and ended up second in the box-office charts. Suddenly Michael J. Fox was the most talked about young actor in America. He'll next be seen in Paul Schrader's *Light of Day*, with singer Joan Jett, and then in Herbert Ross's *Private Affairs*. You guessed it, Michael J. Fox can write his own ticket – to anywhere.

Michael J. Fox.

Whoopi Goldberg, all popping eyes and irresistible grin, emerged from virtual obscurity to grab the lead role in Steven Spielberg's *The Color Purple*. The film, based on Alice Walker's controversial Pulitzer prize-winning novel about Southern blacks, went on to snare 11 Oscar nominations, inlcuding a 'Best Actress' nod for Whoopi. However, as an ultimate snub to Spielberg, the film was left empty-handed after Oscar night (but, then, no black actress has ever won a leading actress statuette). Christened Caryn Johnson, the comedienne later changed her name – to 'Whoopi Cushion', and then her surname to 'Goldberg' – for a joke. Born in Manhattan 'around' 1949, Whoopi landed up in San Diego when she accepted an airline ticket from a friend – not realizing it was one-way. In California, she started acting in repertory theatres (performing in *A Christmas Carol* and taking the lead in *Mother Courage*), and then started an improvization act. Forming a one-woman show based on a series of comic characters, Whoopie found herself back in New York – first, off-Broadway, and then on Broadway at the Lyceum, under Mike Nichols' supervision. The show was an enormous success, ended up on video cassette and HBO, and was caught by Steven Spielberg. *The Color Purple* made the comedienne a star, and she shared with Kathleen Turner (for her role in *Prizzi's Honor*) a Golden Globe award for 'Best Actress' – all the more surprising as it was for a (very) serious role. But Whoopi returns to comedy for her second film, 20th Century–Fox's *Jumpin' Jack Flash*, with Stephen Collins. There's also talk of a re-make of Elia Kazan's 1957 classic, *A Face in the Crowd*. Next: the re-make of *Born Yesterday*, with Walter Matthau, *Public Enemy*, with John Travolta, and another comedy, *Burglar*.

Whoopi Goldberg as Celie in Steven Spielberg's *The Color Purple*.

Christopher Lambert, a short, bespectacled Frenchman, seemed an unlikely choice to play Tarzan. Nevertheless, after an intensive body-sculpting programme, Lambert cut a dashing and unusual figure in chamois leather as the star of Hugh Hudson's enormously successful *Greystoke, The Legend of Tarzan, Lord of the Apes*. Emanating a raw sexuality and a passing resemblance to Jean-Paul Belmondo, Lambert was eagerly snatched up by his native France to star opposite Catherine Deneuve in *Paroles et Musique* and with Isabelle Adjani in *Subway*. The latter film was a huge success in London – breaking records for a foreign-language film – and British producers offered him the lead in *Highlander*: as a 400-year-old Scotsman! Another French film followed, Marco Ferreri's *I Love You*, and there are now plans for Lambert to play Tintin for Steven Spielberg and to star in *The Third Eye*, an Anglo-French project about the Dalai Lama. Christophe (or Christopher as he's been re-christened in the West) Lambert is without doubt the most exciting star to be exported by France in years, a fact more than confirmed by his growing female following.

Christophe(r) Lambert in *Highlander*.

Madonna, it seems, is much more than just a rock personality. Every year, one of them invariably successfully crosses the gulf between vinyl and celluloid: last year it was Prince (with *Purple Rain*); this year Madonna. The brazen, navel-flashing superstar had previously secured a bit part in *Visionquest* (unreleased in Britain) – as a club singer – but with her starring role in *Desperately Seeking Susan* (as Susan), she surprised the critics with her authentic portrayal of a zany, capricious girl-about-town. Born in Bay City, Michigan, the star – christened Madonna Louise Ciccone – began her career as a dancer, studying modern dance, jazz and ballet at the University of Michigan, but switched

Madonna in *Desperately Seeking Susan.*

professions when she was offered the chance to sing in Paris. 'They kept telling me I was going to be the next Edith Piaf,' she said at the time. 'It was a great adventure, but I soon tired of it.' Returning to New York City, the singer augmented her talents by learning to play the guitar, keyboards and drums; she also began to write her own songs. Her first album, simply titled *Madonna*, went double platinum, and spawned two top-ten singles – 'Borderline' and 'Lucky Star'. Since then, Madonna has produced a slew of hit songs, and also had one of the most highly publicized weddings of the century – to temperamental 'Brat Pack'-actor Sean Penn. Inevitably, they quickly teamed for a film: Jim Goddard's romantic adventure *Shanghai Surprise*. Her other projected movie, *Blind Date*, was cancelled due to recording commitments.

Rick Moranis, in *Ghostbusters*, created the ultimate 'nerd'. Short, chinless, heavily bespectacled and downright stupid, Moranis's Louis Tully made one's flesh creep. The film became the biggest-grossing comedy of all time, and Moranis was suddenly a household – well, *schlemiel*. Born in Canada, and now living in Toronto, Moranis started (part-time) in radio and got a job as an on-air 'personality' after his producers became tired of his constant (and witty) suggestions to their DJs. From there, the little comedian became a regular on CBC's *Second City Television*, teamed up with Dave Thomas to create the McKenzie brothers, and soon produced an album – which was duly nominated for a Grammy. Next, Moranis and Thomas wrote, directed and starred in *Strange Brew* (MGM) which became the most successful Canadian film of 1983. A small part in *The Wild Life* followed, then there was another nerd in *Streets of Fire* (as Diane Lane's righteous 'boyfriend'), and finally, *Ghostbusters*. In Ivan Reitman's epic comedy *Club Paradise*, Moranis was elevated to star billing (opposite Robin Williams and Peter O'Toole, no less), and then snatched the star role of Seymour in the large-scale horror musical *Little Shop of Horrors*. Originally a cheap B-movie from Roger Corman, the story of a man-eating plant was transformed into a successful stage musical (in both New York and London), and the new film version – with Moranis in the role of the hapless florist's assistant, with Steve Martin and John Candy in support – is bound to cement Moranis's stardom.

Rick Moranis (right) with Ellen Green and Frank Oz on the set of *Little Shop of Horrors.*

Brigitte Nielsen.

Brigitte Nielsen is 22, Danish and already a very big star. She's also 6 foot tall, constructed of solid muscle and married to the highest-paid actor in the world: Sylvester Stallone. Born in Copenhagen, Brigitte (pronounced with a hard *g*) bought herself a one-way, second-class ticket to Paris (at the tender age of 16) and started modelling almost immediately. Soon, she was jet-setting between Europe and New York. It was a topless pose on the cover of *Photo* magazine that caught the attention of film tycoon Dino De Laurentiis, who promptly cast her in the title role of *Red Sonja*. A sword-and-sorcery epic from the man who created the *Conan* stories, *Red Sonja* saw Brigitte heading a very impressive cast, no one more impressive than Arnold Schwarzenegger as Sonja's brickhouse sidekick, Kalidor. Brigitte and Schwarzenegger became friends, but her sights were aimed even higher. Discovering the address of her favourite actor – Stallone – the model-turned-actress sent him a 8″ x 10″ glossy of herself, accompanied with a note proclaiming that 'Red Sonja' wanted to meet 'Rocky'. The megastar phoned her that night, and in no time at all the couple were engaged. Stallone cast her as his Soviet Nemesis in *Rocky 4*, and the film – surprise, surprise – became a megahit. Next, the powerful pair co-starred in the action-adventure *Cobra*, helmed by *Rambo* director George P. Cosmatos. At the time of going to press, *Cobra* looks set to be one of the biggest moneymakers of 1986.

Judge Reinhold is *not* a nerd. He occasionally looks a bit like one, but generally he plays a decent sort, with some brains, and not a little attraction for the opposite sex. You may remember him as the pizza delivery boy in *Fast Times*, or as one of the young cadets in *The Lords of Discipline*. But it was as the bemused rookie policeman in *Beverly Hills Cop* who befriends Eddie Murphy that launched Judge as a leading comedy talent. The young actor was born in Wilmington, Delaware, attended high school in Virginia and opted to major in drama when he discovered that a lot of girls were doing the same thing. In fact, he landed the lead in the first play for which he auditioned. From children's theatre, to a drama course at the University of Virginia, Judge joined the Burt Reynolds Dinner Theater in Florida. Emigrating to California, he was

Judge Reinhold with Lori-Nan Engler in *Head Office*.

signed up by Paramount Television, did a bit in the *Magnum P.I.* pilot, and then had small roles in the films *Running Scared*, with Ken Wahl, and *Stripes*, with Bill Murray. Then came *Fast Times, The Lords of Discipline* (filmed in England), *Gremlins, Roadhouse '66* and *Beverly Hills Cop*. Since the success of the last-named, Judge got top billing in the starry comedy *Head Office*, top-billed again in *Off-Beat*, with Meg Tilly and stars opposite Bette Midler in Zucker, Zucker and Abrahams' hugely successful *Ruthless People*, another comedy.

Meg Tilly may have lost the chance to play Constanze in *Amadeus* – by tearing the ligaments in her leg the day before shooting started – but she more than made up for it by snatching the title role in *Agnes of God*. Jane Fonda got top billing in the latter film, but it was Meg who walked away with an Oscar nomination. Ironically, it was another accident that originally prompted the young Canadian to take up acting. She was studying to be a ballerina when a disastrous *pas de deux* shattered one of her lumbar vertebrae, forcing her to quit and turn her sights elsewhere. Yet her training aided her in two of her most important film roles: as the leotard-clad Chloe in *The Big Chill*, and as the amateur dancer in Graham Baker's effective thriller *Impulse*. Meg Tilly was born in western Canada, started dance training at 14, and, after her accident, defected to Los Angeles. After a mere six months there, she landed her first film: the female lead in the highly acclaimed *Tex*, opposite Matt Dillon. She fell in love with the film's producer, Tim Zinnemann (who was married), and then broke off the relationship. Six months later they reunited, he divorced his wife and cast Meg in *Impulse*, opposite Tim Matheson. *Psycho II* followed (she was the girl in the shower), and then *The Big Chill*, an enormous critical and commercial triumph. Since the success of *Agnes*, Meg has landed the female lead in *Off-Beat* – a comedy with Judge Reinhold – as a female cop involved in a police benefit dance contest.

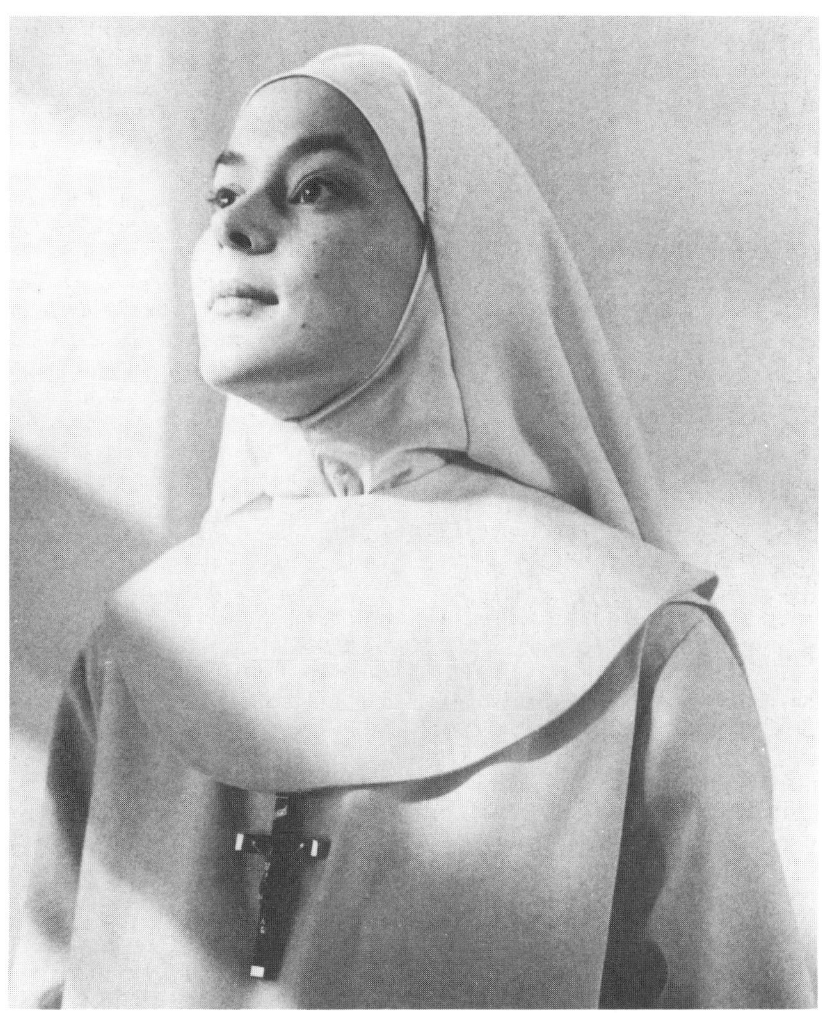

Meg Tilly as *Agnes of God*.

Previous 'Promising Faces of the 'Eighties' (as compiled by James Cameron-Wilson for *Film Review*)

1980	1981	1982	1983	1984	1985
Bo Derek	Karen Allen	Bess Armstrong	Sandahl Bergman	Jennifer Beals	John Candy
Paul Dooley	Dan Akroyd	Lewis Collins	Michael Keaton	Matthew Broderick	Glenn Close
Lisa Eichhorn	Jamie Lee Curtis	Clio Goldsmith	Ben Kingsley	Tom Cruise	Charles Dance
Frederic Forrest	Roberts Hays	Jeremy Irons	Daryl Hannah	Rebecca de Mornay	Emilio Estevez
Mariel Hemingway	William Hurt	Kevin Kline	Eddie Murphy	Rupert Everett	Lucy Gutteridge
Bette Midler	Timothy Hutton	Elizabeth McGovern	Mickey Rourke	Valerie Kaprisky	Kelly LeBrock
Ricky Schroder	Nastassja Kinski	Miles O'Keefe	Greta Scacchi	Sean Penn	John Malkovich
John Savage	Steve Martin	Tom Selleck	Henry Thomas	Cynthia Rhodes	Kelly McGillis
Sigourney Weaver	Jaclyn Smith	Kathleen Turner	Julie Walters	Eric Roberts	Joanna Pacula
Robin Williams	Debra Winger	Rachel Ward	JoBeth Williams	Helen Slater	Prince

The Continental Film

For full details of the films illustrated in these pages, see 'Releases of the Year' section

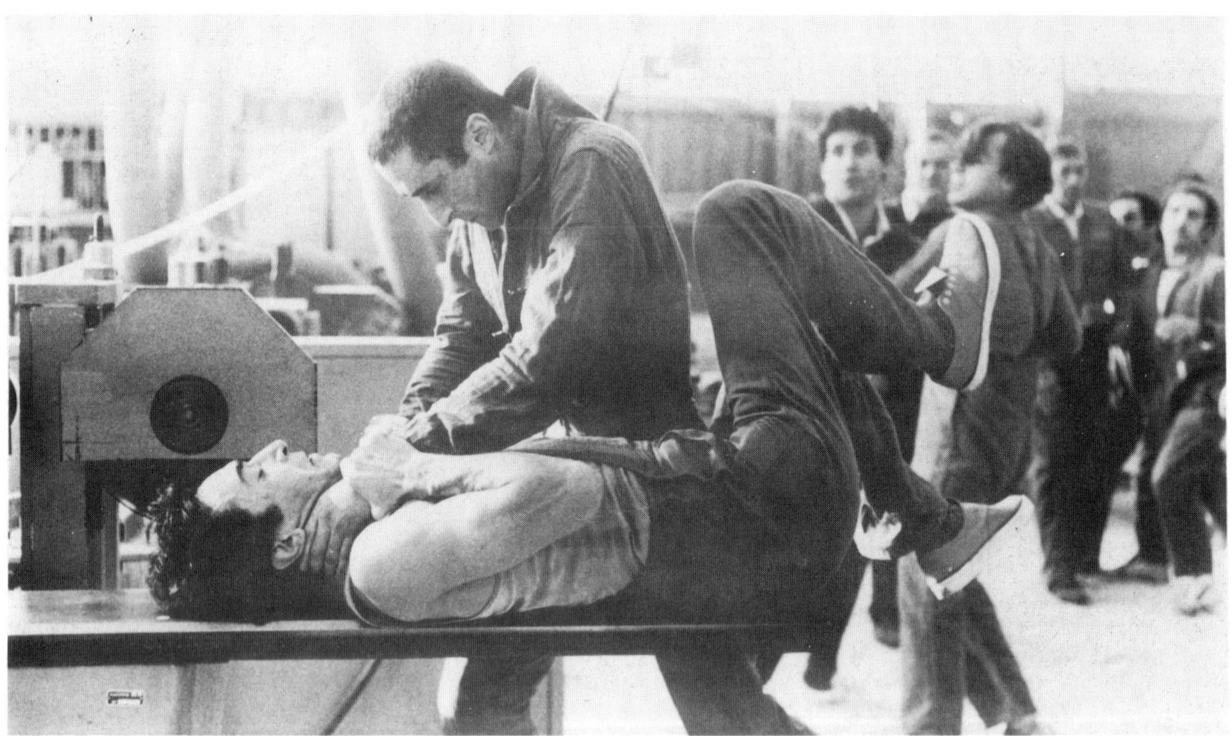

Above, the brutal fight between the unfortunate young actor Bruno (Richard Berry) and the prison bully (Farid Chopel, with the advantage at this point) which will lead to the murder of the latter by the former in Denis Amar's strong French prison drama *L'Addition* (Cannon-Gala). Left, Victoria Abril, as the pretty girl with a taste for caviar which she steals from a supermarket shelf. The young actor comes to her aid, when he thinks the cops are getting a bit rough with her – his first brush with the police and the first subsequent jail sentence. Having fallen in love with Bruno while visiting him in jail, Patty pays her debt to him by helping him escape after the prison killing, and flees with him . . . to a future that will almost inevitably end with recapture. And it was all pretty grim.

Christopher Lambert, who, as you may recall, was the modern-style Ape Man in Hugh Hudson's *Greystoke: The Legend of Tarzan, Lord of the Apes*, has a very different kind of role as the eccentric young Fred in *Subway* (Artificial Eye). Fred repays Isabelle Adjani's (below) invitation to her party by blowing her safe, thereby setting in train pursuit by the cops, which continues for nearly the whole length of the film, set largely in the Paris Metro. Having in his first film *The Last Battle – Le Dernier Combat*, made a very promising writing-directing debut, young Luc Bresson in *Subway* confirmed his – admittedly rather idiosyncratic – originality and command over the medium, and made his future work for the screen well worth watching for.

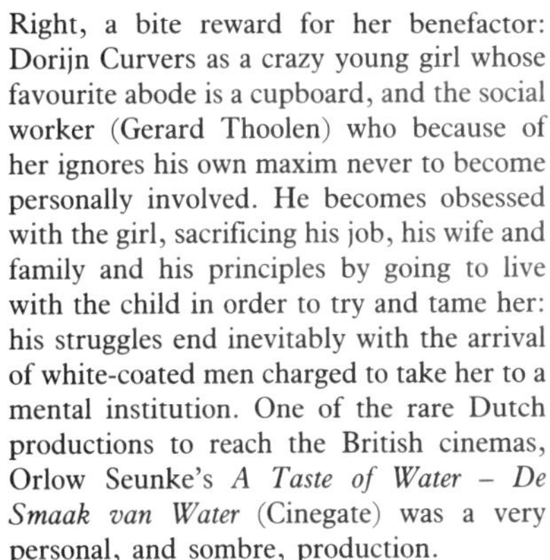

Right, a bite reward for her benefactor: Dorijn Curvers as a crazy young girl whose favourite abode is a cupboard, and the social worker (Gerard Thoolen) who because of her ignores his own maxim never to become personally involved. He becomes obsessed with the girl, sacrificing his job, his wife and family and his principles by going to live with the child in order to try and tame her: his struggles end inevitably with the arrival of white-coated men charged to take her to a mental institution. One of the rare Dutch productions to reach the British cinemas, Orlow Seunke's *A Taste of Water – De Smaak van Water* (Cinegate) was a very personal, and sombre, production.

Will Patton, as Marsh, is caught in an ambush in British director Christopher Petit's West German thriller *Chinese Boxes* (Palace Pictures). The viewer sometimes felt the need for a computer to work out what was going on in a confusingly over-plotted tale primarily concerned with such illegal activities as dope smuggling, murder and other mayhem taking place in West Berlin.

Below, with some promising success, young Polish writer-director Julius Machulski mixed science-fiction, satire and broad comedy in his often witty *Sex Mission – Seksmisja* (Cinegate), a fantastic story about a couple of scientific experimental Rip Van Winkles waking up after a *very* long nap to find themselves apparently the only males in a feminist society which has rejected the rule of the phallus to the extent of doing away with it altogether. But it soon becomes obvious that its attraction to the female is still potent. Though the film met with a mixed critical reception in Britain, few could deny it was full of surprises and imagination, and was well handled.

Erika Ozsda as the 16-year-old 'Princess' in Pal Erdoss' film *The Princess – Adj Kiraly Katonati!* (Cinegate). She's a working girl from the provinces who obtains a job in a Budapest cotton mill and suffers a lot of unkind buffets from fate as she tries to make a reasonable life for herself in the Hungarian capital. But it's a pretty joyless existence for her: rape, abortion, a weakling boyfriend, and on top of that she is forced to return to the real mother the baby she has taken into her care and loves. Were it not for the fact that it comes from Hungary (made in black-and-white) you might be excused for thinking this is a new Victorian melodrama of *East Lynne* proportion.

Below, another grim film from Hungary (again made in black-and-white) was Marta Meszaros' *Diary For My Children – Naplo Gyermekeimnek* (Artificial Eye), which she both wrote and directed. Although backdated to the Stalin era, the film was surprisingly critical of some aspects of general communist tenets in a story about a young girl (Zsuzsa Czinkoczi, centre) who steadfastly rejects her aunt's offers to adopt her: aunty is a strict Party member who rises from newspaper editor to prison governor as reward for unquestioning acceptance of the regime. It showed how even a most useful, hard-working – and non-political – member of society who dares to resist, ends up in jail.

Something of the behind-the-scenes stresses and strains that occurred during production found their way into the finished French-Japanese film *The Fruits of Passion*, (New Realm), the last to be directed by well-known Japanese director-writer (and poet and stage director) Shuji Terayama. He was persuaded to take over direction when the original choice, Nagisa Oshima, walked out of the studio after a row with producer Anatole Dauman, who soon began to see less than eye to eye with Terayama about the way the movie should be made. The script was based – a little vaguely to say the least – on 'Retour a Roissy', the Pauline Reage sequel to her 'Story of O', which continued the shameful life of the evil Sir Stephen (Klaus Kinsky, making 'Sir' a most nasty piece of pornographic work) and the pretty little girl 'O', who he installs in a Hong Kong brothel for his twisted pleasure.

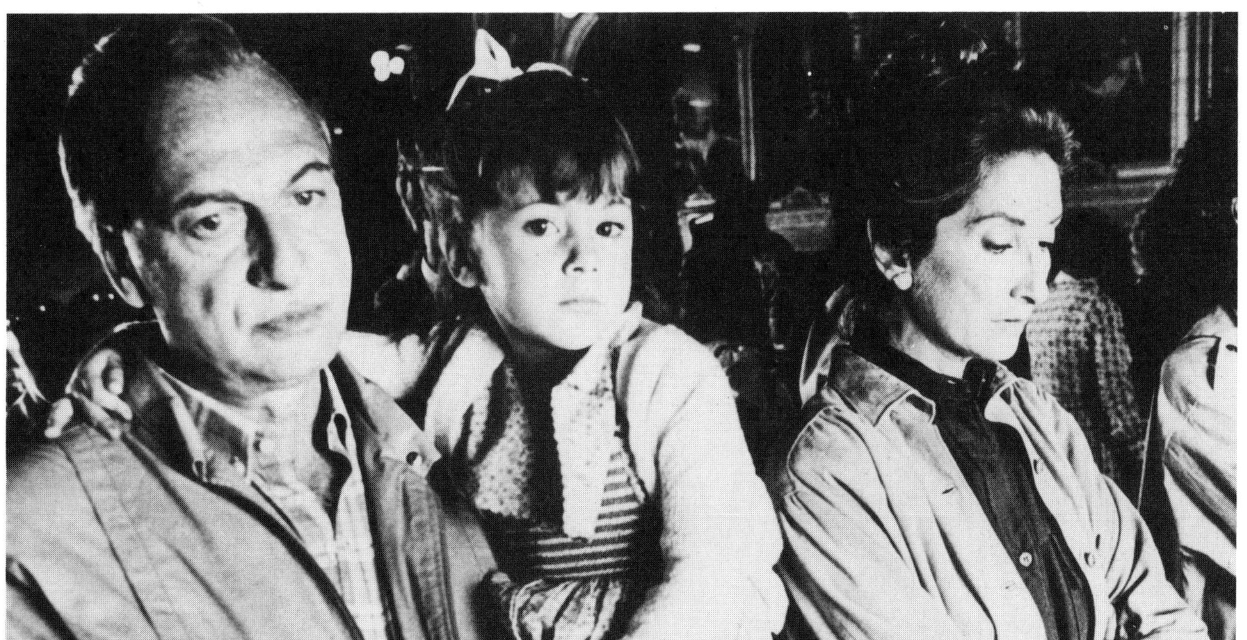

The ending of the iniquitous junta regime in Argentina gave that country's moviemakers a sudden heady freedom, and they rushed into production with the sort of film that previously would have earned them a stiff prison sentence at the very least. Typical of this new celluloid wave was Luis Puenzo's *The Official Version – La Historia Oficial* (Virgin Films), made in Buenos Aires within three months in 1984, but showing no sign of hasty production. Based on the infamous 'vanishing' of those opposed to the regime and the subsequent sale of any babies they might have had to the Generals' supporters, the film portrays a businessman (Hector Alterio, left) who buys a baby (Chunchuna Villafane) for his wife, and grows to love the child. Stresses and strains in the marital relationship begin when his wife, (Norma Aleandro) becomes suspicious of the adoption story and begins an investigation which brings about domestic disaster. Highly dramatic, the film was a firm political statement.

Right, though superficially a historical drama based on fact, with echoes of Heloise and Abelard, *Camila – Camille* (Enterprise Pictures) carried a strong political undercurrent in its depiction of a brutal Argentinian dictatorship of the 1800s. Also boldly critical was the depiction of a Church too afraid to denounce the cruelties of the regime. Susu Pecoraro (centre) played the lovely young Buenos Aires heiress who defied family, the authorities and everything else when she fell in love and ran off with a young Jesuit priest (Imanol Arias), vainly hoping for happiness. Polished, beautifully acted, and skilfully directed, it showed that the Argentine cinema of today, after recent repression, is now a force to be reckoned with.

Few, if any, of the films shown in the 1985–6 period caused more international controversy than Jean Luc-Godard's *Hail Mary – Je Vous Salue, Marie* (released in Britain by The Other Cinema). It was inevitable that Godard's 41st film would meet considerable religious opposition over its allegedly blasphemous treatment of the Virgin Birth, but hardly to be anticipated were the riots it caused in Nantes and other French cities, some near riots outside France, and the climax of the Pope's condemnation: 'It distorted and reviled the spiritual side of the Mother of Jesus.' Typically formless and deliberately provocative, the film re-told the story of Mary in modern France, with shapely (and fully revealed) Myriem Rousel playing a teenage Holy Mother working as assistant at her father's petrol station.

Below left, *Cop au Vin – Poulet au Vinaigre – Chicken with Vinegar* was the teasing title chosen by Claude Chabrol for the latest addition to his witty and wickedly observant films about French provincial life. Below the surface of deceptively routine small-town life are dark, simmering passions, gradually revealed. They climax in a killing, and the out-of-town detective sent to investigate ruthlessly stirs the mud of secret intrigue and villainy. Jean Poiret played the investigator, Michel Bouquet the local notary and one of the worried suspects, with Stéphane Audran (right) as the crippled Madame Cuno, whose refusal to sell her property lies at the root of all the evil.

Racial opponents and eventual collaborators: Arab terrorist Muhamad Bakri, leader of the Arab faction in an Israeli jail, and Hilel Ne'Eman, a Jew serving a sentence for armed robbery, join forces in an attempt to achieve better, more humane conditions in a prison where the policy is to divide and rule. Such was the grim, sordid and unrelievedly depressing story of this Israeli film from Cinegate, *Beyond the Walls – Me'Achorei Hasoragim*.

Right, the Hungarian-Austrian-West German co-production, the award-laden *Colonel Redl – Redl Ezvedes* (Cannon–Gale), renewed the director-star combination of Istvan Szabo and Klaus Maria Brandauer which had such a success in the Oscar-winning *Mephisto*. The story was based on the 'case' of a poor railway worker's son who rose to become head of the Vienna Secret Police: inadvertently he spoilt some plans of the Crown Prince and so was disgraced and forced into suicide, thereby revealing the rottenness at the heart of the Austro-Hungarian Empire at the outbreak of the 1914 war. Among the film's awards are the Jury Prize at the 1985 Cannes Festival, the Best Film and Best Actor prizes at the Hungarian Film Festival, and the Golden Band awards in the same categories of the German film industry.

Agony – Agonia, the Russian film released in Britain by Thorn EMI Classics, had a story of its own equally as fascinating as that it shows on the screen. Made in 1975, it was held back from public showing until a recent Moscow Film Festival for political reasons hard for the non-Russian viewer to understand. Set in the Russia of 1916, a period of political ferment and social upheaval, it portrayed the rise of the evil monk Rasputin, played by Alexei Petrenko.

Below left, Winner of the Grand Prize at the Cannes Film Festival, the Yugoslavian production *When Father Was Away on Business – Otac na sluzbenom putu* took its title from a saying common in Yugoslavia at the time of the country's break with the Soviets, a period when anyone suspected of pro-Stalinism vanished for several years: it meant in fact that the victim had been sent to prison or a labour camp. The film is about a boy's gradual understanding of what his father's 'business trip' really is. A comedy-drama of wit and irony, it contained a number of brilliantly realized family portraits: Miki Manojlovic as the husband and innocent victim of a false denunciation with Mirjana Karanovic as his wife; inset, Mustafa Nadarevic (centre) as her brother, (and the local police commissioner) with Eva Ras (right) as his fiancée and the denouncer.

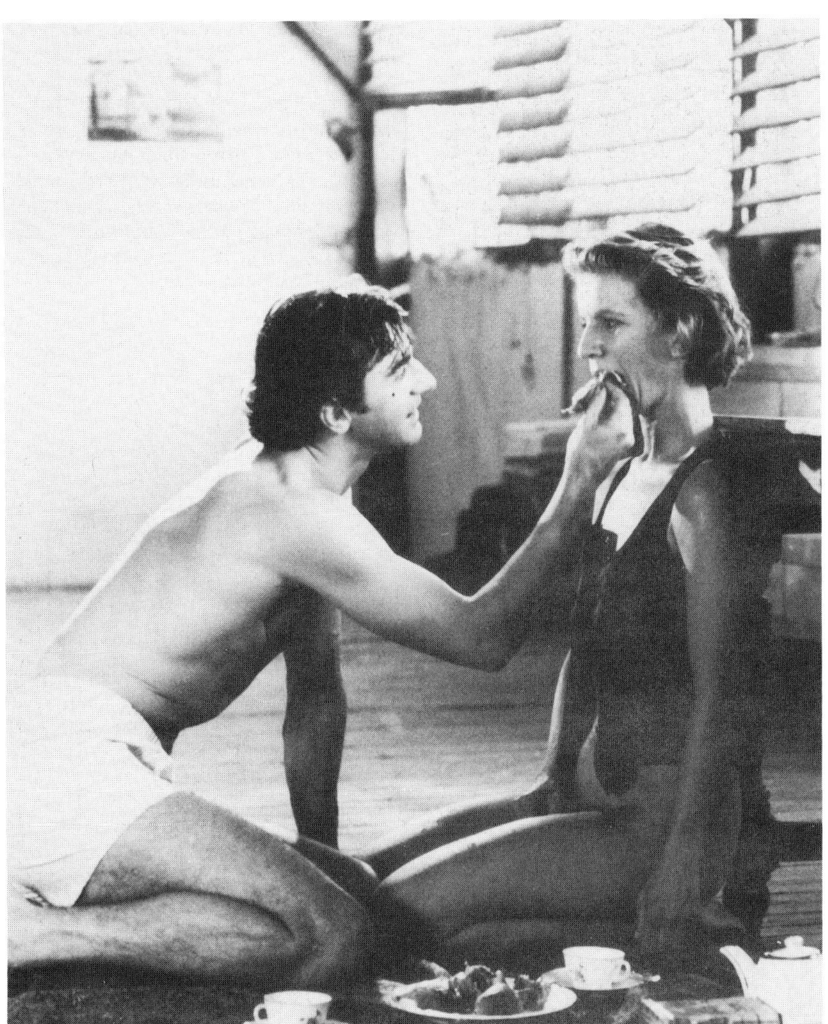

Christophe Malavoy as the somewhat naive young music teacher who surrenders to the erotic advances of his pupil's mother (Nicole Garcia) and so drifts into a dangerous liaison which leads to murder, and the eventual transfer of his amorous intention to the nubile pupil (Anais Jeanneret). Top right, Richard Bohringer as the enigmatic detective who befriends the young teacher, and (below) Anemone as the mysterious neighbour. Though director Michel Deville has been making box-office winners in France since his first film in 1960, *Death in a French Garden – Peril en la Demeure* was his first film to be shown in Britain (An Artificial Eye release).

Right, the scene of unrelated carnage in Jean-Luc Godard's Artificial Eye release *Detective*. Like so much of his work, this had moments of good cinema but they never added up to anything like a normal, coherent film. In fact, there are those who claim – and include this writer – that Godard has never achieved anything better than his first cinematic milestone, his 'New Wave' movie *A Bout de Souffle – Breathless.*

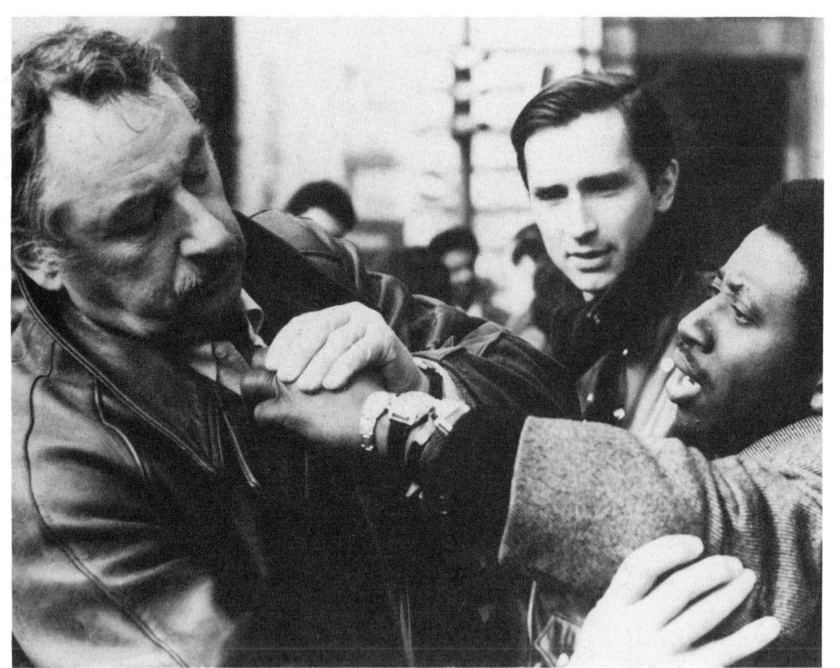

Philippe Noiret gave a fine comedy performance in the Cannon–Gala release *Le Cop – Les Ripoux*, an amusing story about a bent Paris policeman whose law-breaking, when found out, leads to a short, comfy spell in jail and a rich reward when he comes out. Director Claude Zidi, a former cameraman, has some 15 successes to his name, of which previously only one, *French Mustard*, has (from recollection) been released on the British side of the Channel.

Below and inset, a rare example of British-German co-production, Odyssey-Enterprises' *Forbidden* was based on a true story of the last war: a German countess (played so well by Jacqueline Bisset) kept her Jewish lover (Jürgen Prohnow) hidden in her Berlin flat right through the war, marrying him after it ended, and managing to keep secret even from him her work, through the Swedish Church, with the Resistance. Eschewing the obviously tempting melodramatic angle, director Anthony Page kept the tone cool – though often tense – and obtained a fine atmosphere of reality.

An example of Norwegian cinema – rarely seen in this country – Enterprise's *Orion's Belt* was a full-blooded adventure story written by a British scriptwriter (Richard Harris). The most expensive production ever to be made in Norway, it was an adaptation of a Jon Michelet novel. Some pretty ruthless Soviets decide that a trawler blown by a storm near to their secret base can't be allowed to take its story back to Norway, and accordingly they set out to destroy men and boat. But after great privation, one man, played by Helge Jordal (above), lives to tell the tale – only to find that he and his story are less than officially welcome back home.

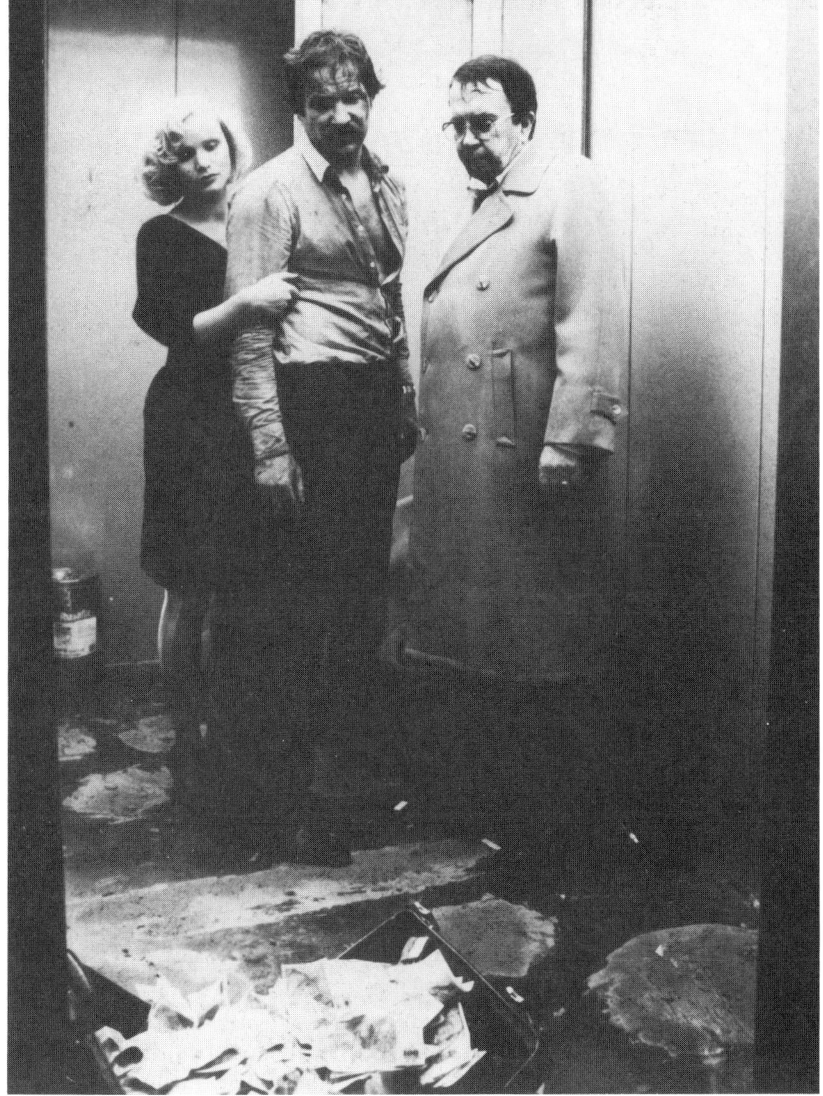

Right, Swiss-born director-writer Carl Schenkel – a former journalist and film critic – has been working in Germany since he was 20, rising from assistant director and general factotum to his present position. His *Out of Order*, a tense, claustrophobic thriller released in Britain by Virgin Films, set four characters in a suddenly out-of-order lift and followed their increasingly panicky reactions, aggravated by the rivalry that develops between two of the men over the girl, and the worry of the fourth occupant about his suitcase full of stolen money, revealed in this scene shared by Renee Soutendijk (the Dutch star), Gotz George and Wolfgang Kieling. Last of the quartet, struggling unseen up the lift shaft was played by Hannes Jaenicke. The film was a good example of brilliant movie-making on a very minor budget.

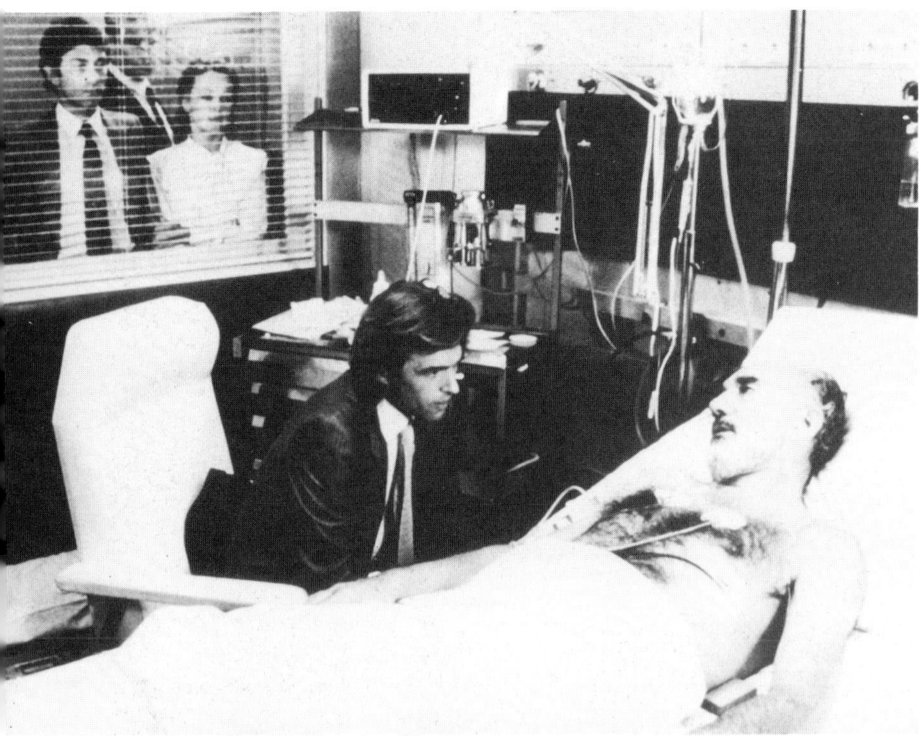

To Swiss writer-director Richard Dembo goes the credit not only for making the first film to be centred on the game of chess but for making it a first-rate, thrilling movie. *Dangerous Moves*, released by Enterprise, proved good enough, indeed, to win a Hollywood Oscar as the best foreign movie of its year. Michel Piccoli, as the old Russian master, plays his young opponent (Alexandre Arbatt) in a final game on his death-bed, with Leslie Caron the onlooker.

Below, the three principal characters in the hybrid (Polish–West German–American) production, *Year of the Quiet Sun – Rok Spokojnego Slonka* (Blue Dolphin release): Scott Wilson is a quiet American soldier, only survivor of a German POW death camp, who falls in love with a sad widow eking out a meagre living by her cooking (Maja Komorowska, below left), and is supported in his gentle wooing by the widow's invalid but strong-willed mother (Hanna Skarzanka). Three outstanding performances in a melancholy but brilliantly directed (Krzysztof Zanussi) film.

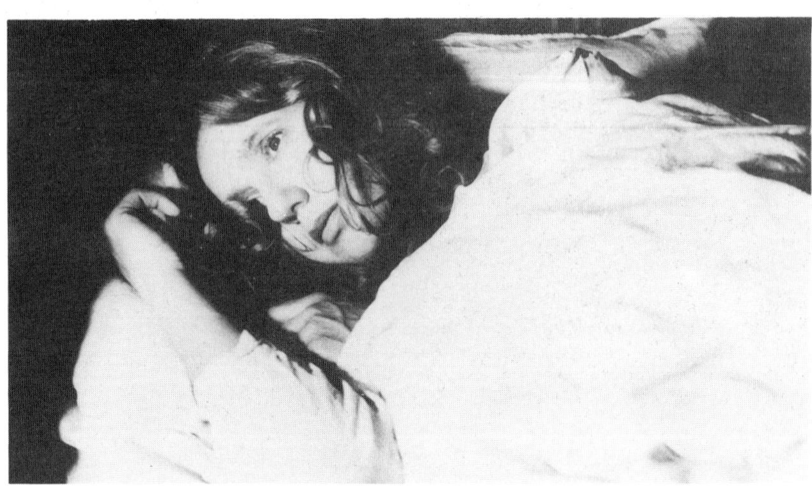

It was some 30 years ago that Akira Kurosawa first turned to Shakespeare for inspiration, using *Macbeth* as the source for his classic *Throne of Blood*. Now, at the age of 75, he returns to the bard, basing his marvellously visual, Virgin-released, *Ran* on that most tragic of Shakespeare's plays, *King Lear*. The centre of this stylish, highly dramatic film are the stunningly spectactular battles, classical sequences using vast numbers of men and horses in swirling action or in banner–flapping stillness, allied to some memorable performances, most notably by Tatsuya Nakadai (top) as the tragic Lord Ichimonji (Lear) and Mieko Harada (above) as the scheming, ruthlessly ambitious Lady Kaede.

Hector Babenco's Palace Pictures release gained for William Hurt the 1985 Best Actor Oscar for his playing of the homosexual prisoner in a South American jail, who breaks down the natural prejudice of his more normal cell-mate. A Brazilian-American production and a rare example of such cinematic collaboration, *The Kiss of the Spider Woman* also starred Sonia Braga as a beautiful woman in one of the tales-within-a-tale which provided a novel angle to the motivation of the movie.

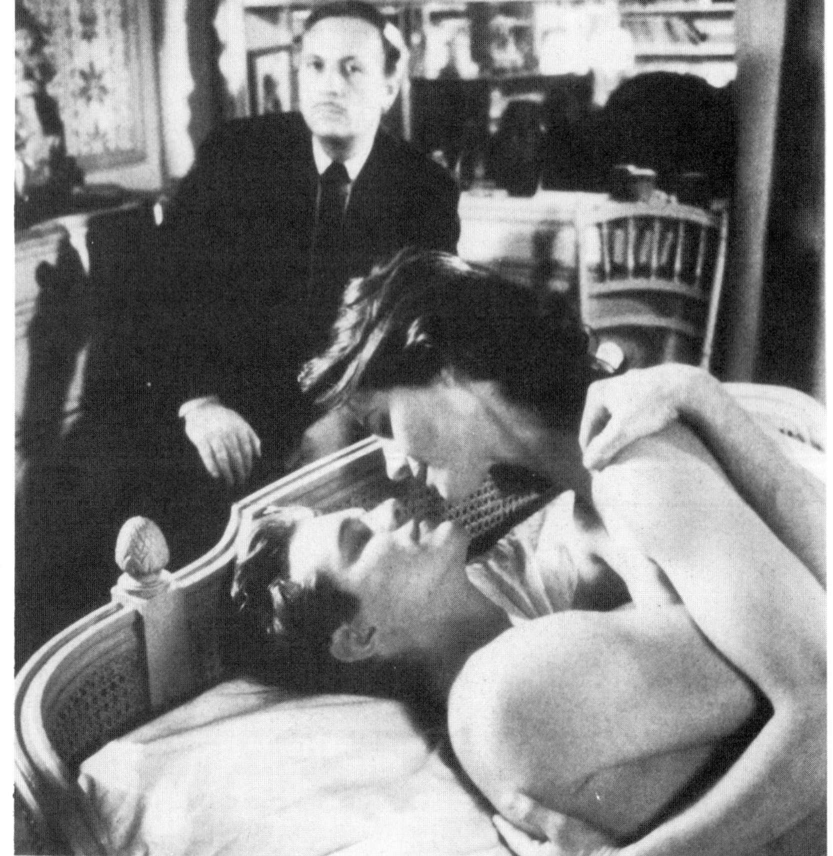

Right, Michel Serrault, as the surprised – and shocked – onlooker, Inspector Staniland, watches the incestuous coupling of Barbara (Charlotte Rampling) and brother Marc (Xavier Duluc) in Jacques Deray's murder mystery *He Died With His Eyes Open – On ne meurt que 2 fois* (a Cannon–Gala release). Serrault, who so deservedly won Best Actor of the Year 'Cesars' for performances in *La Cage Aux Folles* and *Garde a Vue*, contributed another quietly compelling performance to the Deray film, giving the lonely, dedicated sleuth a credible dimension of weak flesh when he falls in love with his puzzling suspect and is seduced by her. It was a performance that raised the French whodunit several notches above the place it would otherwise have occupied.

Sandrine Bonnaire as the female *Vagabonde* (French title: *Sans Toit Ni Loi*, which has been roughly translated to *Without a Roof and Beyond the Law*) in Agnes Varda's grey, cold and formidable film about the discovery of the girl's frozen body in a ditch, and how she reached this bleak end. Refusing to dramatise the story, or at any point suggest that the girl's sordid life and miserable demise were anything but her own obstinate fault, the film did suggest the high price that must sometimes be paid for the ambiguous satisfaction of retaining personal freedom. As the unsympathetic and unlikeable tramp, Mlle. Bonnaire gave a disturbingly good performance, perfectly tuned to Varda's uncompromising intellectual picture, released in Britain by Electric Pictures.

Left, the diaries of Adelaide Herclone Barbin underline the old adage that Truth is Stranger than Fiction. Born a normal male child but given a false female birth certificate through his mother's insane modesty, Barbin (played by cartoonist Philippe Vuillemin, seen here with Valerie Stroh) was sent to a girls' convent school! Somehow escaping detection there, Barbin's secret was revealed when, as a resident teacher at a small school, he seduced the girl in the next bed. Subsequently unable to change the personality grafted on to him, losing his mistress, forced into menial jobs at women's wages, the lonely, miserable man finally committed suicide. Never digging far into the fascinatingly tangled psychological depth of the tale, writer (with Jean Grualt), director and producer Rene Feret nevertheless created in *The Mystery of Alexina* a modest but intriguingly worked film from this bizarre 19th-century case history. An Electric Pictures release.

The ubiquitous Gerard Depardieu made an unusual and unexpected switch to comedy in the Virgin release of the French import *A Woman or Two – Une Femme ou deux*, playing a shambling, dedicated archaeologist who falls in love with two women at once; the first a two-million-year-old little lady he digs up and reconstructs, the second a somewhat warmer and sexier, and by modern standards more beautiful, American advertising executive (played by Sigourney Weaver), who is tempted by circumstance into playing a famous woman archaeologist. Sadly the initial fun got a bit thin: the mistaken identity and kidnapping ingredients of the plot lead to something of an anti-climax when the scene switches to New York.

Left, Gerard Depardieu was back on more familiar ground in Maurice Pialat's Artificial Eye release, *Police*, a very watchable French drama starting at a hectic pace as it followed the tough, rough routine confrontation between cops and robbers in a Paris police station then suddenly slowing down and switching to the personal, psychological problems of one shambling, untidy cop (perfect casting for Depardieu), and his romance with the lovely, shrewd but totally unreliable and constantly lying gangster's girlfriend – played beautifully by Sophie Marceau.

Awards and Festivals

The following does not pretend to be a complete list of the year's many film festivals and awards, more of which seem to be spawned every year. It does, however, include all the major festivals and awards and some of the more interesting minor ones.

The American Academy of Motion Picture Arts and Sciences Awards, March 1986

Best Film: *Out of Africa*, directed by Sydney Pollack, who won the Best Direction Award.

Best Actor: William Hurt, in *The Kiss of the Spider Woman*.

Best Actress: Geraldine Page, in *The Trip to Bountiful*.

Best Supporting Actor: Don Ameche, in *Cocoon*.

Best Supporting Actress: Anjelica Huston, in *Prizzi's Honor*.

Best Original Screenplay/Story: Earl W. Wallace and William Kelly (screenplay) and Kelly and Pamela and E. W. Wallace (story), for *Witness*.

Best Screenplay Adaptation: Kurt Luedtke, for *Out of Africa*.

Best Cinematography: David Watkin, for *Out of Africa*.

Best Foreign Language Film: *The Official Story* (Argentine).

Best Art Direction: Stephen Grimes (art) and Josie MacAvin (set decoration), for *Out of Africa*. Best Costume Design: Emi Wada, for *Ran* (Japan).

Best Shorts, Animated *Anna and Bella* produced by Cilia Van Dijk; Live Action, *Molly's Pilgrim* produced by Jeff Brown.

Best Documentaries: Feature, Maria Florio and Victor Mudd's *Broken Rainbow*; Short, David Goodman's *Witness to War: Dr. Charlie Clements*.

Anjelica Huston, actress daughter of writer-director John Huston (inset), who won the 1986 Best Supporting Actress Oscar for her performance in her father's film *Prizzi's Honor*.

The Jean Hersholt Award to Charles (Buddy) Rogers.

Honorary Awards to Paul Newman in recognition of his many memorable and compelling screen performances and for his personal integrity and dedication and to Alex North in recognition of his brilliant artistry in the creation of memorable music for motion pictures.

The Australian Institute Awards, Sydney, September 1985

Best Film: *Bliss*, directed by Ray Lawrence, who also won the Best Direction Award.

Best Actor: Chris Haywood, in *A Street to Die*.

Best Actress: Noni Hazlehurst, in *Fran*.

Best Supporting Actor: Nique Needles, in *The Boy Who Had Everything*.

Best Supporting Actress: Annie Byron, in *Fran*.

Best Original Screenplay: Glenda Hambly, for *Fran*.

Best Story Adaptation: Ray Lawrence and Peter Carey, for *Bliss*.

Best Cinematography: Peter James, for *Rebel*.

Best Documentary: Bob Weis' *Raoul Wallenberg: Between the Lines*.

Best Short Fiction Film: Robert Marchand's *The Cellist*.

Best Animated Film: Richard Chataway and Michael Cusack's *Waltzing Matilda*.

The Avoriaz Fantasy Film Festival Awards, France, January 1986

Grand Prix: *Dream Lover*, directed by Alan Pakula (USA)

Jury Prize: *Link*, directed by Richard Franklin (USA)

Critics' Prize: *House*, directed by Stephen Miner (USA)

The Dario Argento Award: *Fright Night*, directed by Tom Holland (USA).

The Berlin Film Festival Awards, February 1986

Golden Bear First Prize: Reinhard Hauff's *Stammheim* (West Germany).

Silver Bear Special Jury Prize: Nanni Moretti's *The Mass is Over* (Italy).

Best Actor: Tuncel Kurtiz, in *The Smile of the Lamb* (Israel).

Best Actress: shared between Mercelia Cartaxo, in *The House of the Star* (Brazil) and Charlotte Valandrey, in *Red Kiss* (France)

Best Direction: Georgi Shengelaya, for *Journey of a Young Composer* (USSR).

Special Silver Bear Prize for 'Outstanding Style': Masahiro Shinoda, for *Gonza the Spearman* (Japan).

Shorts prizes: Golden Bear to Dean Parisot, for *Tom Goes to the Bar* (USA). Silver Bear to Csaba Verga's *Augusta Feeds* (Hungary). Prizes also awarded to Gabriel Beristain for his photography in *Caravaggio* (Great Britain). Special mention to Dan Pita for his film *Paso Doble* (Rumania).

The British Academy of Film and Television Arts Awards for 1985

Best Film: *The Purple Rose of Cairo*, directed by Woody Allen – to whom also went the Best Screenplay Award.

Best Actress: Peggy Ashcroft, in *A Passage to India*.

Best Actor: William Hurt, in *Kiss of the Spider Woman*.

Best Supporting Actress: Rosanna Arquette, in *Desperately Seeking Susan*.

Best Supporting Actor: Denholm Elliott, in *Defence of the Realm*.

Best Adapted Screenplay: Richard Condon and Janet Roach, for *Prizzi's Honor*.

Best Foreign Language film: the West German/Austrian/Hungarian *Colonel Redl*.

Best Short: *Careless Talk*.

The BAFTA Fellowship Award to Steven Spielberg and the Michael Balcon Award to Sidney Samuelson, for his longstanding service to the Academy.

The British Critics' Circle Film Awards, November 1985

Best English Language Film: Woody Allen's *The Purple Rose of Cairo*.

Best Foreign Language Film: *Heimat*.

Best Direction: Roland Joffé, for *The Killing Fields*.

Best Screenplay: Alan Bennett, for *A Private Function*.

Best Actor: shared betwen Richard Farnsworth in *The Grey Fox* and James Mason in *The Shooting Party*.

Distributors' Award for being most helpful to the critics: Palace Pictures.

Special awards to (a) Michael Powell and Emeric Pressburger; (b) Kevin Brownlow and David Gill; (c) Donald Murrey.

The Cannes Film Festival Awards, May 1986

Golden Palm for Best Film: *The Mission*, directed by Roland Joffé (Great Britain).

Special Jury Prize: *Sacrifice*, directed by Andrei Tarkovsky (Sweden/France).

Jury Prize: *Thérèse* directed by Alain Cavalier (France).

Best Direction: Martin Scorsese, for *After Hours* (USA)

Best Actor: shared between Bob Hoskins, in *Mona Lisa* (Great Britain), and Michel Blanc, in *Evening Dress – Tenue de Soirée* (France).

Best Actress: shared between Barbara Sukowa, in *Rosa Luxemburg* (West Germany), and Fernanda, in *Love Me Forever or Never* (Brazil).

Golden Camera Award for Best First Feature Film: Claire Devers, for *Black and White* (France).

Best Artistic Contribution: Sven Nykvist, for his cinematography in *Sacrifice*.

Short Film Golden Palm: *Peel*, directed by Jane Campion (Australia)

Prize of the Commission for 'Technical Excellence': *Sacrifice*.

The Chicago International Film Festival Awards, November 1985

Golden Hugo for Best Film: *The Official Story – La Historia Oficial*, directed by Luis Puenzo (Argentina).

Silver Hugo: *Tea in the Harem of Archimedes*, directed by Mehdi Charef (France).

Bronze Hugo: shared between *Alpine Inferno*, directed by Fredi M. Murer (Switzerland/West Germany) and *Oriana*, directed by Fina Torres (Venezuela/France).

Special Silver Hugo for Most Promising New Director: Peter Gados for *The Philadelphia Attraction* (Hungary).

Best Female Performance: the entire all-female cast of *Segreti Segreti*, directed by Giuseppe Bertolucci (Italy).

Best Male Performance: shared between Kamill Feleki and Karoly Eperjes, in *The Philadelphia Attraction*.

Best Supporting Performance: Chunchuna Villafane, in *The Official Story*.

Best Screenplay: Zev Mahler, for *Forget Mozart* (West Germany).

The Festival dei Popoli (Documentary) Prizes, Florence, December 1985

Golden Marzuccos: Robert Gardner's *Forest of Bliss* (USA), Pe A Holquist's *Gaza Ghetto* (Sweden) and Dennis O'Rourke's *Half Life* (Australia).

The French Academy César Awards, February 1986

Best French Film: *Three Men and a Cradle*, by Coline Serreau.

Best Foreign Film: Woody Allen's *The Purple Rose of Cairo*.

Best Direction: Michel Deville, for *Peril en la Demeure*.

Best Actor: Christophe Lambert, in Luc Besson's *Subway*.

Best Actress: Sandrine Bonnaire, in Agnès Varda's *Sans Toit Ni Loi*.

Best Supporting Actor: Michel Boujenah, in *Three Men and a Cradle*.

Best Supporting Actress: Bernadette Lafont, in Claude Miller's *L'Effrontée*.

Best Screenplay: Coline Serreau, for *Three Men and a Cradle*.

Best Cinematography: Jean Penzer, for Jacques Deray's *On Ne Meurt Que Deux Fois*.

Special 'career' Césars to Bette Davis, Rene Feracci (film poster artist), Jean Delannoy (director), Maurice Jarre (film music), Claude Lanzmann for *Shoah*, and The Cinémathèque Française.

The 2nd International Film Festival of Cinema, TV and Video Awards, Rio de Janeiro, December 1985

Best Film: Jorge Ali Triana's *Time To Die – Tiempo Para Morir* (Colombia)
Best Director: Jaoa Botelho, for *A Portuguese Farewell* (Portugal)
Best Actor: Gustavo Angarita in *Time to Die*.
Best Actress: shared between Christine Pak in *90 Days* (Canada) and Glenda Jackson in *Turtle Diary* (Great Britain).
Special Jury Award: *What's the Time, Mr Clock?*, directed by Peter Basco (Hungary).

The Italian David Di Donatello Awards, Rome, June 1986

Best Film: *Let's Hope It's A Girl*, which also won the Awards for Best Direction (Mario Monicelli), Best Producer (Giovanni Di Clemente), Best Supporting Actor (Bernard Blier), Best Supporting Actress (Athina Cenci), Best Editing (Ruggero Mastroianni) and Best Script (Mario Monicelli, Tullio Pinelli, Suso Cecchi d'Amico, Leonardo Benvenuti and Piero de Bernardi).
Best Actor: Marcello Mastroianni, in *Ginger and Fred*.
Best Actress: Angela Molina, in *Camorra*; this film also won the Awards for Best Cinematography (Giuseppe Lanci) and Set Design (Enrico Job).
Best Foreign Film: *Out of Africa*. Best Foreign Direction: Akira Kurosawa, for *Ran*. Best Actress in this category: Meryl Streep, in *Out of Africa*. Best Actor in a Foreign Film: William Hurt, in *Kiss of the Spider Woman*.
Visconti Memorial Award for Career Achievement: Ingmar Bergman.

9th Annual Japanese Academy Awards, February 1986

Best Picture: *Gray Sunset* by Shinohiro Sawai, which also won the Best Direction, Best Screenplay (Hiroo Matsuda) Best Actor (Minoru Chiaki) and several other awards.
Best Foreign Film Award: Miloš Forman, for *Amadeus*.

The Locarno International Film Festival Winners, August 1985

Golden Leopard for Best Film: *Alpine Fire – Hohenfeuer*, directed by Fredi M. Murer (Switzerland).
Silver Leopard: *Yellow Land – Huang Tudi*, directed by Chen Kaige (China).
Second Film Prize: *Stealing Time – Tagediebe*, directed by Marcel Gisler (West Germany).
Bronze Leopard: shared between Helen Shaver, for her performance in *Desert Hearts* (USA), and Mitsuo Yanagimachi, for his direction of *Fire Festival – Himatsuri* (Japan).
Special mentions: Steff Gruber's *Fetish and Dreams* (Switzerland), Rob Nilsson's *Signal 7* (USA) and Luigi Faccini's *Errors – Inaganni* (Italy).
Critics' Prize: Edward Yang's *Taipei Story* (Taiwan). Also special mention for Moustapha Diop's *The Doctor from Gafire* (Niger).

The London *Standard* Film Awards, January 1986

Best Film: *My Beautiful Laundrette*.
Best Actor: Victor Banerjee, in *A Passage to India*.
Best Actress: Miranda Richardson, in *Dance With a Stranger*.
The Peter Sellers Award for Comedy: Michael Palin, in *A Private Function*.
Best Screenplay: Alan Bennett and Malcolm Mowbray, for *A Private Function*.
Outstanding Newcomer: shared between Alexandra Pigg and Margi Clarke, in *A Letter to Brehznev*.
Outstanding Technical Achievement: Norman Garwood, for his work on *Brazil*.
A Special Award to Handmade Films.

The Los Angeles International Animation Celebration, September 1985

First prize for feature of over 30 minutes: *Warriors of the Wind* by Kauzo Komarsurbara (Japan).
First prize for computer-assisted film: *Tony de Peltrie* by Pierre La Chapelle, Philippe Bergeron, Pierre Robidoux and Danielle Langlois (Canada).
First prize for film of 15–30 minutes: *Paradise* by Ishu Patel (Canada).
First prize for film of 5–15 minutes: *Anna and Bella* by Borg Ring (Holland).
First prize for film under 5 minutes: *Sundae in New York* by Jimmy Picker (USA)

The Louis Deluc Prize, Paris, December 1985

This award went to Claude Miller's *The Hussy – L'Effrontée*.

The Madrid (Imagfic) Film Festival Awards, March 1986

Best Film: *Tea in the Harem of Archimedes – Le Thé au Harem d'Archimede*, directed by Mehdi Charef (France).
Best Direction: Sam Raimi, for *Crime Wave* (USA)
Best Screenplay: Bill Baer, Bruno Lawrence and Sam Pillsbury, for *The Quiet Earth* (New Zealand).
Best Acting Performance: Elena Safonova, in *Zimnaya Vishnia* (USSR).
Best Cinematography: Giuseppe Lanci, for *Kaos* (Italy).
Best Technical Credit and Special City of Madrid Jury Prizes to *To Live and Die in L.A.* (USA)
Best Short: *A Good Turn Daily*, by Gerrit Van Dijk (Holland).

The Canadian World Film Festival Awards, September 1985

Grand Prix des Amériques for Best Film: *Our Father*, directed by Francisco Regueiro (Spain).
Best Actor: Armin Mukker-Stahl, in *Bitter Harvest* (West Germany).
Best Actress: Nicole Garcia, in *The Fourth Power* (France)
Special Jury Award: *The Philadelphia Attraction*, directed by Peter Gados (Hungary)
Jury Award: shared between *You Only Die Twice* directed by Jacque Deray (France) and *The Alley Cat*, directed by Jean Beaudin (Canada).
Special Prize to Toshiro Mifune, for his contribution to the knowledge of Japanese cinema in the Western world.
Best Short, Grand Prix: *The Big Snit*, by Richard Condie (Canada)
Jury Prize for Short Film: *Up*, by Mike Hoover and Tim Huntley (USA).

The 14th Moscow Film Festival Awards, July 1985

Golden Prizes: Best Film: *Go and See*, directed by Elem Klimov (USSR), *A Soldier's Story*, directed by Norman Jewison (USA) and *The Descent of the Nine*, directed by Christos Shiopachas (Greece).
Silver Prizes: *Unseen Wonder*, directed by Zivko Nikolie (Yugoslavia), *A Woman in a Hat*, directed by Stanislaw Rozewicz (Poland) and *The Seeds of Vengeance* directed by Zelito Viana (Brazil).
Special Jury Prizes: *Train d'Enfer*, directed by Roger Hanin (France), *The Gist*, (India) and *At the Lifebreak*, directed by Leif Erlsboe (Norway).
Best Actor Prizes: Lars Simonsen, in *Twist and Shout* (Denmark) and Detleff Kugoff, in *Wodzeck* (West Germany).
Best Actress Prizes: Juli Basti in *The Red Countess* (Hungary) and Che Yen Hi, in *Salt* (Korea).

The MystFest Film Festival Awards, Cattolica, Italy, July 1985

Best Direction: Ola Solum, for *Orion's Belte* (Norway).
Best Technical/Artistic Contribution: Michael Lahn, for *Kaminsky* (West Germany).
Best Actor: Jean Poiret in *Poulet au Vinaigre – Chicken in Vinegar* and *La Septième Cible – The Seventh Target* (France)
Best Actress: Kathleen Quinlan, in *Blackout* (USA).
Best Screenplay: Jean Loup Dabadie and Claude Pinoteau for *La Septième Cible*.
Special Prizes: Pierre Chenal and Carlo Rambaldi for their contribution the the cinema; and to actress Maayke Bouten for her screen début performance, in *De Prooi – The Prey* (Holland).

The New York Critics' Circle Awards for 1984–5, December 1985

Best Film: *Prizzi's Honour*.
Best Director: John Huston, for *Prizzi's Honor*.
Best Actor: Jack Nicholson, in *Prizzi's Honor*.
Best Actress: Norma Aleandro, in *The Official Version – La Historia Oficial*.
Best Supporting Actor: Klaus Maria Brandauer, in *Out of Africa*.
Best Supporting Actress: Anjelica Huston, in *Prizzi's Honor*.
Best Screenplay: Woody Allen, for *The Purple Rose of Cairo*.
Best Cinematography: David Watkin, for *Out of Africa*.

The Paris International Science-Fiction and Fantasy Film Festival, March 1986

Golden Unicorn Grand Prix: *House*, by Steve Miner (USA).
Special Jury Prize: *The Hand*, by Oliver Stone (USA), which also won him Best Screenplay award.
Best Actress: Lori Cadille in *Day of the Dead* (USA), which also won the Best Special Effects Prize, and the 'Gore' Award.
No Best Actor Award this year.

The Pula (Yugoslavia) Festival Prize Winners, August 1985

Already a winner at Cannes, Emir Kusurica's *While Father Was Away on Business* more or less swept the board, winning prizes for Best Film, Best Direction, Best Actor (Miki Monojlovic) and Best Actress (Mitjana Karanovic).

The San Sebastian Film Festival Winners, Spain, September 1985

Golden Shell for Best Film: *Yesterday*, directed by Radoslaw Piwowarski (Poland).
Silver Shell for Next Best Film: shared between *Los Motivos De Luz*, directed by Felipe Cazals (Mexico) and *La Corte Del Faraon*, directed by José Luis Garcia Sanchez (Spain).
Best Director: Francisco J. Lombardi for his *La Ciudad y los Perros* (Peru)
Best Actor: Francisco J. Lombardi in *La Ciudad y los Perros* (Peru).
Best Actress: Mercedes Sampietro in *Extramuros* (Spain).
Special Jury Prize: *Zina*, directed by Ken McMullen (Great Britain).

Sitges Film Festival, Sitges, Spain, October 1985

Best Film: *Re-animator*, by Stuart Gordon (USA).
Best Direction: Shuji Terayama, for *Saraba Hakobune* (Japan).
Best Actor: John Walcutt, in *Return* (USA)
Best Actress: Lori Cadille, in *Day of the Dead* (USA).
Best Cinematography: Tatsuo Suzuky, in *Saraba Hakobune* (Japan).
Best Screenplay: Heiner Stadler, for *King Kong Faust* (Germany).
Best Short: *Wings of Death* (USA).
Critics' Prize: *Saraba Hakobune* (Japan).

The 31st Taormina Film Festival Awards, Sicily, July 1985

Golden Charybdis: *Ososhika – Funeral*, directed by Juzo Itami (Japan).
Silver Charybdis: Laszlo Szabo for *Volley for a Black Buffalo* (Hungary/France).
Special Jury Awards: *The Ice Cream Parlor*, directed by Dimitri Frenkel Frank (Holland) and *Leave All Fair*, directed by John Reid (New Zealand).
Golden Mask Prize for Acting Performance: Maggie Smith, in *A Private Function* (Great Britain).
Silver Mask for Acting Performance: shared between Gerard Thoolen, Renée Soutenkijk and Bruno Ganz, in *The Ice Cream Parlor*.
Bronze Mask for Acting Performance: Liz Smith, in *A Private Function*.

The Venice Film Festival Awards, September 1985

Golden Lion for Best Film: *Vagabond – Sans Toit ni loi*, directed by Agnès Varda (France).
Golden Lion 'career award': Manoel de Oliveira (Portugal) and John Huston (USA).
Silver Lion for Best First or Second Feature Film: Marion Hansel, for *Dust* (Belgium).
Special Jury Grand Prix: *Tango: Gardel in Exile – Tango: El Exilio* directed by Fernando Solanos (France/Argentina).
Special Jury Prize: Jerzy Skolimowski's *The Lightship* (USA).
Best Actor: Gérard Départdieu, in Maurice Pialat's *Police* (France).
No Best Actress Award was given this year but there were Special Mentions for: Themis Bazaka, in *The Stone Years* (Greece), Galya Novents, in *Childhood Tango* (USSR) and Sonja Savic, in *Life is Beautiful* (Yugoslavia).
Venice Biennial Golden Lion (career award) to Federico Fellini.
Firresci's (unofficial) Best Film in Competition Prize to Agnès Varda's *Vagabond – Sans Toit ni loi* and Best Film of International Critics' Week prize: *Yesterday*, directed by Radaslaw Piwowarski (Poland).

The 1986 Women's Film Festival Winners, Paris

Grand Prix: Magdalena Lazrakiewics's *Puzez Dotek – The Contract* (Poland).
Best Direction: Suzana Amaral, for *A Hore Da Estrella* (Brazil).
Best Performances: Louise Marleau in *Anne Trister* (Canada) and Jukka-Pekka Palo in *Flucht in den Norden* (West Germany).

A Survey of the Australian Year

JAMES CAMERON-WILSON

During 1985, Australian cinema in Britain was virtually invisible. Down Under, box-office tills were ringing on empty. In America, Australian cinema only meant one thing: Mel Gibson. It was a bad year.

Only three new Australian films opened in Britain during the 1985–6 period covered by this annual – besides *My First Wife* and *Careful, He Might Hear You*, about which I wrote last year. But of the new three, only Sophia Turkiewicz's *Silver City* met with half-way decent reviews. Even this, directed by a Pole, failed to ignite the British box-office. The other two, *The Return of Captain Invincible* and *The Boy Who Had Everything*, were miserable disasters. Also, all three films featured foreign stars. Yes, it was a bad year abroad for the Australian cinema.

At home, the picture was equally black. There was one major box-office winner, but this was hardly a reflection of a new, indigenous industry. As expected, *Mad Max: Beyond Thunderdome* 'mopped up', but fell off quickly at the wickets after a sensational opening. The same box-office story was repeated in Britain and America. A long-winded, plodding sequel to *Mad Max*es One and Two, the film was at least buoyed up by an unusual performance from rock star Tina Turner, but was otherwise too 'preachy' for its own good. The hit songs 'We Don't Need Another Hero' and 'One of the Living' helped concentrate media attention on the film, but that was all.

Mel Gibson, alias Mad Max and Australia's most viable export since Vegamite, retired for the year, but it is rumoured that we shall soon see him starring in a film called *Clean Straw For Nothing*, with Judy Davis, and the American *Lethal Weapons*, with Danny Glover.

However, it was Bryan Brown, star of *Winter of Our Dreams* and TV's *Far East*, who emerged most memorably into the international spotlight. Besides an ignominious supporting role in Paul McCartney's ill-fated *Give My Regards to Broad Street*, the lean, strong actor took the title role in the good-looking British thriller *Parker* and then landed the starring part in the well-received American special-effects suspenser *F/X*. The film performed moderately to well in the States, and prompted producer Rafaella de Laurentiis (*Dune*) to cast Brown in the central role in *Tai Pan*, a part earlier earmarked for Steve McQueen, Sean Connery and Roger Moore respectively.

Back to the performance of native films Down Under, Ray Lawrence's *Bliss* was a surprise success. Although given the thumbs-down at the 1985 Cannes Film Festival, the eccentric black farce snatched the 'Best Film' award at the Aussie Oscars and garnered favourable reviews at both the New York and the London film festivals. It also turned its unlikely leading man, Barry Otto, into a star. After a sizeable amount of trimming and re-editing, the film went on to do exceptional business, and benefited from excellent overseas sales. Watch this space.

However, a far more expensive film, which also attracted rave reviews, died

Ted Hodgeman as Dr Dealgood, the Thunderdome's macabre master of ceremonies, introduces a duel to the death in the Warner release *Mad Max: Beyond Thunderdome*, third and most spectacular (if not actually the best) of the three 'Mad Max' movies.

at the box-office. This was Graeme Clifford's stunning, epic-scale *Burke and Wills*, the true story of two explorers (played by Jack Thompson and Nigel Havers) who died in the Australian interior. Many blamed the film's failure on the simultaneous release of a spoof, *Wills and Burke*, which received terrible notices and confused the public enormously – which, considering that the better film cost in the region of (Australian) $10 million, was nothing short of tragedy.

The spiralling increase in Aussie budgets was another thorn in the side of an ailing industry. Take, for example, the 1971 comedy hit *Stork*. That was shot for a mere $60,000. Today, a medium-budget film is reckoned to cost in the region of $3–4 million. And the expense of *Mad Max: Beyond Thunderdome* was so considerable that to this day the budget remains a secret. Even a light-hearted comedy, Peter Faiman's *Crocodile Dundee* – starring TV comic Paul Hogan – took a staggering $8,900,000 to make. And then, of course, there was the sky-high budget of *Burke and Wills* . . .

In spite of this, Australian film production has taken a marked swing upwards. Last year it was predicted that as much as $115 million could be invested in 1985 production, but in fact the final figure was $200 million – an unprecedented amount. In short, film production has never had it so good, prompting one producer to describe it as a 'great problem. There just are not enough good people to go around.'

After the disappointing box-office returns of 1985 this could be taken as surprising. But the reason for all this optimistic investment is that financiers are *guaranteed* a return, via a pre-sale or distribution advance, of as much as 40 per cent of their outlay. Any non-deductible items in the budget will be picked up by the production company or a government body, entitling the investors to their full 133-per-cent tax write-off. However, this failpoof plan is alarming the Federal Treasury, which sees it as a much-exploited scheme that is draining public revenue: so much so that the government is intending to phase out the incentive within the next year. Consequently, producers are jumping in while the money is still available, regardless of the probable box-office performance of the project.

Of the more impressive films produced in the period 1985–86, there was a new one from Paul Cox, Australia's best new director (previously responsible for *Lonely Hearts, Man of Flowers* and *My First Wife*). Called *Cactus*, it stars Isabelle Huppert as a Frenchwoman who falls in love with a blind Australian.

Bruce Beresford also had a new film before the cameras, *The Fringe Dwellers*, based upon the Nene Gare novel about a semi-Aboriginal family surviving on the outskirts of white society. Tim Burstall finally got his adaptation (from Evan Jones' script) of D.H. Lawrence's *Kangaroo* off the ground with Judy Davis and her actor-husband Colin Friels in the lead roles (it was originally to have starred Olivia Newton-John and Jonathan Pryce). Judy Davis – freshly Oscar-nominated for *A Passage to India* – was also tipped to star (opposite Mel Gibson) in *Clean Straw for Nothing* for Gillian Armstrong, the director who helped the actress become a star seven years earlier with *My Brilliant Career*.

Colin Friels turned up again in *Malcolm* an off-beat comedy about a simple-minded soul whose one talent – inventing electronic devices – lands him in trouble with the law. The film was directed by Nadia Tass, just one of many new exciting female directors; Friels' co-stars were Chris Haywood and John Hargreaves.

Another female director to make an impact was Jackie McKimmie, who made her début with *Australian Dreams* – a humorous 'exposé of the sexual mores of life in a typical middle-class Brisbane suburb'. Sounds promising. And there was Di Drew, another débutante of '85, on *The Right Hand Man*, a big-budget period romance starring England's Rupert Everett.

Another expensive period production was *The Trailblazer*, about a bushman who steals 1,000 head of cattle and drives them 1,200 miles across the Outback with the police in hot pursuit. Carl Schultz, who won the 'Best Director' award in 1983 for *Careful, He Might Hear You*, was in charge.

Talking of the Australian 'Oscar', it would be remiss of me not to recount the major winners. As already mentioned, *Bliss* ran away with the 'Best Film' statuette, as well as awards for 'Best Director' (Ray Lawrence) and for 'Best Adapted Screenplay' (Lawrence, Peter Carey). The versatile rambunctious Chris Haywood won a 'Best Actor' award for his role as a dying Vietnam vet and Agent Orange victim in *A Street to Die*; and for her role as a luckless housewife and mother in *Fran*, Noni Hazlehurst (*Monkey Grip*) was honoured as 'Best Actress'. *Fran* also won an award for 'Best Original Screenplay' (by Glenda Hambley).

Originally made for television on a pauper's wages, and, naturally, shot on 16mm, *Fran* was the surprise success story of the year. Not only was the film inexpensive, but its subject matter was decidedly downbeat. *Fran* ran off with the awards and critical raves *and* did decent business, proving a glimmer of hope in a darkening picture.

Equally surprising was the *failure* of *An Indecent Obsession*. Based on the best-selling novel by Colleen McCullough (of *Thorn Birds* fame) and starring top box-office attraction Wendy Hughes, the film seemed to be a dead cert. However, the reviews were not kind and the film slipped quickly from view.

Other fatalities at the box-office were Chris Thomson's well-directed *The Empty Beach*, starring Bryan Brown as a Sydney detective; the well-meaning and often very funny *Emoh Ruo*, about house-hunting; and Tim Burstall's good-looking, muscular Outback actioner, *The Naked Country*. All three were kicked in the teeth by the critics and all three slid off the face of Down Under.

Still, where some Australians were failing at home, others were succeeding overseas. Peter Weir, for *Witness*, his very first American film, was nominated for an Oscar as 'Best Director'; *Witness* itself was nominated for 'Best Film' and its star, Harrison Ford, for 'Best Actor'. As a result of this success, Peter Weir went on to helm the long-awaited-to-shoot *Mosquito Coast*, with Harrison Ford again starring. Fred Schepisi, recovering from his *Iceman* flop, went on to an enormous critical success with *Plenty*, all the more remarkable as it was such a quintessentially English film. The director elicited superb performances from an awesome cast: Meryl Streep, Charles Dance, Tracey Ullman, John Gielgud, Sting, Ian McKellen and a token Antipodean, Sam Neill.

Not a good year for Australian cinema, perhaps, but nevertheless a year bubbling with promise.

Film Books of the Year

IVAN BUTLER

The boom in film books – many of high quality – continues. To cover, or even to discover, all of them is impossible, but some 80 titles will be found in the following pages. The number of particularly recommendable ones makes the selection of a mere dozen for a short list difficult, but here, in alphabetical order as usual, is a purely personal choice of favourites – for interest, entertainment or reference: *The 'B' Directors*, Wheeler W. Dixon; *Dark Star*, Leatrice Gilbert Fountain; *Hollywood Destinies*, Graham Petrie; *Illustrated Directory of Film Character Actors*, David Quinlan; *Inside Oscar*, Mason Wiley and Damien Bona; *John Boorman*, Michel Ciment; *J. Stuart Blackton*, Marian Blackton Trimble; *Orson Wells*, Barbara Leaming; *The Paramount Story*, John Douglas Eames; *Screen Deco*, Howard Mandelbaum and Eric Myers; *Some Day We'll Laugh* Esther Ralston; *2000 Movies – The Forties*, Robin Cross.

And I must make special mention for two updated reissues: *Hitchcock* by François Truffaut, and the fifth edition of *Halliwell's Film and Video Guide*.

Acts of Murder, Jonathan Goodman; Harrap, £9.95

This fascinating collection of true-life murders with a showbusiness background includes the fullest account we are ever likely to have of Hollywood's famous unsolved mystery – the killing of director William Desmond Taylor in 1922. The book contains a useful plan and photographs of all the chief film stars involved, including Mabel Normand, Mary Miles Minter and Edna Purviance, and there are chapters on the tragedy of Fatty Arbuckle, the shooting of the gangster Dillinger as he emerged from a cinema (after watching the appropriately named film *Manhattan Melodrama*), and another unsolved, and very strange, death mystery – that of the Marx Brothers' glamorous co-star Thelma Todd. Mr Goodman writes wittily and authoritatively, and the theatrical stories are as good as those connected with the cinema. Of guaranteed interest to all those curious (and which of us, if we are frank, is not?) about the seamy side of public life.

All Those Tomorrows, Mai Zetterling; Jonathan Cape, £9.95

Few people who saw her will forget Mai Zetterling's first film performance in *Frenzy*, a haunting Swedish production of 1944 (disappointingly dismissed in a few lines in this autobiography) and the reader who can skim through the rather embarrassing brief first chapter will find many interesting, if at times somewhat depressing, details about her professional life in the cinema and her personal life with husbands Tutte Lemkow and David Hughes, and lovers Herbert Lom, Peter Finch and Tyrone Power. The narrative is rather confusingly interspersed with diary and other extracts, and even a transformation into a third-person romantic storyette; but her style is lively, and though more about her actual work as actress and director might have been welcome, there are compensations such as the pen portrait of Ingmar Bergman and the saga of disillusionment with Hollywood.

All-time Box-office Hits, Joel Finler and Neil Sinyard; Columbus Books, £9.95

A book with this title, described as 'an account of the most popular movies ever made' is bound to induce a sense of *déjà-vu* as one familiar title after another springs into view – from *The Sound of Music* to *Star Wars*. There are, however, some surprises (*Roman Scandals, Peyton Place, How to Marry a Millionaire*), and the authors find some fresh comments to make. It is primarily a picture book, and the illustrations, many of them unfamiliar, are generally very good – though those in colour include some awful examples of garish artificiality (for example, Esther Williams on page 52 and the *Shane* trio on page 85).

NOTE The still at the bottom of page 131 is not of the final ambush of *Bonnie and Clyde* but of the earlier scene in the meadow.

American Dreaming, Raymond Carney; University of California Press, £25.25

A study in depth of the films of John Cassavetes. Known mainly to the general cinemagoer for his acting roles in *Rosemary's Baby, The Dirty Dozen, The Fury* and others, Cassavetes' real interest has lain in the making of a series of highly personal and original films, tracing with subtlety and insight the complications of human relationships. That he is 'America's greatest film-maker' may be open to argument [it most certainly is! Ed.], but that he has been 'astonishingly neglected and misunderstood' is probably true. This detailed, enthusiastic and (except for such occasional, horrific nonwords as 'excerptible') well-written book should go far to widen interest in his work. There is an excellent filmography.

Audrey, Charles Higham; New English Library, £9.95

A good, workman-like (in the best sense) biography of Audrey Hepburn, from her early traumatic years in Holland under the Nazis to her meteoric rise to stardom, following an early helping hand from Alec Guinness – a fact for some reason omitted from the index. Private life and public career are nicely balanced by her experienced biographer, and there is much about her indomitable baroness mother as well as interesting glimpses of Audrey at work – such as her painstaking preparations to play the blind heroine of *Wait Until Dark*. Some very good illustrations and a brief (not to say minuscule) filmography round off a book which sympathetically reveals that even an apparently most successful life may have its full share of troubles.

Bardot, Deneuve and Fonda, Roger Vadim; Weidenfeld & Nicolson, £10.95

A 'setting-the-record-straight' book by a famous director who has had three even more famous women in his life could hardly fail to arouse interest. Vadim's rendition of his own memories is at least as entertaining as the sensational publicity stories it sets out to correct, and there is the added attraction that, despite a great deal of dialogue that surely is not always completely accurately remembered, this time, we are assured, we have the truth. Annette Stroyberg is excluded from the triumvirate of the title but has her place in the text. Lively, often amusing and, of course, 'frank', spiritedly translated by Melinda Porter, and decorated with a good batch of photographs in each case.

The 'B' Directors – A biographical directory, Wheeler W. Dixon; Scarecrow Press, dist. Bailey Bros. & Swinfen, £47.50

The 'B' picture, defined as a film made specifically to fill the first half of a double-feature bill, is generally held to have come into being at the time of the advent of sound, and Mr Dixon takes 1929 as his starting date. By no means every director of a 'B' picture was solely a 'B' picture director, of course, and many names in the book are better known as makers of 'A' films. All, however, appear among the 350-plus gathered here, with complete lists of their productions and a brief biographical commentary in each case. It is a worthy addition to the excellent Scarecrow reference library, with alphabetical lists of major films and serials for easy use and some very rare stills.

Bette Davis, Christopher Nickens; Columbus Books, £7.95

Much has been written about the indestructible Miss Davis, but this book, aptly subtitled 'A Biography in Photographs', is an attractive addition to the collection. The story is told in lengthy captions to the innumerable illustrations. As the latter are excellent and the former both concise and detailed, the result is a well-rounded portrait, pleasantly presented.

Bliss – the Film, Peter Carey and Ray Lawrence; Faber & Faber, £4.95

This is a very good example of how a film script should be presented for general reading: just enough technical detail and no more, an explanatory note where necessary, an informative introduction which includes comments on differences between screenplay and original novel, and a reasonable number of stills. Whether, having read it, one would feel the urge to see this particular film from Australia is another matter.

Burton – the Man Behind the Myth, Penny Junor; Sidgwick & Jackson, £9.95

In some ways, Burton's life – as told in this excellent biography – might be regarded as a truly tragic story – a potentially great artist brought down by flaws in himself – but sadly it has not the stature of tragedy. The dreary promiscuity (and still drearier boasting about it), the violent drunkenness, the occasional unprofessional reluctance to accept direction, the mindless extravagance, the seemingly deliberate wasting of a rare talent – all these are depressing rather than tragic. However, this book is no 'hatchet job'; it is written with sympathy and understanding. What will remain in one's memories of Burton are not the failures but his performances in his (regrettably few) notable films, and – perhaps even more – such masterly recordings as his narration of *Under Milk Wood* and (surprisingly not mentioned in this book) *The Rime of the Ancient Mariner*.

There is some evidence of carelessness – why, for instance, do so many film biographers (or their editors) neglect to check name spellings (Joan 'Blondel', 'Sheila' Graham, even 'Micky' Mouse)? – and some grammatical clumsiness. Apart from such minor errors, however, this is a reasonably penetrating recount of the life of Richard Burton.

Caught in the Act – Sex and Eroticism in the Movies, David Shipman; Elm Tree Books, £12.95

As was to be expected, Mr Shipman's survey of the slow, tortuous but inevitable growth of permissiveness in the film is related with both wit and scholarship. The emphasis is, necessarily, on the early and middle years, which gives plenty of scope for a lot of interesting and rare stills, but the whole story is covered, from the notorious Irwin/Rice osculation of 1896 to the anything-goes-let-it-all-hang-out carryings-on of recent years – the latter probably no more, and possibly less, exciting in their period than the former. Foreign films are also included, from Bernhardt to Bardot. Would-be sensational sexploitation movie books have proliferated: here the subject is dealt with seriously but entertainingly.

(NOTE: The 'husband' on page 43 is Marc MacDermott, not George Fawcett.)

A Certain Tendency of the Hollywood Cinema, 1930–1980, Robert B. Ray; Princeton University Press, £37.50 cloth, £12.95 paper

Yet another book examining the Hollywood films against their sociological, mythical and ideological background. However, in this case the author refreshingly keep his feet on the ground: his arguments and conclusions are firmly based on realities. Instead of vague theorizing, actual films are discussed in detail – five in particular: *Casablanca*, *It's a Wonderful Life*, *The Man Who Shot Liberty Valance*, *The Godfather* and *Taxi Driver*. Too much significance, perhaps, is given to the first of these, an over-rated movie which nobody connected with it apparently knew how on earth to finish! To see it again today is to wonder what all the fuss was about. Apart from these five, however, many other films of the half-century are invoked and analysed, helped by a large number of frame enlargements to illustrate various points.

On the whole, an interesting and stimulating study by a writer who carries his scholarship lightly and conveys it lucidly.

Charlie Chaplin, Maurice Bessy; Thames & Hudson, £20.00

A magnificent collection of over 1000 illustrations: stills and frame enlargements from every film Chaplin made, in addition to personal and production photographs, all excellently reproduced. The author, who was well acquainted with Chaplin, provides essays and a brief biography translated from the French by Jane Brenton. Synopses are provided for all the films and there are numerous quotations from famous persons, as well as 10 sketches by artists and by Chaplin himself. This is a superb tribute to the most famous of all cinema stars, a fine complementary volume to David Robinson's definitive biography, and a huge treasure-house of memories – beautifully printed and handsomely bound.

Charlton Heston, Michael Munn; Robson Books, £10.95

Heston being a man reticent about his private life, which in any case is (as this book implies) 'stable', the author is free to devote most of his space to the films themselves, with glances at various stage appearances. Helped by copious personal comments from Heston himself, he examines these thoroughly and entertainingly, painting a convincing and sympathetic portrait of an actor of skill and integrity – a man who cheerfully accepts the description 'square' and is a credit to that much-abused adjective! This is another in the useful Robson series of workman-like biographies.

Cinéstars, introduced by James Cameron-Wilson; Columbus Books, £15.95

A large-format collection of magnificently reproduced colour photographs of contemporary or near-contemporary female stars – a number of them perhaps quite unfamiliar to the general film-goer. The freakish rather than the beautiful seems to be the aim, and many of them seem to resemble the more extravagant pages of modern fashion magazines. It is as a striking tribute to the photographers' art that the book is notable. As regards the subjects themselves, the actresses of earlier years (even if more soberly posed and in mere black-and-white) need have little to fear from comparison.

The *Citizen Kane* Book, Orson Welles, Herman J. Mankiewicz and Pauline Kael; Methuen, £6.50.

There will be a welcome for the reappearance of this famous book in a neat, strong paperback form. Here are Pauline Kael's controversial pro-Mankiewicz essay 'Raising *Kane*', the complete shooting script and the cutting continuity. Comparisons for those who already possess the previous large-format edition: the new one is much easier to handle than the earlier paperback; it has (mainly) stills in place of frame enlargements, resulting in a gain in clarity but a loss of immediacy; there are fewer illustrations; and the index to the essay is missing, which is a loss, and also the list of Mankiewicz's other credits, which is not.

True *Kane* enthusiasts, even if they already have the earlier edition, may find it handy to possess this one, too. For the majority who may never have had the chance of reading either the script of this great film or Pauline Kael's often criticized article, this new arrival is indeed a matter for rejoicing.

Clockwise, Michael Frayn; Methuen, £1.95
The publishing of film scripts for general reading is becoming almost as customary as that of plays – a very welcome development. This is a good example of how it should be done, as regards both price and presentation. It is also easy to follow, with the necessary minimum of technical details, and extremely entertaining in its own right.

Dark Star – The Meteoric Rise and Eclipse of John Gilbert, Leatrice Gilbert Fountain; Sidgwick & Jackson, £15.00
This superb biography must come high on the list of any year's 'bests'. Here, at last, without any whitewashing but with compassion, frankness and often humour, is the true story of one of the most cruelly mistreated and misrepresented of all the great silent stars. The myth is well known: the 'great lover' who is betrayed at the coming of sound by a squeaky effeminate voice and then drinks himself morosely to death. Here is what really happened – his appalling treatment by the vindictive Louis B. Mayer and the studio for which he made a fortune; his off-and-on but always affectionate relationship with his beautiful second wife Leatrice Joy; his love affair with Garbo, who alternately supported him and let him down – in contrast to Marlene Dietrich who, towards the end of his life, treated him with the utmost kindness and encouragement. Against his drinking and often provocative behaviour (frankly related) can be set the devotion he aroused in so many people, such as his co-star in several films, the unforgettable Renée Adorée. Recent revivals of *The Big Parade* and *Flesh and the Devil* reveal Gilbert as the star he was; *Queen Christina* alone exposes the lie about his voice (a pleasant 'light baritone'). His daughter and her sympathetic collaborator, John R. Maxim, have set the record straight in this fine and moving book, which includes some excellent and rare illustrations.

(*Note*: James Barrie would have been astonished to find himself credited with the authorship of *Bunty Pulls the Strings* – a film adaptation from a play by Graham Moffat.)

Directors – The All-Time Greats, Neil Sinyard; Columbus Books, £6.95
Forty-five famous directors, from D. W. Griffith to Steven Spielberg, from Ingmar Bergman to Satyajit Ray, are included in this survey. The work of each is discussed in a brief but informative essay, and there are about 100 photographs and stills. A very useful introduction to fuller study, with excellent illustrations. An index of names might have proved useful.

The Disney Version, Richard Schickel; Pavilion (Michael Joseph), £12.95
This is an updated and revised version of a book that first appeared in 1968 when, according to the author, it caused some controversy because it regarded the creator of such universally loved animated beings as Dopey, Pinocchio, Bambi and Dumbo in a not wholly uncritical light. Subtitled 'The Life, Times, Art and Commerce of Walt Disney', it is an examination in depth, filling over 400 packed pages. The body of the book has been left untouched, though the author states, in a lengthy epilogue bringing it up to date, that he has since modified certain opinions and now regards the Disney operation as a 'valuable American institution'. His book is an important addition to Disney literature, serious enough to eschew illustrations but an unfailingly interesting 'read'.

Double Act, Michael Denison; Michael Joseph, £12.95
In 1973, Michael Denison saw the publication of his book *Overture and Beginners*, the story of the lives and work of himself and his wife, Dulcie Gray, up to 1948 (it was highly recommended in *Film Review* 1974–5). This sequel brings the account up to date, and is equally enjoyable. Apart from his skill in making the ups and downs of 'a life in the theatre' lively, amusing and, at times, moving, he has a happy knack of vividly etching portraits of the many interesting (and not a few unusual) people he has met and with whom he has worked, in just a few pertinent lines. Perhaps this derives from his skill as a painter as well as an actor. There is also quite a lot about his activities in the actors' union Equity – he makes even such esoteric matters interesting to outsiders – and an abundance, but not a surfeit, of good 'actors' stories. Though both his and Dulcie Gray's work has recently been almost wholly in theatre and television, he discusses a number of films from earlier years which the cinema-goer will remember with pleasure.

Above all, although it is sharply forthright when necessary, this is a generous book and a kindly one – a pleasure in these hatchet-wielding days. Illustrated, with a good index and three useful chronologies.

Eisenstein at Work, Jan Leyda and Zina Voynow; Methuen, £17.95
This is a remarkable, detailed study of the great director, very originally set out – a 'montage', as the jacket blurb accurately states, of how a genius of the cinema created his masterworks. The fairly brief text on each film is embellished with a wealth of illustrations: stills, action and personal photographs, scores of sketches, reproductions of Einenstein's notes (with translations by their side). There is a chronology of his theatre work, together with one for his life as a whole. At first glance, perhaps, the book may appear somewhat scattered and difficult to follow, but as one reads on, it proves to be one of the most penetrating and detailed accounts of a great film-maker's approach to his art. Highly recommended.

Fifty Classic British Films – A Pictorial Record, Anthony Slide; Dover, £9.95
The author's selection, which starts in 1932 with *Rome Express* and ends in 1982 with *Gandhi*, consists in the main of familiar titles, but he has also interestingly included a number of less widely recognized productions, such as *St Martin's Lane* (*Sidewalks of London* in the US), *Wings of the Morning* and – perhaps most overlooked of all – *Mr Perrin and Mr Traill*, from Sir Hugh Walpole's novel (Walpole later denied being either 'Mr Perrin' or 'Mr Traill' but, as Slide suggests, it is probable that he was partly both).

George Formby (*Let George Do It*) and Gracie Fields (*Sing as We Go*) rub comfortably alongside Thomas More (*A Man for All Seasons*) and *Henry V* in this excellently illustrated and authoritatively written study.

Film Theory and Criticism, ed. Gerald Mast and Marshall Cohen; Oxford University Press, £11.50
This is the third edition of a collection of essays on film aesthetics originally published in 1974, with the scope now widened and the contents enlarged to contain 53 items. In period, the range extends from early writers such as Vachell Lindsay, Kracauer, Arnheim and Sadoul to those of the present day. Subjects vary from the practical and particular (Tynan on 'Garbo', Eisenstein on 'Dickens, Griffith and the Film Today', Royal Brown on Herrmann and Hitchcock, Agee's famous 'Golden Age of Comedy' to general – and occasionally somewhat woolly – theorizing. On the whole, a book for the serious student to whom the cinema (or rather 'the film') is more than a mere evening's entertainment.

Finally Truffaut, Don Allen; Secker & Warburg, £10.95
When writing about the original edition of this survey of Truffaut's work (in 1974 – price £2.50 hardback, £1.30 paperback!) I recommended it as 'a disarmingly warm-hearted yet clear-sighted appraisal'. In additional chapters, the author now covers the remaining films and concludes with a fitting summary and tribute, pointing out the grimly appropriate title of the last production – *Finally Sunday*, the day of the week on which he died in 1984 – and listing the projects which, to the regret of every film lover, will never be realized. A generous number of good stills, an excellent filmography and details of Truffaut's other activities round off a useful and perceptive handbook.

Fonda – Her Life in Pictures, James Spada; Sidgwick & Jackson, £12.95

Although this is primarily a picture book, the author, in his introductory essays to the various sections and very full captions to the multitudinous illustrations, provides a full biographical account – not only of Jane Fonda's place in cinema history but also of her more controversial role as 'Hanoi Jane' during the Vietnam war and her other 'radical' activities. The text is lively and authoritative, and the illustrations, whether photographs or stills, are excellent and include a striking section of full-colour studio portraits, which follow her development from sex kitten to mature, attractive woman. There is also a page on 'Jane's Workout'. A filmography or index of films would have been useful, but the book is handsomely produced.

Frank Sinatra, Derek Jewell; Pavilion (Michael Joseph), £12.95

This new addition to the excellent Celebration series comes up against the richly produced biography of her father by Nancy Sinatra. They are, however, complementary rather than repetitive. Few if any of the numerous illustrations in each seem to be repeated from Nancy's book, and the text forms an interesting comparison with the more intimate memoir; the filmography is rather more detailed. George Perry provides a 30-page essay, 'Sinatra on Film', and there is a good list of Sinatra recordings.

Frank Sinatra – My Father, Nancy Sinatra; Hodder & Stoughton, £17.95

In this opulently produced biography, Nancy Sinatra relates the vicissitudes of a legendary career with candour and affection – a change from the recent fashion of disgruntled descendants – and her intimate personal memories are expanded by stories and comments from a large number of her father's friends and associates. The magnificent illustrations include, apart from those throughout the text, a special section of film stills, another of record sleeves and several pages of casual snapshots. Appendices include a chronology, an annotated filmography and a detailed list of recordings. There is a list of names referred to in the text, but no index.

Goddess – The Secret Lives of Marilyn Monroe, Anthony Summers; Gollancz, £12.95

In this detailed and thoroughly documented study, Mr Summers gives an authoritative account of the rumours and counter-rumours that have continued to surround Marilyn Monroe's death. This is, however, only the tragic climax of a full biography of her life, written from the angle suggested in the subtitle. One or two films are mentioned – *The Prince and the Showgirl, Some Like It Hot* – but this is primarily a personal story of her relationships with her friends and associates, her husbands (Joe DiMaggio, Arthur Miller) and her lovers, actual and alleged, in particular the Kennedy brothers. The story is rivettingly told – even if the whole truth can never be revealed – and the evidence that there was some sort of cover-up of her last hours is convincingly presented. Some unusual illustrations include a surprisingly beautiful one of Marilyn without any make-up, and a horrifying one, from police files, after the autopsy had done its work.

Greta Garbo – Portraits 1920–1951, introduced by Klaus-jürgen Sembach; Plexus, £27.95 hardback

This fine collection of photographs (almost 150 of them, all full coffee-table-book size) is a treasure in itself, but its special interest lies in the score or so of early ones, taken in Sweden, Berlin or the United States before Garbo had been handed over to the Hollywood grooming process. These show the 'amazing transformation' (as the jacket blurb accurately puts it) of a part-time mannequin into a cinematic legend. The book concludes with a short section of photographs taken after her early retirement from the screen – a more mature but still matchless face. A brief note explains that the film titles under a number of the portraits refer to the period rather than the films themselves. A short biographical introduction rounds off an album of works by master photographers which is an essential companion to the many books written about the 'One and Only'.

Halliwell's Film and Video Guide (5th Edition), Leslie Halliwell; Granada, £15.00

One of the most surprising things about this gargantuan volume (apart from Mr Halliwell's incredible industry) is that, although (compared to the previous edition in 1983) it contains nearly 200 extra pages and around 2000 extra entries, its price has remained the same. (Oddly enough, he says in his preface to the present edition that 'the three-column setting has reduced the number of pages.' I gently suggest he is mistaken: the number of pages has increased and the three columns were present in the previous edition!)

Changes include increased attention to the thirties – that great period of movie-making – more critical quotations (including publicity 'tag-lines') and an indication when a film is available on video, accompanied by a warning that this particular information may quickly date. Useful sections that have been retained are: alternative titles, foreign film title changes, a note on screen sizes and the famous lament on 'The Decline and Fall of the Movie', with an added postscript. Illustrations – stills and advertisements – are mainly nostalgic.

Halliwell's Harvest, Leslie Halliwell; Grafton Books, £12.95

This is a sequel to *Halliwell's Hundred*, recommended in *Film Review 1983–4*. It follows much the same procedure – essays on his 'choice of entertainment movies from the Golden Age' – the number being reduced to 84, but with the addition of three highly entertaining and stimulating essays, on the best and worst films, forming a movie library, and curious film titles. Famous productions (*The Best Years of Our Lives, Grand Hotel, The Seventh Veil*) and less famous (*Alias Dick Beal, The Enforcer, It's in the Bag*) are combined in a selection which radiates enthusiasm even when it is at its most critical. How pleasant, among many felicities, to find the 'dream ending' to *The Woman in the Window* firmly defended. One good still is provided for each film.

Harold Lloyd – The Man on the Clock, Tom Dardis; Penguin Books, £5.95

Despite several studies of his work as one of the greatest silent film comedians, this book's claim to be the first full-length biography of Lloyd seems to be justified. There certainly was a gap that needed to be filled, and Mr Dardis does this handsomely. An excellent, well-written account, it deals with all the important films in detail, and also reveals sides of Lloyd's personality and life which will surprise the many who think of him as the perpetually cheerful go-getter who amassed a fortune that kept him in comfort during his long years of retirement. Some wonderful old photographs and an excellent filmography round off an affectionate tribute and an important addition to the story of the great silent years of cinema.

Hepburn, James Spada; Columbus Books, £7.95

In this picture-biography, the story of Katharine Hepburn's life and work is told in the lengthy captions accompanying over 200 photographs, many of them both rare and full-page. This is a very good example of a fairly new, attractive and valid way of presenting a showbusiness biography. Mr Spada's text is concise, readable and informative, an admirable accompaniment to the excellent illustrations. It might, however, have been given a name and film-title index.

Hitchcock, François Truffaut; Secker & Warburg, £18.00

The reissue of this famous record of a mammoth interview conducted by one director with another is a matter for celebration, particularly as Truffaut updated the book to take it to Hitchcock's death. Though barely touching on the latter's personal life, it is a mine of fascinating details of Hitchcock's working methods, of his opinions on film-making (and on certain film stars), of his philosophy and his favourite stories. Even if it may be claimed that the 'real' Hitchcock is as elusive as ever, much is revealed. The illustrations have also been revised and re-selected, and are lavish and excellent. They have not, however, always been very well treated: too many are uncaptioned; on page 198, all four captions are incorrectly placed.

Note. It is interesting to see Hitchcock twice remarking that *The Man Who Knew Too Much* was taken from one of Sapper's Bulldog Drummond stories. This appears to be untrue – certainly there is no reference to this fact in the credits of either of Hitchcock's two versions of the film.

Hollywood Destinies, Graham Petrie; Routledge & Kegan Paul, £19.95

This addition to the important Cinema and Society series is concerned with the fortunes of a number of European directors in the United States during the years 1922–31 and examines why they all (with the exception of Lubitsch, Curtiz and perhaps Leni, had he not died in 1939) failed to adjust to the American way of movie life, yet managed to leave their mark on it. Three of them, Lubitsch, Murnau and Sjöstrom (Seastrom) are given special prominence; others such as Stiller and Christensen are more briefly studied. In all cases an account of their pre-American work is included. A scholarly yet eminently readable work covering an important aspect of film history, it makes even lengthy synopses of films we are never likely to see interesting to read. Also included are 50 excellent stills and photographs, copious notes, bibliographical data and a good double index.

Hollywood 1930s, Jack Lodge; Admiral, £5.95

Hollywood 1940s, John Russell Taylor; Admiral £5.95

These are the first two volumes in a series intended to cover each decade. A fairly brief but adequate text accompanies a large number of stills and other photographs from the famous Kobal Collection, and these are strengthened by full captions. The illustrations will probably be the main attraction for potential buyers: a welcome proportion of them are new. Many are full page – indeed, a few are spread over two pages with the inevitable split faces and foreshortened limbs, though these distortions are avoided as far as possible. The second volume also has a number in colour, attractive in the Disney cartoons but not always so successful elsewhere. The prices are modest and the books have a bright and lively appearance; they form useful introductions to more detailed study of the periods covered.

Hollywood on Hollywood, Douglas McClelland; Faber & Faber, £8.95

An entertaining (and often revealing) collection of several hundred opinions – from actors, directors, writers and others – on Tinsel Town from the 'twenties to the present day. Most of the quotes – taken from books, magazines and newspaper articles – are under half-a-dozen lines in length, but there are also a number of much longer personal interviews. Comments range from the sour, snide and embittered to the enthusiastic and affectionate – the former possibly predominant – and many are amusing and sharply observant. Illustrated by over 100 excellent stills and group and production photographs, this is a fine compilation for bedside dipping.

The Illustrated Directory of Film Character Actors, David Quinlan; Batsford, £17.50

David Quinlan's prodigious industry is in evidence again in this latest addition to his series of comprehensive reference books; this one contains some 850 entries, from the silent era to the present day. The great asset of these books is that the film lists are complete – or as complete as the compiler's earnest research can make them – including shorts, films made for television, etc., and many of them are of truly formidable length. As in the other volumes produced by Mr Quinlan, each name is accompanied by a photograph – particularly useful here, where the face/name connection is often not as easy to make as in the case of the big stars. As in all such ventures, there will be film-goers who will ask indignantly why so-and-so was omitted, but to be all-inclusive would surely entail a life sentence of hard labour. The range here is wide and comprehensive enough to satisfy all but the most demanding buffs.

Inside Oscar, Mason Wiley & Damien Bona; Columbus Books, £12.95

Numerous books on the Oscar, both historical and documentary, have already appeared, but this gargantuan volume of 850 pages surely beats them all. Every year receives a filmic 'overview' – a general potted history – followed by a full, at times hilarious, account of the Big Night itself and its aftermath, together with a list of all the presenters and performers at the ceremony, and other practical details. A 200-page appendix records every Oscar ever given, rule changes, brief 'points of interest' and a selection of films and songs which failed to be nominated.

So entertainingly is the whole thing written that it cries out to be read (if and when time permits) from cover to appendix. Illustrations are limited to one relevant photograph per year; stills and stars are, however, available in various other books on the subject – most fully in the large-format paperback *Oscar* (also from Columbus) covered in *Film Review 1984–5*.

Inside Warner Bros. (1935–1951), Rudy Behlmer; Weidenfeld & Nicolson, £15.95

This is a large and fascinating collection of memos, notes, letters, tables, etc. from the files of Warner Bros. during their peak years, concerning such famous films, among many others, as *Dark Victory, The Maltese Falcon, Now, Voyager, Dodge City* and *The Private Lives of Elizabeth and Essex*. A whole section is devoted to *Casablanca*, and a useful 'interlude' in the form of a lengthy article from *Fortune* magazine (1937) summarizes facts about the studio at the time. Here also are the Bette Davis and Olivia de Havilland confrontations, the Davis/Hopkins feud, suggestions and comments from and about Hal Wallis, Cagney, John Huston and dozens of other varied workers in the vast concern. The illustrations are well chosen and pertinent to the text, but the index is a let-down.

International Film Guide 1986, Ed. Peter Cowie; Tantivy, £7.25

The *Film Guide* is firmly established with such reference works as John Willis' *Screen World* (and our own *Film Review*) as an annual beacon to brighten the dark pre-Christmas days. The 23rd edition (500 lavishly illustrated pages) has all the usual features: 'World Survey' as the backbone, 'Festivals', 'Animation', book and magazine reviews, etc. The bonus this year is a 20-page dossier on Australian cinema with 'boxes' on individual directors, players, producers and cinematographers. Stoutly bound, attractively presented and pleasantly solid to handle.

The International Film Poster, Gregory J. Edwards; Columbus Books, £12.95 hardback, £8.95 paperback

This beautifully produced book does belated justice to an aspect of the cinema world that has not, until recently, received the serious attention it deserves, and triumphantly proves the point that the film poster can be much more than a mere 'selling tool'. The author has collected together a wide range of examples from throughout film history and from many countries. The detailed text is full of fascinating historical and technical information, and the posters themselves are excellently reproduced. Those in colour are so crisp and bright as to make one regret that there are not more of them, generous though the proportion is. Recommended for everyone interested in this important ancillary to the cinema, or in fine examples of popular art.

James Cagney – A Celebration, Richard Schickel; Pavilion (Michael Joseph), £12.95

This addition to the handsome Celebration series follows much the same pattern as those on Alec Guinness, Katharine Hepburn, etc., with lavish illustrations (mostly stills, many unfamiliar) and an excellent full filmography. As the author states, it is intended less as a biography than as an analysis of Cagney's career, derived largely from a long interview and other, less formal meetings. Personal and private affairs are – as Cagney himself would have wished – only lightly and coincidently sketched, but there is much about the development of his screen *persona* and how it relates to the social background of the time. Mr Schickel, an experienced writer on the cinema and author of the monumental and definitive work on D. W. Griffith, here presents as fully rounded a portrait of Cagney as we are likely to have, from his early days in the theatre to the last brave but mistaken television appearance in 1984.

James Stewart, Allen Eyles; Comet (W. H. Allen), £5.95
This is the softback edition of the book reviewed in *Film Review 1985–6*, which was welcomed as an enjoyable and worthy biography of a major star who had hitherto received less attention from film historians than others, and in particular for its superbly full filmography. Attractive and stoutly made, it is an even better bargain now.

John Boorman, Michel Ciment; Faber & Faber, £25.00
With only nine films to cover in this large and handsome book (very well translated from the French by Gilbert Adair) the author has plenty of space to devote to each one, and this he does with thoroughness and authority. There is a long analytical essay followed by a personal interview for each production. Also included are sections on his work in general, his life, his TV experience and a reference to his deep admiration for D. W. Griffith. 'Recollections' by a number of professional associates, a full filmography and detailed bibliography complete the study. The book, bound in laminated boards, is not inexpensive – which may be partly accounted for by the large number of superbly presented colour stills.

J. Stuart Blackton, Marian Blackton Trimble; Scarecrow Press, dist. Bailey Bros. & Swinfen, £16.00
A wholly delightful biography by his daughter (who was herself a screenwriter) of one of the most neglected pioneers of the earliest days of moviemaking – co-founder of the once renowned Vitagraph Company, and obviously a man of the utmost charm, impulsiveness and courage. In his foreword, Anthony Slide (who edited the book and has previously written the history of Vitagraph – *The Big V*) describes Mrs Trimble's style as 'perhaps somewhat rococo', and indeed it is both engagingly personal and eminently suited to its subject. It is also a vivid picture of those days – truthful and often hilarious. I defy anyone to read the story of the attempted transformation of Viola, the company cow, into a fierce bull for a scene in *Carmen*, without laughing out loud.

The account of Mrs Trimble's relationship with her father and the inevitable ups and downs of their lives is all the more moving because of its total lack of sentimentality. This comparatively brief book, embellished with a number of rare photographs, will be treasured by all who love the cinema.

Katharine Hepburn, Anne Edwards; Hodder & Stoughton, £12.95
Katharine Hepburn has recently bid fair to rival Humphrey Bogart in the proliferation of books on her life and career.This is one of the fullest – somewhat bland and fulsome, but easy reading, well documented and including an excellent reference section with theatre, film, television, radio and award details, and copious notes. Perhaps the most unexpected and intriguing (if slightly irrelevant) example of the latter is a full account of transvestism in films!

The Last Days of Alfred Hitchcock, David Freeman; Pavilion (Michael Joseph), £12.95
The author worked with Hitchcock for some six months on his last script – a spy story never (sadly) to be filmed – after which he wrote this penetrating, sympathetic and most revealing account of Hitchcock's last days when he was afflicted with pain, depression and occasional lapses of memory, but also showing frequent flashes of the old master. This memoir, which also contains many glimpses of Hitchcock's method of working, is followed by the complete script of the projected film. We can only regret that we shall never see what he would have made of the screenplay, which is full of interest in itself and is presented in a very 'readable' form. The book, which is well illustrated, concludes with notes on the script and a very good filmography. It is an important – indeed, essential – addition to the already not inconsiderable body of Hitchcockiana.

The Last Gentleman – A Tribute to David Niven, Peter Haining; Comet (W. H. Allen), £5.95
After the main tribute by Haining in this lavishly illustrated softback edition, there follow what might be called 'mini-tributes' from about 20 of Niven's close friends and associates, who write with unstinting praise and affection. They include Lauren Bacall, Flora Robson, Laurence Olivier, John Mills, Bette Davis, Maggie Smith and Lord Hailsham. Niven must, indeed, have been an almost perfect human being to have evoked these responses; he was certainly one of the most warmly remembered of film stars. The brief description of his courage during his final, dreadful illness is movingly written.

A comprehensive annotated filmography is useful for quick reference to his career.

Leading Men, Julie Welch and Louise Brody; Conran Octopus, £12.95
Recent years have seen quite a number of photographic glamour albums of movie actresses – with the men, by comparison, unkindly ignored. The balance is handsomely redressed by this large and luscious collection of mainly manly stars, from Valentino to Sean Penn. All the famous are here, but room has been found for some slightly less so – about 300 in all. Illustrations are lavish, often several to a star, and all in crisp black-and-white – none of those dreadful 'masculine glamour' portraits sometimes in hideously false colour. The text, with a charming introduction, is lively, balanced and informative.

Legends – Gary Cooper, ed. John Kobal; Pavilion (Michael Joseph), £6.95
Legends – Ingrid Bergman, ed. John Kobal, Pavilion (Michael Joseph), £6.95
These sturdy softbacks ('paperbacks' is altogether too weak a description) are the first in what should prove to be a very popular series: collections of studio portraits and stills from the famous Kobal Collection, together with lengthy introductions by Richard Schickel (Cooper) and Sheridan Morley (Bergman) and a general note from Kobal himself. The essays, from experienced writers on the cinema, are lively and informative, and the photographs (about 100 in each case) are superb.

Lure of the Tropix, Bill Feret; Proteus, £6.95
The cinema may include Eisenstein and semiology, but it also embraces leopardskins and sarongs, and the latter are the subjects of this pleasant history of what are widely called 'Jungle Films'. Tarzan, Dorothy Lamour and many others are all here, as well as such illustrious names as Marlene Dietrich, Claudette Colbert, Audrey Hepburn and Ava Gardner. Plenty of suitably revealing stills, including some guaranteed to raise a smile – such as that on page 17, where Miss Natalie Kingston lies with wrists bound, overhung by a lascivious-looking ape, wearing the sort of expression which might indicate mild irritation at being made late for an appointment at the hairdresser's. Some interesting old photographs also – who, I wonder, apart from myself, now remembers Dorothy Janis?

The Making of *Citizen Kane*, Robert L. Carringer; John Murray, £8.95
In the author's words, this is a study of the 'collaborative process' in the making of what is generally held to be one of the greatest (and, in the opinion of many, *the* greatest) film of all time. After an opening chapter examining the genesis of the idea of *Kane*, which followed Welles's abortive attempt to film Conrad's *Heart of Darkness*, each aspect of the creative process – financing, scripting, art direction, photography, music, etc. – is discussed in detail, with a final brief glance at *Kane*'s successor, *The Magnificent Ambersons*. Fascinating secrets and tricks of the

cinematographic trade are revealed – such as the famous shot of Susan Alexander's attempted suicide and the construction of the apparently enormous Xanadu palace. In addition, the notorious controversy over Herman Mankiewicz's share in the script is re-examined. A large number of unique illustrations – sketches, frame enlargements, documents, production photographs – and a good index add to the value of the book, which is essential reading for any film student.

(*Note*: the author surely means that the arrival of Amelia Kent had 'fortunate' rather than 'fortuitous' consequences for Welles – an odd error for a professor of English studies!)

Marilyn – Mon Amour, André de Dienes; Sidgwick & Jackson, £12.95

M.M. must rank high – if not highest of all – in the ranks of the most photographed personalities of all time. Even so, this book of beautifully reproduced and presented pictures adds something unique to the mystique. They were taken – all in black-and-white and none the worse for that – between 1945 and 1953 by a young Hungarian photographer who fell in love with and wanted to marry her, and more than many others, these photographs come close to capturing the charm, high spirits and underlying pathos of her personality. De Dienes died in 1985 aged 71, never knowing whether a phone call he was just too late in answering came from her – perhaps a last call for help – on the night of her death. Even those to whom the story of Marilyn means little now may find themselves oddly moved as they look through this fascinatingly varied collection.

Marlon Brando, Gary Carey; Robson Books, £9.50

A welcome addition to the Robson list of concise, workman-like biographies. Gary Carey, author of one of the best books on MGM and L.B. Mayer, writes in lively style of Brando's up-and-down career, and is often wittily sharp in his comments – see the description of the notorious Oscar ceremony when Brando refused to take the award himself. It was time that an informed, well-balanced biography of Brando appeared, and this nicely fills a gap. Plenty of illustrations and a somewhat skeletal filmography.

Martin Scorsese and Michael Cimino, Michael Bliss; Scarecrow Press, dist. Bailey Bros. & Swinfen, £25.00

The author follows up his exhaustive study of Brian De Palma with equally detailed analyses of the works of two more contemporary film-makers in the same series. The procedure is the same: a close examination of each film, a magnificently full filmography with plot synopsis, biographical note and bibliography. The lengthy commentaries are extremely detailed and demand concentration from the reader, but for everyone interested in the careers of these important figures in contemporary cinema the effort is richly rewarding. Of special interest is a full account of the 'sabotaging' of Cimino's *Heaven's Gate*, surely one of the costliest *débâcles* in cinema history. Well illustrated and thoroughly documented.

A Method to Their Madness, Foster Hirsch; W. W. Norton, £14.95

The term 'method acting' will be familiar to most theatre and film enthusiasts, but probably not many will know what it is all about. This very complete and well-documented history of the American Group Theatre and Actors' Studio should satisfy their curiosity, even if it does not materially widen their understanding. If anyone wants to know about the 'affective memory' or what might be termed the 'as if' approach to the Art of the Actor, it is all here. Fortunately, Mr Hirsch's writing is a lot less affected than some of the theories and practices he has to describe – which, frankly, often seem to veer between the pretentious and the platitudinous, the solemnly obscure and the painfully obvious. At times, one remembers with relief Noel Coward's succinct advice to aspiring actors: 'Learn your lines and don't trip over the furniture.'

Names of interest to film-goers include Brando, James Dean, Paul Newman, Elia Kazan, Shelley Winters, Estelle Parsons, Arthur Penn, Geraldine Page, Al Pacino, Sandy Dennis – who, after director Lee Strasberg yelled at her, told him, 'You can't speak to me this way. I'm a human being.'

Money into Light, John Boorman; Faber & Faber, £4.95

While making *The Emerald Forest*, a film based on the hunt for a kidnapped boy in Brazil, John Boorman kept a journal; this well-produced and very interesting paperback is the result. It deals with all the aspects of the complex matter of creating a movie – not only the actual shooting but the financing, the casting, the personal problems, the logistics . . . in short, the lot. It covers, however, a good deal more: there are references to many other films, his own and other people's, and to many business associates, and there are some excellent photographs and frame enlargements. Two minor defects: a cast-and-credit list and, in particular, an index would have been useful.

The Movie Directors' Story, Joel W. Finler; Octopus Books, £12.95

Concentrating on the 'mainstream Anglo-American cinema', this handsomely produced book is among the best on its subject. Here are represented 140 directors, in three sections, from 1920 to 1985. Each entry contains a lengthy biographical and critical entry and a number of excellent stills and production photographs. All the big names are included, but room is found for a number of lesser-known film-makers such as Bob Rafelson and John M. Stahl. Three good indexes list directors, films and other personnel. A large-format volume eminently suitable for either study or nostalgic browsing.

My Life in the Silver Screen, Gerald Kaufman; Faber & Faber, £9.95

Judging by this book, the author, a Labour MP, certainly deserves the title of 'Parliament's leading film buff'. It is a lively account of a devotion to the cinema that has lasted some 50 years, told with a salty mixture of affection and acerbity. If some of his castigations appear to stem from a desire to be controversial merely for controversy's sake (an occupational hazard, perhaps), there is also some sound common sense. The lines at the top of page 72, for instance, might be heeded by many film critics. He makes a praiseworthy attack on the monstrous practice of dubbing foreign-language films, and dismisses *Chariots of Fire* and *Gandhi*, the twin pillars of the 'British film revival', in two caustic words. He is also frank enough to admit to political prejudice in some of his judgements. Lightweight but quite enjoyable.

My Mother's Keeper – A Candid Portrait of Bette Davis, B. D. Hyman; Michael Joseph, £10.95

After Crawford, Sellers and Crosby, it is now Bette Davis' turn to be portrayed with something less than total adulation by her offspring. Though almost inevitably the book will be described as yet another 'hatchet job', it is by no means wholly destructive: an underlying admiration and wish for affection can be glimpsed through the murk. Nevertheless, this portrait of a woman whose outbursts of temper are tediously peppered with the fashionable insults of the day is a fairly unpleasant one. There is no index, but this book, which with its mass of supposedly recollected dialogue reads like a sensational novel, hardly calls for one. Reprehensible though it may be, most of us enjoy reading a modicum of scandal and – human nature being what it is – this lively and often diverting account will doubtless attract a wide circle of readers.

National Heroes, Alexander Walker; Harrap, £10.95

In 1974, Alexander Walker published *Hollywood, England*, an absorbing account of the British film industry during the 1960s. The present book is a sequel, dealing with the position in the 'seventies and 'eighties. It is, in some respects, a weightier work, dealing more with the 'people in power' (producers, financiers, entrepreneurs, corporate bosses) than with actual film-makers. Fewer films are discussed in detail, and more space is devoted to the wheeling and dealing and selling and buying and merging and dissolving that so involve the industry today. The title of his book, Walker states, is partly ironic. However, he threads his way through the maze with such lucidity and *élan* (and humour) that the importance and serious purpose of the study in no way detracts from its entertainment value.

(*Note*: It is welcome news that Walker's previous book, which has been out of print for some time, will be available again before this review is published.)

Nightmare Movies, Kim Newman; Proteus, £11.95 hardback, £6.95 paperback

The stills in this survey of horror and Gothic films since 1968 are mainly of the glutinous-gore-and-battered-eyeball variety, but the text is another matter.Starting from and frequently referring back to, the seminal *Night of the Living Dead* (Romero), the author has written a lively, informative, perceptive and often amusing account, summarizing and dissecting hundreds of films and, on occasion, shedding new light on them. When necessary, the comments are pretty scathing too, with nice touches of excoriation. Indicative chapters include 'The British Horror Film', 'California Gothic', 'Devil Movies', 'Ghost Stories', 'Psycho Moves On', culminating in 'Apocalypse Now!'. There is a chapter on recent Italian horror, and appendices include a chronology and a useful list of alternative titles. The index has a few errors, including a pleasant reference to 'Pink Flod' . . .

The Once and Future Film, John Walker; Methuen, £5.95

A useful compact handbook of British cinema 1970–84, with much lucidly written information on business convolutions, and prophesies and developments in video, cable and even personally computer-controlled television films. Several interviews with leading film-makers, notably David Puttnam and Michael Winner, contain much good sense and many interesting ideas. The final outlook is, on the whole, optimistic. No illustrations, but a good index and a very welcome annotated list of directors and the films they made during the period.

Orson Welles, Barbara Leaming; Weidenfeld & Nicolson, £14.95

This massive book – over 500 large pages – is obviously one of the biographies of the year. It was written with Welles's full co-operation, and is presented in a form which combines straight narrative with fascinating glimpses of the writer's interviews with her subject and with his friends and associates. Personal life and professional career are, on the whole, well balanced, the weight perhaps somewhat favouring the former. Of the films, *Citizen Kane* not unexpectedly is given prominence – some 30 pages packed with interest, both on the technical side and for the various turmoils surrounding its production. In addition, new light is thrown on the notorious Pauline Kael essay on the authorship of the script. The frustrations and disappointments (and final greatness) of the unforgettable *Chimes at Midnight* are movingly related. One might perhaps have wished for more on films in which Welles appeared as actor, and (in a book of this importance) a chronology of film and stage appearances, but on the whole, the often misused description 'definitive' might suitably be applied here.

The Other Side of the Moon, Sheridan Morley; Weidenfeld & Nicolson, £10.95

To those acquainted only with David Niven's jocular autobiographies (*The Moon's a Balloon, Bring on the Empty Horses*), this fine (unauthorized) biography will come as both an eye-opener and a salutary corrective, revealing a darker side and a more complex and considerably more interesting personality behind the amusing but somewhat superficial façade. Mr Morley explores the truth with candour and sympathy, dealing with private life and professional career in equally fascinating detail.

The book adopts the eminently sensible idea of heading each chapter with the year or years that it covers – a practice many a reader, after searching frustratingly to trace a missing date, might like to see used more widely. A film list, an index (not sufficiently detailed) and generous sections of illustrations round off an informative and most 'readable' book.

The Paramount Story, John Douglas Eames; Octopus Books, £12.95

The highest compliment one can pay to this splendid studio history is to say that it is well up to the rest of the series. Year by year, 1916–1984, every important film from Paramount is featured with a commentary, synopsis, leading players and a still – the last sometimes full-page, sometimes small, but always reproduced with crystal clarity. Brief paragraphs cover minor productions. The total, we are assured, amounts to 2805 films. At the opening of each significant period, the story of the studio itself is brought up to date. Academy Awards are listed, and the book, containing some 350 large pages, concludes with two comprehensive indexes. Studios already covered in the series are Warner, RKO Radio, Universal and MGM – the latter also written by Mr Eames.

Peter Cushing – An Autobiography; Weidenfeld & Nicolson, £9.95

Peter Cushing closes his most enjoyable and heart-warming (and excellently illustrated) autobiography on 14 January 1971, the day on which his wife died and his life 'as he knew and loved it' ended. In a style combining wit and humour, and with a disarming modesty, he recounts his early and often tough struggles to earn a living as actor on stage and screen in Britain and, briefly, in America, until, following his appearance as Osric in Olivier's *Hamlet*, he rose fairly steadily to such prominence that he became known (before his connection with Hammer films) as 'the Horror Man of the BBC', and ultimately achieved the final accolade of receiving a letter from America which reached him without difficulty having been addressed simply, 'PETER CUSHING, ENGLAND'. On the way he relates adventures and misadventures so entertainingly as to cause at least *this* unwary reader the embarrassment – on more than one occasion – of laughing out loud in a public place.

It is, however, when he writes of his wonderful relationship with his late wife, Helen, that the book becomes more than another showbusiness career story. No one, surely could read the closing pages without being deeply moved: a worthy memorial to a most inspiring and courageous woman.

Portraits of the British Cinema, John Russell Taylor and John Kobal; Aurum Press, £17.95

A part of the effort during 1985–6 to celebrate and revive British cinema, this is a collection of studio photographs and stills worthy of being set beside the best volumes of Hollywood stars and cameramen. Following a note on the photographers, around 150 actors and actresses are represented, from Edna Best and Herbert Marshall in 1930 to the well-known names of today. An introduction incorporates pictures of studios and a few earlier portraits.

Raising Hell, Terence Pettigrew; Columbus Books, £7.95

The main part of this interesting and attractively produced softback considers the lives and careers of some famous Hollywood rebels (Cagney, Brando, Dean, Eastwood, McQueen and others) against the historical and sociological events of their period – the Depression, the Cold War, the permissive 'sixties, Vietnam, etc. Science fiction and films dealing with contemporary problems, from *The Invasion of the Body Snatchers* to *The Best Years of Our Lives* and *Death Wish*, are also touched upon in this wide-ranging survey. Stills and portraits, both rare and familiar, are well produced.

Rex Harrison, Allen Eyles; W. H. Allen, £9.95

This biography, as the author states, concentrates on Harrison's career rather than his personal life, the latter being referred to only in passing when it has affected the former. There is a very full account of Harrison's work in both cinema and theatre. The plays and, in particular, the films are treated in great detail, often with full synopsis and critical analysis in this relatively short book, together with numerous quotations from interviews Harrison has given over the years. The reference section is also commendably detailed, with full cast lists of both plays and films whenever possible.

Scandal, Colin Wilson and Donald Seaman; Weidenfeld & Nicolson, £12.95

Poor old Hollywood comes once again under the microscope in this collection of reprehensible but (if we are frank) fascinating examples of human nature at its less than edifying. It contains brief but pithy accounts of the murder of William Desmond Taylor and the activities of Clara Bow, Chaplin, Flynn, Arbuckle, Polanski and others.

NOTE Perhaps one day the question of Mary Miles Minter's age at the time of the Taylor murder will be settled: at present opinions vary from 17 to 20 (the most popular) to the unlikely 30 suggested here.

Science-Fiction Films of the 'Seventies, Craig W. Anderson; McFarland & Co., dist. Bailey Bros. & Swinfen, £15.95

The author covers 50 films, arranged by year, giving each a synopsis, lengthy commentary and cast-and-credit list, with copious references to other films along the way. Titles range from *The Andromeda Strain, A Clockwork Orange, Star Wars, Superman* and other leaders to lesser-known productions such as *Phase IV, Dark Star* and *Americathon*. In entertaining style he is equally vigorous in praise or condemnation (his excoriation of Corman and his works is awe-inspiring), has many original points to make and knows his subject with exemplary thoroughness. His book, one feels, deserves a more attractive presentation than it receives in its paperback form.

Screen Deco, Howard Mandelbaum and Eric Myers; Columbus Books, £12.95

While the dictionary weakly evades the issue by defining 'art deco' as 'the decorative art style of 1920s and 1930s', the authors of this very beautifully produced book gallantly attempt a more illuminating definition, then trace its origins from France to America in the films of the period. Admittedly the spiky geometrical lines and clean curves, etc. are easier to recognize by sight than through verbal descriptions, and the admirably lucid and entertaining text is accompanied by a huge number of excellently crisp photographs and stills which include, in the settings, many stars and supporting players. Among the many topics discussed are, for instance, the anachronisms in such 'historical' films as *Cleopatra* (1934) and *The Warrior's Husband* (1933), deliberately introduced to give a *stylized* impression of a reality which would give only a *false* impression if accurately presented to the eye of the film camera. This is a valuable addition to one of the less frequently examined components of film-making.

Screen World 1985, John Willis; Muller, £14.95

Once again, this indispensable review of the American cinema scene (during 1984) appears in its usual bright and attractive format. If, as the years pass, it is difficult to find fresh words in which to recommend it, this is simply because its excellent standard has been consistently maintained. Details: 1,000 photographs (stills and portraits), superbly full cast lists; sections on awards, biographical data, promising new actors, obituaries, etc.; and an enormous – really enormous – index of names and film titles. This year's 'dedicatee' is Clarence Brown, famed director of such films as *Flesh and the Devil* (1927), *The Trail of '98* (1928), *Anna Christie* (1930), *Ah! Wilderness* (1935), *The Rains Came* (1939), *National Velvet* (1945) and *The Yearling* (1947).

The Secret Life of Danny Kaye, Michael Freedland; W. H. Allen, £10.95

The author was, of course, handed the title for his biography of this Hollywood 'Walter Mitty' on a plate, but he does, in fact, look quite closely into a personality more complex than the apparently ebullient and extrovert entertainer might suggest. It is also a good standard account of a brilliant performer who enjoyed a meteoric rise some 35 years ago, but did not perhaps remain on the pinnacle of success for as long as might have been expected. This is an eminently readable book which, for many people, will conjure up pleasant memories. Two sections of illustrations but – alas! – no index, though it deserves one.

Someday We'll Laugh, Esther Ralston; Scarecrow Press, dist. Bailey Bros. & Swinfen, £16.00

The author of this enchanting autobiography is now 83 years old; in the 'twenties and 'thirties she was one of the brightest stars in the Hollywood firmament. Nowadays, except for an occasional screening of the British *Rome Express* (in which she is not seen to best advantage), her films are rarely if ever shown. One of the best, *The Case of Lena Smith*, is currently listed among the famous 'lost films'. Her story, written in a delightfully individual style, is above all one of courage, from her early days in a sort of one-family travelling show to her totally unself-pitying recognition that she was 'no longer a star'. She draws a warmly affectionate picture (on the whole) of the film capital and of her many professional friends and associates, and a devastatingly frank one of her three mainly disastrous marriages. Her own story ends with the break-up of the third, but her editor, Anthony Slide, gives a brief summary of her life since then, from saleswoman and lighting consultant for an electricity supply company to 'actress in countless TV commercials'. This is a book of charm and humour, and a vivid portrait of the Hollywood of the period, embellished with a generous selection of rare photographs.

Star Billing – Tell-Tale Trivia from Hollywood, David Brown; Weidenfeld & Nicolson, £4.95

The book's subtitle tells all – this is a light-hearted collection of gossip, lists of all kinds, odd facts, etc. about dozens of stars, early and late, under a multitude of headings from 'Six Reasons for Marilyn Monroe's Insecurity' to 'Ten Crucial Pieces of Advice from the Stars'. Ideal for parties, or wherever two or three film buffs are gathered together, with something in it to interest or amuse most people. Someone might even spot the misspelt name on page 99.

Such Devoted Sisters – Those Fabulous Gabors, Peter H. Brown; Robson Books, £9.95

As might be suspected from the title, this long and gossipy book about Zsa Zsa, Eva and Magda (and mother Jolie) reads more like a novel – or, to be frank, a novelette – than a true triple biography. It is full of (surely) invented dialogue and sentences such as 'Her face flushed and her eyes narrowed'. Did they, indeed? Despite its length and quite pleasant appearance it is a very lightweight addition to the cinema bookshelf: not up to the general standard of the modest but efficient Robson biographies, though probably acceptable casual reading for the indiscriminate showbiz browser.

That's Dancing, Tony Thomas; Penguin Books, £14.95

The musical film has been fairly well covered in books, but Tony Thomas has managed to collect together a large number of rarely seen stills (together with frame enlargements) for this beautifully produced, large-format, softback volume. After a long introductory survey, largely in the form of lengthy picture captions, he has written concise biographies of ten great masters of the film musical, ranging alphabetically from Astaire and Busby Berkeley to Donald O'Connor and Eleanor Powell. It is a pity, though perhaps inevitable, that some of the splendid stills have had to be cut down the middle to cover a double-page spread, but care has obviously been taken in this instance to ensure that the division is as little destructive as possible.

2000 Movies – The Forties, Robin Cross; Sidgwick & Jackson, £12.95

A gargantuan collection of stills, one to each film, 200 per year, accompanied by the names of the director and stars, and a two-to-three-line commentary. Each decade is prefaced by a short essay, and the films are subdivided into *genres*, with additional sections on 'B' movies, and British and European productions. An enormous index makes titles and players easy to trace. Some of the stills are necessarily rather small but nearly all are crisply reproduced. An added attraction is the inclusion of a large number of almost, or totally, forgotten films, not easily found elsewhere. A wonderful nostalgic wallow, but also useful for reference or as a memory jogger, and handsomely produced.

Index